TAOIST RITUAL AND POPULAR CULTS OF

SOUTHEAST CHINA

TAOIST RITUAL
AND POPULAR CULTS OF
SOUTHEAST CHINA

Kenneth Dean

PRINCETON UNIVERSITY PRESS

PRINCETON, NEW JERSEY

LIBRARY OF CONGRESS CATALOGING-IN-PUBLICATION DATA
DEAN, KENNETH, 1956–
TAOIST RITUAL AND POPULAR CULTS OF SOUTHEAST CHINA/
KENNETH DEAN
P. CM.
INCLUDES BIBLIOGRAPHICAL REFERENCES AND INDEX
ISBN 0-691-07417-8
ISBN 0-691-04473-2 (PBK.)
1. TAOISM—CHINA—RITUALS. 2. TAOISM—TAIWAN—RITUALS
3. CULTS—CHINA. 4. CULTS—TAIWAN. I. TITLE.
BL1923.D43 1993   299'.51438'0951209048—DC20   92-21047 CIP

PUBLICATION OF THIS BOOK HAS BEEN AIDED BY A GRANT FROM THE
CHIANG CHING-KUO FOUNDATION FOR INTERNATIONAL
SCHOLARLY EXCHANGE

THIS BOOK HAS BEEN COMPOSED IN LINOTRON GALLIARD

PRINCETON UNIVERSITY PRESS BOOKS ARE PRINTED ON ACID-FREE
PAPER AND MEET THE GUIDELINES FOR PERMANENCE AND
DURABILITY OF THE COMMITTEE ON PRODUCTION
GUIDELINES FOR BOOK LONGEVITY OF THE
COUNCIL ON LIBRARY RESOURCES

FIRST PAPERBACK PRINTING, 1995

PRINTED IN THE UNITED STATES OF AMERICA

3 5 7 9 10 8 6 4 2

To David and Mary Alice Dean,

WITH THANKS FOR HAVING TAKEN

ME TO CHINA IN THE

FIRST PLACE

CONTENTS

LIST OF ILLUSTRATIONS

Map

Plates and Figures

(All photos by author)

LIST OF TABLES AND CHARTS

Tables

Charts

ACKNOWLEDGMENTS

THE FIELDWORK and research that led to this book was conducted in Fujian from 1985–1987, with support from the Committee on Scholarly Communications with the People's Republic of China and its funding agencies, the National Endowment for the Humanities and the Department of Education. A year of fieldwork with Taoist priests in Taiwan in 1984–1985, supported by a Fulbright-IIE Fellowship, enabled me to gain an understanding of the ritual traditions of the Minnan region of Southeast China. A final period of fieldwork in Fujian and Taiwan over several months in 1989–1991 was supported by the CSCPRC and the Chiang Ching-kuo Foundation. I thank all these organizations for their generous support.

I would like to express my gratitude to my host institution in China, the History Department of Xiamen University, and to the International Education Center, the Overseas Correspondence College, the Foreign Students Section, the Xiamen University Library, and the Foreign Affairs Office of Xiamen University. I would also like to acknowledge the assistance of the Fujian Bureau of Higher Education; the Bureau of Religious Affairs; the Fujian Provincial Library; and the district level offices of the United Front Division; the Bureau of Culture; and the Foreign Affairs Offices in Fuzhou, Quanzhou, Xiamen, Zhangzhou, Shantou, Chaozhou, Gutian, Putian, Xianyou, Hui'an, Jinjiang, Nan'an, Dehua, Yongchun, Anxi, Tongan, Longhai, Zhangpu, Pinghe, Yunxiao, Zhao'an, Dongshan, and Jiexi xian in Northeast Guangdong.

Many individuals assisted me in my work. I would like to thank in particular Michel Strickmann, a brilliant scholar and an inspiring teacher, for introducing me to Taoist studies, and for the stimulating guidance and constant support he provided throughout my research. My thanks also to K. M. Schipper, leading authority on Taoist studies, for his penetrating insight and guidance, and the many hours he spent discussing my research. In many ways, this study explores new paths opened up by his research in Taiwan. I appreciate the patience and kindness shown me by Taoist Master Ch'en Yong-sheng of Tainan. The Mary McCleod Lewis Foundation supported the preliminary writing up of my research results in 1987–1988 as a dissertation in Chinese at Stanford University. I appreciate the helpful comments of the members of the reading committee: Albert Dien, Michel Strickmann, G. W. Skinner, and David Nivison. I would also like to thank Catherine Herrmann, John Lagerwey, James Wilkerson, Ho Ts'ui-p'ing, Brian Massumi, Brigitte Berthier, Terry Kleeman,

Dennis Allistone, Steve Jones, Lucy Ivy, Cora, and David. I am most grateful to Chinese friends and colleagues in Fujian who helped me reach an understanding of religion in Southeast China. These include Yang Guozhen, Zheng Zhenman, Ke Jiaoli, the late Xiao Yiping, Lin Guoping, Li Ting, and Guo Tianyuan. The index was prepared by Robert Palmer. Bill Laznovsky improved the text by his careful copyediting. My thanks as well to Margaret Case and Ann Wald for the patience and skill with which they have edited this volume. These friends, colleagues, and the foundations mentioned above are of course not responsible for any errors in fact or judgement in the text.

TAOIST RITUAL AND POPULAR CULTS OF

SOUTHEAST CHINA

1. Taoists in front of community representatives before a temple in the Zhangzhou area.

INTRODUCTION

SOURCES AND METHODOLOGY

THE FESTIVALS on the birthdays of the local gods bring one, where they still exist, to the temples and their leaders. At the festivals, affiliated communities visit one another, and so the general organization of religious institutions in the region is gradually revealed. The different levels of religious activity in any one locale can only become clear after a long immersion in the area. The festivals are a crucial structuring element of local life. During these extraordinary occasions, the different religious specialists perform rituals. The most visible of these, in Taiwan and in Southern Fujian, are the Ritual Masters and the spirit mediums. They are usually connected to specific temples, and work together in the open courtyard between the temple and the stage. The courtyard is a volatile space of sacrifice. Offerings of animal and vegetable substances are set out in this space by the community. Surrounded by tumultuous crowds, thick clouds of smoke from exploding firecrackers, and heavy fumes of incense, the mediums are brought into a state of trance through chanting, drumming, and dancing. Possessed by the gods, they cut at themselves with swords or skewer their flesh until the blood flows from their bodies. Inside the temples, Taoist or Buddhist priests, who serve as religious specialists for a great number of temples and individuals over a wide area, perform extremely elaborate classical rituals. Ecstatic possession and bloody sacrifice work side by side with highly refined, sublime ancient liturgical forms.

Given the complexity of these interactions between classical liturgy and popular religion, and their continued prominence during the festivals of the gods, it seems clear that the study of Chinese religion in the modern period must begin with the study of the cults of the gods. The cults which are discussed in this study all took form in Fujian in the Five Dynasties and Tang period, and all provide an insight into certain aspects of the ongoing interaction between Taoism and popular religion. Schipper has defined Taoism in this context as the written tradition of local cults (Schipper, 1985a). It will be shown in this study that Taoist ritual functions as the main structuring element in the vast liturgical framework that supports the festival of the local gods.

Unknown to most outside observers of contemporary China who believe it to be monolithic, atheistic and materialist, and wholly divorced from its traditions, an enormous resurgence of traditional rituals, local cults, and popular culture has been gathering force since 1979, when the

Chinese government relaxed its controls on the practice of religion. In the face of continuing government restrictions and prohibitions, villagers in isolated areas of southeast China have begun a significant effort to restore traditions suppressed since the Communists took power and almost completely destroyed during the Cultural Revolution of the 1960s and 1970s.

In one sense, this activity represents an important but as yet little-known aspect of the reforms underway in China. Similar policy shifts in the past have often resulted in temporary liberalization of the Party policies on religion (Skinner and Winckler, 1969). The current bundle of reforms seems to have forced local cadres to relinquish control of day-to-day economic life and production. With the ascendance of *chengbao* (guaranteed field system) and the growing acceptance, especially in the relatively "open" Southeastern Chinese coastal region, of the *getihu* (individual household system), economic activity boomed, and the first thing that people who had made money did was not to buy televisions and refrigerators but to rebuild temples to their local cult god that had been destroyed during the Cultural Revolution. Large-scale religious rituals were openly performed in parts of Fujian in 1979, after the Fall of the Gang of Four, for the first time in decades. By 1980 repairs or reconstruction of local temples had been undertaken.

These temples had to be consecrated, so local Taoists and Buddhists were implored or enticed back to work. Moreover, newly carved god statues required the services of Taoists for *kaiguang dianyan* (rituals of consecration of the god involving dotting the eyes with blood or red ink to open them to the light). These rites were performed in many temples in 1981. On such occasions, the young males of the community were often organized to carry the newly carved gods of the temple over a pile of glowing coals into the temple, a process called *guohuo* (crossing the fire).

The *China Daily* reported in 1986 that, of 3,500 Buddhist temples in Fujian before the Cultural Revolution, over 2,400 had been restored.[1] My estimate of the total number of temples restored in Fujian since 1979 would be close to 30,000. Cultural authorities in Tongan xian estimated 3,000 temples in their county. An official working on local gazetteers in Zhao'an estimated over 450 temples in that county. United Front officials in Xianyou and Putian acknowledged the existence of over 700 *Sanyi jiao* (Three-in-One) temples devoted to the cult of Lin Zhao'en (1517–98), as well as an even greater number of temples dedicated to other local gods.[2]

Proceeding simultaneously with the restoration of temples, lineage organizations were reforming. These began holding rites of ancestor worship, although they lacked any corporate property. Later, ancestral halls were built in many areas, and large gatherings bringing far-flung branches of the lineage back together were held. "Amateur" theater groups were forming at a rapid pace but still had trouble meeting the escalating demand. Gods' birthdays, temple consecrations, and in some areas, individuals' birthdays, weddings, and funerals: all called for theatrical presentations. Another possibly unintended effect of the reforms was a boom in house-building. Large amounts of granite have been quarried in coastal Fujian, and whole villages of stone have sprung up, particularly in the stone-producing areas of Hui'an and Jinjiang. Many of these houses required the services of a Buddhist or Taoist priest for a house-settling consecration.

Several years of economic prosperity in a row, together with a sense of the possibilities inherent in the complex, evolving political situation, led many communities, beginning in 1984, to celebrate by holding elaborate Taoist *jiao* communal sacrifices for the first time in thirty-five or forty years. Moreover, around this time, many local temples began conducting yearly pilgrimages to the sites of the ancestral temples of their local deity. Several of these major temples were renovated during this period.

Much of the reconstruction described above was actively assisted by donations from overseas Chinese. They began to return in large numbers to attend religious rituals and to bury their dead—or at least hold a service in their place of origin for those who had died overseas. Local cadres quickly learned that they could be persuaded to make substantial contributions to local schools, hospitals, and roads, once they had been allowed to spend money on rituals. Some areas even instituted a tax on ritual expenditure.

This entire process can be viewed as a response to both the failures of the ideals of the Cultural Revolution and to the pressures for modernization coming from an increasingly undisciplined market sector. The collapse of ideals and the loss of education for many young people during the Cultural Revolution, combined with a blind, unrealizable desire to imitate Western ways, regardless of the means, has led, in the view of many village elders, to a dangerous decline in public morality and national sense of purpose. Their solution was to return to their own local traditions, the source-bed of Chinese culture. Their efforts have not gone unchallenged. Cadres still angered by their loss of power in the economic sphere sometimes foil local efforts to organize religious celebrations.

On the other hand, many cadres feel that the values fostered by these traditional community performances deserve support. More and more, cadres feel that it is appropriate for them to take part in their own families' elaborate traditional funeral rites, although few yet dare openly take part in communal jiao sacrifices. This clearly puts them in an awkward position, for in Southeast China, as throughout China, involvement in religious activity is inseparable from social standing and is a precondition of involvement in local organization and local decision-making.

. . . . .

There were, of course, many things that I could not see in China. The uneven development of the restoration of traditions in different areas meant that it was often difficult to assemble a clear picture of the distribution of religious specialists in one area. Was the current situation a traditional pattern, or was it the result of fluctuations in policies directed toward religion? Were the group of Zhangzhou Taoists I met avoiding funerals because of the laws demanding cremation in large cities and local ordinances against elaborate funerals, or was this part of their tradition? Were other groups of Taoists formerly funeral specialists? But how was it that these same Taoists had been trained at the Dongyue Miao, Temple of the Eastern Peak—in traditional times a central point for the performance of funerals for those who had died a bad death? Were the Taoists covering up their past, or adapting to contemporary needs?

Sources

Despite the widespread destruction of ritual texts and traditions, along with an enormous number of religious artifacts and stone inscriptions during the "Fifteen-Year Disaster" (1966–79) of the Cultural Revolution, I was able to find a considerable body of source materials on cults and ritual traditions. I visited over one hundred temples and attended over sixty Taoist and Buddhist rituals. The field notes that I have published elsewhere on this material represent the first ethnographic material on the role of religion in Southeast China to emerge in fifty, or in some cases, almost one hundred years (Dean 1986; 1988a,b; 1989a,b; 1990a,b).

My research in Fujian was greatly facilitated by the findings of J.J.M. de Groot (1854–1921), who did research in Xiamen one hundred years before me, first in 1877–1878, and then in 1886–1890. De Groot's penetrating descriptions of the annual festivals and Buddhist funerals of Amoy in the 1880s, the religious system of China, and sectarian religions all provide a valuable point of reference for contemporary research in Southeast China and Taiwan (De Groot, 1878, 1884, 1886, 1892–1910, 1903–4). In general, extraordinary as it may sound, one could say that everything described in De Groot is still happening in Southeast China, but no longer all in any one place. The immediate qualification, of course, is that the role of Confucian mandarins is no more. Many of the posted announcements, notices, and formal condolences written in literary Chinese are no longer in use. However, Confucian ritual has always been the preserve of the patresfamilias, and, as such, it retains its influence, as seen in the restoration of traditional funeral rites and ancestral worship. Religious activity in cities is extremely limited both by government supervision and rapidly changing social customs. In most major cities of Fujian the dead must be cremated within twenty-four hours. But only a few miles out of town in the countryside the largest traditional festivals and funerals in four decades are being held. De Groot's detailed studies proved invaluable to my research. Japanese ethnography on Taiwan, and recent Chinese and Western anthropological studies of Taiwan, Guangdong, and Southeast Asia were also essential references for my work (Strickmann, 1980).

De Groot (1886) describes the Taoist rituals surrounding the cults of several of the principal deities of Fujian. He described a number of the central cult temples. I discovered that the restoration of these cult temples and their affiliated temples had resulted in the revival of Taoist and Buddhist ritual traditions. As I mentioned above, Taoists are indispensable for the consecration of the restored or rebuilt temples and the god statues within them. Buddhists in some communities are traditionally called upon to perform the important *Pudu* rituals. These groups had begun reassembling their collections of liturgical manuscripts. I too was able to collect a large number of these manuscripts.

The manuscripts collected from Taoist, Buddhist, and sectarian religious specialists include some scriptures dedicated to local gods. These can be compared to several similar scriptures included in the Taoist Canon. Significantly, several local gods from Southeast China such as Mazu, the Immortal Xu brothers, and Wen Yuanshuai had scriptures, ritual texts, mediumistic accounts, and literary or hagiographic accounts included in the Taoist Canon. Many of the scriptures were written in standard form, which reveals a great deal about the process of universalization of local cults. Variant themes in the manuscript version of the scriptures reveal late developments in the cults. Occasionally there are also manuscript or printed accounts of a mediumistic nature. These encounters with the local gods also show certain standard formal features which shed light on the cult, as well as on the role of mediumism. In the case of those scriptures that are not included in the Canon, much new material on the legends and hagiography of the local gods is provided.[3]

Some of the temples I visited still preserved unpublished stone inscriptions providing essential materials on the history of the cults. These inscriptions enable one to trace the development of regional *fenxiang* (division of incense) networks. They provide documentation on the sponsorship and local organization of cult centers. Some provide the names of generations of spirit mediums. Some detail the organization of local irrigation system, others discuss the distribution of temple lands. Many provide data on the hagiography of the gods. These materials will be published in the near future (Dean and Zheng, 1993).

A third body of source material I collected is gazetteers of temples. A few temples, or the leaders of unofficial temple committees, had kept rare temple gazetteers unavailable elsewhere. The temple gazetteers I gathered were compiled toward the end of the Qing dynasty by Fujian literati. Some compilers, such as Chen Xishi, an Anxi *juren* (Provincial Graduate), were local men interested in publicizing the glory of their local cult. Others, like Yang Jun (1830–90), a Fuzhou juren, wrote to fulfill vows. One gazetteer, the *Guoshan miaozhi*, was written in 1897 by a local member of the elite, a second ranked Hanlin academician who had served in the Chinese Documents section of the Grand Secretariat named Dai Fengyi, to provide a Confucian reinterpretation of a local cult. Some gazetteers were printed to be distributed locally in limited numbers. Others were sponsored by devotees and companies and published, again in small numbers, in Fuzhou. These gazetteers tend to draw upon earlier materials on the cults. These include religious pamphlets providing a hagiography of the god written and printed locally as a form of religious propaganda. These were distributed at the temples of the cults.

The gazetteers can provide more complete coverage of the development of the cult than the surviving epigraphy, although editorial bias is often an issue. They list the principal repairs and inscriptions on the temple over the ages. They discuss the geographic and geomantic properties of the temple site, the physical dimensions of the temple, and the variety of subsidiary buildings and temples. Next they provide a standard written version of the legend of the god. They list the titles of enfeoffment received by the god over the ages, occasionally including the documentation—the texts of the edict conferring the title and the local and provincial reports that led to the bestowal of the title. Other sections cover the miracles performed by the god. There are long collections of literary pieces written in honor of the temple and the cult. There are also lists of the plaque inscriptions and carved or painted couplets around the temple. Sometimes material is included on the temple lands. One can sometimes also find material on the rituals designed for the god. Occasionally one finds the Taoist scripture of the god and the divinatory poetry of the temple. Rare but valuable material is occasionally included on unusual local customs surrounding the cult.

Aside from Taoist scriptures, liturgical manuscripts, epigraphy, and temple gazetteers, I collected a considerable body of oral accounts on the legends of the gods, as well as local history on the development of the cults, the vicissitudes of temples, the traditional networks and ritual traditions, and the family backgrounds of Taoist ritual specialists. The fact that much of this is now oral history has to do with the widespread destruction of genealogical records and temple inscriptions. These accounts provide new perspectives on the cults and on the gods. Every temple contains a collection of gods around the central figure of the principal deity. To understand a cult in its social context one must unravel the connections of these subsidiary deities to the god, the temple, and the community. Only the most prominent of the god's attendants will have made their way into the written sources.

Another body of oral accounts refers to the current revival of religious traditions. Bureaucrats in charge of religious affairs explain the shifting policies on "religion" as opposed to "superstition." Local elders discuss the problems of bringing the younger generation to an understanding of the underlying values of the traditions. Young people talk about their excitement and pride in their community festivities, and the part they play in them. Bureaucrats avoid certain issues, and local elders do more than they say to ensure the survival of local traditions. Oral accounts and observations of contemporary efforts to maintain ancient traditions and alternative networks in a complex society form one aspect of the materials to be discussed below.

I was able to see something of the confrontation between local government and temple committees over the pace of the restoration of religious traditions. For example, if one village in a certain area managed to successfully perform a jiao communal sacrifice, then all the other nearby villages will begin planning to perform one as soon as possible. They will want to reestablish the traditional links between villages, the ritual visits back and forth, and the participation in each others' temple festivals. But the official policy is to condone but not encourage religious activity. They generally will allow a jiao and a procession to take place if it does not exceed the boundaries of the village, does not disrupt traffic, does not lead to disorder, and if no firecrackers are exploded. In practice this allows a great deal of leeway to local governments to act as they see fit. The permissibility of a ritual depends a great deal on the determination of the local people, the relationship of the village Party secretary with the villagers and with the local government, the extent of overseas Chinese connections, the wealth and influence of the community, and the constantly changing "political atmosphere." Every ritual puts all these issues on the line.

The ancient standoff between the state and the locality requires extremely sophisticated handling in contemporary China. One can only hope that the government will come to allow a broader interpretation of

2. Community procession bearing King boat (Zhangzhou area).

the "freedom of religion" clause in the new Constitution. The effort to save local popular culture before it perishes with the last generation of priests and performers deserves support.

Chinese and Western scholars can help by providing balanced assessments of popular culture and by clarifying the central role of Chinese religion in popular culture and local society. Many conceptual problems need to be solved and brought to the attention of both local and central officials and cultural authorities.

Methodological Issues

The variety of materials that I gathered in Fujian naturally allow a variety of angles of approach. Because my research in Taiwan had been primarily on the Taoist liturgical tradition, I at first sought to center my research on that topic. However, my field data clearly showed that the revival of liturgical practices by Taoists and Buddhists was very much subsidiary to the revival of cult temples and the increased wealth of individual families. Therefore, this study will center on these developments and discuss developments in Taoist, and to a lesser extent Buddhist liturgy, in relation to these changes.

The purpose of this study is to move beyond widely available documentary sources (the Taoist Canon, regional gazetteers, published epigraphical sources) to explore new sources (temple gazetteers, unpublished epigraphy, Taoist scriptures and liturgical manuscripts, temple records, genealogies, contemporary observances, etc.) on the interaction of Taoism and local cults in the context of local history and contemporary society. Inevitably, the research environment in China from 1985 to 1990 has imposed certain limitations on this project. It was not possible to arrange to spend extended periods of time in one area, examining current practices and following up leads on locally held manuscripts relating to the history of one particular cult, its immediate ecological setting, the locality and its lineages, the wider network of temples that divided off from the cult center, and the ritual traditions preserved by local Taoist ritual specialists. Instead, my tactic was to keep moving between open cities and a group of cult centers and their ritual cachement areas, looking into each of these questions to the degree possible, in order to build up a general picture of several dimensions of the interaction between Taoism and popular cults as a guide to future research. Studies of this process of interaction should be conducted in different parts of China and Taiwan, employing historical, anthropological, and religious studies approaches to the study of Chinese religion in historical context.[4]

Although it is certain that cults played a major role in the local history and economy of Fujian, the role of cults in local village organization, or the religious aspects of the organization of merchant organizations and guilds in the towns, are rarely mentioned in the secondary literature on Fujian. If they are mentioned, the religious aspects are unfortunately discussed in a generally crude and unsophisticated way. The same is true for historical studies on the cults and canonizations of the gods, in which a great expertise in texts and official documents is not matched with an equal sophistication in the history of religions. Duara's (1988) recent study of the cultural nexus of power in Republican period North Chinese villages strikes out in a new direction, outlining the importance of temple committees in interaction with lineage groups and state organizations. Sangren (1987) also highlights the importance of religion in Chinese society by tracing the impact of temple networks and pilgrimage routes on local market systems. Neither of these studies focuses, however, on the role of ritual specialists or liturgical frameworks.

Despite recent advances in scholarship, the fact that there is still no adequate, developed model of the role of religion in the evolution of modern Chinese society means that this study must break some new ground. One of the central issues in this study is the still poorly defined relationship between the two elements in the title: popular cults and Taoist liturgy. As I mentioned above, this relationship as judged from the historical material at hand is fraught with contradictions. If, as Michel Strickmann and Rolf Stein have clearly shown, liturgical Taoism in its early development rejected the shamanistic cults with their bloody sacrifices, this did not mean that Taoism did not have its own locally based sanctuaries and cultic organizations (Strickmann, 1979a, 1981; Stein, 1979).

This fact is apparent from early sources like the *Liexian zhuan* (Yu Jiaxi, 1980). Of the seventy-one hagiographies contained in the book, twenty-two explicitly mention cults and corresponding temples (Kaltenmark, 1953). Moreover, in later movements such as the Maoshan tradition, the Mao brothers were, at the same time, the objects of a local cult and incorporated into the Taoist pantheon. Similar situations can be found in the cases of the cults of Wu Meng and Xu Xun studied by Miyakawa (Miyakawa, 1979, 1983). Even when the Taoists reject a certain type of popular cult, they recognized other cults.[5]

An issue that still awaits research is the nature and scope of the Taoist liturgical organization during the medieval period. The system of grades of initiation outlined in the writings of Zhang Wanfu and others implies the existence of a unified Taoist ecclesia. Sources dating from the Tang point to the existence of communities which strongly bonded together clergy and laymen. Clergy appear to have had considerable control over the activities of their parishioners. Coming-of-age and marriage rites, under close supervision by Taoist priests, moved parishioners through a series of Taoist investitures with registers of gods of the body. Sources on the Taoist ordination of Tang princesses reveals that ordination into even the higher ranks of the clergy was conferred on laymen (Schipper, 1985b; Benn, 1991).

The period from the end of the Tang to the beginning of the Northern Song would seem to represent a major turning point in Chinese society, economy, and therefore, religion as well. The rise of merchant centers in the Jiangnan region created a new social order and a new balance of power. The local organizations organized around cults of their saints and gods achieved emancipation into nationwide networks of economic, political, and cultural corporations. Schipper has argued that this emancipation led these cult groups to enter into the Taoist liturgical tradition (Schipper, 1985d). Akizuki has traced the development of the cult of Xu Xun as it evolved into a local Taoist movement by the end of the Tang.

He goes on to show how the movement was made in the Song to take on Confucian, nationalistic overtones (Akizuki, 1978).

After this point, one finds Taoists in the employ of local cults, rather than in charge of communities. They performed rituals and wrote scriptures that absorbed local cults into the universal Taoist pantheon. The unity of medieval Taoism fell apart under the rapid development of new revelations and local movements. Nevertheless, the extraordinary unity of the underlying structure of the Taoist ritual tradition was preserved.

To a certain extent, a similar situation still holds true today. Cult groups with fenxiang networks are extremely autonomous, not only politically but from a religious point of view as well. At every central point in their liturgical practice, however, the participation of one or more Taoist Masters is indispensable. Taoists must consecrate the temples. The festival of the gods must be blessed by Taoists. Purification ceremonies are conducted by Taoists. Processions are initiated and led by Taoists. Great offerings are consecrated by Taoists. I present several examples of this involvement in the discussion below on the contemporary observances surrounding these cults. I also discuss instances of Buddhist participation, but these are generally of a secondary nature.

Even more fundamentally, the process of the development of a cult from a local spirit to one of the highest members of the heavenly pantheon is conceived according to the dictates of Taoist theology. The hagiography of the local god is inevitably phrased in terms established in Taoist literature. Even city gods are often conceived of as local spirits who receive ordinations and assignments from the Taoist Celestial Master. Even so, the communal celebrations around a cult remain a complex ensemble of contradictory elements. Each segment of the local or regional society remains highly autonomous, and freely invests into the celebration its own desires, values, and ideology through the way in which they participate. For affiliated group participation it is primarily a matter of pilgrimage. They visit, burn incense, make offerings, and return home with incense from the main cult center. For the local militia groups, and the performing arts troupes, the celebration is an occasion for vying in the procession of the gods. For the local elite, the celebrations may offer an occasion for a Confucian-style sacrifice to the god.

These different points of view result in a theological identity that becomes highly contradictory. These contradictions are clear to many of the participants, but the contradictions are not allowed to erupt: a taboo against confronting contradictions seems to take effect. For at the same time, all these contradictory elements must be present so that all the groups can identify themselves in one or another aspect. That this all holds together is primarily due to the fact that Taoism never imposes doctrinal dogma. This is a fundamental principle of Taoism, which spontaneously recognizes in all these different aspects so many facets of its panthe-istic worldview. These different aspects of the deity have their place in the liturgical framework. Different representations find their place on the same Taoist altar. These manifold representations relate to a fundamental Taoist assumption that all forms of spiritual power, *ling*, are efficacious, and should therefore receive a cult (Schipper, 1985c).

An appreciation of the role of ritual and liturgy is the missing link in our understanding of the history and functioning of local community in Chinese civilization. Obviously these are not exclusively Taoist. Confu-cian ritual shapes family and lineage domestic and ancestral worship, and many life-crisis rituals, especially funerary ritual (Watson, 1988). Bud-dhist rituals such as the Pudu (which could also be performed by Taoists) bring together communities around notions of their indebtedness to the dead, and provides ritual means for the transferral of merit to the dead (especially the hungry, dangerous dead) via the Sangha (Teiser, 1988; Weller, 1987). At the communal level, however, Taoist liturgy plays the predominant role in structuring cult worship.

Needham (1974) discovered in Taoist liturgy the missing link in the history of alchemy in China. I suggest that one can conceive of Taoist liturgy as the alchemy of Chinese society. Sivin (1966) has explained that alchemy in China could be an end in itself, a means of merging with the creative forces of the universe. As Needham put it, "let us . . . follow a path that leads off in a highly unexpected direction, through a scented forest in fact, at first penetration very foreign to anything with which we are familiar, but on closer acquaintance much less so." (Needham, vol. 5.2 (1974): 128).[6]

My usage of the term "the Taoist liturgical framework" differs some-what from the definition of "liturgical" corporate group structures in the comparative social and economic theory of Max Weber (1864–1920). Weber borrowed the term from German economic-historical studies of Classical Antiquity, where the root sense was derived from the Greek *lei-tourgia*, *leitos* (public), *ergon* (work). He applied it to a wide range of associations in different cultures performing public services elsewhere carried out by the state. In the Chinese case he applied the term to kinship and village groups, the *baojia* system, the *tongxiang hui* or Landsmann-schaften, and guilds (Weber, 1951; 1979). My use of the term "Taoist liturgical framework" derives from the late Greek sense of the term *lei-tourgia* (a public service dedicated to the gods). I argue that communal celebrations (i.e., liturgies) structured by Taoist rituals marked social hier-archy while maintaining communal integration. Local elites performed their "liturgical" functions through participation in temple committees and cult worship. In other words, it is necessary to reassess the function of religious ritual within the liturgical organizations surveyed by Weber.

Three aspects of Weber's treatment of liturgical organizations and religion in China deserve further attention. First of all, as I mentioned, Weber applied the term liturgical governance to village level kinship groups and the baojia system. He found that these organizations performed essential public services. However, he believed that the village temple was seldom used for religious purposes (Weber, 1951). The work of anthropologists in the last several decades has demonstrated the frequency and centrality of religious ritual centered in the temple for village life (Gallin, 1966; Jordan, 1972; Sangren, 1987). The temple is the scene of daily as well as annual observances. Moreover, the regular performance of Taoist jiao at least once every sixty years is required in most villages (Gallin, 1966; Schipper, 1974). Natural disasters call for special rituals in the temples. I would suggest that an essential dimension of the public work of the local-level liturgical organizations involved the sponsorship of temples and rituals and the participation in local cult worship, particularly the communal Taoist jiao sacrifice. Moreover, through these activities the social standing of the liturgical leadership was reaffirmed through a reinvestiture before the universal gods of the Taoist pantheon (Schipper, 1977).

Secondly, Weber noted that the tongxiang hui and guilds of China were organized around religious rituals. Mann (1987) also notes this in passing[7] as does Negeshi Tadashi (1953), who provides figures on the costs of a Shanghai rice guilds's Taoist jiao. Dou Jiliang's (1943) short pamphlet on tongxiang hui does insist on the centrality of these features, but he does not develop this point. Niida (1950) discusses the religious organization of guilds in Beijing. However, much more work needs to be done on the ritual dimension of guild and merchant associations. An awareness of the centrality of religious ritual to merchant associations should cast doubt on Weber's theories of the impact of religion on Chinese economic development. One could argue instead that the rituals functioned to solidify a potent new economic organization which contributed substantially to the economic growth of late imperial China.[8]

The third point is that Weber's entire treatment of Taoism as an *individually* oriented *magical* religion relies on biased early treatments of partial sources.[9] He was unable to draw upon the path-breaking work of Henri Maspero, who researched the Taoist Canon in the 1920s, shortly after it became publicly available for the first time in centuries. These sources provide a wealth of material on the impact of Taoism on Chinese society. Maspero discovered that Taoism should be seen as the indigenous higher religion of China. Kristofer Schipper's fieldwork in Taiwan in the 1960s led to the discovery of the extraordinary underlying unity and continuity of the Taoist liturgical tradition from the Six Dynasties period to the present day. Their discoveries and ongoing research in Tao-

3. Procession entering the outskirts of Zhangzhou.

ist studies demonstrate the profound impact of Taoism on local Chinese society. One can now begin to assess the impact of Taoism at the communal level in China.

In the chapters below, I emphasize the historical and structural role of Taoist liturgy in the contemporary revival of religious practice. In Southeast China, cultural activity and economic and political decision-making center around the main temple or lineage hall of the village. The Taoist or Buddhist priest performing rituals in the temple is at the center of a circle traced by the movements of the god's procession around the boundaries of his spiritual precinct. Making up the procession is every genre of popular performing arts in the regional culture. Outside the temple theatrical troupes performed for the gods and the community, while in the space between the stage and the temple, community and family representatives set out a variety of offerings in correlation with specific rituals. Inside the temple, following the movements of the priest, are the village *huishou* (headsmen), who have sponsored much of the ritual. They have set out Lamps of Destiny on the altar to attract the attention and blessings of the gods. All these offerings, together with the texts sacrificed by the Taoist priests, represent a liturgical system that has much to reveal. The ritual, the procession, the offerings, and the theatre are intimately interrelated. There is a rhythm and a flow of intensities throughout the course of the entire community performance. Each performance by the priests of a ritual text is unique. Each community brings its own desires to bear upon the selection of elements from the regional culture and ritual tradition. Unique connections between different sectors occur at each ritual, crisscrossing the structural unity.

From the perspective of cultural reproduction, Taoism provides the liturgical framework which enables local cults to expand and develop. Taoism was always looking for ways to channel the energies of China's "shamanistic substratum" (van der Loon, 1977). While early sources emphasize the rejection of blood sacrifice by Taoism, fieldwork reveals that blood sacrifice has been replaced inside the temple by the sacrifice of texts (Schipper, 1982), while outside the temple blood sacrifice has been marginalized but allowed to survive under certain restrictions. The interaction between Taoist liturgy and cult observances generates a rich, constantly changing, play of forces embedded in powerfully charged cosmological symbols. The role of Taoist liturgy in community organization in Southeast China has also changed over time.

After briefly tracing the history of Taoism in Fujian, and describing general features of Taoist ritual in the first chapter, each of the following chapters provide case studies of a particular cult. These are the cults of *Baosheng Dadi* (the Great Emperor Who Protects Life), *Qingshui Zushi* (the Patriarch of the Clear Stream), and *Guangze Zunwang* (Reverent

Lord of Broad Compassion). Each case study focuses on one particular aspect of the history and structure of every cult, namely, the spread of the cult temple network, the processions of the gods, and the elaboration of specifically marked rituals for different social groups in a community. These cults have been chosen not only because they are among the most important regional cults of Fujian, but also because they span the Three Religions. Thus, the Great Emperor Who Protects Life is popularly identified as a Taoist doctor, the Patriarch of the Clear Stream was a Buddhist monk, and the Reverent Lord of Broad Compassion is represented as a paragon of Confucian filial piety. In each case study, however, I point out the role of Taoist ritual specialists in providing a framework for the universalization of the local cult. This process of interaction between Taoism and popular cults is reflected in the composition of invocationary songs, hagiographies, and Taoist scriptures for the local god as well as by the ongoing integration of contemporary cult observances into the Taoist liturgical framework.

The writing in Classical Chinese of holy scriptures devoted to local gods in particular represents a major step in the process of incorporation of local cults into the universalistic Taoist liturgical framework (Schipper, 1985a). This usually involves the identification of the esoteric identity of the god as a Taoist astral deity. The printing of these scriptures implies a developed political-economic substructure to the cult. The appearance of the god's legend in official memorials and ultimately, in the official pantheon and register of sacrifices suggests that the political-economic factors have achieved considerable momentum. The recovery of a measure of that momentum under vastly different circumstances is an index of local power in contemporary China.

In the course of this study I document examples of the ongoing confrontation between the *State* and the *Locale* over the pace of the restoration of traditions. Tensions within individual communities over the role of tradition in modernization are also discussed. Generally speaking, the description of each cult begins with a section based on contemporary observances. In the Conclusion I raise the question of the state's capacity for response to this process of revival. By raising these issues, I do not intend to contrast a sinologist's dreamlike vision of an ideal traditional China made up of ritually self-contained, culturally rich villages in opposition to a modern society deprived of essential cultural resources by the strict imposition of state control. Instead, it is crucial to keep in mind that religious traditions are constantly remade and adapted to changing social surroundings. Power may be defined as the *interaction* of forces, creative and repressive, oppressive and evasive, cooperative and cooptive. Individuals reconstruct their community and their culture by actively adapting ancient symbols and ritual forms.[10]

Unfortunately, for decades now in China, religious traditions have been indiscriminately labeled as "feudal superstition." The situation is rapidly changing, however, and scholarly attention is beginning to be devoted to the religious traditions of China and their role in Chinese society. As China struggles to shake loose restrictive ways of thinking to meet the challenges of economic reform, the time has come to reevaluate the categories under which religion has been perceived. Further ethnographic studies, combined with greater critical reflexivity, will help reveal the enduring functions of traditions that refuse to die.

Note on Transliteration

Chinese names and titles have generally been transliterated using *pinyin*, with the exception of some Taiwanese terms and personal names. The term "Taoist" has been used because of its familiarity.

4. Taoist altar painting of Laozi, the Ancient Infant, as the *Daodetianzun* (Heavenly Venerable of the Way and Its Power), from Tongan.

ONE

TAOISM IN FUJIAN

Historical Background

THE THREE CULTS discussed in this book are located in the Minnan area of Southeast Fujian. The time frame takes up developments in the cults beginning at the end of the Five Dynasties period and continuing up to 1990. The coastal province of Fujian is largely made up of mountains, crossed by rivers flowing to the sea, four major coastal plains, and a large number of isolated narrow mountain valleys that have preserved a great diversity of local dialects and subcultures. Inland communication with the rest of China is difficult; one must cross over one of a small number of hazardous mountain passes (see Rawski, 1972, map 3, p. 58).

Skinner (1985) has mapped out the four principal geographically defined economic systems of the Southeast Chinese coast, each organized around river valleys linking inland mountainous hinterlands to coastal greater-city trading systems. To an astonishing degree, these areas have preserved distinct regional subcultures, marked by differences of dialect, local theatrical traditions, architecture, food, and musical traditions. Within each of these regional subcultures there can be a considerable variety of social forms and usages.

The three cults discussed below all originated and flourished within the Minnan "Zhang-Quan" economic region as shown in Skinner (1985, map 2, p. 277). They have since spread beyond Fujian to other areas of coastal China, Taiwan, and Southeast Asia. The Zhang-Quan region forms a triangle that is made up on the western side by the Daiyun Mountain range. The great Jiulong River flows to the sea through the center and the southern portion of the region (Zhangzhou), and the smaller Eastern and Western streams flow to the sea in the north (Quanzhou). The mountainous interior half of this region relies on transportation routes along riverbeds to the two interconnected coastal plains around the two greater-city systems of Zhangzhou and Quanzhou. Xiamen and Jinmen Islands rest in the deepwater bay in between these two systems.[1]

Han Chinese emigration to Fujian began slowly in the Han and began to accelerate in the Tang. The spread of Han settlements in Fujian over this period has been mapped out by Bielenstein (1959). Schafer (1954) has chronicled the short-lived empire of Min at the end of the Five Dy-

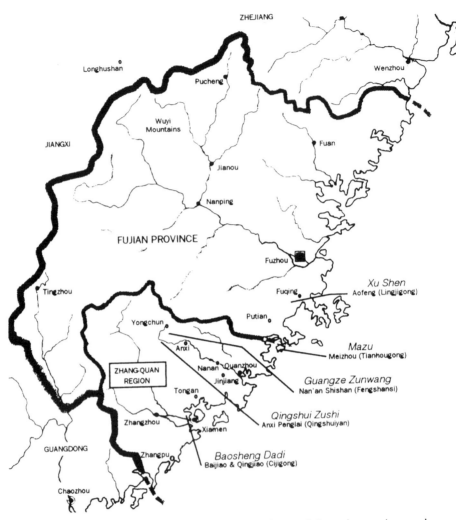

ZHEJIANG

Longhushan

Wenzhou

Pucheng

Wuyi
Mountains

Fuan

JIANGXI

Jianou

Nanping

FUJIAN PROVINCE

Fuzhou

Xu Shen
Aofeng (Lingjigong)

Tingzhou

Fuqing

Yongchun

Putian

Anxi

Mazu
Meizhou (Tianhougong)

Nanan Quanzhou

ZHANG-QUAN
REGION

Jinjiang

Guangze Zunwang
Nan'an Shishan (Fengshansi)

Tongan

Qingshui Zushi
Anxi Penglai (Qingshuiyan)

Zhangzhou

Xiamen

GUANGDONG

Zhangpu

Baosheng Dadi
Baijiao & Qingjiao (Cijigong)

Chaozhou

Map of Fujian Province, showing the Zhangzhou and Quanzhou regions and
the locations of Five Founding Temples of local cults.

nasties period. Skinner (1985) has charted the principal economic macro-cycles of the Fujian area beginning with the Song dynasty. Briefly, the periods of rising and falling economic development are: (1) the period of economic expansion centering on Quanzhou up to 1300; (2) the period of bans on overseas shipping beginning in 1371 and the decline of the Quanzhou economic cycle which reached its lowest point around 1500; (3) the rapid increase in trade with Portuguese and Spanish leading to the establishment of Haicheng as an open port in 1567 culminating in the last years of the Ming (1646–58); and (4) the coastal evacuation in response to the Zheng regime on Taiwan from 1661 to 1683 which broke the upward cycle. The ensuing downward cycle was further accelerated by restrictions on overseas trade in 1717, the designation of Guangzhou as the only open port in 1757, and by rising population pressures and emigration.

Ng (1983) has argued that the region saw a marked expansion in coastal trade and in trade with and development of Taiwan centering in Xiamen from 1683–1735 but the impression remains that higher levels of commercial activity were still inadequate to support growing demographic pressures. Finally, in 1840 Xiamen was made an open port, and another upward economic cycle began under increasing foreign influence (Skinner, 1985). This cycle got off to a shaky start due to major local uprisings in the 1850s and the intrusion of the remnants of the Taiping armies in the early 1860s.

The social history of Fujian since the Song dynasty has been characterized by the growth of single-lineage villages and higher-order lineages (Freedman, 1958, 1966), increasing commercialization propelled by overseas trading, smuggling, and the establishment of an interregional network of Fujian merchant associations (Rawski, 1972; Ng, 1983), growing population pressure and large-scale emigration to Taiwan and Southeast Asia, and an ominous escalation of the level of militarization of local society and social violence, particularly lineage-feuding (Freedman, 1966; Lamley, 1977b). I argue that another central feature in the social history of this period was the development of local cult networks structured by the Taoist liturgical framework.

The development of lineages has been of crucial importance in Fujian. Post-49 land reform figures indicate that jointly owned lineage lands accounted for a hefty proportion of cultivatable land in Fujian: 75.8%–77.98% in Minbei, 50% in Mindong, and 20%–30% in coastal Minnan. (Zheng Zhenman, 1992). Such commonly held property was considered by Freedman to be a necessary condition for a lineage (Freedman, 1966). Recent studies in other parts of China reveal the Southeastern case to be rather the exception than the rule (Ebrey and Watson, eds., 1986). Nonetheless, in Fujian one can still find a very large number of single-surname villages or higher-order lineages spread over several nearby villages. Geographic conditions and agricultural requirements of the area facilitated the evolution of complex lineages.

It is difficult to overemphasize the central importance of territorially based lineages in every aspect of Ming and Qing Fujianese society. In order to understand the cultural forces that enabled lineages to expand into wider arenas of cooperation and conflict, one must examine the role of local and regional cults. And in order to understand the processes by which a cult transcends localism and becomes a vehicle for wider social action, it is necessary to explore the role of Taoism in Fujian.

Taoist Traditions in Fujian

The history of Taoist traditions in Fujian is still largely unexplored. The name of the god of Wuyi Mountains in northwest Fujian appears on early earth contracts found in graves dating from at least the Six Dynasties period (Seidel, 1987; Kleeman, 1984). The same god appears on similar documents in funerals conducted by Taoists in Fujian and Taiwan today. The Wuyi Mountains have long been a center of Taoist traditions. Legends link the mountains with Pengzu, the Chinese Methuselah, and with Taimu, a mother goddess. In the Tang the mountain was listed as the sixteenth of the thirty-two grotto heavens, superior to the seventy-two blessed lands. These grotto heavens were believed to be linked together underground and accessible only to Taoists. A Taoist *guan* temple was established in the Wuyi Mountains in the Tianbao period (740). The mountains were a hotbed of religious activity in the Song when the great neo-Confucian Zhu Xi befriended the estimable Taoist Master Bai Yu-chan (White Jade Toad). Six Taoist temples survived in the mountains until the end of the Qing dynasty (*Wuyi shanzhi*, 1981 [1751]:j.3). A separate study could be devoted to the rise and decline of Taoism in the Wuyi Mountains.[2]

With the exception of certain Quanzhen monastic centers in Northern Fujian, including some in the Wuyi Mountains, Taoists in Fujian have always been Zhengyi (Orthodox Unity) Taoists, otherwise known as *Tianshi* (Celestial Master or Heavenly Master) Taoists.[3] Their ritual tradition is ultimately based on the early Celestial Master Movement of the late Han. Essential elements of their cosmology and their liturgy took shape during the Maoshan revelations of the fourth century, the Lingbao revelations of the fifth century, the Tang codification of Taoist traditions, and the Song Taoist renaissance. This ritual tradition differs from that of the Quanzhen Taoist tradition, founded in the Song, with its emphasis on internal alchemy and its monastic organization and Buddhist-style

5. Taoist altar painting of Zhang Daoling, founder of the
Taoist religion, from Tongan.

daily worship schedule. In contrast, the Orthodox Unity Celestial Master tradition, as it was revived in the Song dynasty on Longhushan (Dragon Tiger Mountain) in Jiangxi, is primarily a tradition of *huoju* (hearth-dwelling) Taoists. These ritual specialists work out of their homes, and provide ritual services to temples, families, and individuals within a large area determined by local traditions and the extent of their own reputations. This is a hereditary priesthood, which generally selects one son in each generation to act as the chief priest, Master of High Merit, while others in the family serve as acolytes. The temples to which they are invited to perform rituals are for the most part dedicated to local gods. Taoists perform rituals in such temples on many occasions, such as the birthday of the local god, or in commemoration of the restoration of a temple, or to consecrate a new god statue. In many areas, Taoists can also perform funeral services and conduct individual rites including exorcisms and prophylactic rites.

The Celestial Master movement was founded in Sichuan in the late Han, as the result of a new revelation by Lord Lao (the deified form of the putative author of the *Daodejing*) to Zhang Daoling. The revelation involved the transfer of registers of the gods and talismans. These materials outlined the early Taoist pantheon and conferred control over many deities to the Zhang family. Many elements of earlier Taoist tradition were integrated into the new theocratic order established in Sichuan. Twenty-four parishes were established, with regular contributions of five bushels of rice from the adherents. Ritual traditions centered on the confession of sins and the administration of talismans to cure disease. Recent research has explored the ritual traditions and scriptural background to the movement (Seidel, 1969, 1970, 1978, 1990; Kaltenmark, 1979; Cedzich, 1987).

The influence of the early Celestial Master movement on the subsequent development of Taoism was profound. The leaders of the movement capitulated to the Wei commander Cao Cao, bringing their ritual traditions into his court and leading to a compromise with secular authorities that positioned Taoism to oversee the spiritual realm. Such arrangements are reflected in the elaboration of Taoist ceremonies of Imperial investiture in the Northern Dynasties and Six Dynasties period (Seidel, 1983).

The loss of north-central China to the Toba and other groups led the court to move south to Jianyang (Nanjing), bringing with them the Celestial Master ritual traditions. These traditions were absorbed into and altered by existing southern occult traditions. Southern aristocratic families sponsored Taoist revelations that confirmed the spiritual primacy of their ancestral lines and local ritual and alchemical traditions. The most significant of these revelations centered on Yang Xi (fl. 365), a visionary in the service of the Xu family. The series of revelations of new deities, visionary and meditational techniques, alchemical recipes, Taoist poetry and song, etc., lasted for several years. These revelations were reverently and scrupulously collated by the great polymath and Taoist master Tao Hongjing (456–536). These writings are known as the Maoshan revelations (Strickmann, 1977, 1979a, 1981; Robinet, 1984).

The importance of Fujian to the Maoshan revelations can be seen in Tao Hongjing's search for the divine headquarters of Wei Huacun (251–334), the divine instructress of the Maoshan revelations, and Mao Ying (145–1 B.C.), Director of Destinies and Minister of the East, in the Daiyun Mountains north of Nan'an in Fujian between 508–512 (Strickmann, 1979a).

The Maoshan revelations were primarily concerned with visionary, meditational, and alchemical techniques suitable for aristocrats convinced of the imminent end of the world. A major turn in the evolution of Taoist ritual traditions occurred in the Lingbao revelations of Ge Chaofu (fl. 415). These took place some fifty years later in the same milieu as the Maoshan revelations and largely in response to them. However, they are distinguished by a greater degree of borrowing from Buddhist traditions and pantheons (Bokenkamp, 1983; Zurcher, 1980). These revelations were codified and worked into ritual texts by Lu Xiujing (406–77). Lu Xiujing's ritual codification would provide the basic framework for subsequent developments in the evolution of Taoist ritual over the centuries (Bell, 1988).

Imperial efforts were also underway to systematize Taoist doctrine, as evidenced by the early Taoist encyclopedia, the *Wushang biyao*, compiled in the Northern Zhou (Lagerwey, 1981). The Tang dynasty furthered the Imperial promotion of Taoism. The Imperial family claimed direct descent from the deified Lord Laozi, and claimed divine aid in the establishment of their dynasty (Seidel, 1970; Benn, 1977). The Tang marked a period of systematization of the various Taoist traditions that had emerged over the preceding five centuries. Adherents were initiated into progressively higher levels in the religion, beginning with the basic texts and pantheon of the Orthodox Unity tradition. Each initiation involved the conferral of a *lu* register of gods, a set of scriptures central to a specific revelation or ritual tradition, a list of related prohibitions, vestments, talismans, spells, and sacred charts (Schipper, 1985b; Benn, 1991).

As mentioned in the introduction, the end of the Tang marks a watershed in the social and religious history of China. The great aristocratic clans lost their grip on bureaucratic office, local centers of power began to emerge, especially in the Jiangnan region, and newly prominent lineages adopted strategies to consolidate local economic power while promoting access to bureaucratic office (Hartwell, 1982). This was also, not surprisingly, a period of proliferating local cults.

Schafer (1954) has stressed the importance of Taoism in the court of the Emperors of Min in Fuzhou, Fujian, at the end of the Tang during the Five Dynasties period. Schafer mentions the extremely influential role of the Taoist Chen Shouyuan in the court of Wang Yanjun, First Emperor of Min. In 932 Emperor Wang received a Taoist ordination complete with talismans and registers of the Taoist gods (see *Ordination Certificate* below). He built Taoist temples for the Taoist Master Chen, and for Tan Zixiao, whom he dubbed Celestial Master.[4] Berthier (1988) has recently analyzed the mythological connections between Taoist Master Chen Shouyuan and his "cousin," Chen Jinggu, the goddess Linshui Furen, the Women by the Side of the Waters. Her cult is closely linked with the myths of the founding and fertility of Min. Her legend is still very much alive in the minds of northern Fujianese. Her cult was the source of a set of rites and ritual techniques associated with the dangers of childbirth and the difficulties of childhood that combine shamanistic and classical Taoist elements. These rites, sometimes referred to as *Sannai* (Three Maidens), or Lushan rites, have spread across Fujian and southern China, and represent one of the most significant regional Taoist movements in Fujian.[5]

The Song dynasty was a period of a renewed outburst of Taoist revelation. Many of these new Taoist movements sought the support of the Imperial court. The best known of these movements was the Shenxiao revelations of Lin Lingsu. Other movements included the Tongchu (Youth's Incipience); Tianxin zhengfa (Orthodox Methods of the Heart of Heaven) movement; the distinct Lingbao movements (Spiritual Treasure) on Longhu Mountain and on Tiantai Mountain; and the Qingwei (Pure Tenebrity) movement. Each of these movements has left its mark on the contemporary Taoist ritual traditions of Fujian (Strickmann, 1979b; Boltz, 1987). As will be seen below, many of these traditions have left an echo in the ritual titles of contemporary Taoist priests in Fujian.[6]

During the Southern Song, the great Taoist Master Bai Yuchan (fl. 1209–24), considered the sixth patriarch of the Southern branch of Quanzhen Taoism, based himself in the Wuyi Mountains of Northern Fujian. Through the work of Taoist Masters like Bai, the Thunder Rites of Shenxiao Taoism made their way into Fujian. Bai commented on many of the variant local movements of Fujian Taoism in his (CT 1307) *Haiqiong Bai chenren yulu* (The Recorded Sayings of the Realized Being Bai Haiqiong). There are many disparaging references to rival Taoist traditions as well as detailed discussions of sectarian religious rituals and doctrine. His own activities in Fujian are described in his *Wuyi ji* (Anthology from the Wuyi Mountains) included in CT 263 *Xiuzhen shishu* (Ten Writings on the Refinement of Perfection). Further information on the evolution of Taoist traditions in Fujian in the Song dynasty can be found in Hong Mai's (1123–1202) *Yijianzhi*. Several anecdotes refer to the strong traditions of mediumism of the Minnan region. Other anecdotes relate the zealous exorcistic efforts of Tianxin Taoists in Northern Fujian. These Taoists often joined forces with government officials to suppress local cults.

Other sources on popular religion in this period include the writings of important Fujian-born neo-Confucians such as Zhu Xi and his disciple Chen Chun (1159–1222), author of the *Beixi ciyi* (*Neo-Confucian Terms Explained*). Chen strongly condemned the proliferation and official recognition of local cults of the Fujian region in his day.

Emperor Song Huizong (r.1101–25) saw through the compilation of a Taoist Canon in the Song. As a center of publishing, Fuzhou was chosen as the site of the first printing of the Taoist Canon between 1118–1120 (Strickmann, 1980; van der Loon, 1984; Boltz, 1987). Song Huizong's effort to gather and print a Taoist Canon is paralleled by his attempts to gather up local cults all over the empire into a unified, officially sanctioned pantheon in which he would play the key role (see *Song Inscriptions* below). Both enterprises reflect a desire to reestablish imperial power in a cosmic continuum, a hierarchy of perfection, or great chain of Being similar to that of Tang Taoism. Such a system proved increasingly difficult to maintain under the pressure of contentious regional Taoist movements in ever-increasing interaction with more and more powerful local popular cults. These tensions become more manifest in the Ming edition of the Taoist Canon, in which much Song material has been lost, but new material on local cults and Taoist ritual traditions can be found.

There is some question as to the extent of the distribution of the copies of the various editions of the Taoist Canon. It is certain that sets of the Canon compiled under Ming Chengzu (1403–24) were distributed to major Taoist temples in 1447. A set of the next Taoist Canon, compiled during the Zhengtong period in 1598 by Emperor Shenzong on behalf of his mother, Empress Dowager Li, was sent to the Wuyi Mountains, according to a stele inscription of 1602 entitled "*Huangdi chiyu Wuyishan Chongyouguan juchi ji Daozhongrendeng*" (Imperial Proclamation to the Abbot and Taoists of the Belvedere of Surging Blessings of the Wuyi Mountains) (*Wuyi shanzhi*, 1981:3.5b–6a; Chen Yuan 1988:1298–99). The inscription mentions a set of 480 cases of books that should be sent "to the Taoist belvederes of the renowned mountains of the Empire."

This set most likely did not include the *Xu Taozang* (Appendices to the Canon), which was added to the Zhengtong Taoist Canon in 1607. At any rate, only three intact sets of the final version of the Taoist Canon survived in China into this century (van der Loon, 1984; Boltz, 1987).[7]

Taoist Sources and Local Cults

By examining the relationship between Taoism and popular cults in Fujian as reflected in the Taoist Canon of the Ming Zhengtong period, one can establish some hypotheses regarding temporal and spatial aspects of the process of interaction between Taoism and popular religion in different regions. A considerable amount of material dating from the early Ming was incorporated into this last Taoist Canon. An analysis of the nature of these materials enables us to distinguish four categories of cults. A cult with the closest connections between official Taoist and government circles might be expected to have the fullest documentation, ranging from liturgical texts and scriptures dedicated to the local deity to temple gazetteers and mediumistic chants of invocation. Other cults with less pronounced official connections might have only some of these different kinds of materials included in the Canon, while others could still be found in the manuscript collections of local Taoist priests. Major local cults with little official contact might escape mention in the Canon altogether. However, Taoist scriptures or liturgies might still be found in the working manuscript collections of local Taoists. A final category of cults would neither be represented in the Canon, nor yet have evolved Taoist scriptures. However, invocationary chants giving the titles and attributes of the god or goddess would circulate among lower-level Taoist Ritual Masters and the mediums they direct.

An example of the first type of cult is that dedicated to the Xu brothers, Xu Zhizheng and Xu Zhi'e (fl. 945), originally military men who may have intervened to aid Fuzhou in the tenth century shortly before the founding of the Min Empire (Davis, 1985; Lagerwey, 1987a, chap. 15). The founding temple of this cult is in Fuqing, south of Fuzhou. In this case, the Taoist Canon includes a full range of texts including a scripture (CT 317), eight liturgical texts (CT 468–475), historical records and mediumistic records (CT 476, CT 1468–70), and divinatory poetry (CT 1301–2). The cult was supported by Ming Chengzu, who built a temple to the Xu brothers in Beijing in 1417. This high concentration of materials indicates a high level of interaction between the court, official Taoist circles, and the popular cult. In fact, a lowly temple keeper in Fuqing had been instrumental in providing a remedy for the ailing Emperor. In reward, his entire family was moved into a temple dedicated to the god built in Beijing and provided with land and emoluments. The scriptures and liturgies are all placed in prominent positions within the subcategories of the Ming Taoist Canon, underlining their importance in official eyes. In 1419, over seven thousand Taoist priests from Zhejiang, Hunan, Jiangxi, and Fujian were gathered into the Fuqing temple to perform a seven-day Taoist ritual of thanksgiving under the direction of the thirtieth-generation Celestial Master, Zhang Yuqing. The texts of the cult describe the spread of the fenxiang network emanating out of the cult center in Fuqing throughout north and central Fujian.

A second category of popular cults includes those like the cult to Mazu, Goddess of the Sea. The mother temple of this cult is located on Meizhou Island off the coast of Putian district, sixty miles south of Fuzhou. In this case, the Taoist Canon has preserved a scripture to the goddess (CT 649), which has been translated by Judith Boltz (1986). However, no liturgical texts devoted to the goddess can be found in the Canon. But such texts do exist in the working collections of Taoist ritual specialists in Putian, Quanzhou, Zhangzhou, and Taiwan. Liturgical manuscripts of *Haijiao* (Sacrificial Offerings for the Oceans), dedicated to Mazu, and written in the mid nineteenth century in Zhangzhou, are also preserved in the British Museum. Nor in this case does the Taoist Canon include any of the temple gazetteers, historical records, theatrical scripts, and even a novel which were produced in the late Ming and Qing periods as the cult grew in importance and eventually was co-opted by the state as an official cult of the Qing dynasty. The inclusion of the scripture of the goddess in the Canon provides evidence of a close connection between the cult and official Taoist circles around the time of the compilation of the Ming Taoist Canon. However, the additional material not included in the Canon provides further evidence of interactions between local-level Taoists and Buddhists, temple committees, and government officials (Li, 1979; Watson, 1985; Jiang, 1990).

A third category of cults would include those major cults of the Minnan region of Fujian to be discussed in chapters 2 and 4 below such as those of The Great Emperor Who Protects Life, Baosheng Dadi, and the Reverent Lord of Broad Compassion, Guangze Zunwang. In these cases, neither scriptures nor liturgies were included in the Taoist Canon. In fact, these cults are not mentioned at all in the Canon. However, Taoist scriptures for these deities have been written by local Taoist priests and survive in their collections and in the collections of the major temples of these cults. Of course, the lack of inclusion in the Taoist Canon by no means indicates that a cult was insignificant in terms of local history.

A fourth category of cults, by far the most numerous, would include such cults as that of the Patriarch of the Clear Stream, Qingshui Zushi, discussed in chapter 3, and the vast majority of other local gods. In these cases, even Taoist scriptures may not yet have been written by local Taoist priests, but the legends of the god are transmitted in the form of invocations chanted by locally based Taoist Ritual Masters when they invoke local gods while performing minor rites or when leading processions in honor of the god. These songs of invocations may be written down but are not liturgical texts, since their presence is not required on the altar during rituals.

One might surmise that the first phase of interaction between Taoists and local cults would lead to the composition of songs of invocation, summarizing the god or goddess's accomplishments. The next phase of interaction requires the major step of the writing of a Taoist scripture for the god. Finally, the degree of official recognition of the cult, within officially sanctioned Taoist circles as well as within the court canonization process, may be reflected in the degree to which additional Taoist sources are elaborated for the cult and included in the Canon.

Certain hypotheses could also be fashioned with regard to the spatial aspects of the interaction between Taoism and popular cults in Southeast China. The reader familiar with Fujian geography (see map) may have noticed that the four types of cults outlined above can be plotted geographically from north to south, from close proximity to government administrative centers to more and more peripheral regions. The impact of the court can be seen most clearly in the cult of the Xu brothers, located near Fuzhou, provincial capital of Fujian. A more complex picture of local sponsorship, mercantile backing, and official co-option can be seen in the case of the Mazu cult further south in Putian district. Local cults such as those to the Great Emperor Who Protects Life, the Reverent Lord of Broad Compassion in the third category, and the Patriarch of the Clear Stream in the fourth, take shape in peripheral regions where they have played a significant role in defining the parameters of local nongovernmental collective action. The specific history of each of these cults needs to be studied in context over time.

In addition to the shifting social and economic conditions in Fujian, the historical context also includes the discrete histories of competing ritual traditions in particular areas. Fujian was of course known as the *Nan foguo* (Southern Buddhist Kingdom), and the growth of Buddhist monasteries from the Song dynasty onward was phenomenal. Liang Kejia's *Sanshanzhi* (Gazetteer of Three Mountains, compiled in 1182 and printed in 1240) provides comparative figures on the expansion of Buddhist monasteries and Taoist temples in the greater Fuzhou area of northeast Fujian (j.10, *banji* [Registration] and j.33–38, *siguan* [Buddhist monasteries and Taoist temples]). To begin with the Buddhists, in the greater Fuzhou area alone some 38 monasteries were established in the Southern and Northern Dynasties, and another 80 were added in the Tang. The Min Empire saw the establishment of 267, and another 331 were added soon after. The Song dynasty saw the establishment of 1406 monasteries. Some 1523 monasteries were still active in the Shaoxing period. At a high point, earlier population registration records gave a figure of 51,233 monks and novices for the Northern Fujian area.

Given the predominance of the household-based tradition of hereditary Taoists, it is not surprising that the Buddhist monasteries greatly outnumbered the Taoist temples. While the Taoists could only boast of 9 temples in this area in 1140 the Buddhists had over 1500. The number of registered Taoists at that time was about 175, while registered Buddhists numbered 15,445. These religious establishments controlled between one-fourth to one-third of cultivated land in Song Fujian (23.05% according to the chart in *Fujian jingji fazhan jianshi* [A Brief Economic History of Fujian], 1989:108; but see Chikusa, 1982). The non-Buddhist population of this region had approximately 5 *mu* of land per person (6 mu equals one acre), compared to 114.5 mu for each monk. Further south the situation was similar. Contemporary estimates suggest that Buddhist landholdings in the Zhangzhou region outnumbered private holdings by a ratio of 6:1 (*Fujian jingji fazhan jianshi*, 1989:109, quoting Chen Chun in the *Zhangzhou fuzhi*).

The section on temple lands in the *Ninghua District Gazetteer* of 1653 provides a succinct overview of the dismantling of these landholdings during the Ming and Qing dynasties. Originally Buddhist monastic estates were expected to perform major construction jobs such as the building of roads and bridges in a kind of tacit fulfillment of responsibilities they managed to avoid through exemptions from taxation. But the burgeoning population of Southern China and the growth of piracy stretched the administrative capabilities of the declining Ming dynasty in Fujian. In the Wanli period lands were seized from Buddhist monasteries to pay for defense against piracy. Once powerful lineages and covetous officials realized the weakness of the monastic estates, they continued to appropriate resources from them. Judging from Fujianese genealogical records, the lineages had in many cases first established Buddhist Halls of Merit for their ancestors so as to ensure continuous services for the dead. These Halls and their monks were supplied with lands and rental properties. Toward the end of the Ming, these halls were repossessed by the lineages and lost their independent bases of financing (Zheng Zhenman, 1992). Tian Rukang (1990) has closely documented the decline of Buddhist landholdings in Fujian in the late Ming and early Qing.

Multiple inscriptions in older temples dedicated to local cults established in the Song enable us to trace a common trend in development beginning with the founding of a temple organized and directed by resident Taoist priests or Buddhist monks in the Song. The next phase (late Ming or early Qing) is usually a restoration effort sponsored by a local lineage that has absorbed the temple into its sphere of influence, or which may be using the temple to extend its influence beyond lineage bounds into a wider regional alliance. These inscriptions tend to be written by literati and include a high proportion of local-level gentry—not necessarily officeholders, but usually men of influence in local society. These materials suggest that lineages and local gentry had in effect taken over most major aspects of local administration by the end of the Ming. Involvement in temple committees was a new way to organize communal projects. For men of position, this involved considerable financial sacrifice, but there were concrete gains in social esteem and power. In theory, membership in such temple committees was open to all in the community served by the temple.[8]

Many of these temples had multiple deities, representing cooperation between distinct localities and social groups. Numerous spirit associations (shenminghui) were formed around individual gods in these temples in the late Ming, judging from mentions in genealogies and occasional inscriptions. These groups often pooled financial resources for the benefit of their members. The later mid-Qing inscriptions in these temples suggest that sponsorship of repairs and rituals had spread to a wider range of social groups, including commercial units such as shops and guilds. The leading role of local lineages can usually still be seen, but the patterns of interaction with local economic forces have changed decisively. The following excerpts from various inscriptions illustrate these trends.

Song Inscriptions

In the foothills of the Qingyuan Mountains, beyond the north gate of Quanzhou, a massive stone sculpture of Laozi was carved in the Song, and it survives to this day. Other sources mention Taoist belvederes and Taoist figures in the Zhang-Quan area, such as two Song inscriptions, the *Zhangpuxian Shengzudian ji* (Record of the Hall of the Saintly Ancestor of Zhangpu District) and the *Quanzhou zimaoshan jinsuguan ji* (Record of the Golden Millet Belvedere of Purple Cap Mountain of Quanzhou) (Chen Yuan et al., *Daojia jinshi lue* 1988:387, 392–93).

Traces can be found in Fujian of the impact of the Southeast Chinese Taoist Lin Lingsu (1076–1120) from Wenzhou, who captured the imagination of Emperor Huizong. Lin's success in persuading Huizong that the latter was in fact the incarnation of the Taoist Grand Sovereign of Long Life of the freshly revealed supreme celestial region of Shenxiao (Strickmann, 1978; Boltz, 1987) resulted in important changes in religious policy. These revelations appear to have been prompted by Huizong's call in 1114 for the submission of texts to be included in the Taoist Canon. Several Shenxiao scriptures and ritual compendiums survive in the Ming Taoist Canon. Further evidence of the impact of the inspired emperor's interest in the Taoist movement is a stele written by Huizong establishing a Shenxiao Taoist temple in Putian. The stele survives to this day. The temple has been renamed the Temple of the Eastern Peak. The text is entitled *Shenxiao yuqing wanshou gong* (The Temple of Great Longevity of Jade Purity of the Divine Empyrean), composed and written by the Emperor (Chen Qiren *Minzhong jinshilue* 1934: 5.8:7b-10a). The stone measures 7'9" by 3'2", with sixteen lines of forty words each. The carved top of the stele, with the title of the inscription, had broken off and sunk into the ground but had been recently unearthed when Chen wrote his account. A blank space had been filled in with the names of court editorial officials and local officials who erected the stone in 1119/9/22, two months before Lin Lingsu returned in disgrace to Wenzhou.

Strickmann (1978) has demonstrated the role of the Shenxiao revelations in an attack on Buddhism, and particularly the sale of blank ordination forms. He has also noted the impact of the movement on the organization of the Taoist Canon from the Song to the Ming. Thus, efforts to translate new Taoist revelations and divinities into temples throughout the Empire represent one extreme instance of imperial involvement with, and overcoding of, local-level popular religion.

Another somewhat later surviving Song stele from Putian illustrates the more usual flow from the local level to the court already institutionalized in Huizong's reign. The *Xiangying miaoji* (Record of the Temple of Auspicious Responses), was composed in 1138 by the Grand Master for Court Audiences, Administrator of the Taishou Taoist Belvedere for the Veneration of the Tao, Fang Lue (fl. 1107–29) and written by Grand Master for Closing Court, Vice-Director of the Branch Bureau of Equipment of the Ministry of War, Fang Zhaobing. The text is given in Chen Qiren, *Minzhong jinshilue* (1934: 5.8:20b-25b). The original stone was 5'4" high and 3'4" wide. The inscription is made up of thirty-three lines of sixty-three words each (approx. 2079 words), written in *zheng* calligraphy. The title was written in seal script. The temple was ten li (three miles) to the north of Putian City. Originally the temple, called Daguan miao (Temple of the Great Official), housed a large group of local gods, without any one principal deity. In 1107 Huizong worshiped the "hundred gods" in the southern suburban sacrifice. He commanded that all those gods of the mountains and rivers and the hundred gods that had performed meritorious deeds for the people should be reported to the Circuit Fiscal Commissioners. Therefore, the deeds of the gods of the Temple of the Great Official were reported to the court which responded to the request of the people and presented the temple with an official name.

Nine years later (1116), another worship of the "hundred gods," conducted by Huizong in the Ming Tang, led to another report and a request for a title for the god of the temple. This was accepted by the Court of

Imperial Sacrifices and signed with pleasure by the Emperor. The title of "Duke of Auspicious Responses" was granted in 1122.

The authors next recount the miraculous origin of the temple in a lightning storm. Then they remark on the geomancy of the site, and quote the comments of knowledgeable (diviners):

> There are many members of a great surname group and excellent clan living around the temple who will be selected to be officials in special examinations. Everything was as the diviner had said. There is a legend that the Great Official Temple was so named because after local people had become great officials, they would retire and live out their old age in their home village. They would lead their children and grandchildren together with the [village] elders . . . each year on the day of the *she*, village festival, to pray for abundant harvests before the god. They would carefully set out the plates and goblets, spread forth the ritual food vessels, and then bow and ascend into the hall by order of age with great filial piety. This was like the ancient [custom of] village wine-drinking.

This passage illustrates the trend whereby the great bureaucratic service lineages of the Northern Song were turning their attention toward their local villages and lineage affairs (Hartwell, 1982; Hymes, 1986; Hansen, 1990). After listing further miracles involving divine protection from locust plagues in 1117, bandits in 1120, and rebel bands of soldiers attacking Fuzhou in 1129 and 1130, several passages describe the assistance rendered by the god to local merchants on their journeys by sea both along the China coast and overseas.

> A Quanzhou merchant named Zhu Fang sailed to Sanfoqi [in Indonesia]. Before leaving he also asked for the god's incense ash and carefully worshiped it. His boat traveled swiftly and without trouble. The round-trip voyage was completed within a year, and his profit was a hundred times that of the original outlay. Since no one who did business overseas had ever done this well, everyone agreed that the credit for this was due to the god. From this time onwards, whenever merchants were travelling on a distant journey, they would first come and pray to the god.

This passage illustrates the increasing involvement of local gods with the growing commercial sector in the Song documented in Hansen (1990).

The author concludes by suggesting that the god could use an enhancement of his title to match the splendor of the newly restored temple and augmented rituals addressed to him by the local people. He reminisces about having been dragged to the temple as a boy for solemn rituals, only to run and play in the dirt outside as soon as he could break away. Now at the end of his thirty-year official career, he can think of nothing more gratifying than to leave it all behind and join the elders in their long, white, cotton gowns, leaning on their staffs as they go to worship and offer wine in the temple of the god. He mentions that the repairs were led by a Vice Director of the Imperial Court of Sacrifices, Fang Qiao (*jinshi*, 1034), who donated land and expanded the temple in 1083. Then in 1116, Supervisor of the Household of the Heir Apparent, Fang Hui (*jinshi*, 1076), led in restoring the temple. The most recent repairs cited were carried out from 1134–1136, and involved building a hall with eighty-two beams at a cost of ten thousand strings of cash.

In this inscription one can see evidence of the interaction between powerful officials, wealthy merchants, and a large lineage centered around a temple to a local deity. The requests for enhanced enfeoffments refer to the pace of local improvements. Should not the court recognize these changes? In the two Song inscriptions one finds both the direct impact of Taoist revelation on the court and the local level as well as efforts on the part of the court to absorb local gods upward into the imperially worshiped pantheon. The entire process of the standardization of the canonization process can be seen as an attempt to expand Imperial ritual and reaffirm the Imperial role in an ideologically coded cosmic continuum of power, by absorbing local forces and cults that have reached a certain level of development, usually within the framework of the Taoist liturgical tradition.

The second inscription raises the issue of the role of the lineage in the development of the cult. While the general trend was for lineages to control the expansion of the cult, including the regulation of its lands and the hiring of Taoist or Buddhist ritual specialists for its ritual observances, one can find occasional references to other sorts of relationships between lineages and Taoism. An entry in the *Putian xianzhi* (1926: 4:46) describes a certain Fang Guangweng who, in the Yuan dynasty, gave up his official position as a Salt and Iron Commissioner, and became a Taoist priest. He had the many halls and towers of the Wanshou gong (known as the New Belvedere, in distinction from the Shenxiao Wanshougong—later known as the Yuanmiao Guan [Belvedere of Primordial Mystery] mentioned above) built in 1314, and set aside some 1500 shi of land-rent grain, along with extensive aquacultural properties for the temple. This capital could only be passed down to his male descendants if they became Taoist priests and took charge of the temple. This practice continued for a hundred years, until, in the early 1400s, it was found necessary to bring in outside Taoists with different surnames to run the somewhat diminished holdings of the temple. The temple appears to have remained in the hands of Taoists for some time, for it was rebuilt in 1613 by Taoist Master Lin Jian. When, sometime thereafter, government officials were considering repossessing some of the temple lands, the lineage rose up to protect their holdings, and established an ancestral shrine dedicated to Fang Guangweng, and other illustrious members of the lineage, within the temple compound.

Ming and Qing Inscriptions

At the outset of the Ming Dynasty, the government attempted to achieve a greater degree of control over local Taoist groups by establishing a nationwide Office of Taoist Affairs at the provincial, prefectural, and district levels. Taoists were expected to obtain certificates of ordination from the Celestial Masters of the Zhang line ensconced in the Celestial Master Headquarters on Longhu shan (Dragon Tiger Mountain) in the town of Shangqing (Supreme Purity) in the district of Guixi in Jiangxi. This site is some thirty miles north of the pass into the Shaowu region of northwest Fujian, beyond the Wuyi Mountain range. The Ming Emperors continued to favor the Celestial Masters of Longhu shan, sponsoring the construction of the massive Shangqing Temple near the Tianshi fu, and inviting the Tianshi to court to perform immense rituals and equally immense scholastic tasks such as the editing of the Ming Taoist Canon. However, it is very difficult to determine to what extent this effort at controlling the spreading localization of Taoist movements had any success. The Office of Taoist Affairs survived in some districts of Fujian until modern times (in some areas of Fujian and in Taiwan), but in others had already fallen into disuse by the Qing (*Anxi xianzhi*, 1757, j.5.1, 1969 rpt., 143).

For the Ming and Qing periods there are over a dozen extant unpublished steles in the Minnan region (including Xinghua) that were composed by or name local-level Taoist priests. From these inscriptions, one can gain a sense of the institutional as well as the extrainstitutional setting of Taoists in Fujian during this period. Most district-level cities had a major Taoist belvedere, founded in the Song dynasty. When these belvederes were restored in the Ming, there is clear evidence of the high level of support of the local administration for these temples, which often became the site of the Office of Taoist Affairs. By the beginning of the Ming, at the latest, and in line with national policy, these cities also had Taoist priests residing in City God temples (Taylor, 1990). Another group of Taoists were associated with the Temples of the Eastern Peak, specializing in difficult death rituals.

The Office of Taoist Affairs in Tongan district of Quanzhou prefecture was established in the Ming dynasty in the Chaoyuan guan (Taoist Belvedere of the Audience with the Primordial), just outside the Chaoyuan gate at the west of the city. This Taoist belvedere was first built in 1238. After being destroyed by fire in battles in 1354, a Taoist named Chen Yining built the Jade Emperor Hall on the foundations of the old temple in 1372. In 1382 one Lin Sizhen added the Three Pure Ones Hall. In 1388 one Gu Huishi built the Yuantan Gong (Palace of the Primordial Altar). In 1413 the Taoist Officer of Tongan, Shi Daoming, set up his altar there. Shi secured the cooperation of two district magistrates to restore the temple. He recorded these deeds in the *Chongxiu chaoyuanguan bei* (Stele Inscription on the Restoration of the Audience before the Primordial Belvedere), written in 1419. The inscription first records the leading role and contributions of the Taoist officials of the belvedere, and then goes on to record the names of the District Magistrate, the Confucian Instructor, and the rest of the local official hierarchy at the end of the list. Shi Daoming could scarcely contain his pride:

> The learning of Laozi consists in emptiness and non-action. For with emptiness there is spiritual power, just as non-being brings forth being. Using (these teachings) one can control demons and spirits, drive thunder and rain, call up the transformations of Yin and Yang, emerge from and enter into Creation. The merit of the teaching is adequate to harmonize the five degrees, to nourish the people and support the Way of the world. Now, as for the Taoist Belvedere of Tongan District, if there is a drought then prayers there will bring dark clouds and rain; if disease breaks out, then efficacious remedies will be found. The people revere and trust in the Belvedere even more than a son reveres and trusts in his own father and mother. Thus the assistance rendered by the two Magistrates is nothing other than inviting in good fortune in response to the requests of the people, and praying for longevity for the Imperial throne.

By the Ming and early Qing, in addition to their presence in Taoist Belvederes and City God temples, Taoist priests were occasionally based in temples dedicated to local deities (especially when the deity was an established member of the Taoist pantheon). However, many such temples to local deities were occupied by Buddhist priests, rather than Taoists. The decline in the great Buddhist monasteries of Fujian had released a flow of impoverished bonzes. Already by the early Qing one begins to find evidence of Taoists being forced out of local cult temples.[9]

In the Qing, relations between the court and official Taoist circles became strained, and Taoism went into a sharp decline. Taoism became associated in the government's mind with millenarian movements and anti-Manchu agitation (Kuhn, 1990). Statutes in the legal codes since Ming times strictly regulating Taoists, Buddhists, sectarians, and popular religious worship were enforced with great severity (de Groot, 1903–4). The growing pressure of the Western powers led to early instances of iconoclastic attacks on popular religion, such as that of the Taiping troops who burned down the headquarters of the Celestial Masters on Longhu shan, along with countless temples to local gods they encountered on their march across South China. Even prior to this time, the central role of the Longhu shan Celestial Masters appears to have declined due to the lack of court backing, and the continuing regionalization of locally based Taoist ritual traditions.

An inscription from Hui'an in the late Qing demonstrates the degree to which Taoist priests had become integrated into an extrainstitutional local regional network, in opposition to the hierarchical powers of the officialdom and the local gentry.

The *Hui'anxian zhengtang xushijin* (Prohibitory proclamation of the Hui'an district yamen) was written in 1909, and quotes the complaint of a group of local gentry to the effect that

> whenever private families carry out sacrifices for auspicious or inauspicious purposes, they inevitably invite the two surnames (Taoist and/or Buddhist priests). . . . [These] Buddhist and Taoist priests set up their own vulgar rites in order to obtain wealth by deceit. They even dare to falsely claim that each ward belongs to a particular **shizhu** (main temple, [lit., 'master of dispensation']), and that they have hereditary relationships with [these temples] due to the fact that their forebears have conducted sacrifices and established merit within the ward, so that whenever anyone within the ward (wishes to) hire a Buddhist or Taoist priest, that matter must be handled by the main temple, and people may not hire anyone else (but them), nor may anyone else take the job for personal profit.

The authors of the complaint point out that this situation has led to territorial disputes and, in particular, allowed certain Taoists to extort high fees for their services and oppress the people of the ward. The Taoist master Zhang Fu of Liangjin ward is singled out for having accepted payments but not provided services, while simultaneously forbidding others from performing the rites. The authors remark: "As for the term 'master of dispensation,' we do not know when it came into use, although it seems to mean that there is one master of dispensation per ward. Now how could it be that Hui'an district, with its seventy-two wards, has never posted a proclamation [officially] listing its 'masters of dispensation'?" In response, the yamen issued a proclamation decreeing that in the future, people could hire Buddhists and Taoists at their own convenience, and that the temples (and their associated priests) had no right to interfere and cause trouble. Reading beyond the evident disdain for Taoists on the parts of the authors of the accusation and the official proclamation, one can begin to get a sense of the degree to which Taoism had penetrated local-level society in late Imperial China.

Despite official oppression and clear signs of decline, the downward dispersal of Taoism has left a mark in the records of early ethnographers like deGroot and missionaries like Doolittle who testify to the continued importance of Taoist ritual practitioners in Fujian at the end of the Imperial era. The underlying attitudes of traditional Confucian literati continued, however, to be opposed to popular religion and to Taoism. Popular religion was subsequently rejected as backward and traditionalistic by iconoclastic, reform-minded Chinese intellectuals involved in the May 4 movement, by modern-state-building KMT reformers, and by CCP revolutionaries. Many temples to local gods were taken over by the Republican government and converted into schools or other government offices (Duara, 1991). Both the KMT and the CCP maintained positions of hostility toward traditional popular religion after 1949 (Agnacost, 1987; Ahern and Gates, 1981b; Weller, 1987). Large quantities of irreplaceable sources on the history of Taoism in Fujian were destroyed during the Socialist Education Campaign and the Cultural Revolution.

The Distribution of Taoist Traditions in Fujian

It would be premature to attempt to delineate the different Taoist ritual traditions of Fujian as they survive today. Some general observations can however be made. As mentioned above, almost all the Taoists in Fujian are Zhengyi Taoists, working within families out of their homes. According to questionable statistics quoted in a publication on Fujian compiled by the *Fujian Daily* in 1981, there were 46 Taoist *guan* and 2,500 Taoists in Fujian in 1949. By 1960 the numbers had drastically declined: only 8 Taoist guan (belvedere) remained and only 450 Taoists were registered. I have seen meeting attendance books belonging to the Taoist Association of Quanzhou dating from 1958. The names of twenty to thirty Taoists are listed as having taken part in such campaigns as the "Elimination of the Five Pests," etc. Nowadays only two or three Taoists are active in the city.

During the Cultural Revolution all these temples were closed, and many Taoists were subjected to imprisonment. Taoist manuscripts, paintings, vestments, ritual implements, etc., were destroyed or impounded. Since 1979, however, many Taoists have been called back to perform rituals for the reviving of local cults and lineage organizations. According to remarks by the Director of the Bureau of Religious Affairs for Fujian, and reports in *Zhongguo Daojiao*, the number of Taoist priests in Fujian is now over 4,000 (Zhang Jiyu, 1989; but for larger estimates see Lin Qing, 1989). Of this number, 171 were said to be Quanzhen Taoists. If one were to include the number of acolytes and apprentice Taoists, I would estimate that the actual number would reach well over 10,000.

Very few Taoist guan have yet been returned to Taoist control, despite a general policy assigning not only Taoist temples, but also popular cult temples, to the Taoist Association. So far in Fujian, the Taoist Association has had little success in organizing Taoists since it is perceived as a regulatory body that would interfere with the freedom to perform rituals in the countryside.

Taoist rituals consist of a variety of forms of either *jiao* (communal sacrifices), *gongde* (family requiem services), or *quxie* or *xiaofa* (exorcistic, or "minor" rites for individuals). The jiao and the gongde can last between half a day to up to seven or even nine days. A core set of some fifteen rites can be abbreviated or expanded, while additional rites can be added in to a total of over thirty rites depending on the time and cost of the complete ritual. Generally speaking, one could divide the surviving ritual traditions of Fujian, as they have been surveyed so far, into five or six general categories:

1. Along the coastal Minnan area including Quanzhou, Jinjiang, Zhangzhou, Longhai, and on south to Zhao'an one finds Zhengyi Lingbao (Orthodox Unity Spiritual Treasure) Taoists with ritual traditions quite similar to those of Tainan Taoist Masters such as Chen Rongsheng. These Taoists perform jiao as well as gongde funerals, and can perform many xiaofa minor rituals, as well.

2. In inland Zhao'an and Pinghe, where Hakka and Hoklos live in close proximity, one finds a Zhengyi tradition very close to that of the Northern Taiwanese Taoists. In these areas, Taoists perform only jiao and certain exorcistic rites, but do not do gongde funerals. The latter are performed by family-based "Buddhist" ritual specialists. (Lagerwey, 1988, 1989)

3. Gutian in Northern Fujian (Minbei) is the center of the Lushan ritual tradition, with its mixture of shamanistic and classical elements. This tradition has spread throughout Fujian and over to Taiwan, but it appears to be strongest in Minbei and in Minxi (Longyan). In the latter area plays based on the legend of Chen Jinggu, the principal goddess of the Lushan tradition, are interspersed into a very sketchy jiao service.

4. The Taoist traditions of Fuzhou are quite distinct from the others in that they include purely lay liturgical groups, in addition to the more familiar specialists in Lushan exorcistic rites.

5. Putian and Xianyou have rich Taoist traditions that appear in some respects to be similar to (1) above, but with a strong Qingwei ritual tradition as well.

6. Certain areas, such as upper Nan'an, appear closer to (1) above in their funeral services, but lack the elaborate jiao rituals. They also have been influenced by Lushan traditions (3 above), but worship a local deity, Zhang Daoyuan, as the founder of that tradition, rather than Chen Jinggu.

Further research will reveal more about the various ritual traditions of the Zhengyi Taoists of Fujian, and the manuscript lineages that link certain of their traditions to those in Taiwan and Southeast Asia. For the moment let us take a closer look at the life experiences of a practicing Taoist priest in Southeast China.

Taoist Priests in Contemporary Fujian

There are many links to past Taoist ritual traditions that can be found in Fujian. For example, I met an old Taoist in Tongan who had received his training in the Belvedere of Audience with the Primordial in Tongan, mentioned above. He counts himself as belonging to the eighteenth generation of Shi Taoists (a different surname group from that of Shi Daoming). He was adopted as a child by the fraternity of Shi Taoists, and lived in the Chaoyuan guan until the age of sixteen. Another group of Shi Taoist priests worked in the Temple of the Eastern Peak to the east of the city. The Belvedere was abandoned during the war, and is now in ruins.[10] As a result, Master Shi now works out of his home in a nearby market town. All of his manuscripts were destroyed during the Cultural Revolution. He was imprisoned and tortured, and forced to write many confessions. He often contemplated suicide but persevered out of concern for his elderly mother. He still thanks her for having given him the strength to survive the torments of the times.

His family did manage to save a good collection of beautiful Taoist altar hangings by burying them in a pigsty. These include representations of the Three Pure Ones, Ziwei, Yuhuang, Leisheng Puhua Tianzun, Zhang Tianshi, and Xuantian Shangdi, as well as the Ranks of the Immortals to the East and the West. They are almost identical in style and iconography to the paintings used in Tainan by Master Chen Rongsheng.

Master Shi is an excellent musician and calligrapher. He can play courtly Nanguan ballads on the Southern *pipa* (lute), as well as exuberant *sona* (oboe) pieces in the Stirring of the Hall prior to and after a Taoist ritual. He is most proud of his ability to produce piercing notes on his buffalo horn, used to summon spirit soldiers. His calligraphy ranges from carefully drawn miniature characters, through special Taoist flattened characters for placards and certain documents, to fluidly drawn talismans. He was able to re-create the bulk of his manuscript tradition from memory, but laments that many rituals are lost without the original texts. He is proficient at all kinds of paper-cutting and artwork necessary for the construction of funeral homes, soul banners, Taoist altar hangings, representations of the Lords of the Five Directions, the Six Animals, the Earth God, the White Tiger, and various substitute bodies employed in certain rituals. Master Shi is now over sixty years old. He is currently training his son in Taoist rituals. His own ritual tradition has finally rewarded him in recent years. He now lives in a newly built, two-story home with his son's family, including one grandson. But he is less than optimistic about the future. He worries that policies toward religion may change again, as they so often have in the past four decades.

Taoist Master Shi represents the common condition of Taoists in Fujian, struggling in relative isolation to rebuild his ritual tradition, often without original texts. An example of the opposite end of the spectrum is a small single-surname village in Jinjiang in which virtually every single male out of fifty in the community could perform some aspect of a Taoist ritual, either as a priest, an acolyte, a musician, a decorator of altars, or a fabricator of paper puppets, soul palaces, Marshals, etc. Other traveling

6. The Jade Emperor (papier-mâché; from Zhangzhou).

groups of artisans from Jinjiang specialized in carving god statues, or painting temple murals. The scope and extravagance of funerals in Jinjiang are legendary throughout the Minnan region. Everything is thrown in, including Western brass bands, disco music, and of course the entire gamut of traditional processional troupes, theater, music, dancing lions and dragons, etc.

Like many Taoist Masters currently working in Southeast China, Master Shi keeps a list of temples in the area to which he is regularly invited to perform rituals, along with the dates of the birthdays of the local deities in those temples. In some areas, where the principal temples are more intact, one can get a sense of the levels of importance of the various temples, as reflected in the relative elaborateness of the rituals scheduled for their festivals.

Master Shi did not go to the headquarters of the Celestial Masters, the descendants of Zhang Daoling, at Longhu shan in nearby Jiangxi to receive his ordination. He received it directly from other senior members of the Shi fraternity. His home altar is designated as the *Ningzhenjing jingxuantan* (Realm of Crystallized Perfection, Altar of Purified Mystery). His ritual name is *Faxuan* (Ritual Mystery). His Taoist title is *Zhengyi mengwei jinglu xuanhua dachi xianguan kaojiao youming xianshi* (Immortal Officer Who Proclaims the Great Commands of the Scriptures and Registers of the Sworn Powers of Orthodox Unity, Interrogator of Immortal and Underworld Affairs). Shi's ordination certificates were destroyed along with his family genealogy and many liturgical manuscripts in the late 1960s. I was only able to find one such ordination document among the dozens of Taoist priests I met in Fujian. This is translated below at the end of the chapter.

Structural Features of Taoist Ritual

It would be possible to conduct an archaeology of Taoist ritual beginning with the careful, comparative study of current Taoist ritual traditions. The performance of these rituals and their manuscripts reveal the processes of accretion, displacement, and substitution between the layers of the evolving tradition, which result in redundancies, metaphysical elaborations, and a loss of narrative comprehensibility. Such historical and philological investigation will reveal a great deal about the rules of ritual elaboration over time (Dean, 1990a). A formal study of contemporary Taoist ritual can also elucidate the rules of ritual structure. Hubert and Mauss presented some suggestions along these lines in their work (1964 [1898]), and recently Frits Staal has demonstrated the usefulness of this approach in his study of the Vedic *Agni* ritual (1983).

The following generalizations are based on some fifteen jiao communal sacrifices that I attended in Fujian between 1985 and 1991. Fairly exhaustive descriptions of Taoist altars and rituals as performed in Taiwan are now available (Schipper, 1975, 1982, 1984; Ofuchi, 1983; Lagerwey, 1987a), and since the ritual traditions of Fujian and Taiwan are very similar (see above), I will not go into great detail here. It is important to note that the Taoist altar is portable. Paintings of the highest anthropomorphic emanations of the Tao, the *Sanqing* (Three Pure Ones) are arranged at the back of the local god's temple. The statue of the god is moved to the position of a guest, facing the Taoist high gods from the (ritually) south side of the temple. Along the walls next to the Sanqing are arrayed paintings of Zhang Daoling (stage left) and Xuantian Shangdi (stage right). The Taoist altar, with incense burner, ritual implements, the liturgical manuscript, and various offerings is set in front of the paintings. Another altar, for the gods of the Three Realms, is set just inside the entrance, facing the Taoist deities. Around the room, along the walls, other altar tables are set with placards indicating the seat of the gods invited to the ritual. Upon these altars, or on additional tables, are arrayed the *doudeng* (Lamps of Destiny) of the community representatives. Five buckets of rice are distributed around the four directions and the central altar. The ritual setting out of the Five Real Writings into these containers during the Evening Overture rite, usually at the end of the first day of the ritual, symbolizes the creation of a Sacred Space, the Land of the Tao.

In many areas, the temple, normally open to all, is cordoned off during a jiao communal sacrifice, and only the Taoists and the community representatives are allowed in. Outside the temple, one normally finds a courtyard which is used to set up tables of offerings at certain times, and at other times as a spectator's space for theatrical performances which take place on the stage facing the temple across the courtyard.

Lagerwey (1981, 1987a) has shown the continuity of the three fundamental phases of early Taoist ritual within more complex, contemporary ritual. These phases are the *Suqi* (Evening Overture), the *Xingdao* (Walking the Way), and the *Yangong* (Announcement of Merit). Schipper (1984) argues for an underlying dyadic formal structure within Taoist ritual consisting of (1) the establishment of a Sacred Space and the *zhai* (Retreat), and (2) the jiao (Sacrifice of Texts) and the Deconstruction of the Sacred Space. Within the first set, one finds elaborate rites of (a) entry; (b) purification; (c) invocation; and (d) distribution of the Five True (Talismanic) Writings. Each of these subsets is composed of the particular rituals that are structured in the same way as the overall ritual. They each include the burning of one or more of a variety of documents. The second set is, as Hubert and Mauss have suggested, the inverse of the first, and includes the parallel subsets of (d) sacrifice of the texts, or in some rites, libations; (c) send-off of the gods: (b) purification; and (a) exit. To the first set correspond the rituals of Invitation of the Gods, Division of

Lamps, Sealing of the Altar, Evening Overture, and the Audience Rituals (Sacred Space, Morning, Noon and Evening Audiences). In the second set one finds first the Presentation of the Memorial and the True Sacrifice, followed by the Dispersal of the Altar and the Send-off of the Gods.

The ritual is further complicated by the performance of an internal ritual by the chief priest simultaneous with the external ritual. Schipper (1984) points out that early Taoist liturgy involved two settings, the *jing-shi*, Meditation Chamber, and the *Tan*, outdoor Altar. Both of these have been conflated into the single Sacred Altar Space for many contemporary rituals, although the Presentation of Memorial still takes place on a stage platform outside the temple. Recall that the Taoist body is a microcosm, in which the ritual is carried out. Internal changes affect the external world. The gods are within. The second phase of the first set is crucial. In it a Sacred Space is established by the placement of the Five True Talismanic Writings around a Sacred Space. Then the pure offerings are brought before the gods, anthropomorphic emanations of the Tao. Next, a message is presented to the gods, transformed by fire, and sent to them. Finally, the Five True Talismanic Writings are burned, and the Sacred Space is deconstructed. The Taoist telescopes time and space by constructing a universe, then speeds up cosmic cycles through the recitation and oblation of divine texts and the dispersal of the sacred space in order to generate merit for himself, the community representatives, the village, and for all the beings and spirits along the Great Chain of Being. Every being is promoted upward on the cosmic scale. The ritual thus reenacts the Taoist's own ordination while saving all beings.

In referring to a "Sacrifice of Texts" I am clearly far from the game of death that concerns Luc de Heusch (1985). K. M. Schipper has used the term "le sacrifice des écritures" in his book, *Le Corps Taoiste* (1982). "Écritures" means both writing and Scripture. Schipper is pointing out something unique in Taoist ritual that may extend our conception of sacrifice. Recall Hubert and Mauss's (1964) emphasis on the establishment of communication with the gods through some medium which is destroyed in the course of the ritual. In Taoist ritual the medium consists of words and signs. In fact, the Five True Talismanic Writings are not words but talismanic configurations of primordial, numinous energy. In some traditions they are not even written down; instead, a brush and ink are set before a blank sheet of paper in each of the Five Measures of Rice (*wu dou mi*, also the name of an early Taoist movement).

Some documents are sent to underworld officials, demanding the release of the soul. Others are divided in halves and sent to two parties—the soul and the underworld official, for example—who can then reconnect the halves for verification. Some are kept by the soul as records or receipts for the rituals performed on his behalf, or the paper spirit money spent to repay his debt to life.[11]

Clearly this vast amount of bureaucratic paperwork reflects the influence, or perhaps the usurpation of the Imperial Government apparatus. Emily Ahern has claimed that "people use charms, as well as documents in funeral ceremonies and the *chiao* [jiao], just as they would use other documents in the world of men: to bring the authority of figures in positions of power to bear on others" (Ahern, 1981a:29). However, there is a danger in being too literal. Certain Taoist documents, such as the Five Real Talismans, have the power to create a universe. It is difficult to imagine a similar worldly document. We must turn our attention to the theory of the origin of these signs in the Taoist scriptural tradition in order to understand their function.

Several central Taoist scriptures such as the *Duren jing* (Scripture of Salvation), the first in the Taoist Canon, present an account of their own origins in the following terms: In the beginning the primordial breath, *qi*, filled the Void. The Breath gradually congealed into immense cloud-seal characters. These emitted light and sound. Eons later they were transcribed by heavenly scribes on gold tablets, and preserved in libraries of the stellar court. After many more eons they were revealed to the Taoist elect, usually in the context of a visitation from a divine messenger, a "hierogamy." Contemporary Taoist liturgical manuscripts, passed down within a family for centuries, also refer to cloud-seal characters. In this case, it is the smoke of the incense burned in the ritual that rises into heaven, forming characters legible to the gods alone. The transformation of texts by burning would seem to produce a similar translation. Thus the scriptures would return to their origins, completing a cosmic cycle. Recall the lengthy eons between successive phases of the revelation of scriptures mentioned above. These are in fact prescribed. The holier the scripture, the lengthier the period of storage and the resultant delay in revelation. The recitation of several scriptures within the re-created universe of the Sacred Space established by the placement of the Five True Talismanic Writings, followed by the burning of these talismans represents an acceleration of the process of revelation and return, and is thus the engine of merit-making in the ritual.

The ritual is also proceeding within the body of the chief priest. The medieval liturgical manuals reveal that the talismanic-orders were not only burned and sent to the gods or to the souls. Some were burned and then the ashes were consumed by the priest. Descending into his body, they could effect the summoning of the gods within his body, whom the priest would then send forth to merge with their counterparts in the macrocosm. In contemporary ritual, the gods within the body of the Taoist priest are invoked and sent forth during the Opening of the Incense Burner segment of rites such as the Presentation of the Memorial through meditation and visualization.

Having thus united the inner and outer realms, the Taoist priest was

7. Sketch to assist a Taoist priest's visualization of the journey to the star palaces during meditation (from the *Jiutian yunlu tujue* "Illustrated Instructions on the Cloudy Way through the Nine Heavens," manuscript from Putian).

prepared to hold audience with the highest emanations of the Tao. During this visualized meeting he would present the message of the ritual, before merging with the Tao to effect the ritual. An illustrated manuscript from Xianyou provides an example of just how this audience between the chief Taoist priest and the Three Pure Ones was visualized within one ritual tradition. One first sees the high priest kneeling before the altar between two acolytes. The altar is called Heming shan, the site of Laozi's revelation of sacred texts to Zhang Daoling, the first Celestial Master. The next image shows the high priest in flight atop a crane about to enter the gateway of the Sun, the Moon, and the Stars (see figure 7). The final image shows the priest kneeling before the Three Pure Ones, where he will read the Memorial explaining the purpose of the ritual.

The Structuring of Community Involvement
in Taoist Ritual

The activities of the entire community—the setting out of different categories of offerings, the performance of ritual theater, the processions of the gods, and the worship conducted by the community representatives inside the temple—are all structured by the sequence of rituals performed by the Taoist priests.

At the most obvious level, the timing of these different aspects of the festival is determined by the timing of the Taoist ritual. At a deeper level, the liturgical framework organizes distinct groups along parallel lines. Finally, at the level of cultural construction of reality, the liturgical framework generates a complex process model of spiritual power in a multifaceted interaction with local systems of power.

The funding for rituals is gathered according to two systems; on the one hand every person in the village is expected to contribute the same small amount. Similarly, every family sends a male representative to the temple, and each one takes turns casting divination blocks. The men with the most successive affirmative casts are selected as the huishou. Depending on the rank they attain in this fashion, they are expected to make a major contribution to the cost of the festival. On the other hand, individuals may contribute additional amounts if they so choose, within certain limits, depending on the locality. Individuals can also choose to contribute or to demonstrate their wealth and standing by sponsoring extra theatrical performances, or throwing lavish feasts.

Every family brings a table out into the courtyard before the temple and arrays a set of offerings appropriate to the rite being conducted by the Taoists. For example, in a jiao I attended in 1986 near Zhangzhou, when the Taoists emerged from the temple on the third day of the ritual to ascend the stage set up facing the temple across a courtyard, each family in the community had prepared an offering table in the courtyard facing northward toward the stage. This table contained offerings symbolically keyed to the significance of the Taoist's ritual, with gifts for the high gods. When the Taoists emerged again the next day to perform the Pudu, Feast for the Universal Deliverance of Hungry Ghosts, another set of offerings keyed to the needs of the dead was laid out by each family facing east toward the Pudu altar. A third set of offerings was also arranged (Dean, 1990b).

Theater is an integral part of the liturgical framework. In a fundamental sense, it is performed for the gods, as an offering, rather than for the spectators. Indeed, before human actors can perform, marionettes consecrate the stage and the marionette god of theater emerges at midnight to sing of the Supreme Harmony brought by song to the mortal

8. Opera singers presenting a dollbaby symbolizing the children of the
community to the gods (Zhangzhou).

realm. Prior to the afternoon and evening performances of the regional
repertoire, short ritual plays are performed. These performances are
timed to coincide with certain Taoist rites. Ch'u Kunliang (Qiu Kun-
liang) (1986) has charted the synchronous correspondences between ritual theatrical presentations by a *Beiguan* troupe and a Taoist ritual sequence during a three-day jiao in northern Taiwan. Three out of six ritual
presentations were obligatory performances at the beginning and end of
ordinary theatrical shows. The other three were linked to rituals going on
inside the temple. The first took place simultaneously with the opening
rituals on the first night. The second took place just prior to the Presentation of the Memorial. The third was the exorcistic dance of Zhong Kui,
itself modeled on the Taoist Sealing of the Altar, which was performed
on the evening of the last day during the reopening of the doors of the
temple.[12]

Alan Kagan (1989) has pointed out that the various groups involved
in a ritual share certain structural features. The priests, the community
representatives, the puppet troupe or theater group and the musicians,
and the entire community follow parallel prohibitions during the course

of the ritual. Most groups are marked by special clothing; the community representatives make a brave showing in traditional Qing scholar robes while the Taoist priests are bedecked in embroidered vestments. A multitude of performing arts and militia troupes dress up for the procession of the gods, which frames the ritual and reinscribes the boundary of the cult.

The community representatives follow the actions of the Taoist priests during the course of the ritual. They emerge during the inspection of the offerings at set times throughout the ritual. After the central inner rites have been completed, they follow the Taoists out and follow them up onto the stage (in some areas only the *Zongli*, or General Manager, ascends the stage). Here the Taoists perform the *Jinbiao* (Presentation of the Memorial), a descendant of the *Yangong* (Announcement of Merit) ritual of medieval Taoism. This ritual is addressed to the Jade Emperor, the high god of the popular pantheon, in full view of the entire community. The climb to the stage platform, transformed by the ritual into the Golden Gates of Heaven, surely symbolizes the elevation of the local leaders before the gods and above the people.

At various points in the ritual, outside the temple, in traditional times and when possible nowadays, the Ritual Master leads spirit mediums in recitations of chants detailing the hagiographies of the local gods. Manuscripts of these chants are often written in vernacular Chinese. Occasionally the medium will go into a trance, and enter into the temple. This usually occurs at some point in the ritual that calls for dramatic emphasis. The rites performed by these groups are complementary to the rituals performed by Taoist priests (Schipper, 1985a).

Inside the temple, the local gods are invited to special "seats" on the Taoists' altar. If the cult has achieved the necessary qualitative leap in its development, the priests will recite a Taoist scripture dedicated to this god, identifying him as a Taoist astral divinity. Often the god will be identified as a transformation of the Pole Star, *Ziwei*. This god is usually pictured on the right of the Taoist altar, in the fifth place after the Sanqing, anthropomorphic representations of the abstract Tao, and Yuhuang Shangdi (The Jade Emperor), chief of the popular pantheon. The scripture, written in classical Chinese, will present the god's essential qualities and divine mission as revealed in the form of an audience with the Yuanshi Tianzun, the Heavenly Worthy of Primordial Commencement, before the entire universal Taoist pantheon. In these ways the universal qualities of the Taoist liturgical framework are illustrated.

At the same time, the various and sometimes contradictory representations of the god illustrate the role of contradictory elements invested by different social groups which are nevertheless absorbed into the Taoist liturgical framework. Thus one sees the god represented in the trance of spirit-mediums outside the temple, in carved statues carried around the spiritual parameters of the village, in special "seats" upon the altar, and in his underlying form as the Pole Star among the highest emanations of the Tao. Taoism would also appear to be playing a contradictory role in en-feoffing the local leadership in the eyes of the local gods while at the same time claiming these gods were part of a universal pantheon. These local leaders included the very officials who when in office had often sup-pressed local cult celebrations similarly structured by Taoism. Should one interpret Taoist ritual as a symbolic affirmation of local authority, appeal-ing to the cosmic spiritual hierarchy that encompassed the imperial order? In that case, Taoism could be seen to serve the imperial metaphor (see the conclusion). Or can one see to a deeper level, at which Taoism refuses to be drawn into either the bureaucratic metaphor erected by the despotic signifier, or the local codes of territoriality and blood ties. Perhaps Tao-ism served to scramble the codes, creating floating signifiers that distinct groups in Chinese society could fix upon to fashion their own interpreta-tions of the significance of their own participation in the ritual festival.

A Taoist Ordination Certificate from Putian (1981)

As noted above, ordination is a central ritual action in Taoism. In prepa-ration for ordination, the aspiring Taoist Master recopies the scriptures and liturgical manuscripts in his father's working collection. Moreover, Taoist liturgy is itself based upon the model of an ordination ritual (Schipper, 1982, 1984). Each ritual re-presents the revelation of sacred texts. The sacrifice of these texts completes a cosmic cycle. The chief priest conducts an inner ritual which includes an audience with the highest em-anations of the Tao. The merit generated by these accelerated cycles of revelation results in advancement for all in the community along the path to perfection. In many ways, the process of providing a "Taoist enfeoff-ment" for the local gods described in chapter 2 resembles an ordination into the astral ranks of the Taoist universal pantheon. The Ordination Certificate translated below was bestowed in 1981. The Certificate is di-vided into three separate documents. In addition, the ordained priest also receives a lamp, a seal, a horn, and other ritual implements. The Ordina-tion Certificate is, in fact, a register of the ritual methods and the ritual texts passed on to the new priest, as well as a list of deities at his com-mand. In modern practice, all the ritual texts mentioned are usually not passed on and may not exist any longer. The titles no longer correspond to mastery over all the discrete ritual traditions listed. (In Southern Tai-wan such titles are selected by divination.) The priest is expected to copy out a manuscript collection of essential ritual texts for his personal use. Note that although the text of the certificate claims that the Taoist priest has traveled to Longhu shan to receive his ordination, the actual rite was in fact carried out locally in Putian. (Zhang Jiyu [1989] mentions pre-1949 visits to Longhu shan).

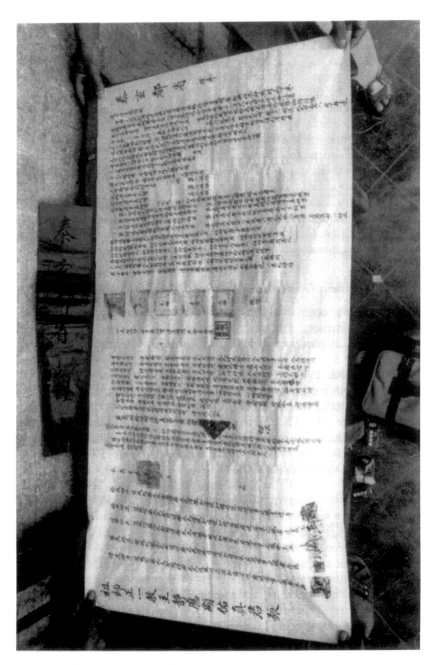

9. Taoist Ordination certificate (Putian).

The Ministry of the Most Mysterious, Taixuan, reverently receive: The order of the Tao conferring the following certificate on Huang XX, hereditary disciple who has not yet been ordained, whose name has been memorialized, who serves the Tao and thereby extends his life, who dwells in the realm of Spiritual Response of Xinxing she of the Temple of Awesome Manifestations of X li of X **xiang** *of Putian District in Xinghua, of Fujian Province, of the People's Republic of China. His ritual name is Chuanhong. His palace of destiny is [based on the moment of his birth] in the xinmao year [1951], the twelfth month, eighteenth day at the xu hour. His Fundamental Destiny depends above on the Northern Dipper. The palace of the Stellar Lord Wen Qu illumines his [actions below]. The aforementioned Chuanhong has been fortunate to bathe in the mercy of the Mysteries. He kowtows, begging to be allowed to carry on his [family's] ancestral teachings. But he fears that he has not comprehended the marvellous meaning [of the Tao], nor comprehended the [means] of refining [himself] to perfection. He desires to enter the ranks of the Immortals. [In this matter], relying upon the Emperor's strength, in the mid-autumn of the* **xinyou** *year [1981], the Master of Transformations, equipped with ritual staff, was ordered to proceed to Longhushan, Dragon Tiger Mountain, to the Great Ancestral Altar of Ten-Thousand Ritual Methods of the Headquarters of the Perfected Being, Master of the Religion, Hereditary Descendant of the Han Dynasty Heavenly Master, and received a Register of the Scriptures of a Libationer of the Officer of the Capital of the Three and the Five of the Most High, Hereditary Ritual Office of the Perfect Register and Scriptures of the Pact with the Powers of True Unity. One each of silk and rings are given to him. They will always guard his body and protect his life. All this is the fruit of the actions of former generations. With all these pledges and with incense, he beseeches Master Zheng of the Temple of Chaotic Origin of the realm of Mysterious Response to be the Chief Priest of the ritual, and to memorialize his name, [transmitting] his oath to uphold the prohibitions, cultivate perfection, proclaim transformations on behalf of Heaven, dissolve disasters, save from cataclysms, lift up and save the dead, resolve their entanglements, pile up merit, perform with utmost purity the mysterious subtleties of the empty receptacle, so that family and State will be benefited. Having taken the oath, he will gladly leave the sea of bitterness, relying on the Merciful Venerables to send down their humanity and protection. Reverently, on the ninth day of the seventh month in Mingan Temple they worshipfully established a Taoist Altar of the Most High and Merciful for an Ordination ritual to prolong Life, and communicated the name [of the ordained], memorialized concerning the Registers and proclaimed the prohibitions. Both the Retreat and the Sacrifice were modeled on the Sovereign Heavens. We begged for the bestowal of good fortune and blessings for this altar. These matters, in addition to the register and reports, were clearly memorialized to all the Heavens and the Three Realms. Notifications were* *sent to all the Officers of the Bureaus. In addition to this it was necessary to announce to Heaven the transmission of ritual methods. Before the Headquarters of the Supreme Emperor we have presented documents to the ordained [listing] the three refuges. The first is to take refuge in the Ritual King of Primordial Commencement, the Perfected Heavenly Treasure. The second is to take refuge in the Most High Lord of the Tao, the Perfected Scriptural Treasure. The third is to take refuge in the Most High Lord Lao, the Perfected Treasure of the Spirit. The nine prohibitions are: (1) The initial Perfection: Respectfully behave with filial piety towards one's parents. This results in a good long life. (2) The prohibition of thoughtfulness: One should be loyal to one's kings and overlords. This results in intelligence and wisdom. (3) The upholding of perfection: Do not kill. Mercifully free animals. This results in riches and power. (4). Holding perfection: Do not tempt yourself with things. This results in good luck and happiness. (5). Protecting Perfection: Do not steal for this means harming yourself. This results in purity and a good name. (6). Cultivating perfection: Do not express anger or hatred towards people. This results in prosperity and tranquillity. (7). Completing perfection: Do not lie or harm the good. This results in satisfaction in all things. (8). Attaining perfection: Do not cheat or be tricky. This results in attaining the Correct Methods of the Great Tao. (9). Ascending to perfection: Do not turn against what one worships, uphold the prohibitions. This results in man and heaven both moving towards the good. The name of our ancestral line [zupai] is True Marvel **Zhenmiao**. The first ancestral Master was the Wei Yuanjun of High Prime, Purity and Perfection, of the Purple Void, the Goddess of the Qingwei (Pure Tenebrity) teachings, Lady of the Southern Sacred Mountain, High Minister of the Golden Gates, [then came] Ancestral Master of the Central Alliance, True Lord Chen, Ancestral Master of Scrutiny with Penetrating Vision, True Lord Lin, Ancestral Master Great Gentleman of Great Simplicity [Taisu] . . . [the list goes on to give eleven Masters, some True Lords and others Perfected Ones, of the Western River, Surpression of Demons, Thunder Valley, Purity and Simplicity, Controller of Wind and Rain, Controller of Records. The list concludes], all the masters through time of the line that branched off from the Small Chamber of Mount Song that had received the true transmission from the Southern Sacred Mountain. To memorialize on the Ritual Title [of the ordained]: **Shenxiao yufu zhangjiao xianguan zhi beiji fumo fushishi taishang zhengyi mengwei jinglu jiutian jinque shiyudaifu yufujiuchashi**. (Immortal Officer in Charge of the Teachings of the Jade Headquarters of the Divine Empyrean [**Shenxiao**], Vice-Commissioner in charge of the Powers of the North Pole for the Suppression of Demons, Attendant Censor of the Golden Gates of the Nine Heavens of the Scriptures and Registers of the Sworn Alliance of Most High Orthodox Unity, Judicial Investigator of the Jade Headquarters.)*

*This position puts him in command of the affairs appropriately handled by all the various offices, institutes, and messengers. We memorialize on the emblems [of the ritual traditions] presented to him: The Ministry of Taixuan, the Great Ritual Office of the Spiritual Treasure, the Ministry of Thunder and Lightning, the Left Headquarters of the Yellow Register of Qingxuan, the Great Ritual Institute of Mt. Lu, the Exorcistic Institute of the North Pole. We memorialize on the seals offered as proof [of the transmission of these traditions] [There follow six, square, red-ink seals inscribed with black ink as follows: Three Treasures, Pangu, Taiji, Spiritual Treasure, North Pole, and Seal of Office]. We memorialize concerning the bestowal of the heart-seal. [There follows the ordained priest's name and birthdate as well as his seal.] [There follows a list of thirty-five offices and institutes now under the control of the ordained priest.] We memorialize upon the ritual items presented to the ordained: The Thunder Seal and a **lingpai** [a wooden block for slapping on the altar when giving orders], a ritual measuring stick and a ritual incense burner, an "immortal sieve" and "immortal divining blocks," Taoist vestments and robes, Taoist cap and wooden sandals, a "jade court tablet" and a "golden" bell, a precious sword and a ritual whip, wooden divining blocks made from a bamboo root, a divine flag and a soul banner, a gold bell and a jade sounding-bowl, and a wooden fish [on which the tempo is beaten], a rhinoceros horn and a ritual drum, an ivory court tablet and sceptre [in a **ruyi** shape]. The General Rule: Whosoever amongst the disciples who have received [training in] the rites cultivates and refines himself, piling up good deeds through his actions, will only then be qualified to receive a transmission of the ritual methods and be initiated into the Order.*

The above Dispatch has been presented to the disciple cultivating perfection, Huang XX, ritual name Chuanhong. [Over the ritual name the left triangular half of a diamond-shaped seal is imprinted, the right-side half having been imprinted on the copy of the document sent to the Taixuan Ministry by transformation through burning.] Indeed, the August Emperor of the Chaotic Origin [i.e., Laozi] established the Teachings in the Zhou Dynasty. The Ancestral Master of the True Unity [movement, i.e., Zhang Daoling] let shine the Fundamental Teachings in the Han Dynasty. For generations these teachings have led people to cultivate perfection. Thus at the present time our ritual methods include the Mysterious Writings which show how to grasp lead and refine mercury into the elixir of ninefold transformations. [Guided by these writings] we build up the breath, visualize the spirits, and cultivate the body into pure Yang [energy]. When we employ the marvellous [secret] instructions, thunder peals and lightning strikes. In the area where we pace the Mainstays of Heaven, stones roll and sand flies. With perfected power we attack evil. The six demonic spirits all are annihilated. The merciful power shakes up the Underworld. The dead hun souls of those in the Nine Regions [of the Underworld] all ascend, attracted by the excellent proclamation of the True Teachings, and attain a state of eternal desirelessness. The True Words [mantras] pronounced secretly sweep away all sorts of disaster and difficulty. Finally one joins the Heavenly Officials and lives in the Realm of the Immortals forever.

[This document is dated the seventh month of the xinyou year [1981], and was presented by (the following five Taoist priests who all have the same basic title, although their functions in this ritual are differentiated.) The title is:]

Zhengyi mengwei jing lu jiutian jinque shi yu daifu qingwei hongdaoshi jusiyuanfushi yishizhizhi _____ Attendant Censor of the Golden Gates of the Nine Heavens of the Scriptures and Registers of the Sworn Alliance of Orthodox Unity, Commissioner (in charge) of Expanding the Way of Pure Tenebrity (Qingwei), Commissioner of the various Bureaus, Agencies, and Headquarters (or Prefectures), entrusted with the office(s) of:

The Master who Confirms the Prohibitions, Lu XX, [seal and signature].

The Master who Examines the Secret Instructions, Huang XX, [seal and signature].

The Master who Recommends and Guarantees the Initiate, Lin XX, [seal and signature].

The Master who Examines the Initiation, Huang XX, [seal and signature].

The Master who Transmits the Initiation, Zheng XX, [seal and signature].

[On the left margin, in large characters:] Ancestral Master and Founder of the Teachings of True Unity, the True Lord of Quiescent Response and Manifest Aid, Zhang.

The Taoist priest also received a second document, written with black ink on a yellow sheet of paper two feet high and over four feet long, entitled "The Precious Command of the Great Merciful Most High Three Heavens, reverently worshiped by the disciple of the Three Heavens." This document begins in the same way as the one translated above. In the central portion, three talismans are presented to the initiate. These are the Precious Talisman of the Supreme Emperor of Jade Purity that initiates one into Sainthood, the Precious Talisman of the Supreme Emperor of Supreme Purity that initiates one into the Ascent to Perfection, and the Precious Talisman of the Supreme Emperor of Great Perfection that initiates one into the ranks of the Flying Immortals. This document was signed by the Master who Transmits the Initiation, Zheng XX, [seal and signature].

10. The Great Emperor Who Protects Life (from an incense pouch
distributed at the Baijiao temple).

TWO

THE GREAT EMPEROR WHO PROTECTS LIFE:

THE DIVISION OF INCENSE

Pilgrimages to the Founding Temple

T HE *Tong an County Gazetteer* of 1929 includes a fascinating list of "Ten Superstitions" which provide useful material on local cults. Under Superstition Number Five, one finds:

As for welcoming the god, every shrine and temple does this but the [celebrations around] the cult of Baosheng Dadi are the greatest. When worshipping the Great Emperor, they go to Baijiao to present incense. Upon returning, they hold elaborate rituals, with colored banners, god's palanquins, and decorated processional floats drawn by horses. Performing processional troupes sing stories. Drum music shakes the sky as they march around the town. Each *bao* has to prepare a performing arts troupe. Welcoming the god is called "greeting the incense." It is said that in this way one invites the god's protection. Those who worship the Saintly Mother [Mazu] go to Meizhou in Xinghua to present incense. Those who worship Guangze Zunwang go to the Fengshansi in Nan'an to "ask for fire." When these groups return they do the same [celebration]. There is also [the cult of] the Perfected Linshui Zhenren. People who come down from the provincial capital [Fuzhou] [worship] the image of the Emperor (Baosheng Dadi) in Xiamen. As for those who come down from Quanzhou prefecture, their paths all lead through Tongan . . . I estimate that at each such god festival one thousand in gold or at least several hundred is wasted. (Vol.1.22:611–13)

De Groot (1977, 1:271–73) remarks:

When it is a matter of procuring a soul for a new god, the procession repairs if possible to the original temple of the divinity: for example, for Mazupo, people prefer to seek the soul in Meizhou, and for Guo Shengwang [Guangze Zunwang] in Anxi [*sic*: should be Nan'an—see chapter 4]. This is, however, sometimes too long a journey, and so people content themselves with a temple that has already been consecrated to the god in question, taking care to select where possible the most well known in the environs. Along with the new soul, they retrieve incense ash. . . . The most brilliant of the processions of this sort conducted in Amoy in 1877 took place in the latter half of the 3rd month on the little island of Gulangyu, in honor of the Great God-Patron of Production [De Groot's translation of Baosheng Dadi, which has to do with his dubious efforts to link the god to a solar cult], in a temple on the island across from the cricket field, and whose principal festival is celebrated on the 15th of the third month. . . . [His] cult has taken on great proportions all around Amoy, and there are many temples consecrated to his worship on the mainland. We cannot say anything with certainty about his origins and the Chinese themselves do not have many accounts on this subject. The people of coastal Fujian say that he was originally a Taoist priest, called Wu the Excellent [Wu Zhenren], and that he achieved such renown in the practice of the art of curing disease that by this he merited being given the rank of patron of the Chinese Aesculapians. There is a beautiful temple in the vicinity of Haicang in the village of Baijiao right on the mouth of the [Nine] Dragon River, where people say he was born. This is the famous "Temple of Baijiao," one of the most beautiful examples of its kind in the province, ornamented all over its facade with sculptures, frescoes and other paintings, and altogether worthy of being visited by those who go to that region.

The Setting

The village of Baijiao today has perhaps twenty-five hundred residents. Most families divide up the labor, with one son involved in farming, another in fishing; and if there are more, they try to find work as laborers in Xiamen. The majority are surnamed Wang, and they worship their clan ancestor and namesake, the Kaimin Shengwang (Saintly King who Developed Fujian) Wang Shengzhi (r. 909–25).[1] A statue of the god and his consort stands behind a statue of Baosheng Dadi as a little boy, in the back hall of the Ciji gong (Temple of Merciful Salvation). This god is paraded about the streets of the village on the fifteenth of the first month.

The village is situated near the northern side of the long mouth of the Nine Dragon River, which passes next to Zhangzhou. The river has silted up and is no longer navigable all the way to Zhangzhou. The process of reclaiming land from the sea to expand the four coastal plains of Fujian has gone on for centuries, aided by the silting in of the major rivers. The silting has led to the rise and fall of major harbors in the area—first Quanzhou from the twelfth century to the fifteenth, then Haicheng, across the broad mouth of the river from Baijiao in the sixteenth and seventeenth centuries, and finally Xiamen, which from the mid seventeenth century on would eventually supersede all these central Minnan ports (Ng, 1983). To reach Baijiao from Xiamen now, one must rely on the tides. A passenger boat takes over an hour to reach Haicang. From there one can walk forty-five minutes into the village, passing first Hongluo, then Qingjiao. A ten-minute walk between Qingjiao and Baijiao proceeds on a raised dirt road above rice fields and vegetable gardens. One enters the village and walks toward its center along a narrow lane between brick and wood houses. Suddenly one emerges onto a vast square; immediately on one's right is an enormous temple with five entranceways and a two-story front hall with an inner balcony with drum and bell in the left and right inner wings. To the left across the square is a large concrete stage facing the temple. Inside the temple there are two side courtyards with front and back halls, and a central courtyard with a well and a protruding open stone altar. Behind it one sees the central hall, with statues of Baosheng Dadi at the center. To his left and right are cases holding statues of thirty-six generals, representing the thirty-six *tiangang* (stellar spirits of the Polar Star constellation). Two side altars house images of the god as a young boy. Behind the central hall and up a flight of stairs is the back hall. There are six altars to other divinities, including one for Guanyin.

The open stone altar is the oldest part of the building, very likely dating to the Song. The altar was no doubt used for Taoist rituals, and the rituals would have been viewed from the balcony. Schipper (1990) refers to the altar as a *jinbiao tan* (Altar for the Presentation of Taoist Memorials), and the balcony as a *guanli tai* (Platform for Viewing the Rituals). Relief carvings of flying devas playing flutes adorn the sides of the altar, and on top at the front sits a stone lion with a seal in its paw, held face outward. Upstairs, Qing frescoes cover the walls. A bell cast in 1873 hangs in the second-story balcony opposite a large, recently made drum. There are five doors into the temple, a sign of the high status of the god. The walls of the entrance hall and the central hall are covered with fifteen steles, which describe the temples that had branched off from this temple and that were, at that time, sponsoring renovations of the ancestral temple. These stelae, listed in note 4, begin in the Qing Jiaqing period and continue up to 1984. With their assistance, and drawing on local gazetteers, it is possible to chart the spread of the cult first from the Song to 1799, and then in greater detail on to the present day.

This temple is known as the Western temple. In a recent redrawing of county boundaries, the village has been assigned to Longhai xian (county seat, Shima, across the mouth of the river). Originally Baijiao belonged to Tongan xian, and the temples that have branched off from it come almost exclusively from the greater Quanzhou region to the north. Xiamen also belonged to Tongan, although it was fought over by Quanzhou and Zhangzhou bureaucrats over the centuries (Ng, 1983). Many affiliated temples of this ancestral temple are on Taiwan (Chou, 1981; Schipper, 1990). This may partially explain the good condition of the temple. The support offered by overseas Chinese encourages government support and interest in the Baijiao temple. The impressive carved stone dragon pillars in front of this temple were reputedly shipped over from Taiwan in the 1930s.

A half-mile's walk northwest across the spine of the peninsula takes one to the Eastern temple in Qingjiao. This temple was once even larger and more impressive than the Western temple, but it is now in much worse repair. When I first visited in 1985, the roof of the back hall had collapsed, and the side halls were in ruins. The floor of the second-story balcony threatened to collapse. Fortunately, major restorations were sponsored in 1989 by an affiliated Taiwanese temple from Taizhong. In their prime, both temples originally housed *shuyuan* (Confucian academies). Both temples have altars to Guanyin, originally established in the right wing of each temple. The Qingjiao temple is across the county line into the Xiamen City expanded limits. Originally, the temple belonged to Longxi District, and served the greater Zhangzhou region, especially Haicheng. Five steles in this temple, beginning with one from 1697 in the Kangxi period and continuing to 1923, give the names of affiliated temples from Haicheng to Zhangpu. The names of the affiliated temples that visited the temples in 1987 were also posted.[2]

Contemporary Observances

I attended the celebrations surrounding the birthday of the god on lunar 3/15 (1987). A vast number of temples sent groups of young men and older men to pay homage at the temple. Groups arrived by tractor-trailer, truck, chartered bus, or boat. Visiting groups of overseas Chinese were greeted with tea and pleas for aid in reconstruction. Most local temple groups were led by a man holding a banner giving the name of their temple and its location. Behind him came two or three sona players, and a few drum and gong men. Then came a group of four to eight men shouldering a god's palanquin. Many of the groups also brought a medium, usually an older man, who would direct the gathering of incense from the temple burners and the placement of offerings on the altar (sometimes by climbing on top of the altar and placing them himself). Upon entering the great temple, he would go into a trance and lead the group in a mad clockwise dash around the temple. Finally, he would lead the god chair to the open stone altar in the courtyard before the main altar. The god would be set down facing the original god statue (actually a 1982 duplicate of the original destroyed in the Cultural Revolution). After sufficient

11. Mediums in front of the Baijiao Baosheng Dadi temple running with a sedan chair carrying a visiting god statue.

time had passed for the incense of the offerings to communicate the sincere intentions of the group to the god, the medium would signal the departure, and the sedan chair would race, counterclockwise, out of the temple. Out in the courtyard the chair would dart about seemingly under the power of the god as vast numbers of firecrackers exploded all about it. Finally, they would load the god onto a truck and drive off in yet another burst of firecrackers.

There were many variations on this pattern. Interestingly, a number of groups came without a god because they belong to temples that have not yet been rebuilt. This was the case for four or five groups from Xiamen. Newly built temple groups making their first visit to the temple were filled with exuberance and put on a good show. Many groups from Tong-an were led by young mediums in traditional yellow medium's aprons, who worked with four young men dressed in aprons of four different colors. These troupes represent the five spirit soldier camps that protect many villages in this region. They would chant long rhythmic passages to a pounding drum, then assist the medium as he went into a trance. A god's silk umbrella was lowered over the medium's head as a skewer was stuck through his cheek. Then the medium would continue dancing and leaping wildly about as the chanting went on. At each drum beat all five men would hop. The medium would begin beating himself with a sword or a mace of nails. Some of the men would try to protect him from inflicting too much damage by blocking his blows with whisk brooms. Finally, the medium would cry out and leap into the air. The others rushed to catch him and lowered the umbrella over his head and removed the skewer.

Some of the men in the aprons of the five camps were much older and were probably Ritual Masters responsible for the training of this young generation. At least one Taoist priest dared to don his robes briefly at the entrance of one large group. The mediums were fitted out with swords, flags with the dipper star design, and whips of hempen rope. They took scoops of incense on the end of their swords and placed them in incense burners from the home temple carefully transported in sealed wooden boxes shaped like miniature temples.

The most spectacular showing was made by a group of villages from Tongan, all belonging to the same higher-order lineage, who arrived in thirty large boats. They numbered almost fifteen hundred, as virtually every male in the five or six villages was taking part. They marched up the road from Haicang, pausing to paste printed strips of paper announcing the passage of the god onto doorways along the way. When they were out of view of the town, ten mediums, varying in age from early twenties to mid-sixties, climbed atop ten god's palanquins and were carried through the fields to the temple. The group then fanned out across the courtyard before the temple, and the mediums dismounted. They began leaping about, possessed, flailing at themselves with an assortment of weapons. Drums, gongs, oboes, and firecrackers combined with the roar of excited onlookers. Then they charged into the temple, first pausing to rush forward and then back three times by way of saluting the god. Great clouds of incense smoke filled the air of the temple. Several mediums climbed atop the altar and passed a forest of glowing incense sticks into the huge burner, which was now a bonfire. Bands of mediums and chanters set to chanting. The temple committee was frantically struggling to record the names of all the donations and to pass out talismans and souvenirs with photos of the god. The entire episode lasted less than an hour, and soon everyone was outside again, regrouping according to their villages and their gods. They marched back in high spirits to the dock, loaded the heavy sedan chairs with their god statues aboard their boats, and sailed back into the setting sun.

All these visits from temples that had branched off occured before the actual birthdate of the god, for local custom reserves the worship of the god on that day for the residents of the village of Baijiao. The night before, elaborate preparations were made for all the young men in the village to go barefoot and carry the newly carved, thirty-six attendant generals over a pile of red-hot coals into the temple. This is called *guohuo*, and De Groot again provides a glowing description of the rites involving a barefoot Taoist priest, the barefoot lads, and the male members of the temple community. De Groot feels that these rites are closely connected to the cult of Baosheng Dadi. But he does note that similar rituals were performed on the fifteenth of the first month before many temples. At that time the Taoist wears a tiger's mask when he leaps across the bonfire. Such rituals are always performed at the consecration of a new temple, and so have been very common in Southeast China in the last few years. I observed one medium in Tongan throw himself back-first into a bonfire at the conclusion of a long, entranced dance. Unfortunately, the Taoist priest who had been summoned some time before did not appear by the chosen hour on the dawn of the god's birthday and so the ritual had to be postponed.

Photographs in the Qingjiao temple show large processions with marching bands, singing troupes (*huagu* or *yaogu*) in uniforms, men in traditional long blue gowns, and god chairs carried by enthusiastic young men. Interestingly, De Groot's description focuses on the absence of literati and the filthiness of the "dirty coolies" who carry the god chairs. Nowadays, by contrast, in most villages in Taiwan and increasingly in the Fujian countryside as well, it is considered an honor to carry the god.

The Baijiao temple committee told me that one of the most important Baosheng Dadi temples in Jinjiang was planning to make a major pilgrimage that year (1988) or the next. They planned to have all the men in the village follow the traditional route in the customary manner, walking the entire way in traditional costume and carrying the gods. They estimated the trip would take a week. They hoped to stop along the way in villages with other Baosheng Dadi temples with which the village had connections. They would sponsor theatrical performances each evening. What they have in mind sounds very much like the Dajia pilgrimage to Beigang in Taiwan in honor of Mazu. One does occasionally see processions with mediums in god chairs along the major highway connecting Chaozhou (and Guangzhou) with Fuzhou. But something of this scope has yet to be attempted.

The temple committee informed me that, during the year, the donations usually came to about two thousand yuan a month, but that, during the fortnight around the god's birthday, they collected at least that much each day. They pointed out quite accurately that these funds were still not adequate for the extensive repairs that needed to be made to preserve the building and to maintain the Chinese and Western clinic in the temple.

12. Medium at the birthday of Baosheng Dadi.

They complained that it was difficult to persuade Cultural Officials to assign the temple the status of a provincial cultural relic, which would free up some government money for repairs.

Division of Incense and Presentation of Incense

Looking back to trace the development of the cult of Baosheng Dadi, one can draw upon De Groot's detailed descriptions of the rituals for the consecration of a new god and for subsequent birthdays of a god. These accounts emphasize that the division of incense and later return-presentation of incense were central to the structure of god worship. His detailed depictions of the "barefoot lads," "exorcists," "group chiefs," and Taoist priests deserve to be quoted at length. However, there are problems with his analysis. As Schipper (1985a) points out, De Groot combines all these groups under the general rubric of "Wuism," or shamanism. By doing so, he ignores the implications of his own observations as to the different functions and methods of these groups. I would call his "barefoot lads" a group of potential mediums and potential Ritual Masters, depending on their susceptibility to trance and guided suggestion on the one hand, and their interest in ritual training on the other. When they are in trance, they may or may not self-flagellate, becoming the "exorcists" in De Groot's descriptions. On the basis of my observations in Taiwan, the Penghu Islands, and Fujian, the "group leader" who strikes the gong is quite likely to be the Ritual Master. He is often not marked by distinctive clothing, although such Masters in Southern Taiwan often wear an elaborate headdress over a red headcloth. The Taoist priests De Groot refers to may also perform as Ritual Masters, during portions of the "Opening of the (God's) Eyes" ritual or the "Crossing of Fire" ritual, or even when performing individual exorcisms for the ill. But during the jiao, communal sacrifices, or "Masses," they are performing roles distinct from, and usually beyond the ability of, a Ritual Master.

Sources on the Cult

Early sources on the evolution of the cult are scanty and frequently couched in disapproving terms. Fortunately, however, temple gazetteers and Taoist scriptures written for some of the central god cults of Fujian were collected and published by a late Qing scholar and bibliophile from Jinjiang, named Yang Jun (1830–90).[3] In 1887 he published his *Sishen zhilue* (Brief Record of Four Gods), which included brief accounts of the temples, legends, honors, literature, and miracles of Guangze Zunwang, Baosheng Dadi, Qingshui Zushi, and Tianfei (Mazu). He also provided collections of divinatory poems for each of the gods, as well as scriptures for the first two and for the last. He appended an edition of the *Yuli* (Jade Calendar), a chronicle of the tribunals of the Underworld. The printing of this work was sponsored by contributions from eight individuals and fifteen shops. These contributions came to thirty-eight English pounds and one hundred thousand wen.

Yang mentions some of the sources from which he drew his accounts. A few of these survive in provincial and regional libraries or local district Cultural Bureau collections. Yang's work provoked at least one response from a scholar-gentry in Shishan, who produced a very detailed gazetteer on Guangze Zunwang. More complete gazetteers also exist for Qingshui Zushi and Tianfei. Nevertheless, Yang's penchant for delving into the miraculous power of local gods and his interest in Taoist scriptures and divinatory poems has resulted in the preservation of a great deal of valuable material. Aside from Yang's material, the principal sources for the study of Baosheng Dadi's cult include two Song inscriptions recorded in later gazetteers, the 1209 *Cijigong bei* by Yang Zhi and the *Cijigong bei* by Zhuang Xia (*jinshi*, 1181; died 1271), later records in Ming and Qing regional gazetteers, over twenty stele inscriptions still kept in the two temples, and the Taoist scripture included in Yang Jun's temple gazetteer.[4]

The Legend

The legend of Wu Tao, the Divine Doctor, can be divided into the following episodes: (1) birth; (2) "hierogamy" (a liaison with a divine preceptress): visit to the Queen Mother of the West at age 17; (3) mastery of medical methods and Taoist ritual pacing; (4) resurrection of an official's pageboy; (5) miracles during his lifetime: deliverance of the village from famine, deliverance of the region from plague; (6) geomantic selection of the site of his temple; (7) death and/or ascension; and (8) posthumous miracles such as the divine defeat of invading pirates, divine aid to Emperor Song Gaozong, divine aid to Emperor Ming Taizu, and the divine prognosis and cure of the inflamed breast of Empress Wen.

(1) Birth

Zhuang Xia's Song inscription simply records the dates of the birth and death of Wu Tao as 979–1035, and lists early enfeoffments of the god. He says nothing about portentous omens or dreams. Nor does Yang Zhi, our other Song dynasty source. The *Min Shu* is also silent on this issue.

The short hagiography in the *Haicheng xianzhi* of 1762 may be the first mention of the dream in which Wu Tao's mother saw a white turtle and conceived. The undated Qing *Record of the True Lord Wu*, by Yan Lan, inscribed on a stele in the Zhenjun Temple in Tongan, and drawn upon in Yang Jun's synoptic hagiography, provides a much more vivid legend. There it is stated that soon before Wu Tao's mother was due to give birth, she dreamt that five Taoist Ancients appeared in long gowns and offered congratulations on the imminent birth. These were the (three) spirits of the Santai constellation, the Nanling Shizhe (Messenger of the Southern Slope), and the Beidou Xingjun (Stellar Lord of the Northern Dipper). They were escorting an infant whom they introduced as the Ziwei Shenren (The Spiritual Being of the Purple Rose). The character *wei* is most likely a mistake for *wei*, as this is the title of the fifth highest Taoist god of Purple Tenebrity, ruler of the stellar court. This is a standard identification, and it is given in one scripture translated below, but in fact the god will be identified more precisely as a Shenxiao divinity in the fifteenth century. Shorter versions of this epiphany have the woman dreaming that a star enters her as she conceives the god. Huang Jiading's *Investigation of the True Facts Concerning the Investitures (with Titles and Honors) of the Perfected One, Wu Tao*, included in the 1893 edition of the *Maxian tingzhi*, has only one Great Immortal in the dream on the night of the fourteenth day of the third month. This spirit escorts the infant into the room and introduces him as Ziwei Shenren. He records the hour of birth as between 7–9 a.m.

(2) Hierogamy

After an unusual childhood and adolescence of vegetarianism, sexual abstinence, precocious reading which extended to medical works, and a compassionate urge to help mankind, the next major event in the legend is a visit to Xi Wangmu, the Queen Mother of the West. Again, neither Song source records this story, but Yan Lan's inscription provides the details. While the god was wandering along a river, a man on a raft offered him a ride. The landscape changed dramatically, and soon they were in the Kunlun Mountains.

> Hitching up his robes, Wu Tao climbed to the highest peak, where he saw the Queen Mother of the West. He stayed for seven days. [She] transmitted to him divine methods of saving the world, and the arts of exorcising demons and driving away evil influences. Upon setting out to return he suddenly found himself back home and thus attained enlightenment. He cultivated perfection and eschewed rank and honors.

Yang Jun offers an embroidered account of the same episode.[5]

(3) Taoist Medical Methods

Zhuang Xia describes Wu Tao's medical technique in thes following way:

> He prescribed medicine that struck like an arrow and destroyed [the illness].
> Sometimes by breathing in air and spitting out water the cure took effect.
> Even if the sick person was suffering from a serious chronic disease or an
> inexplicable ailment, he could cure them. Therefore, those stricken with
> plague, or covered with sores, or suffering from carbuncles, ulcers, and ab-
> scesses, people on stretchers and those supported by [others] crowded his
> doorway every day. He never asked about their wealth or status, but saw and
> cured them all. Everyone who came to him got what he desired. Far and
> near, everyone believed him to be a god.

Yang Zhi's description of his healing practices have a distinctly Taoist
tone.

> People with wounds and infections would not visit other doctors but only
> waited for him. He would sprinkle purificatory salt and water from a recep-
> tacle, and hold a sword horizontally before them. Then he would burn in-
> cense and pray silently, and serious illnesses were cast off.

The 1762 *Haicheng xianzhi* suggests, along with Yang Zhi, that during
his travels Wu Tao attained divine techniques, which they identify as the
"Method of the Flying Pace of the Three and the Five." Huang Jiading
(*Maxiang tingzhi*, 1893) describes the episode this way: "At seventeen
years of age he met an extraordinary being who gave him a green satchel
and a jade register. Thus he obtained 'the Method of the Flying Pace of
the Three and the Five.'" Huang's account suggests a ritual Taoist ordination, complete with the transmission of precious texts and a register of
the gods at the command of the initiate.

(4) Resurrecting the Dead

Yan Lan is the first to record the episode of Wu Tao bringing a pageboy
to life. Yang Jun reworks it into his account, and other versions are given
in Huang Jiading's essay in the *1893 Maxiang tingzhi*. This episode is
probably related to the early patronage of the cult by a local official. According to the legend, a certain Jiang Shaofeng (some sources give his
name as Jiang Xianguan [Immortal Official], was en route to the imperial
exams when a tiger attacked him and killed his pageboy after first tearing
off a leg and devouring it. Jiang drove off the tiger at last but was too
pressed for time to properly bury the pageboy and so went sadly on his
way. Sometime later Baosheng Dadi was traveling through this part of
Henan and saw the bones of the boy lying scattered by the wayside. He
reassembled them in order, replaced the missing limb with a willow

branch, and performed a spell and sprayed spirit-water on them. The corpse came to life. Later Jiang, who had passed the exam and been assigned to be District Magistrate of Tongan, saw his pageboy walking with Wu Tao. At first he did not believe it was the same man, so Wu Tao sprayed water on him and he decomposed again, revealing the willow branch where the leg had been. Jiang decided to give up his office and become Wu Tao's disciple. A second official, Assistant Magistrate Zhang, also became Wu Tao's disciple.[6] Several legendary local medical figures became his disciples and figure among the thirty-six generals who stand guard around his idol in temples today. Huang Jiading (*Maxiang tingzhi*, 1893) says that raising the dead is nothing extraordinary and that he saw someone successfully reconnect the severed heads of two victims of a bandit raid.

(5) Miracles

Yan Lan records that Wu Tao was summoned to the court of Renzong (r. 1023–64), and cured the Emperor's wife, but refused the offer of a position as Censor as a reward. Then in Mingdao 2 (1033), there was a great drought in Quanzhou and Zhangzhou. The god used his ritual arts to bring grain shipments in by boat. Two years later, in 1035, plague struck and the god saved thousands with his arts.

(6) Geomantic Skill

Yang Zhi records that, while traveling with a next-door neighbor named Huang Yu, he passed the site of the current Qingjiao temple and pointed it out, saying "[Whoever] attains this spot will flourish. He who gets here first will be the Master." Then he buried three porcelain jars and made an oath. Later when his temple was being built by the side of the Yunqiao yuan, a workman "ecstatically, as though drunk and crazy, shouted in a loud voice, 'This is not my former residence. On the south side of Longqiu [stream] I formerly made a pledge.' He raced to the spot. They dug several feet into the ground and found the three jars still intact. A green snake was coiled inside one. Everyone who saw this was impressed by the divine sign."

(7) Death/Ascension

Zhuang Xia records that Wu Tao died in Jingyou 6 (1039), but the Jingyou reign-period only lasted from 1034 to 1037. Later sources give the date as Jingyou 3 (1036), fifth month, second day (May 5, 1036). Zhuang maintains that he died at home, whereas Yan Lan and others describe how his entire household ascended into heaven in broad daylight, followed by all their chickens and dogs. Huang Huaji's *Summary Account of the Filiations of Baosheng Dadi*, preface 1831 (included in Yang Zhi's *Baijiao zhilue*) records that he ascended into heaven on a crane. Several sources beginning with Yang Zhi relate that immediately after his death, the elders of the village (*xiang zhi fulao*) privately gave him the posthumous name of Yiling Zhenren (The Perfected of Medical Power). They carved his image and put it in the Longqiu Shrine. The artisan at first had no idea how to proceed with the carving and was troubled for days. Finally, one night he had a dream in which the god told him, "My appearance is similar to that of Wang Ruhua in the East Village, but if you examine his aspect, then make it a slightly broader forehead and then carve it." Zhuang also notes that shortly after his death, people were moved by his good deeds and competed in carving statues of him and offering him a cult.

(8) Posthumous Miracles

Shortly after his death a large group of pirates attacked the area. The people of Baijiao prayed to Wu Tao, and imperial soldiers arrived, captured, and executed the three leaders of the pirates. Soon afterward a flood threatened to destroy the region. Then Wu Tao was seen riding on a crane above the waves, pointing at the water. The flood withdrew. Thereupon people built a shrine with the god's image in it. When Gaozong was escaping from the Jin, the god helped him by covering him in mist. (Gaozong's flight from the Mongols is described in the *Sung Shi, Gaozong benji*.)

In 1150 a temple was built in Baijiao by imperial decree. The next year (1151) Yan Shilu (1119–1193, *jinshi*, 1142), a Minister of the Ministry of Personnel, and a man from the Qingjiao area, petitioned the court for permission to build a second temple in Qingjiao.[7] In the Qiandao reign-period (1165–73), according to Yang Jun, one Liang Zheng Gong petitioned the Cabinet, which issued in response a plaque for the temple with the name Ciji (Merciful Salvation) and the official posthumous title for Wu Tao of *zhenren* (Perfected Being).

At the onset of the Song Qingyuan reign-period (1195–1200), pirates again attacked the Quanzhou, Zhangzhou region, but dared not attack the villages protected by the god's banner. At this time an unspecified "great official" successfully petitioned the court to raise the god's title to that of Duke. The villagers meanwhile decided to enlarge the temple but feared that their funds were inadequate. Suddenly a well sprang up beneath the steps of the temple with miraculous curative properties. People from far and near came to drink from it and make contributions to the new temple. In 1206 pirates were again frightened off by the Duke's banners. In 1207, an epidemic of measles struck down every neighboring county but did not affect the area around the god's temples. In the Jiaxi period (1237–40), the Censor Zhao Ya pointed out that the god was not greedy for honors but deserved to be elevated to the rank of *zhenjun* (Perfected Lord).

Later, when Ming Taizu (r. 1368–98) was inspecting troops on the Pingyang Lake, a storm arose and threatened to drown him. The god came to his aid, calming the storm and leaving his signature in the clouds. He received another enfeoffment in recognition of his service. During the reign of Chengzu (1403–21), the Empress Wen suffered from an inflamed breast. A Taoist priest offered his skills, but the Emperor tested him by having him take her pulse with a string held on the other side of her bedroom wall. First the Emperor attached it to a cat. The Taoist said, "Not a bear, no not bear, it's a cat." Then the Emperor tied the string to a doorknob. The Taoist said that it was something of metal and wood, and not a human pulse. Finally, the Emperor tied the string to the woman's breast and the Taoist said that the liver pulse was inflamed and the blood clotted, and that this indicated a breast infection which had to be treated by moxibustion. He offered to perform the operation by dangling a cord over the wall. He cured the ailment and vanished, refusing a reward of gold and office. In He Qiaoyuan's version, the Emperor inquired about his name and discovered that he was the long-deceased Divine Doctor Wu Tao. In gratitude, the Emperor enfeoffed the god as Wanshou wuji baosheng dadi (Emperor Who Protects Life of Limitless Longevity).

In Huang Huaji's and Yang Jun's version, the Taoist disappeared by flying off on a crane and shouted out in the sky that he was the one who had aided Gaozong (r. 1127–62) in his battle on Lake Pingyang. The Crown Prince Zhu Gaoshi, subsequently enthroned as Renzong (r. 1425) then realized who he was and further enfeoffed him, after attaining the throne in 1425, with the title *Haotian jinque yushi ciji yiling chongying huguo fuhui puyou miaodao zhenjun wanshou wuji baosheng dadi* (Censor of the Golden Gates of August Heaven, True Lord of the Marvelous Tao, Merciful Salvation, Efficacious Spiritual Power, Instant Response, Protector of the Nation with Trustworthy Benevolence and Universal Aid, Great Emperor Who Protects Life of Limitless Longevity). These late sources claim that the common legend that attributed the healing of Empress Wen to the two Immortal Lords, the Xu brothers, was mistaken. In fact, what seems more likely is that such episodes of divine healing of the Imperial family form a motif that many local cults adopt for themselves. After all, the cures of the Yongle Emperor effected by an obscure temple keeper of the Xu cult center in Fuqing had led to the immediate and spectacular promotion of the cult to the center of the Empire (see chapter 1).

The contradictory information on the history of the god's enfeoffments is set forth in table 1. Several points merit our attention. With the exception of the petition by Yan Shilu that is mentioned in Yang Zhi's inscription and Yan Qingying's preface, there is no conclusive evidence of the flow of requests for endorsements, titles, and plaques from local scholar-gentry to district officials, then to provincial officials, and finally to the Inner Secretariat. However, the final decision rested with the Emperor, and payments and bribes for enfeoffments and ordinations went directly into the pockets of the Imperial Household. This may explain why some of the titles, particularly the later high titles, are not reported in official sources.

The *Haicheng xianzhi* mentions a Censor named Zhao Ya who petitioned the throne in 1240 to raise the god's title to *Chongying zhenren* (Perfected Being of Instantaneous Responses), but gives no further information on this man. Yang Jun mentions a few other petitioners, but does not give any sources or reprint any evidence. Evidence of the return flow of titles and endorsements from the central government after the Shaoxing period is similarly nonexistent. By comparison with the cult of Mazu, where examples of material of both kinds is abundant, or the cult of Qingshui Zushi, where at least the Imperial decrees of enfeoffment have been recorded, in Baosheng Dadi's case there is little to work with. The *Song Huiyao*, generally reliable on these matters, records only two enfeoffments, the first involving a plaque changing the Lingyi si (Shrine of the Divine Doctor), to Ciji (Merciful Salvation) in 1166. The second entry is from 1207, and records that the title Yinghui (Heroic and Benevolent) was added to that of the Zhongxian hou (Duke of Loyal Manifestations).

The confusion over titles is all the more strange in view of the heights the god's rank attained, equaled by such powerful deities as Guandi among those gods officially recognized by the Qing court. The confusion over dating in table 1 is one result. This appears to be an example of a local cult's receiving a strong local push in which Taoists have stepped in to provide suggestions as to the title of the god. It is probable that during the Ming dynasty, the leaders of the god's cult, with the aid of local Taoists, decided to enhance the title of the god by associating him with one of the central Taoist divinities linked with the Song court Taoist pantheon, the Jiutian Siming Cangguang Baosheng Dadi (Great Emperor Who Protects Life, Darkly Gleaming Commander of Destiny of the Nine Heavens). This deity first appeared in a dream to Song Zhenzong in 1008 (see the comments in the CT 1221 *Shangching lingbao dafa* 10.4b., cited in Schipper, 1990:411, n.20). Sometimes on expanded Taoist altars, this Taoist deity is added after the following five central deities: Yuanshi Tianzun (The Heavenly Venerable of Primordial Commencement); Ling-

TABLE 1
Titles Bestowed upon the Great Emperor Who Protects Life (A.D. 1101–1450)

979–1035	吳本 (tao)	
1150	紹興 20	Baijiao temple built
1151	紹興 21	Qingjiao temple built 靑礁
1165–1173	乾道年間	慈濟眞人 (F)
1165	乾道 1	慈濟靈官 (I, J)
1166	乾道 2	Temple plaque "慈濟" (A, D)
1180?	乾道 15 (sic)	顯佑眞人 (F)
1195–1200	慶元年間	忠顯侯 (E)
1195	慶元 1	忠顯侯 (B)
1196	慶元 2	忠顯侯 (D, I, J)
1207	開禧 3	英惠侯 (B, E, F, G)
1207–1228	嘉定年間	英惠侯 and 康佑侯 (D) 英惠侯 (I, J)
1207	嘉定 1	忠顯英惠侯 (A) 英惠侯 (C)
1227	寶慶 3	康佑侯 (J, I)
1235	端平 2	靈護侯 (D, I)
1239	嘉熙 3	晉正祐公 (D) 正祐公 (I, J)
1240	嘉熙 4	沖應眞人 (D, I, J)
1241	淳祐 1	詔廟爲宮 (D) 嘉熙 5 (sic) 妙道眞君 (I, J)
1242	淳祐 2	孚慧眞君 (I)
1245	淳祐 5	孚慧眞君 (J)
1257	寶祐 5	守道眞人 (F)
1264	景定 5	廣慧眞人
1266	咸淳 2	孚慧眞君 (I, J) 孚慧眞人 (F)
1275	德祐 1	普祐眞君 (F) 孚慧妙道眞君 (I, J)
1372	洪武 5	昊天御史醫靈眞君 (H) (I, J 洪武初)
1409	永樂 7	萬壽無極大帝 (F) 萬壽無極保生大帝 (I)
1419	永樂 17	恩主昊天醫靈妙道眞君萬壽無極保生大帝 (E, F)
1421	永樂 22	保生大帝 (F)
1425	洪熙 1	昊天金闕御史慈濟醫靈沖應榎國孚慧普祐妙道眞君萬壽無極保生大帝 (I, J)

Sources: A = 宋會要輯稿 B = 莊夏碑文 C = 楊志碑文 D = 海澄縣志 E = 泉州府志 F = 漳州府志 G = 福建通志 H = 顏蘭碑文 I = 黃化機譜係 J = 楊浚白礁志略

bao Tianzun (Heavenly Venerable of Precious Treasure); Daode Tianzun (Heavenly Venerable of the Way and Its Power; i.e., Laozi); Yuhuang Shangdi (The Supreme August Jade Emperor); and Ziwei Dadi (The Great Emperor of Purple Tenebrity). Whether or not a separate altar is set up for the god, he is invoked on many occasions throughout contemporary Taoist liturgy. Schipper (1990) notes that the principal guardian among the thirty-six attendant generals is Marshal Zhao Gongming, also the guardian spirit of the Song Dynasty. (Variant lists of these guardians are given in Yang Jun's *Baijiao zhilue* and in the *Taipei Bao'an gong zhi*.) Schipper suggests that local leaders of the cult took the title from the Taoists performing liturgical services in their temples. Again, the similarities with the high titles bequeathed by the Yongle Emperor on the Xu brothers (Great Emperors of the Jade and Golden Gates, equivalent to the rank of the Jade Emperor) are striking. Schipper notes that

> By giving such an extravagant title to a local saint, the Yongle Emperor created, perhaps unwittingly, a strong rallying point for local interests. If we consider that, together with metaphorical imperial status, the canonization conferred the right to carry imperial insignia and paraphernalia, as well as the possibility to obtain, by purchase or influence, an official rank for the local saint—the authority of which was allowed to be exercised, in the saint's name, by the local leaders—such a canonization amounted to giving the region and its liturgical organization a status of semi-independence versus the administration and making it into a kind of little kingdom. (Schipper, 1990:412)

Schipper goes on to point out that this is not actually so much a territorial entity as a nonhierarchical communications network that established transversal relations between more or less equal parties within and beyond their home regions. If this hypothesis as to the origins of the title of the god is correct, then this could be described as an example of Taoist "enfeoffment" in contrast to (but perhaps underlying) the official canonization procedures to be explored in chapter 3 below. Further insight into the cult of the god and the role of Taoism in providing frameworks for interpreting it can be gained by an examination of the scripture of the god, translated at the end of this chapter.

Implications of the Scripture

Based on internal evidence, it would appear that *The True Scripture of Baosheng Dadi* was written after the middle of the fifteenth century. The text claims to have been revealed over three hundred years after Wu Tao's life (963–1035). The date *guiyou* year, fourth (lunar) month, seventh day, could be any year, in cycles of sixty, beginning with 1273, close to the fall of China to the Mongols. In the opening passage, the god is referred to as *Dadi* (Great Emperor). Elsewhere in the text, he is called either *Ciji zhenjun* or *Fuhui zhenjun*. These titles were probably conferred in the Song (see List of Titles). If one assumes, based on the comments in He Qiaoyuan's *Min Shu* of circa 1620, that the title *Baosheng Dadi* came into use sometime in the Yongle period (1403–24), the scripture should have been written after that time. There is, however, no mention of the treatment of Empress Wen, an anecdote reported by He Qiaoyuan, and frequently repeated in various gazetteers. The association of the god with Guanyin, in particular with the cult of Guanyin on Bohai Island, suggests the importance of that Buddhist cult. Boltz (1986) has discussed the similar claims on the Mazu cult in a set of Taoist scriptures in K. M. Schipper's collection. She seems to date the later redactions, which include these claims, around 1631. She notes that these versions preserve a fuller sense of the goddess's Fujian origins but only at the price of trading Taoist celestial status for rank as an avatar of Guanyin. In the scripture translated above, the association has been made by a medium in trance. Apparently, no contradiction is felt between the many Taoist features of the god and his underlying Buddhist nature. It is possible that the mediumistic spell and closing remarks were added later, but the entire text breathes an apocalyptic air, full of portents and threatened disasters, and could readily have been the product of a mediumistic revelation. Unfortunately, I cannot offer an interpretation of the prophecy in the text, except to say that it seems to involve an eclipse of the moon.[8]

Not only is the Taoist god under the command of Taishang Laojun, and at the same time the transformed body of Guanyin, he is also associated with the Center, surrounded by the four heraldic powers. At the Center he is also in the position of Commander of the Camps of the Five Spirit Soldiers, whose chanting bands of "barefoot lads" and mediums I described above.[9] Baosheng Dadi's cult seems especially connected to mediumism. This has to do with local traditions, and with the role of medicine and exorcism in the cult. Some elders in Anxi maintained that different gods require different things of their adherents; for example, Guanyin would never want her devotees to spill blood, but Baosheng Dadi's mediums would do things that a Wangye (Pestilence God) medium would not do, such as ride on a sedan chair of knives.

I would like to draw attention to the scripture's request that people hire Buddhist or Taoist priests or form scripture-recitation associations to chant it. Such associations survive to this day around the Mazu cult in Putian, and represent another vehicle for the expansion of a cult.[10] The promised rewards appear to be primarily addressed to peasant agricultural concerns. In the Qing period, Lin Tinggui observed that "scholars pray to the god for success, and peasants pray for an abundant harvest." Still, the paucity of the surviving historical materials on the god suggests that his cult was primarily based in the merchant, trader, peasant, and lower classes (see discussion of temple sponsorship below).

Another way in which the cult spread was through printed pamphlets on the god's legend. Yan Qingying, in his prefatory remarks to the republication of Lin Tinggui's *Record* (1848), states that the book had been purchased as one aspect of a restoration of the Qingjiao temple (probably the restoration commemorated by the 1854 stele), which he had organized in the tradition of his ancestor Yan Shilu.

> We purchased the *Record of the Great Emperor* and spread it widely about so that people nowadays could see it. We knew that his meritorious deeds were incomparable. [At first] no books could be found, having vanished without a trace. We were only able to obtain the book personally compiled by Lin Tinggui of Xiamen. It was in fragments, and far from perfect. Had not the pure actions and great merit of the Great Emperor nearly faded away and ceased to shine? Therefore we added several lines at the head of the book, printed and distributed it, hoping that the learning, acts of salvation and services of the Great Emperor would appear before people's eyes and ears, like the sun crossing the skies and the rivers flowing over the earth.

The *Record* included Yan Lan's Qing dynasty inscription from the Zhenjun Temple in Tongan. Probably the most important point about the inscription is the identification of Wu Tao with the Taoist divinity Ziwei (*Zhoutian xingzhu beiji ziwei dadi* [Great Emperor of Purple Tenebrity of the North Polestar, Ruler of the Stars of all the Heavens]; see Ofuchi, 1983:195–96). After what has been said above about the likely sources for the title of the *Baosheng Dadi*, it is perhaps easier to understand the widespread conviction that local gods were transformed versions of Taoist astral deities. For everyday purposes of esoteric identification, the star-god of the North Pole is the Taoist counterpart of the Boddhisatva Guanyin. A poem written in 1815 by one He Shanyan encapsulates the legend of the god and points to his underlying identity as a Taoist deity.

Praise Poem on a Painting of the God Refining an Elixir to Save the World

> Riding on clouds into the distance,
> The white crane is far off.
> Refining the elixir, gathering drugs,
> The Queen Mother transmitted the scriptures.
> He found a scattered corpse,
> And substituted a willow branch.

The breast was enflamed and he drew near the bedcurtain.
He saved from starvation and plague.
Supported the life of the people.
He assisted with martial deeds,
And struck with bolts of lightning.
In all this aiding the people and preserving the nation.
Not interested in enfeoffments and honors,
His virtue is fragrant.
The world all worship him as the Divine Doctor.
They don't know that into this life he was born
The Imperial Star of Purple Tenebrity.

A second scripture for the god Baosheng Dadi exists. This version, sent to me by K. M. Schipper, is a recently printed edition from the Xingji Temple in Tainan, which was rebuilt in 1797 (not founded then, as Qiu Dezai [Ch'iu Te-ts'ai, 1981] indicates). The temple at that time already had a Buddhist monk in charge. The temple still has a strong Buddhist orientation, and the scripture is sandwiched between Buddhist scriptures and prayers. The text is probably much later than that translated above, as the incident of the treatment of the Empress's breast is alluded to. The god is referred to at one point as *Jinque yushi yiling puji miaodao dazhenjun* and elsewhere as *Jinque yushi wanshou wuji baosheng dadi*, both late Ming titles (see table 1). Midway through the scripture one finds the Sacred Spell of divine responses that eliminates disasters and expels illness. This begins, "The Emperor was originally the Star of Purple Tenebrity." Another important point brought out by this scripture is the god's control over thunder. Thunder sounds when he opens his mouth. His hands send forth lightning bolts. Such powers are associated with the Five Thunder Rituals of the Qingwei school of Taoism, which was founded in the thirteenth century and had a profound impact on Minnan Taoist ritual traditions.

The scripture is basically a retelling of the god's legend with moral admonitions included toward the end. Aside from the usual Taoist scriptural elements, like the opening purificatory chants followed by invocations of Taoist (and some miscellaneous Buddhist) deities, and the inclusion of some *zhouwen* (sacred spells) and the god's Precious Sobriquet, the scripture does not follow the standard model. Instead of the usual audience with the Heavenly Venerable Most High Lord Lao (see above), who decries the state of the world and sends the god to save it, one finds here the narrative device of the god telling his own story. The text nevertheless provides a fascinating instance of Buddhist packaging of a Taoist divinity, although it stops short of introducing Guanyin's transformed body.

Thus the scripture, inscriptions, pamphlets, and poetry all associate the god with either the Taoist divinity Baosheng Dadi, Ziwei, or the Bod-dhisatva Guanyin. These scriptures reveal certain standard features that suggest that their compilation was a major step in an effort by local leaders working with local Taoist and Buddhist religious specialists to transcend localism. No specific Taoist rituals seem, however, to have been elaborated around the cult. The ultimate title of the god, however, reveals the influence of Taoist ritual specialists in the enhancement and aggrandizement of the cult.

The following brief discussion of the god was included in a collection of talismans belonging to a Zhangzhou Taoist family. The sixty-year-old Taoist had studied with his father in the Dongyue miao (Temple of the Eastern Peak) in Zhangzhou, until age sixteen, when the temple was destroyed and his father sent off to do labor. He hauled carts and did menial work for forty years, only starting up as a Taoist ritual specialist again in 1979. Nevertheless, building on the basis of the few ritual texts of his father he had managed to save, and copying manuscripts from children of his father's associates, he reassembled a collection that enabled him to perform a three-day jiao communal sacrifice. The collection of talismans included primarily those for specific purposes, such as ease in childbirth, love magic, etc. The text also contained talismans and brief descriptions for five local gods.[11] Under Dadao Gong (The Duke of the Great Tao), one reads the following:

> The Duke of the Great Way is surnamed Wu, his name is Tao. He was born on the 15th of the 3rd month. He was a Quanzhou man but lived in Zhangzhou. He resided in Baijiao. He performed rituals, and practiced the ways of the Four Saints. He refined the elixir to save the world. He treated the Empress and cured her. In the Wanli period (1573–1619), the Emperor enfeoffed him as Baosheng Dadi, Great Emperor Who Protects Life. Accordingly, he refined the Three Teachings. Ten thousand spirits obey him and have become his Officials and Generals. (K. Dean, 1989b: KD. MSS. 18. ZZ. 18)

Although other sources suggest that the date of enfeoffment as Baosheng Dadi was probably in the Yongle period rather than the later 1500s, this source reveals a close familiarity with the legend of the god. Such handbooks of talismans in the collections of local Taoist priests were another avenue for the spread of information on the god. Similar kinds of knowledge in the hands of local Taoist priests enabled them to play a key role in the development of local cults.

A second issue raised by the Taoist handbook's summary of the god is the interaction of the Three Religions in the activities of the cult. Although Wu Tao is made out to be a Taoist medical saint in his standard written hagiographical accounts (which borrow from the Life of Xu Xun [239–292 / 374?] and Sun Simiao [581?—died after 673? (Sivin, 1968)] as Schipper [1990] points out—only the oral accounts of his failed marriage with Mazu, his subsequent illicit affair with her in and around Xiamen, and his magical battles with the goddess [on Taiwan] contain new materials), the cult does not demand adherence on the part of its followers to Taoist doctrines. The first temple built for Baosheng Dadi was in a Buddhist nunnery called the Longqiu an. Buddhists frequently made their way into temples, as in the case of some of the Baosheng Dadi temples, but this did not mean that adherents were expected to be Buddhists. I have already mentioned the Confucian academies set up inside the temples. Thus the remark in the Taoist's summary, that Wu Tao "refined the Three Teachings" reveals the interplay of these traditions in cult organizations. Nonetheless, the importance of Taoist ritual in cult worship suggests the underlying role of the Taoist liturgical framework in the ritual dimension of the Three Teachings.

The Spread of the Cult

The cult of Baosheng Dadi has spread far inland in Fujian and along the coast of Southeast China. The cult has also spread to Taiwan and Southeast Asia. Zhuang Xia commented that in the seventy-odd years after the end of the Shaoxing reign period (1131–62), the cult had spread north to Puyang, Changle, and Jianjian, and south to Tingzhou, Chaozhou, and on into Guangdong and Guangxi. Huang Jiading, in his detailed essay on the investitures of the god in the *Maxiang tingzhi* of 1893, lists six temples built during the Song Dynasty. He mentions that, in addition to the Ciji gong in Baijiao in Tongan and what he calls the Wu Zhenren si in Qingjiao, the Quanzhou Huaqiao gong was built in the Shaoxing period. This temple is still an active center of the god's cult (see below). A temple known as the Yutou miao was built on Shangjie in Zhangzhou City in the Song. Huang mentions two other temples built in the Song, both named Ciji gong. The *Zhangzhou fuzhi* of 1877 provides the date of one of these, built in Xintai in Longxi in 1157 (j.40.30b). Another temple was built outside the northern gate of the City of Zhao'an. The same source records a Ziji gong built in Changtai in 1398. Huang Jiading goes on to list two temples built in the Yuan. These are the Ciji gong at Longjin qiao in Changtai and the Wu Zhenren si in Nan'an. Three temples are mentioned for the Ming period: the Qingxi gong in Hushi in Anxi, the Huitang gong in Rende in Tongan, and the Honggun miao in Zushan she in Haicheng. Two early Qing temples include the Anxi Shimenguang Wuzhenren si and the Haicheng Xinsheng jie Zhenjun an. Local gazetteers from the mid-Qing record temples in Anxi, Nan'an, Tongan, Longxi, Hai-cheng, and Zhangzhou. After 1409, and the promotion of the god to Emperor, temples like the major Xiamen temple were called Wanshou gong (Temple of Vast Longevity). In the course of my travels in Fujian, I found elaborate temples to the god outside the City of Dehua and throughout the Quanzhou region. Ch'iu Te-ts'ai (1981) maintains that the god is worshiped in Zhejiang and Jiangsu as well.

The cult of the god must certainly have received a strong impetus from the rise of Haicheng as an important coastal port in 1567 (Rawski, 1972), and the later rise of Xiamen from 1686 onward (Ng, 1983). An account in the *Haicheng xianzhi* of 1767 describes the exciting scene of the presentation of incense on the god's birthday:

> The fifteenth day of the third [lunar] month is the birthday of the Heroic and Compassionate Duke Wu of The Temple of Merciful Salvation in Qingjiao. People of Haicheng all worship in their local temples, holding [Taoist] jiao Offerings. After the jiao has ended, they "welcome the god." People of each *she* beat drums and play music and carry banners and pen-nants. Elaborately decorated floats take part in the procession. They lead [their god statues] to the Temple of Merciful Salvation and transfer incense and then return home. This is called, in local dialect, "presenting incense." Usually this is done once a year. When they return home and enter their doorways, their cloths are covered with an inch of incense dust, and talis-mans are stuck to the sides of their heads. Old men, old women, young women, and boys and girls delight in the processions, the processions that come to gather incense. (15:14a,b.)

The steles in Baijiao and Qingjiao listed above allow us to trace devel-opments in the cult during the Qing dynasty. They indicate that restora-tions of the Baijiao temple took place in 1799, 1814, 1840, 1878, 1923, and 1984, that is, at expanding intervals of twenty-five, twenty-six, thirty-four, forty-five, and sixty-one years. Renewal of a temple at least once every sixty-year cycle is a sign of the health of the cult. Such occa-sions require the performance of a Taoist jiao. The Qingjiao temple was repaired in 1697, 1814, 1854, and 1896. Judging from the inscriptions, one can assume that there were restorations between 1697 and 1814, and that restorations continued at a regular pace until the turn of the century. Judging from the state of the temple today, however, there have probably not been any major repairs in eighty years. The list of funds provided by visiting *jinxiang* groups in 1987 is not too impressive. The largest amount offered was 180 yuan ($30), and most contributions were only 10 yuan. The relative success and splendor of the Baijiao temple has en-abled it to attract new fenxiang temples from the greater Zhangzhou area traditionally reserved for the Eastern Temple.

There are 145 temples listed on the Jiaqing 21 (1816) stele in Baijiao. Of these only 38 indicate their home district: 5 from Quanzhou, 20 from Xiamen, 2 from Jinmen, 6 from Tongan, 2 from Nan'an, 1 from Hui'an, and 1 from Anxi. These are all districts in the greater Quanzhou region. There are 136 temples listed on the 1984 stele: 7 are from Xiamen, 2 from Quanzhou City, 34 from Jinjiang (one of the growth areas of the cult these days), 11 from Nan'an, 13 from Tongan, and 1 from Hui'an. However, there are also 3 from Haicheng, 2 from Pinghe, 1 from Changtai, 1 from Zhangzhou City, 1 from Shima, and 1 from Longhai, all in the traditional Zhangzhou region.

I have elsewhere drawn up a map indicating the locations of the temples that visited the Baijiao and the Qingjiao temple in 1987 (Dean, 1988: map 3 and table 10). The total number of registered jinxiang temples that visited Baijiao that year came to 111. Twenty-eight were from Xiamen, 13 from Tongan, 12 from Nan'an, 32 from Jinjiang, 2 from Quanzhou, 1 from Hui'an, 22 from the traditional Zhangzhou area: 14 from Longhai (10 from former Haicheng xian and 4 from former Longxi xian), 2 from Zhangzhou City, 1 from Changtai, 2 from Nanjing, and 3 from Pinghe.

The 83 temples that visited the Qingjiao temple in 1987 came from the following regions: 17 from Xiamen, 3 from Zhangzhou City, 37 from Longhai district, 2 from Zhangpu, 1 from Hua'an, 11 from Pinghe, 7 from Changtai, 4 from Nanjing, and only 1 renegade from Tongan. These lists provide a clear picture of the present spread of the cult from Hui'an to Pinghe. Temple committee members reminded me that only those who contributed appear on the lists, and that many groups simply carry out a ritual visit without making a contribution. Other temples make jinxiang visits periodically, once every three years. Thus the total of Baosheng Dadi fenxiang temples in Fujian could be well over 300. If one assumes a ratio of one temple to a village, and an average population of five thousand to a village, then one obtains a figure of 1.5 million people in Fujian who are affected directly by the cult.[12]

Schipper (1990) has mapped the spread and general distribution of 169 Baosheng Dadi temples on Taiwan. He notes that dates given in Qiu Dezai's *Taiwan miaoshen juan* (1981) are often erroneous and, where possible, should be checked against reproductions of the original steles collected in *Taiwan Nanbu beiwen ji* (1966) and other sources. He discovers a high concentration at the early period in the Tainan region, where the Fengjia Cijigong still maintains the greatest festival for the god on the fifteenth of the third lunar month (Schipper, 1990). The *Taiwan Shentan* gives the figures for 1969: out of a total of 140 temples to the god (note that ten years later in Qiu's count there were 162 temples), 38 were in Tainan County, 31 in Jiayi (Chia-i) County, and another 19 were in

Tainan City. Thus 78 temples, over half of the total, are clustered in the center of this region. Schipper finds that 130 of the 169 Baosheng Dadi temples are concentrated in the traditional area.

Schipper (1990) notes that twenty-two temples on Taiwan claim direct affiliation with Baijiao. In 1989 the Yuanbao gong of Taizhong laid claim to Qingjiao. While some temples were founded as regional associations, like the Tongan merchant *huiguan* in the Taibei Bao'an gong, others like the Tainan County Xuejia gong sought to bolster local education with a Confucian academy. Still other temples were developed around Wu family shrines. Rather than insisting on particular doctrines, the cults encompassed the Three Teachings. Their primary function was to provide participation in "a circuit of communication and cooperation," including cultural, political, economic, and military spheres of activity.

The surviving inscriptions in Baijiao and Qingjiao also provide information on the sponsorship of the temple restoration projects. The earliest inscription in the Qingjiao temple dates to the Kangxi period (dated 1697). The inscription was composed and written by a *jinshi* (Metropolitan Graduate), named Wu Zhong (from Zhenhai wei in Fujian, *jinshi*, 1694). The list of donors gives 112 names, beginning with two *jiabidan* (*gabidan* in Hokkien), which is a transliteration of the Portuguese "Capitano." Altogether, 14 names are listed with those of the two principal Captains. These are followed by 78 names of *xinshi* (believers), and five temple committee members, headed by two men surnamed "Yan." The stone must have been recarved, for it was set up by *shoushi* (headman in charge), one Yan Zhongying, who also set up two steles in 1814. These steles are divided into two categories, one for individuals and the other for contributions by affiliated temples.

Both inscriptions were composed by a *xiangjinshizi* (an unofficial reference to a *juren* [Provincial Graduate]) named Cai Weishan who had been locally recommended (Chang, 1955: p. 30). He was currently the District Magistrate of Wu'an. On the first stele, he remarked that the site of the Qingjiao temple had always belonged to the Yan lineage, and that restorations were still organized by the Yans, in commemoration of the founding of the temple by their ancestor Yan Shilu (see above). This stele goes on to list seventy-six names of individuals, arranged according first to the value of their contributions and then to their ranks. Of these the first was a *jinshi*; two were officials in the General Surveillance and Military Defense Circuit; five held honorary titles such as "Gentleman-litterateur,"and "such and such Grand Masters"; one was a *suijinshi* (Tribute Student, otherwise known as *gongsheng*); twenty were *daxuesheng* (Student in the National University); two were *shengyuan* (Government Students); and forty-five had no titles. The companion stele lists contributions by 167 temples, but also includes two large contributions from two wealthy Yans. Both steles conclude with the name of the Director of the Temple Committee, Yan Zhongying.

The Xianfeng stele of 1854 lists 192 contributors, by order of the amounts contributed, again combining individuals and affiliated temples. Titles were given for eleven individuals, of whom four were *gongsheng*; five were *daxuesheng*; one was a *buzhengsi jingli* (Registrar in the Provincial Administration Commission); and another was a *guanchashi* (Provincial Administration Commissioner), by the name of Ma Zhenhua.

The two Guangxu steles of 1896 list over one thousand individuals and temples mixed together, with little information on the social status of the contributors. One overall impression that arises from an examination of these inscriptions is the close identification between the Yan lineage and the fate of the temple. This impression is borne out by the recent restorations to the back hall of the temple, where an altar has been set up, complete with statues, to the founder of the temple, Yan Shilu. The current temple committee is made up of members of the twenty-seventh to thirtieth generations of descendants of Yan Shilu.

The majority of steles in the Baijiao temple are primarily lists of affiliated temples, or lists mixing temples with individuals. Certain steles indicate the importance of the local Wang lineage in the development of the temple. Indeed, an altar has been set up in the back hall dedicated to their ostensible ancestor, Wang Shengzhi, first Emperor of Min, later deified as Kaimin Shengwang (Divine King Who Opened Up Fujian).

The stele of 1816 provides evidence of high-level patronage. This stele was written by Wang Delu, at the time the Provincial Military Commander of the Naval Forces of Fujian and Commander of the Naval and Land Forces of Taiwan and the Penghu Islands.[13] After noting that the temple was in need of repairs, Wang continued:

> The "filial and scrupulous" [locally recommended *xiangjinshi* = juren] Master Wang Ruizhang came to me and asked me to give funds and raise contributions to expand the temple lands. I reflected that six or seven years had passed since 1809 when I swept the pirates from the seas. I had bathed in the mercy of Baosheng Dadi. He had protected me on several occasions. Thus I took this opportunity to fulfill my former vows. I reverently raised a contribution for the Buddha of 2,000 silver dollars. I lovingly gathered together like-minded men and performed this righteous deed. Now it is accomplished. Therefore I write this record and compose this preface to the stele [listing] the surnames of the contributors. May this last forever!

Following Wang's title and decree commanding the carving of the stone, one finds listed contributions of 200 yuan each by Adjutant Assistant Regional Commander Chen and Left Assistant Councillor of the

Deputy Supreme Commander Yang. Next, one finds 200 yuan offered by each of two *yanghang* (foreign trade guild-leaders) identified as "Jin," a pseudo-surname employed by the guilds dealing with foreign trade in Xiamen. A *shengyuan* named "Su" gave 180 yuan. Next followed the donations given by the "greater and smaller guilds and merchants," listing ten more "Jins" and one man named Huang. Last but not least, one finds that the locally recommended jinshi Wang Ruizhang donated a complete carved palanquin for the god.

Wang Delu was originally from Zhuluo (now called Jiayi) in Taiwan. He played a role in the Qing suppression of the Lin Shuangwen rebellion of 1786–1787, and was awarded the fifth rank and promoted within the Naval chain of command. He continued Li Changgeng's efforts to apprehend Cai Qian, the Taiwanese rebel-pirate. He was ultimately successful in 1809. As a reward, he was awarded the official rank of "2b," hereditary honors and titles for his descendants, and special peacock feathers for his cap. In accordance with Qing sumptuary regulations, he also wore a red coral button on his cap, an embroidered military mandarin square featuring a lion on his chest, and a clasp of gold set in rubies at his waist. He was among the most powerful, highest-ranked men in the Zhang-Quan area. After his long successful career in putting down rebels and pirates, he retired to Xiamen in 1821.

From these inscriptions one can sense the inadequacy of the distinctions usually drawn by historians between elite and popular cultural spheres in late Imperial China. Instead of Confucian scholar-gentry committed to a secular, rational ethic consciously avoiding interaction with the superstitious masses, one finds direct evidence of the involvement of high officials, local scholar-gentry, local lineage leaders, and wealthy merchants in sponsoring the restoration of cult centers. Such restorations were inevitably celebrated with Taoist jiao rituals. The same elite groups must have taken part in these rituals. Cult networks were capable of absorbing gentry sponsorship as well as local popular worship.

If cult networks cut across vertical social class distinctions, what sort of horizontal interactions characterized the relations between different cult networks? I found that Baosheng Dadi is worshiped alongside Mazu in Jiangkou in Putianxian. This interesting juxtaposition is especially evident in Xiamen and Tongan. Several temples where the two gods are worshiped together are listed in the *Tongan xianzhi* of 1798. The *Xiamen zhi* of 1832 is even more indicative of this trend. Out of seventy-six temples listed, twenty-four are devoted to the worship of the two gods together. Separate temples also exist, nine for Tianhou (including the official government-supported temple) and four for Baosheng Dadi. Thus thirty-seven temples, half of all the temples in Xiamen at the time, were devoted to these two gods. A closing note remarks that every village had its god temple, and that those devoted to Tianhou and Wuzhenren were beyond number. In the colorful Lantern Festival god processions of Quanzhou, the two gods were carried around the city together (see chapter 3 below on processions). Schipper (1990) suggests that this joint worship is evidence of the overlapping of cult networks based on the confluence of two trading systems (coastal and international for Mazu, and riverine for Baosheng Dadi). The Mazu cult had spread all along the coast of China from the Dalian to Hainan. At Xiamen the cult merged with the local Quanzhou coastal cult of Baosheng Dadi. Oral traditions suggest an illicit affair between the two deities.

But on Taiwan, popular legends describe a battle of cosmic powers between the two gods in which each attempts to humiliate the other. This explains the winds on the 15th day of the 3d lunar month (designed to blow Baosheng Dadi's hat off) and the rain on the 23d day, designed to soak Mazu's clothing during her procession. It seems possible to me that the coastal cult of the goddess of the sea merged with the local protector deity cult in ports like Xiamen, but that inland adherents of the cult may have opposed unification of the cults. Furthermore, the joint worship of these gods does not seem to have been associated with the Zhangzhou cult of Baosheng Dadi, and one may have here yet another manifestation of that long-standing subethnic conflict as it developed on Taiwan. A modern source noticed that the god is referred to differently in different regions. In Quanzhou he is "Baosheng Dadi," in Zhangzhou most commonly "Dadao Gong," and in Chaozhou, "Wu Zhenren."

These tensions are apparent in the case of the powerful Bao'an gong founded in 1742 in Taibei, which celebrated the thousandth birthday of the god in 1979 with the publication of a temple gazetteer. In it one reads of the attacks on the temple by Zhangzhou groups in the 1850s. Similar attacks by Zhangzhou groups are mentioned on the Longshan si, itself affiliated with the Anhai Longshan si in Jinjiang. The Bao'an gong remains an important institution in Taibei today.[14] The gazetteer boasts that the temple is the grandest of all Taibei temples. This is attributed to the miraculous power of the god. However, careful attention is given to a description of the rotation of responsibilities for the costs of the rituals and theatricals that make up the festival of the god. These are borne in rotation by several surname groups in the neighborhood of the temple. Interestingly, the gazetteer also mentions that a statue of Mazu was originally housed in the Bao'an gong but was moved to a separate temple in the 1860s.

This example serves to demonstrate that cult networks function to channel social forces and tensions, whether these be cooperative links based around flows of riverine and coastal shipping or aggressive flows of attack between rival interest groups.

The Legacy of the Divine Doctor

The cult of Baosheng Dadi has been used here to illustrate a particular feature of cult organization, namely the networks of incense-division. Before turning to another cult, and another aspect of cult organization, it would be worthwhile to pause and consider the particular powers attributed to this god.

Baosheng Dadi is known as the Divine Doctor. The list of "Ten Superstitions" from the 1929 *Tongan xianzhi* provides interesting data on the relation of the god to medicine. The first entry reads as follows:

(1) Shouldering gods [in their palanquins—literally "boddhisatvas," a common term for all classes of gods in Fujian]. The vulgar believe in shamans and ghosts and trust them when it comes to medicine. When someone is ill two people to a side shoulder the poles on a god's palanquin. People mostly carry Baosheng Dadi. One person strikes a gong and follows behind. They wind their way through the streets. When they pass a home in which medicinal drugs are hidden, the god stops and will not move. This is called "begging for medicine." The family [so entreated] then burns incense and in a low voice, recites the names of the drugs. The god advances and retreats to indicate his decision as to which ones to take. The god sometimes races in circles and then charges forward. Then people cast divination blocks [bamboo crescents with one flat side and one convex side]. If they get a *sheng* [saintly, i.e., positive cast, with one side up and one side down] then the god agrees. If they get a *xiao* [laughing response, two flat sides up], then the god rejects the drug. Sometimes they go to a pharmacy and the druggist sings the names of the drugs. Choices are then made by divination. Whether or not the drugs are appropriate to the disease and whether or not the chosen source is willing, people take the drugs without any doubt in their minds. (24:6b.[610])

A medium in Anxi informed me that similar practices were maintained in secret even during the Cultural Revolution. At that time, someone who was ill would approach the medium, and they would arrange to get a group to carry the god's palanquin (in this case Qingshui Zushi, on whom see below) out into the hills late at night. There in the dark the palanquin would rush to and fro seemingly with a life of its own until suddenly one of the front handlebars would become unbelievably heavy and settle on a shrub. Several different plants would be selected in this way and brought back to the temple. There the god would indicate the proper dosages by pounding the handlebars of the palanquin on the altar a certain number of times for each ingredient. De Groot (1979, 1:288–94) gives a similar account of visits to the pharmacist by gods in palanquins in Amoy in 1877.

When I enquired about who became a medium during the Cultural Revolution, one medium explained that, after all the well-known mediums in a particular village had been arrested and sent away or set to labor, five or six devout men, including himself, got together in a local temple and asked the god to select one of them by divination. He was chosen and immediately fell into a trance for the first time in his life. Since then he has helped innumerable people with the god's aid. He was free to do this since he was old and retired. He had a friendly air, old and almost care-free, yet somehow still very cautious when it came to people. He seemed like someone who is often in contact with a nonhuman realm.[15]

Both the Baijiao Cijigong and the Quanzhou Huaqiao gong continue to maintain medical clinics with both Chinese and Western medicine. The Cijigong has a large set of medicinal divinatory poems divided into internal and external medicine, and pediatrics. The Huaqiao gong became a free clinic in 1878, and provided medicine, food at New Year's for the needy, and coffins for impoverished mourners as well. The *Quanzhou hua-qiao zengyaochu geyan* (The Evolution of the Quanzhou Flower Bridge Free Clinic), a pamphlet written by Wu Zexu in 1982, outlines the background and procedures of the clinic. The clinic survived the factional struggles of the Cultural Revolution by maintaining neutrality and helping all in need, much in the spirit of the god. One of the more unusual medical supplies they keep in stock is human excrement, which they store in earthen crocks for thirty years, after which time it is used in certain recipes. The name for this ingredient is "golden liquor." Upstairs there is still an image of the god, but it is only shown to devotees on demand. A staff of retired doctors, specializing in either Chinese or Western-style medicine, staff the clinic. Contributions from overseas Chinese and local people pay for the drugs, some of which are very costly.

Another Legacy—Cultural Unity?

Interestingly enough, Wu Zexu's pamphlet applauds the success of the Baijiao temple at raising funds to carry out repairs in 1981–1982, be-cause this would excite the devotees of the cult on Taiwan, which would be advantageous to the cause of national reunification. The pamphlet goes on to quote reports in the *Fujian Daily* describing the visits of over one thousand Taiwanese to the Baijiao temple. Next, they quote Taiwanese papers as reporting a procession with thirty-six flower carts, over eighty different kinds of popular performing arts troupes, and tens of thousands of devotees who gather at the Tainan County Xuejia temple each year on the 15th day of the 3d lunar month and then march to the seaside and hold a ceremony worshiping the god across the Straits. The pamphlet concludes that the Huaqiao temple should also be allowed to restore its original form, and that it should be treated as a historical monument. At the Baijiao temple, I often observed officials of the Taiwan Division of the United Front escorting Taiwanese visiting the temple. A Philippine overseas Chinese group on a tour of the major god temples of Fujian had observed a Taoist priest from Taiwan performing a *kaiguang* consecration of a small statue of the god they planned to take back to Taiwan.

The possibility of a temple that branched off from a second- or third-generation temple visiting the ancestral temple to establish a direct connection is an intrinsic dimension of the fenxiang system. Such visits often are made when the local cult is moving into a new phase, that is, building a new temple, or enlarging an older one. The number of god statues on an altar may represent these different phases in the history of the temple (Schipper, 1990). Perhaps the most dramatic and significant event of this kind in recent years was the visit by the Taiwanese pilgrims of Dajia to the Mazu temple in Meizhou in 1988. For many years, the eight-day pilgrimage on foot of the Dajia worshipers to the great Mazu temple of Beigang was the most impressive and traditional dimension of the rapidly changing celebration around the goddess's birthday. In 1988 Dajia went instead to Meizhou, fulfilling a dream of thousands of Taiwanese temples to revisit the ancestral center of their cult. To mark the significance of the move, they did not participate in the Beigang celebrations.[16]

This form of concrete involvement (and substantial investment) in local cults of Fujian by Taiwanese temple organizations has provoked an interesting response from the Chinese government. In the interest of promoting contacts across the "two shores," a series of academic conferences on local gods have been organized. Intellectuals who until recently had been under strict orders to avoid topics contaminated by feudal superstition find themselves searching for something to say about the role of these cults in Fujian history. Three conferences have already been held for Baosheng Dadi.

In April of 1990 the latest in a series of "Conferences of the Gods" was held in Putian in honor of Mazu's birthday. This international conference was subsidized by the Chaotian gong Mazu temple of Beigang, Taiwan, which has a great deal to gain by reestablishing its prominence in relation to the fenxiang system originating out of the mother temple on Meizhou Island.

These developments have led to new organizational formations among the fenxiang networks on Taiwan as well as raising interesting possibilities for cult networks in China. As in Taiwan, official involvement in cult celebrations immediately transforms the nature of the celebration, forcing out much of the original ecstatic possession and inserting brass bands and stereotypical dragon dances in their place. But as long as this form of grudging government recognition is forthcoming, there is at least some possibility for a dialogue between traditional sectors, intellectuals, and government officials responsible for religious policy.[17]

The True Scripture of The Great Emperor

(Quanzhou Flower Bridge Temple Edition Printed by donations collected by the Snowy Sea [studio] of Yang Jun of [Fujian] Commandery.)

Raising our heads we invoke the August Heavenly Great Emperor Wu. He lived in the Quanzhou Commandery but was born near Zhangzhou. His brave and valiant awesome spiritual powers arose from his merciful heart. Because he used Ritual powers he became a Medicine King. To the masses of the people he brought most abundant advantages. His fulfillment of his merit moved the Jade Sovereign. He was asked by Imperial decree what karmic path he had followed. [He replied that] upon obtaining correct knowledge and perception [he] expanded the Tao. [The Jade Emperor] commanded that the great lofty title of the numinous doctor be enhanced. Also, he sent [as subordinates] an Immortal Medical Official named Huang, the Awesome Martial Retainer Jiang Si shi, the Perfect Man of the Green Kerchief and two pages, the Six Ding Generals [who are] Strong Soldiers who Expel Evil, Maiden Qin, the Taiyi Female Physician, together with the Great Messenger who Flies to Heaven. [All of these] work together to support the weak and expel disease and misfortune.

I today with all my heart and with complete obedience, express my desire that you will be happy to let fall your mercy at my recitation [of your names].

Chant for the Opening of the Scripture:
Great Saint, Physician Spirit, Perfected Lord Wu
Wrote Talismans, let fall seal-script [revelations], and proclaimed scriptures
Swearing a vow that his Sacred Spell would have awesome power,
And bring auspiciousness, gather good fortune, and avoid disaster.

Formerly, the Perfected Lord of Merciful Salvation, attended an audience in the Taiqing Palace within the Hall of the Three Origins. All the gods of the Stars were gathered round. The Heavenly Venerable said:

Now when I observe the 3,000 million worlds below, and the multitudes dwelling in Jambudvipa, [they are] all practising the 10 evils and the 5 disobediences, disloyal and unfilial, unmannered and unrighteous, not revering the Three Treasures, ignorant of charity, unwilling to provide assistance, frequently carrying out evil deeds, killing living beings, behaving licentiously, stealing, coveting and getting angry, entangling themselves in a web of culpability, and disrupting the nation. [There] both kings and men are unjust; those above do not measure by the Tao, and those below do not uphold the Laws.

The innocent are slaughtered, their spirits do not scatter, but instead turn into demonic flying zombies. Therefore the foreign borderland peoples raised up weapons of war, and the people of South China, in cold and hot seasons, fell victim to malarial miasmas and yellow fever, became dumb and died horrible painful deaths. Then arose a mosquito borne plague of measles, with symptoms of red eyes and dysentery. Pigs, sheep, oxen, and horses became afflicted and died. Mountain demons and pythons, vipers, tigers, and elephants, birds, beasts, and sea monsters [arose]. Wild winds drove the boats; dragons and demonic waves destroyed city walls and fords, and there were many floods and fires. And then there was trouble with [Imperial] Laws, for every year brought hunger and starvation, the five grains did not raise up. As for those of you who performed charity, but for whom things did not work out as you wished, you should know that this is the [work of] demons. These demons are all martial fellows and stout soldiers, with brave and valiant divine energy. They [formerly] aided heavenly spirits to move clouds and spread vapours, so that winds and rain were seasonal, and the grains and rice grew ripe, and the Empire enjoyed Great Peace. Yet today they have all increased in number to a total of 84,000 and have suddenly raised up tornadoes and floods. The 404 diseases circulate through the seasons, bringing little good fortune to the world. The evil and rebellious masses encounter disasters and die. The Heavenly Venerable took pity on those people who had cultivated good fortune [by carrying out] the 10 good deeds. [He then] extended divine protection to them. Study the words of the prophecy:

> *A green dog barks*
> *A wooden pig squeals,*
> *A rooster [crows] at the rabbit [in the] moon*
> *A round moon without lustre.*
> *Three disasters strike*
> *Nine rebellions arise.*

In the jia and yi years there will be military ravages
In the bing and ding years fearful fires
In the wu and ji years locusts will spread plague
In the geng and ren years storms and flood,
Thus from jia year to the gui year,
The first five years will have barren harvests,
The last five years will have good harvests.
Alas we have come to the end of the world
The revolving [sun marked by the] gnomon is about to stop
All the Buddhas will attain Nirvana
Saints and Sages will hide away
Common men and ignorant women are unaware and do not understand
Therefore I have transmitted this scripture
So that it may broadly save the world.

And pronounce this gatha:
The dog barks, the pig squeals
The bad will vanish, the good will survive
Take refuge in the Three Treasures
Uphold and recite this Scripture.
Revere it wherever you go
And it will always hold down demonic soldiers
Heavenly spirits will protect you
Family and nation will be at peace
Widely transmit the Way of the Scripture
Pass it all around

The Most High Lord Lao said:
Whensoever any good man or faithful woman worships the Three Treasures, and delights in charitable deeds, then on the gengshen, and jiazi days, and on the days of the Three Origins, the Seven [Dipper Stars], the Day of Destiny, and the winter sacrifice, they should fast and purify their hearts, recite this scripture, and revere these True Writings. Then spontaneously, heavenly spirits will protect them and they will not encounter any hardship. I, [Lord Lao], will carry on this great work, and obtain for them good fortune and longevity. I [hereby] issue secret instructions and sacred talismans, altogether 120, and announce to the Perfected Lord of Merciful Salvation: Your Tao is complete and your Virtue prepared. Your good deeds are pure and resplendent. In heaven you [observe the] prohibitions, and have thereby established marvellous powers of wisdom. On earth you have mercy and compassion and the great mission of the salvation of [humankind]. Amongst men you have the honorable title of Perfected Lord of Trustworthy Benevolence. You can move between the Three Realms. You can subdue these demons and transmit the message of this Scripture. Save and deliver the masses, bring them all back together to the Great Tao.

When the Most High had finished speaking, the Heavenly Venerable rode away, the spirits of the stars all made their farewells and withdrew. Then the Perfected Lord of Merciful Salvation carried out the command from on high, swiftly ordering the miraculous realm. In the **guiyou** year, in the 4th month, on the 7th day, he Paced the Mainstays [of Heaven] and sprayed out vapor. An earthquake struck three times. Then he descended into a true medium, and pronounced this scripture and made this spell:

> *Transformation body of Guanyin*
> *Gathered up the sprites on Bohai Island*
> *My heart sinks in the six Harmonies*
> *My chi revolves the five Elements*
> *Compassionately I save the world*
> *Saving from disease, I am a Physician Spirit*
> *A glass of water with seven salts*

My precious sword held straight out
I pace the Mainstays, breathing in and out
The masses of demons all collapse
A thousand disasters forever annihilated
A myriad blessing arrive
In the space opened up by the smoke of incense
The sacred form ascends
Recite my sacred spell
And I will descend in my true shape
Om, swiftly, swiftly, in accordance with the ordinances.

The True Medium spoke:
In my life I dwelt in Quanzhou commandery, and left traces [of my deeds] near Zhangzhou. From then until now through over 300 years I have piled up merit in laborious deeds. Fine honors were commended and bestowed [upon me]. Formerly I shipped grain to save [people] in a drought. Also I led spirit soldiers and drove away pirate robbers. Recently I let flow a sweet spring to put an end to the sufferings of sickness. Now I transmit the Methods and Scriptures of the Spiritual Treasure in order to save the people of the world. If any man or woman obtain my true scripture with its marvelous seal, faithfully keep and worship them. Either invite Buddhist or Taoist priests to recite the scripture, or organize an association to read and recite it. Widely order its dissemination. Then as for anything your heart desires there will be nothing that does not satisfy your wishes. Whensoever anyone begins to build a well or a stove, or constructs a house or a tomb, or an enclosure for pigs, sheep, oxen, horses, chickens or ducks, and at that time there be vapors bearing sickness, then they may arrange incense, flowers, lamps, and tea, and offer up outstanding fruit, recite this scripture and repeat my spell seven times successively, and write with red vermillion the talismans and [recite] the incantations that I have revealed, placing them upon the door, then demons of disaster will spontaneously dissipate, and members of the family will be fine. That which I desire with all my heart is that you will all ascend to the banks of the Tao. After the True Medium had finished speaking, he exhaled the soul and came to.

Perfected Lord, Perfected Lord
Regulate evil and behead plague [demons].
Employ your talisman, spells and [purificatory] water
Broadly save the myriad peoples
Pace the Mainstays with correct chi
Forever cutting off the roots of misfortune
Awesome radiance shines brightly
Your illustrious sobriquet has been successively enhanced
With incense and temple sacrifices
Morning and night we earnestly worship you
The myriad spirits all pray

That they might all bathe in your divine merit
Recite my sacred spell
Sweep away the masses of evil
Swiftly, swiftly, in accordance with the ordinances.
[Spell for Commanding Water:]
Perfected Lord of Trustworthy Benevolence
Transformation body of Guanyin
Compassionately you broadly save [people]
Your spirit descends once invoked
Moving clouds and spreading vapors
Curing illness and eliminating adversity
His fire vehicle removes poison
His water vehicle all strike home
His wind vehicle and chi vehicle
Penetrate to the mysterious obscurity
The green dragon guards wood
The white tiger protects metal
The red pheasant guards fire
The Dark Warrior is the spirit of Water
I am the Lord of Earth,
Chaotic Origin,
Ancestor of the Tao
Pacing the Mainstays with correct breaths
I protect the myriad beings
My merit is accomplished
Ascend with me
Swiftly, swiftly, in accordance with the ordinances
The Physician Spirit's honored name is proclaimed far and wide
Brightly shone his Spiritual Skill at his birth near Zhangzhou
Formerly the responsive transformation body of Guanyin
Removed by Ritual means the mass of demons and sprites from Bohai Island
Three shocks from the earthquake and the medium was possessed
Proclaimed the scripture and saves all beings
People of the world, burn incense and earnestly recite the scripture
A thousand disasters will be forever ended
And good fortune and longevity will come to you.
[Talisman]

It is said that this scripture specifically cures periodic outbreaks of pestilence. Reciting it can liberate the masses from hardship. At the end of the original copy there was appended the Marvelous Scripture of Immortal Maiden of Merciful Salvation Who Saves [Those in] Childbirth, which still awaits reprinting. (Noted by Yang [Jun].)

13. Song dynasty stele with architectural plan of the Temple of the
Patriarch of the Clear Stream.

THREE

THE PATRIARCH OF THE CLEAR STREAM:

PROCESSIONS OF THE GODS

The Iconography and Organization of
Religious Processions

DE GROOT REMARKED after the description of the Baosheng Dadi procession translated above, that "It goes without saying that all processions are not put together in the same way as the one we have just described. There are great differences depending on the divinity in whose honor the procession is held and depending on the caprice and fantasy of the organizers. It would take an entire volume to describe in a complete manner all the different sorts of processions which are held in China" (1977, 1:285). By way of an exploration of the iconography, organization, and social functions of religious processions in contemporary China, I will discuss the cult of Qingshui Zushi, Patriarch of the Clear Stream, Chen Puzu (1045–1101).

Contemporary Observances:
Description of the 1986 and 1987 Processions

The plain of Penglai township forms a long, thin oval ringed all around by mountains that rise steeply from the plain. The view from these mountains is one of the loveliest in Fujian. The plain is bisected by a river which emerges from the northernmost edge of the oval and flows into a larger river moving perpendicular to it. This river is crossed by a high stone bridge perhaps 250 yards long and 30 yards high. Tea grows along the rim of mountains, and it is deservedly renowned. Lower down the unbelievable terraces begin, with their intricate irrigation systems providing water for rice beds high on the mountain slopes. On the valley floor, rice paddies stand next to banana groves and vegetable patches. The area is remote and the people are poor. Most homes are built of mud bricks, with black tile sloping roofs. But families with overseas Chinese relatives have homes built of stone, complete with televisions and electric appliances. Some sixty thousand people live in the Penglai area. The present population of the county of Anxi, in which Penglai is located, is close to one million. The overseas Chinese from Anxi exceed this number. This is a testimony to the poverty and hardship of life in Anxi in the last century.[1]

The county is completely mountainous, and there are still a few places without electricity where even kerosene is rationed. The waterways connect Penglai with the county capital Anxi, and thence to Quanzhou and the sea. This was the route followed by the tea trade in the eighteenth century. But after its collapse, the region sank back into poverty. The waterways have silted up and are no longer navigable by large boats. Fortunately, overseas Chinese have returned in large numbers, especially in recent years, and contributed greatly to the building of schools, hospitals, roads, and temples. They have played a major role in the revival of religious traditions and popular culture in the area. Overseas Chinese also provided the bulk of the funding for the restoration of the main temple in the area.

Midway along the mountain rim to the east, at the highest point, stands the Qingshui Zushi gong (Temple of the Patriarch of the Clear Stream). Founded in 1089, it is the center of a cult which has spread across Southeast Asia. A rare stele dating from the Song gives a diagram of the original shape of the temple. This was used to guide restoration work after the ravages of the Cultural Revolution. The original statue of the god, the temple gazetteer, and certain other precious items belonging to the temple, had been concealed "amongst the people" during the Cultural Revolution. Restoration was contemplated as early as 1975, and actual reconstruction was commenced in 1978. All was ready in 1980 for the consecration of the temple. This was performed by Buddhists, although Taoists can do it as well. There is a considerable overlapping of ritual functions between the two groups in the countryside. Three elderly Buddhists now live in the temple. During the Cultural Revolution they were driven out of the temple, forced to do hard labor, to repudiate their faith and marry, and to repeatedly confess their alleged crimes. Now they have children who assist them in their rituals. There are about ten monks in the area who can pool resources for particularly important occasions. The monks in the temple are very literate and refined. They compose poetry, write excellent calligraphy, and sing Minnan Nanyin songs beautifully. Aside from birthdays of the Patriarch and the Buddhas, everyday religious observances are confined to morning and evening recitations by the monks. The Buddhists leave the temple to go to private homes to conduct funeral services, and go from one village to the next throughout the seventh lunar month set aside for the Deliverance of the Hungry Ghosts, Pudu. Visitors to the temple burn incense and paper money, pray, and consult divination blocks.

Perhaps the earliest surname group to arrive in the area was one named Peng, judging from ancient place names, but they have almost disappeared by now. The Yang surname group was followed into the area by a group named Lin, who arrived over six hundred years ago, as shown in a carefully guarded local family genealogy. Later the Liu, the Su, the Cai, and the Chen surname groups all moved into the valley. The Ke surname group was the last to arrive, sometime toward the end of the Ming dynasty. Most of these surname groups eventually organized themselves into lineages. They brought their own gods and set up their own communities, ancestral halls, and temples. The Lin lineage claims that the Xuantian Shangdi god they brought was the first god in the valley. In time the valley came to be divided into three *antang* (altars), called simply upper, central, and lower. These stretch from south to north along both sides of the river with very precise boundaries observed by local custom. Currently the upper division contains Zhang, Su, Cai, and Yang lineages, and some members of the Chen lineage. The middle division has the Lin, Liu, and Ke lineages, with a handful of Chen families. The lower division is primarily populated by members of the lineage Chen, with members of the Liu, Li, Chou, Lu, and Cheng lineages as well. Across the major river a stretch also considered to be part of the lower altar includes Chen, Zheng, and Lu lineage members, as well as other surname groups. The route taken by the procession covers the entire valley, which is made up of two counties. Some of the stops on the procession are traditional, the surname in question having long since died out. Each altar-division has nine stops. Changing geographic conditions are worked into the routing. Thus lunch breaks are often held in schoolgrounds or temple squares.

There may be as many as fifty temples scattered around the valley and in the hills. Two of the largest are in the central altar. One is devoted to Guanyin, and used to be the endpoint of the god procession; another houses the San Daren (the Three Great Lords), Wangye whose cult came from Nan'an and won a great following. These three gods are honored with the second largest religious festival of the year, on the first through the third of the tenth lunar month. Every community sets out offerings and holds a feast for these gods. This temple is the center of an active medium cult. These temples serve their immediate surrounding communities. The Chief Community Representatives, selected by divination (although I heard charges that some purchased the position to enhance their social standing), each raise a pig for a sacrifice before the temple. The pig is actually led into the temple. The Taoist consecrates the knife, and a butcher hauls the pig out of the temple, holds it across a bench just outside the door, and kills it. The other families slaughter a pig at home and bring the head and tail to the temple with other offerings. A Taoist jiao

14. Local gods, including black-faced Patriarch of the Clear Stream, set on an altar below the paintings of Taoist deities.

is held, and opera is performed. Twice the Taoists emerge and circle the offering tables. More offerings are added for the second round, according to local people, because the first is only for local gods, while the second is for the Emperor of Heaven, invited by the Taoists, and all his accompanying troops. Note the central role of Taoist liturgy in transcending the local god's domain and bringing villagers in direct contact with representatives of the universal pantheon. Similar community-defined god birthdays are held at other temples around the valley. Only the Patriarch's celebration brings all these communities and lineages together for a week's time each year.

Certainly the major religious and cultural event of the year is the celebration of the birthday of the Patriarch of the Clear Stream. This coincides with the New Year's festivities as the date is the sixth of the first lunar month. In former times thirty thousand people would come on foot from beyond the valley to take part in the procession. On the first day of the third lunar month local village leaders would gather to determine the exact moment of the commencement of the procession by divination and then send announcements, written in red on yellow posters, which were posted in the major cities in the Minnan region. Nanguan troupes came from Quanzhou, Jinjiang, and Hua'an; large drum and bell ensembles, with children providing slow drumbeats while riding in a sedan chair, came from Zhangzhou. There were local Nanguan troupes as well, plus huagu and dagu drum troupes, dancing dragons and lions, and costumed couples in sedan chairs singing Nanguan ballads. Outsiders camped along the hills near the northern end of the river, just across from the ferry. They brought tents and provisions and set up temporary kitchens. Merchants and peddlers proffered their wares in a festive atmosphere. The procession lasted five days, counting the opening ceremonies on the first day and the return of the god to the temple on the fifth. Each of the three days the god was actually on the move were spent in one of the altar-divisions, starting from the upper and proceeding northward. The honor of housing the god for a night was divided up among the lineages within each altar-division by rotation. Elaborate altars were set up inside the ancestral halls, or largest dwellings of the respective lineages. At every settlement along the way, tables of offerings were set up to greet the god. The Taoists were called on to perform the opening ceremonies and to bless the tables of offerings. Buddhists from the temple followed after the sedan chair of the gods dispensing stamped talismans.[2]

All this stopped during the Cultural Revolution, though smaller-scale religious activities continued in secret. Only in the last three years has the procession gradually been revived. But this is a very complex and difficult process, requiring very sophisticated handling by village leaders. Despite its new policy of freedom of religion, the government is alarmed by religious events of any large scale. Another problem is the desire of the people of Penglai to invite the god statue from the temple down the mountain and into the procession. This traditionally meant closing the temple for five days. But this is peak season for temple revenues, and cadres in charge of the temple are loath to cooperate with something they can only call "feudal superstition." Village elders are working to train the younger generation in participating in such a procession. They have to be shown how to behave so as not to discredit the restoration of popular traditions. Then there is the pressure to speed up the process of restoring traditions, both from older men who fear that much of great value will soon be lost and from overseas Chinese who fervently support the restoration.

Thus it happened that the first procession was carried out in secret largely at night, on a small scale. The following year the procession was larger, and slightly more open, but still very cautious. Then in 1985 things seemed to have taken a turn for the better. The monks from the temple were allowed to come down and participate, many traditional aspects of the procession were revived, and it grew to a great size and marched openly around the valley. Plans were made to make the following year's procession even more complete and magnificent. Communications with the government were not entirely negative. Local officials were naturally more supportive. One remarked to a village leader, "We just don't want you all to do anything that would blacken the face of the god." This was an ambiguous comment, not least because the god's face is black. Such are the intricacies of local decision making. Overseas Chinese donated thirteen thousand yuan toward the construction and carving of an extraordinary sedan chair for the god. A craftsman from Zhejiang spent six months carving and gilding the chair in a workshop in the temple. Two other sedan chairs were ordered from local craftsmen, along with three sets of wooden temple arms to be carried before the god's chairs. The clans selected within each altar-division made elaborate preparations; pigs were selected or purchased to be specially raised for sacrifice; altar hangings, paper lanterns, and massive incense sticks were gathered; and performing arts troupes were formed and drilled for months—often new costumes and instruments were purchased.

On the first two or three days of each New Year, vast numbers of Chinese visit renowned temples to pray for the upcoming year. On the second day of the 1986 New Year the crowds along the mountain path to the Penglai Patriarch of the Clear Stream temple grew too large and several people were forced over the edge, falling twenty feet or so. One girl was seriously injured and was rushed to the hospital in a tractor-cart by her brothers. Sadly, the cart overturned and the girl died. This unfortunate event drew a lot of attention to the temple and the impending procession. A branch police office was set up in the temple. Officials from the district capital and the provincial level came to inspect the situation. The villagers began to get the cold shoulder when requesting permission to proceed as planned with the procession. The cadres in charge of the temple refused to close the temple during the parade. The Propaganda Department sent its propaganda-mobile along the main road of the valley decrying "feudal superstition" through its loudspeakers. Then the Public Security Department posted notices declaring it illegal for "spiritual charlatans" to milk money from the public or for anyone to engage in "feudal superstitious practices that disturb the public order." The people of the Penglai plain were nervous but went on with their preparations. The opening rituals for the procession were set for the evening of the seventh day of the first month.

On the evening prior to the sixth day, the actual birthday of the Patriarch of the Clear Stream, several busloads of lay Buddhists arrived from Zhangzhou. They recited scriptures all night from 8:00 until 6:00 the next morning. From 2:00 until 3:30 a.m. they were spelled by the local temple monks. The latter recited scriptures and sang beautiful Nanguan songs including the *Guanyin can* (Praise-poem for Guanyin). The visitors brought mountains of offerings, hundreds of glutinous long-life, turtle-shaped rice-cakes, paper money, firecrackers, bowls of meat, noodles, fish, fruit, etc. The next morning it was almost impossible to squeeze into the temple due to the crowds. The air was thick with incense and it was difficult to walk without accidentally treading on someone kowtowing or kicking someone's divination blocks. The *Anxi Gazetteer* of 1969 written in Taiwan and quoted above mentions these visits and claimed that they were believed to "bring a great wind" which would blow harmful insects from the valley during the next two days.

On the evening of the seventh, the opening ritual sequence was to begin with the *kaixiang*, an offering of incense by the Taoist priest and a blessing of the pigs and other offerings. Next, he was to perform the *fengqi* and the *jiqi* (blessing of the great banner and presenting offerings to the banner). The banner, inscribed with the full title of the god and made of a massive, twenty-eight-foot bamboo pole, was set standing in a field before the lower division altar. A kaixiang service was to be carried out simultaneously by three different Taoists in each of the altar-divisions. The ritual was to have started at 11:00 p.m. At 9:00 p.m. the police moved in and arrested the Taoists from the central and upper altars. The headman of the lower altar was told to report to district police headquarters the following morning at 8:00 sharp. When I arrived at the lower altar at 11:00 a.m. the offerings were still being brought in; some families had brought pigs in from mountain villages hours away by foot. Each pig had a red ribbon round its neck and a cookie, an orange, and some paper money in its mouth. Also hanging from their necks were lanterns inscribed, "*Qingshui Zushi kaixiang*" (the Patriarch of the Clear Stream lights the incense). Tables of offerings, including *wuxing* (the five kinds of meat), candies, fruit, candles, etc., were set up before the pigs. There were roughly fifty pigs sacrificed at that altar, five more at the central altar (the surname-group chosen to house the god was very small), and probably over fifty in the upper altar. People were extremely upset. The young Taoist could not be persuaded to perform the ritual. I went on to the central altar, where I heard a burst of firecrackers from the lower altar. I concluded that they had decided to skip the ritual and just burn paper money and set off firecrackers. But in fact the people stayed on at the lower altar, waiting to see if any authorities would show up. At about 3:00 a.m. the Taoist performed a quick blessing in the dark, and people took their pigs home, relieved that they had been consecrated. Other Taoists were sent for from outlying areas and they performed the rituals at the central and upper altars late in the night.

The next day tensions were high. The Taoists had not been released, and the lower altar headman had gone to the district capital to report as ordered. The traditional feast of the god's birthday was held at midday, and everyone was glum or angry. Many people wanted to know why the government had let them make all these preparations and then acted to disrupt the festival. Much speculation focused on the cadre in the temple and his play for power before the visiting provincial authorities. Most people just ate in silence. There was little of the usual toasting. The portions of the pigs and offering foods not consumed at the feast were divided up and given to guests to take home.

That evening three men who had trained for months for the task were supposed to climb the hill to the temple, first stopping to pray at the Sanyi gong (Temple to the Three Righteous Ones), near the temple at the top of the hill. Then they were to proceed to the temple, stopping every three paces to bow and to set off a firecracker-gun three times. Exactly 108 paces would bring them to the temple, where they were to offer incense, collect fire from the temple burner to light incense sticks during the procession, and escort the god down the hill. These three young men had been carefully selected. They had practiced abstinence for three months. They had carefully trained how to load a firecracker-gun from a large gunpowder horn and how to load the fuse-holes from a smaller horn. They could light the gun with a long slow fuse of dried banyan rope coiled around their shoulders. I went up to the upper altar around nightfall to watch them make their prayers before starting the ascent. The police had just been there and had arrested the three men. As I arrived another young man was being shown how to work the firecracker-gun. He cast divination blocks to see if he was acceptable to the god. The answer was affirmative. He managed to set off the gun, nearly dropping it in the process.

Later that night he was joined by two men from the other altars. They quickly went up the mountain by a back path. A statue of the god that had been selected by the people for use in place of the god-statue locked in the temple was sent up the mountain by a different path, along with the great banner. Around 3:00 a.m. they began setting off the guns. Since they were unskilled and rain was falling, they had to resort to setting off firecrackers at every third pace. They were allowed to collect fire at the temple. The monks would no doubt have wished to join them but dared not. At 5:00 a.m. I went to a farmhouse a third of the way up the mountain, supposedly the site of the Saint's foster-mother's home, to wait for the god to descend. Finally, at 8:00 a.m., the procession appeared. Led by musicians playing drums and sonas, the group carrying the banner (horizontally) came before a small sedan chair with a tea plant in it. The tea plant had 108 flowers: 76 red and 32 white. Shortly after the opening ceremonies it would be torn apart, and people would determine the number and sex of their future offspring from the color of the flowers (red = male; white = female). Behind the mountain tea plant was a sedan chair containing a metal pan filled with bits of wood lit by the temple's incense fire. Throughout the procession, people would rush forward and light their incense sticks from this fire. Finally came the god in a temporary sedan chair. When they arrived, the banner was set upright. This would occur only once again at the conclusion of the procession. In former times, it was erected at each grouping of offering tables (called *jing*) along the way. But fear of damaging overhead power lines led local leaders to make the change. The god was taken out of the sedan chair and placed on an altar-table. The man who moved him might have been carrying his mother. He changed the god's clothes, putting on a valuable orange *zhasha*, or Buddhist robe, offered by the upper altar division. Then the god was placed in the new magnificent sedan chair. Into the other two sedan chairs were placed a wooden tablet believed to have been sent by the Emperor after the death of the god and engraved with his first title, and a small statue of his adopted mother, the Xiangshan Fanmu. At this point a man with a broom of sprigs and a sign reading *huibi* (stand clear), known as the *kailu* man, pushed back the crowd. He traditionally should have worn an inverted sheepskin coat. His sign should also have had inscribed upon it the traditional message of the Spring Official, on whom more below. But in the confusion of the events the message was left out. As recited to me from memory by an old man who had been a Spring Official in the thirties, the text comes to some 144 characters:

> I have been given the post of Illustrious and Diligent Inspector of the Borders of the Clear Stream. In order that benefit may be brought to a sagely age and an excellent people, let there everywhere be peace throughout these days, and let the people make merry together. Spring has come and I have been appointed Lord of Spring. During this first month of the year this community will invite the Patriarch of the Clear Stream down the mountain and on a tour of the boundaries. Driving away disaster and accumulating rain; all will be harmonious. We will offer incense and the music of drums and bells. Pray that the nation will be well and the people at peace. That all affairs will be accomplished. Now we await the god as though we were dancing and drunken. This Spring Official greets the God, who is moved to respond. Now we shall proceed through this area. I desire that all good men and trustworthy women, limit the quarreling over boundary lines. I officially allow dancing and gambling (during this festival). I order that people obey. I pray that you welcome the god so that our land may be enriched. I will not tolerate any breach in tradition. I have completed the reading of my commission. May everyone act in accordance. (date)

Legend has it that the itineraria of the god[3] was originally led by the Taishou (the Prefect), or later by the governor of the province. One year when the Taishou was coming to take part in the procession, there was a flood. His mother's sedan chair could not safely cross the river, so the

Taishou entrusted this role to a Spring Official selected from among the local people. Such an office is mentioned in the *Zhou Li* (The Rites of Chou), an anachronistic Han reconstruction of Zhou Dynasty bureaucratic hierarchy. The Spring Official should be a man of great moral standing. In the Republican period the mayor of Penglai often filled this role. In the past two years the role has gone to overseas Chinese, who make a large contribution to the festival. Traditionally, the Spring Official was carried in a sedan chair among the procession, attended by family members and led by a group of lictors and soldiers, appropriate to a Mandarin's office. But owing to the situation, the Spring Official was laying low, and had entrusted his position to a stand-in, a local young man renowned for his courage.

As soon as the sedan chairs were ready, the procession moved over to the first jing nearby in front of a school. The sedan chairs first circled the rows of tables of offerings, then took up a position facing the tables, resting on benches. First the three firecracker-gunmen came forward and fired three times, then bowed three times. Next came the relatives of the Spring Official, and finally the stand-in. No Taoists were to be seen, nor any Buddhist monks. A vast number of firecrackers were exploded and people all around bowed or knelt with incense sticks they had lit from the fire in the sedan chair. The procession made its way down the main road, though there had been talk of taking smaller paths and avoiding confrontation with the police. But people were stirred by the solemnity of the occasion and inspired by their ever-growing numbers. Streams of people kept arriving, including all kinds of costumed drum brigades. The procession was led by the kailu man who cleared the way with his broom and "Stand Clear" sign. After this came the depleted tea-plant, which people continued to shred down to nothing, then the fire-pot, then the great banner, then men carrying a wooden trunk with all the gowns and costumes they should have been wearing. Next came an ornately carved sedan chair with a drum set in it (dagu) carried by four men with a fifth on the drum. Next followed a group of children bearing banners inscribed with the title "Patriarch of the Clear Stream" and the "Office of the Spring Official." Next came four white pinions with the words, "Dragons and Tigers Clear the Way." Then came four large paper lanterns, one for each of the three sponsoring lineages and one for the Spring Official. These were followed by children carrying the weapons of the god. The Spring Official and his entourage followed on foot. After them came the three great sedan chairs with at least eight men carrying each one. These were followed by a great assortment of drum-troupes and incense-bearing worshipers.

As they marched up the main road, people scurried to set out offering tables with incense while the god passed by. Most families had feared to set up a table, but everyone got swept up in the spirit of the procession. Midway up the road into town the procession was passed by the jeep of the County Leader, but there was no stopping now, and what was one jeep to several hundred people? The procession stopped in another large schoolground and repeated the process described above. This was the most public space and closest to town so far, and one could sense the tension and determination of the people. The tables of offerings were arranged in two long rows with a table across the front of them, which served as an altar. It had flowers and candles and an incense burner. Each offering along the long row of tables was from a different family. Each had a miniature house made of paper money called a *dadeng* as a backdrop. (The local paper money consists of green figures printed with woodblocks onto yellow strips of paper which are in turn pasted onto larger red sheets. These sheets can be of three sizes: *shang*, *zhong*, and *xia*. A normal offering of paper money includes four "upper" sheets, eight "middle" sheets and twelve "lower" sheets, along with *jinzhi*, white sheets of paper stamped with a red and gold design including the character "longevity.") Set before these paper money houses with their doorways inscribed with the god's name and their attendant paper figurines, were incense burners with incense, stacks of paper money, and plates of food: pig's heads, slices of meat, whole chickens, mushrooms and dried food, fruit, cakes, and sweets. People formed in a great crowd around the tables, keeping an eye on their offerings and watching the excitement. When the procession arrived they had to be pushed back by the kailu man, whom tradition granted the right to whack anyone in his way with his broom. He was utterly hoarse from shouting by the end of the three days.

When the procession left the main road and started heading along narrow, slippery paths through rice paddies in the rain, a noticeable sense of relief was apparent. Despite the rain, the procession continued to grow, with Nanguan troupes and more huagu and dagu troupes joining in. The procession paused for lunch outside the principal hall of the sponsoring lineage in the upper altar-division. Everyone following the procession was handed a slip of red paper inviting them to such and such a family of the lineage for lunch. The procession would halt for two hours and then visit several more jing in the afternoon. Then the god would return to pass the night in the clan hall.

I was walking back to the clan hall altar in the late afternoon when I saw a great crowd following several policemen who were leading a man away. It turned out that this man had been one of the many sedan chair bearers and that he had been chosen somewhat at random as an example. But the police had not anticipated the reaction of the people. They had driven their police van up the narrow road leading to the lineage settlement. The road was slippery from the rain and there was no way to turn it around. So after putting the man inside they were forced to ignominiously reverse slowly down the long hill. The van was almost surrounded by a crowd of angry people, which slowed their descent. Some people were suggesting helping the van over the side of the road. Others were complaining to the policemen about their behavior, which everyone felt was uncalled for and unlawful. The police were so frazzled by this that, when the van did get back down to the town, the prisoner slipped away and could not be found. As it turned out, this was the last time the police attempted to interfere with the procession. The elderly headman from the lower altar had returned that morning with instructions not to take part in the proceedings. He was so confounded and annoyed by the turn of events that he had rather rashly named several other people involved in the event, as if to say, "You see, everyone of standing and good sense is involved." Some of these men were later called in and questioned. Meanwhile, when the authorities learned that the kaixiang rituals had been carried out they arrested two more of the Taoists involved. They had also arrested three Buddhist monks from a nearby village who had planned to join the procession. Thus the Taoists and the Buddhists shared a room for five nights. They were given tea and ordered to write self-confessions. Later, they were charged one yuan per night for their accommodations. The Taoists were fined thirty yuan, and were told that they must have made plenty more in the rituals for the gods at the end of the last year (hints of unreported earnings). Village leaders tried to console them when they returned home, explaining that, as Mao had said, any one thing must be looked at from both sides, and that in a way their being kept away from the procession protected them from greater accusations. They also gave them some money. These Taoists, like most of their generation, had suffered greatly in the Cultural Revolution. They were always the scapegoats, the first to be paraded about and reviled. They had done hard labor and written many a forced confession before. After the Fall of the Gang of Four, the more destitute received substantial aid from their neighbors. One Taoist's house was largely built for him by the community after he was moved from the Guanyin Temple. In any case, the more that were arrested, the more were brought in to take their places.

The procession started up again that evening despite the disruption. That night there were plays and movies performed. The next morning every element of the god's entourage and the gilded carvings on the sedan chairs were carefully counted and compared by representatives of the upper and the central altar-divisions. An elaborate transferral of the god was made at the boundary between the two areas, where everything was again counted up and compared. Then the procession took off through the central altar-division. A young Taoist went along. Wearing everyday clothes and acting as a sona player, he would quickly come before the altar of each jing, whip out a Taoist skullcap and a buffalo horn, and make a rapid prayer invoking the Patriarch of the Clear Stream and beseeching him to partake of and bless the offerings. Then he would toss his hat to a friend, hand his horn to someone else, and disappear into the crowd. The Spring Official also appeared for the first time on this second day of the procession, walking with his family. The weather improved by midday, and with it the spirits of the crowd. By the afternoon the entourage of the Spring Official had donned their long blue robes, and he had taken his place in a sedan chair. The great gong that rightfully should have been second in place in the procession was brought out, and the children put on costumes of traditional soldiers, with the words *bing* (soldier) on the fronts of their jackets and *yong* (brave) on the backs, and wicker hats on their heads. They blew on trumpets five feet long which produce only two notes. Many more banners representing the divinities of local temples joined the procession. Some of the jing visited on the zigzag course across the valley were extraordinarily lavish with large crowds gathered around.

The installment of the god in the central altar that evening was very solemn. Eight paper palaces for the god lined the doorway. In the courtyard were five freshly slaughtered pigs. Before the altar stood three five-foot sticks of incense. Tables of offerings were set out in the left- and right-hand hallways. Before the ancestral altar an altar had been set up for the god, with an empty seat waiting at the highest level. Above it was a richly embroidered ten-foot-square canopy featuring the eight immortals. The sides of the altar were decorated with cones of peanuts and candies fashioned so as to spell out the name of the god. The god was carefully placed on the altar. The craftsman who had carved the god as well as the elaborate chair arranged his clothes and beads. It took him at least twenty minutes until he was satisfied with the results. Finally, the Taoist was persuaded to put on his robe and perform a brief service.

By the third day of the procession everyone felt that it was a success despite the disruptions, and so even greater crowds took part. A Buddhist monk, fully robed, performed a service for the jing outside his home with the Taoist doing his best to keep time to the music on the cymbals. At another jing a Taoist in full robes did a fifteen-minute service. The procession crossed over the great bridge and moved along the highway on the other side of the river. This made a very imposing sight. All sorts of popular performing arts troupes were putting on a show at the same time, attracting large circles of onlookers. Martial arts troupes demonstrated the uses of different types of traditional weapons, costumed children sang folk songs that had not been heard in over thirty years, girls danced with drums, Nanguan troupes performed, lion-dance troupes leaped about, and huagu and dagu drum companies vied for attention.

15. Procession of the Patriarch of the Clear Stream crossing a bridge.

Then, as the procession was reaching the last jing, there was suddenly a tussle as youths from that village demanded that the great banner be raised. Local leaders rushed to calm them down, and one or two got tossed into vegetable patches. The next morning the god was led to a pavilion in the exact center of the valley. He was placed on the altar, and bows were made by the firecracker-gunmen; the incense-bearing entourage of the Spring Official; and the three men who had carried the Incense Trays, with their three-legged flower vases symbolizing *jinding* or *chuding* (an abundance of children), and their small Guanyin statues. Finally came the substitute Spring Official who had refused to sit in his sedan chair throughout most of the procession. That afternoon there was a brief Taoist service for the god. Traditionally, at this point the great banner should have been raised and let fall in the direction of the temple. Then everyone would rush forward and tear off a piece of the cloth as a talisman. But elders explained that youngsters nowadays were too crude and selfish; that in the past, if someone had torn a large strip off, he would have divided it with others, but that today people would rather trample someone to death than give anything away. But they felt sure that, in time, better habits would arise, as people began to respect the god and participate reverently in the procession.

The procession of 1987 took place in the chill of the recent dismissal of Hu Yaobang, and the doubt as to what that event signified. This time overseas Chinese had commissioned two more elaborate, expensive god's sedan chairs. But on the evening of the ascent of the hill to collect the god and the incense fire, the local cadre was observed meeting with police officers. Later that evening the groups went up the hill only to find police making an inspection. The god's sedan chair and props were hidden behind a bend in the path, and everyone watched the police in silence until they left. Then the firecracker-gun bearers went to the temple and succeeded in getting the three god sedan chairs out. The elderly monk followed them and performed a ritual in the Sanyi Miao. Then they waited until morning to proceed to the starting point of the procession. But at that time, the police arrived and insisted that the gods' chairs be returned to the temple, "for safekeeping." Later that day the procession was again hindered by police, who staged a spectacular but ill-timed raid with five vanloads of police officers. However, the local people's information system was too good for them, and the procession was already far up the valley on impassable paths by the time the vans drove up to the large square before a school where noontime performances were going on. They drove off in pursuit, but before they could reach the end of the road a tractor driver dumped a pile of stones across their path. When angry policemen ordered him to remove the stones, he refused, and a scuffle took place. A hot-tempered policeman fired off his revolver, and soon they had arrested the man. It seems he was from Jinjiang, and had friends back home, because a call came through enquiring about him from Jinjiang police headquarters. In any event, as the police were apprehending him, a fifteen-year-old youngster ran up and shouted that this was their procession and that, even if Deng Xiaoping told them to stop, they wouldn't. He became an instant local hero and his words were repeated around the valley. There was only one other arrest of a sedan chair bearer on the second day of the procession. The Taoist priests were allowed to take part in the procession and bless each jing. A local man with many sons was the Spring Official, but he only dared ride in his sedan chair for a few minutes over the course of the procession.

The festivities were affected by the police action and the political atmosphere, and the procession literally raced around the course, accomplishing in three hours, early each morning, what had taken a whole day the year before. The overall assessment was that although people were relieved that the procession had been possible, they felt that it had not been up to the performance of the previous year. They moreover pointed out that the behavior of the police was uncalled for and becoming intolerable. Local leaders confronted governmental authorities over the issue of the gods' chairs, pointing out that overseas Chinese sponsors would be very

16. Final stop on the procession of the Patriarch. Young women in costume sing songs of the seasons (*right foreground*). A Taoist priest blesses offerings, behind which sit the three sedan chairs of the god.

unhappy to hear that the gods' chairs had not been used, although of course they agreed that the government had a responsibility to see to their safekeeping. Flustered officials rushed to the leading overseas Chinese visitor and pleaded with him not to spread word of this, and that things would be worked out by next year. They are clearly in a difficult position. I discuss the policy implications of the current stand-off in the conclusion.

In the Penglai valley the procession of the Patriarch of the Clear Stream transcends village and lineage boundaries and holds the entire valley together. The threat of relations between the component groups degenerating into large-scale feuds is a constant one. The role of the force of commitment to the traditional routing and the acceptance of one's place in the traditional organization of the procession serves the recognized function of preserving unity within the valley. At the same time as the tensions between groups are brought out into the open, they are defused by the involvement of all the groups in a larger process which they can ill afford to disrupt.

On the other hand, the community-based local god temples serve to solidify intragroup solidarity. One interesting example of this is the Zhongting Miao, which has been connected to the Clear Water Cliff temple complex since its original construction in 1317. The square before the temple is still an important stop on the middle day of the procession. But the temple is not one of the *fotoucu* (Buddha houses) where the god spends the night. In fact, the temple is now devoted to the cult of the Three Great Men—the Wangye Zhu, Xing, and Li. The temple is most active on the birthday of those gods on 10/3, when the five thousand people in the immediate community, primarily members of the Lin lineage, but including some Chen families, gather for a Taoist jiao service. The Patriarch stays in lineage halls or the major homes of members of specific surname groups, not in community temples.

In many areas, including Penglai, certain decisions are made by divination within a prearranged framework. The selection of the Spring Official, for example, is made by divination, months in advance, from a pool of candidates who have put their names forward for consideration. Naturally this allows only the wealthy and prominent to compete for the honor. But note that there has been a certain multiplication of functions in the recent processions, with kaixiang consecration ceremonies held at the altar-center of each altar-division, and with firecracker-gunmen selected from each division as well. Perhaps the clearest effort to enhance the mutual involvement of the different groups has been the decision to spread the banner-carrying responsibility to a group of strong men, drawn from each of the divisions of the valley who will not be swayed by demands from individual communities to raise the banner along the way. However, this too is complicated, and during the 1987 procession, a group from the central altar managed to gain control of the banner-carrying party and hoisted the banner in the midst of the second day of the procession as it moved through their central altar-division.

The procession of the Patriarch of the Clear Stream around Penglai township involves several higher-order lineages, passes twenty-nine offering centers, stops before a dozen major and minor temples, and involves some sixty thousand people. Many aspects of the underlying divisiveness between groups that has been worked into a complex interacting whole reappear symbolically in the exchange of the god at the borders of each of the three altar-divisions.[4]

The process of counting all the ornate removable god figures that ordain the elaborately carved and gilded sedan chairs can take hours. First the giver carries out a count, then the receiver. One is reminded of the formalized battles waged between lineages in many parts of Fujian over the last three or four centuries. In the early phase, these battles had many ritual dimensions. The time and place of battle were arranged by lineage representatives beforehand. Then the warriors of the lineage would swear an oath in the lineage hall or local temple to uphold the honor of the clan. A battle would often result in the loss of life. The dead were counted, and more battles waged until a parity in the dead of the two sides emerged.

17. Old woman teaching a young boy how to kneel with incense before
the god's procession.

Later, as monetary factors and the state legal system came to play a larger role in the process, other people could voluntarily stand in for the actual killers and be executed by the state, thus satisfying the demanded ratio of deaths. The families of these stand-ins were supported by their lineage.[5]

Descriptions of the God's Procession in the Anxi District Gazetteer

The *Anxi District Gazetteer* written in Taiwan in 1969 under the auspices of the Taipei Kunshen Patriarch of the Clear Stream temple, includes an *Essay on Clear Water Temple* by Lin Sishui which describes the processions of the god around the vast valleybed of Penglai, upon the birthday of the god early in the New Year (1/6). These descriptions were based on observations made in the twenties and thirties.

> Every month, on the 1st and the 15th, people invited the Patriarch to the public shrine of the headman and performed theater [for the god]; this was called *zuowei*. Traditionally, the entire county was divided into three altars [*antang*], and these rotated the management of the rituals. On 3/1, they performed the *zuodawei*, and representatives from the three altars would gather and divide lots to determine who would be the *chitouchishou* [head of the banner and banner holder]; who would be the *duhuitong* [chief gunmen]; and who would be *zhuang chunguan* [the Spring Official]. The "head of the banner and banner holder" refers to the [men who hold the] great banner that heads the procession of the god and is made of an enormous bamboo, eighteen to twenty-four feet long, both tall and large. Several days before the procession, the two men who would be the head of the banner and the banner holder would climb up Tayan Mountain to the Niaolan peak to select an appropriate bamboo. Then they would ask the Ancestral Master's permission by dropping divination blocks, and then first set out offerings and only then cut down the bamboo. The banner was worshiped at the Opening of the Incense ritual. On it was written, "Enfeoffed by Imperial Decree: Bodhisatva Great Master of Excellent Benefits, Merciful Salvation, Broad Benevolence, and Brilliant Responses." According to the stories told by elders, for three days after the banner had been worshiped, rats were not able to open their mouths, so the food set out to worship the gods and to feast one's guests could be left out and not put away. This great banner determines which stop [of the procession] belongs to which surname. One may not transgress the boundaries by so much as a step; this will lead to a fight, and sometimes a great free-for-all ensues, which can grow so serious as to turn into a feud [*xiedou*]. Because of this, in the autocratic age [i.e., Imperial times], the District Magistrate would personally come take part in the three-day great procession, and hold down [violence] with the force of his posi-

tion. Later, because the District Magistrate couldn't get away [from his work], a relatively well-known local gentry was selected by the County and the *li* to fill the role of Spring Official. Whenever there were quarrels, he could adjudicate, and later this became the established rule. As for the "chief gunmen," this group of men would present themselves before the Patriarch's seat and make vows, and give a monetary contribution. They would purify their bodies and, for three months before the procession, would abstain from sleeping with their wives, and abstain even more strictly from any contact with pregnant women. On the afternoon before the Opening of the Incense, the Patriarch would go up the cliff [with them], and only descend from his seat [in the temple] early the next morning. First they would *jinxiang* [present incense] at the temple of the Three Righteous Ones, then the chief gunmen would walk along the temple cliffside path, taking two steps and firing their guns, for a total of 108 steps. The barrels of the guns would by then have turned red, but if any of the gunmen were burned they took it as a sign that they were not sincere and pure enough. The afore-mentioned banner carriers, gunmen and Spring Official were selected by lots on 3/1, and each altar got only one. As for the Opening of the Incense, this generally took place each year on the 1/7, 8 and 9. The actual date was also determined on the preceding 3/1 by divination addressed to the Patriarch. Each altar had a *fotoucu* [Head Buddha House], where lanterns and decorations were hung up. A great feast would be held there, and several hundred to a thousand pigs were slaughtered. The Incense Headman who invited the most guests won the greatest glory. The day after the Opening of the Incense, the Patriarch was escorted to the Upper Altar. On the second day he went to the Middle Altar. On the third day he was escorted to the Lower Altar. During these three days there were *zhuang zhaojun* [children dressed in opera costume], *zhuang gelou* [decorated floats], Song Jiang [martial arts group processional performances], *nongshi* [lion dances], *nanbeiguan* [Beiguan and Nanguan musical ensembles], and *yuqian qingqu* [concerts of Nanguan before the gods in the temples], and every kind of popular entertainment. On the third day they proceeded to the Yangzhong Pavilion in the center of the valley and Dispersed the Incense. The god was passed to the next surname group, and this is commonly called, *jie fotou* [receiving the Buddha]. The costs of all this are substantial. (*Anxi xianzhi: Fubian zhong*:179)

Sources: Textual History of the Temple Gazetteers

Sources on the evolution of the cult of the Patriarch of the Clear Stream have been gathered in successive editions of Qingshuiyan (Clear Stream Cliff) temple gazetteers. The earliest sources include four Song edicts conferring progressively higher titles upon the god. Yang Jun reports in his edition of the Gazetteer that an Anxi man named Yu Keji (*jinshi*,

1191), who served as Office Manager in Changping and later as Prefect of Meizhou, and was a Gentleman for Governmental Participation, had the edicts printed in the Song. Yang states that this edition survived into the Ming. An inscription written on the mountain gateway to the temple in Hongguang reign-period (1645) by the District Magistrate of Anxi, one Dongou Zhou Zongbi, mentioned that the calligraphy of the edicts was in the hand of one Kou Laigong. These edicts are translated in appendix I.[6]

The Legend of the God in the Min Shu

The legend of the god received fairly complete treatment in He Qiao-yuan's *Min Shu* (ca. 1629):

Penglai Mountain was originally called Zhangyan Mountain. The springs are clear and so it was named Clear Water Cliff. The Song Chan Master Puzu had his ritual altar there. Puzu was a Yongchun man. When he was young he left home and went to the Great Cloud Monastery. When he was older, he built a shrine in Gaotai Mountain. He left to serve the Chan Master of Dajing Mountain. When his tasks were done and he was preparing to leave, the Master urged him to build bridges in over ten places to enable people to pass to and fro. Later he moved his shrine to Mazhang where he pleaded for rain on behalf of the multitudes. [Rain] fell whenever he beckoned it. In 1083 there was a great drought in Qingxi, and the Biancun surnamed Liu, conspired with the villagers of the area to go to him and invite him. When he arrived, rain followed and soaked the earth. The people were delighted. There was a bamboo dwelling for him to prolong his stay in, and subsequently, several buildings were built on Zhangyan Mountain. This [complex] was named Clear Water Cliff, and was the reverent abode [of the Master]. Puzu's arts spread over Jian[ou], Ding[zhou], Jian[an], and Zhang[zhou]. Alms poured in. He resided in the temple for nineteen years. He built the Yongcheng, Gukou, Taikou, and other bridges. He paved the Yangzhong road, which cost a vast amount of money, all of which came from alms. At the beginning of the construction, his disciple Yang Daozhouming, piled up boulders to form two towers on the edge of the cliff. They overhung a precipitous ravine. This was not the work of human hands. There had been invisible aid. Food for the workers came directly out of the rocks. This outpouring ceased when a worker cut off his hand. Amongst the workers was a very bright man named Liu Gongrui who had practiced vegetarianism for a long time and upheld the Buddhist vows. Puzu loved him and one day instructed him about his preparations for death. After singing a *gatha*, he sat in meditation and died. He was 57 at his death. He died on the 13th of the 5th month of 1101 [May 12, 1101]. Everyone from far and near gathered together and observed the rites and sang praises and expressed grief. After three days his body had still not changed color, whereupon [the people] built a stupa [to house his body] and carved a statue of him and worshipped it. If one was even slightly insincere, then thunder roared and lightning struck. Formerly great boulders blocked the path to the temple, making it inconvenient for visitors. Then one night they moved to the side of the road. There was a [pregnant] woman seeking refuge on the cliffside when suddenly hemp and bamboo sprung up all around and she dared not enter. [The god] finds time to answer [those] who present offerings, manifesting [lit.] his shadow to eat [offerings] of soup. Whatever one prayed for he responded to. In the Song he was successively enfeoffed as Zhaoying guanghui ciji shanhe dashi [The Great Master of Superior Harmony, Merciful Salvation, Broad Compassion and Brilliant Responses]. The statues of Puzu mostly are black. The popular legend is that when he first was building the temple on the mountain, there was a demon cave, in which the *She* demons hid away. Puzu made a deal with them, saying, "Do you agree to a struggle of magical powers?" The demons agreed. They put Puzu in the cave and smoked him for seven days and nights. Puzu didn't die, but emerged and said, "You must submit to my control." He hung a cloth from the side of the cliff and had the demons climb onto it and sit down. They did so and then the cloth broke and they all fell to the bottom of the cliff. Then he sealed them into the cave. The reason why his image is now black is that the demons smoked him until he became that way. There is another legend which states that a mountain bandit arrived and chopped off the statue's nose. A monk picked it up and tried to reattach it, when it disappeared without a trace. Looking again he saw it was back in its original position. If the god is dissatisfied, the nose disappears. If you search for it you might find it in your sleeve or your pocket, or inside your clothes. Up to the present day, when people pray for rain they must invite the god and worship him. (Quoted in Yang, 3:1a-2b)

The references in this legend to a "magical battle" with the She minority gives a further indication of the complexity of the society of Song Fujian. A similar legend is recounted at the ancestral temple of the Sanping Zushigong cult in Pinghe. The deified monk there is said to have been a disciple of Chen Puzu. The legends of several other gods of Fujian involve conquest of the She.[7]

The Song Canonization Process

The Patriarch of the Clear Stream received four Imperial Decrees and Mandates of Enfeoffment during the Song Dynasty. In 1164, he was made the Great Master of Brilliant Responses. In 1184 he became the Great Master of Merciful Salvation and Brilliant Responses. In 1201 he was enfeoffed as the Great Master of Merciful Salvation, Broad Benevolence, and Brilliant Responses. Finally, in 1210 he became the Great Master of Superior Benefits, Merciful Salvation, Broad Benevolence, and Brilliant Responses. Valerie Hanson has outlined the process of canonization by first quoting inscriptions citing late twelfth-century law for the local end of the process and then summarizing the court bureaucratic process:

> The prefect should report and guarantee to the fiscal intendants [translated as "fiscal commissioners" below in line with Hucker (1985)] the claims of all the temples and Buddhist and Daoist practitioners of each circuit who have performed miracles in response to prayers and who should be given titles and plaques. The fiscal intendant will send an official from a neighboring prefecture to check the claim personally. Then he will send another official who is not involved to double-check the claim. When these checks are completed, he will report the actual situation to the Emperor. (Hansen, 1990: 91, quoting the *Wuxing jinshi*, 12:4a; *Liangzhe jinshi*, 12:39b). The fiscal intendant's petition to the emperor was automatically forwarded to the Imperial Secretariat [here translated as Department of State Affairs, after Hucker (1985)], who sent it to the Board of Rites to check the claim one more time. Once they approved it, they sent it to the Court of Imperial Sacrifices to receive a provisional title (*nifeng*). The Court of Imperial Sacrifices then sent it back to the Board of Rites for approval; they then sent it back to the Imperial Secretariat who drafted the edict bestowing the title as well as a full report documenting all the investigations which had taken place on the local and national levels. (Hansen, 1990:91–92)

The first edict gives an impression of the process of petition for endorsement of local god cults by groups connected to the cult. Just how mechanical a process this all was is unclear. Surely local pressure groups and bribery must have played a significant role. In chapter 4, I discuss some late Qing examples of this genre, and examine changes in the endorsement process.

More of the issues at stake in this process become clear in the second edict, issued in 1184. There one finds the claim that the cult is not a "licentious cult," that the miracles are no ordinary coincidences, and that the cult merits official endorsement in the form of enhanced titles, commemorative plaques, and entries in the official Register of Sacrifices. From the miracles cited one can see the growth of the cult from a local to a regional one. Finally, one sees the cult absorbed into the official cult and achieving local government endorsement. The memorials guaranteeing the truth of these observations become more insistent in tone and exhaustive in their presentation of the evidence. The appeal to the example of other Buddhist Masters who have been recognized by the court suggests a spirit of competition and possibly mutual assistance between expanding Buddhist temples.[8]

The third edict confirms the rise of the cult to national recognition. Quite conceivably, this recognition may have had to do with the power at the court of Fujian-born Ministers-of-State.[9] The fourth edict presents a striking picture of the power the cult had assumed in relation to the local government and to other cults in Quanzhou.

From these edicts one sees the cult moving in fifty years' time from a local marvel to a savior of an entire region, commanding national attention. The subsequent history of the cult was less spectacular, experiencing periodic decline and renovation, but consistent official support. Moreover, the fenxiang network experienced steady growth. No sources can be found in the temple on affiliated temples, but Taiwanese sources enable us to trace the spread of ninety-nine affiliated temples on Taiwan. A rare stele outside the ancestral temple dating to the Song dynasty provides the layout of the temple and has been the model for all restorations over the ages. Yang Jun's gazetteer includes twenty-two inscriptions, prefaces, and ritual memorials, as well as sixty-six poems written over seven centuries. The overwhelming majority of the authors were officials or advanced scholar-gentry; many were in the Anxi or Quanzhou government.

Later Sources on the Cult

Yang Jun's *Gazetteer* includes twenty-two prayers and inscriptions relating to the god and the main temple, dating from the Song dynasty to the late Qing. In addition, there is a considerable body of poetry. Three important groups of poems merit special attention. These include the early poems by Yu Keji, written in 1196, and by Zeng Conglong (*jinshi*, 1199) in 1199. Both of these men would soon rise to positions of importance where their support for the cult would be crucial. Yu became Magistrate of Changtai around the time of the drought of 1210. He led the local government in praising the god and had the texts of the edicts inscribed. Zeng became Grand Councillor and may have led the Court in recognizing the god as a deity of national importance.[10]

Next, one finds poems by Chen Mi, District Magistrate of Anxi in 1210, thanking the god for rain. Thus Yu's *Postscript to a Prayer to the Patriarch for Rain* of 1210 and Chen's poem fill in the picture of the prayers to the god to bring rain to save the greater Quanzhou region sketched out in the fourth Edict of 1210. The Quanzhou Prefect Zhen Dexiu's (1178–1235, *jinshi*, 1212) *Ritual Memorial Praying for Rain* of 1216 provides an example of the texts addressed to the gods on such occasions.

A third important group of poems is the cycle of works written by the "Six Old Men," who visited the monastery in 1563. These were Education Intendant of Jiangxi Zhuang Guozhen (*jinshi*, 1562), from Jinjiang;

Zhifu District Magistrate Lin Yuncheng (*jinshi*, 1565), from Jinjiang; Fushi Ouyang Mo (*jinshi*, 1559), from Nan'an; Minister Huang Fengxiang (*jinshi pangyan*, 1568), Second Metropolitan Graduate from Jinjiang; Censor and Governor of Guizhou Lin Qiaoxiang (*jinshi*, 1562) from Jinjiang; and Censor and Minister of the Board of Punishments Chan Yangbi (*jinshi*, 1565), a local Anxi man. Another Minister of the Board of Punishment, He Qiaoyuan, also from Anxi, later visited and directed the construction of a Pavilion. He's version of the legend of the god, included in his *Min Shu*, has already been cited above. The presence of all these high-ranking Fujian officials together at the temple suggests that the cult still had power as a symbol of regional unity.

Historical Survey of the Founding Temple

These sources document the evolution of the temple and the continued power of the cult. This history has been give a brief account in the *Anxi Xianzhi* of 1969, published in Taibei under the auspices of the Taibei Qingshuiyan Temple. After reviewing the life of Chen Puzu and the rise of his cult through the events of 1210, attention is drawn to the date of 1216, when the temple began to expand under the direction of Monk Huiqing Shangren and with the assistance of Anxi District Magistrate Zhao Zunfu. The central hall of the temple was rebuilt, and a Dazang lou (Library Hall for the Buddhist Canon) was built, along with a tower and a pavilion below the temple.

In 1277 the temple was destroyed by fire, although the god's statue miraculously moved itself out of harm's way. Monk Yiguo Shangren took charge of the reconstruction effort but died before it was complete. He was succeeded by Monk Chong Yuan, who completed the work and added the Zhongting Temple and Longjin bridge in 1317. The temple was visited during the reconstruction in 1301 by a pair of officials, one Chinese and the other Mongolian. These were the Anxi District Magistrate and Agricultural Proponent Chen Jun and the Quanzhou region Anxi Daluhuachi Tuohulu. They held a sacrifice for the god.

In 1329 another drought struck Quanzhou. The gods of the city proved to be of no avail, and a Taoist Ritual Master named Yang Zhongyi suggested that the Prefect invite the Great Master. He sent Official Huang to invite the god. As soon as the god had been seated on the altar, rain fell. Anxi District Magistrate Chang Juren describes these events in his 1332 *Brief Account of Prayers for Rain*.

In 1564 the people of Penglai invited a monk from the Kaiyuan si in Quanzhou to direct the temple and organize much-needed repairs. Only one hall and three rooms remained intact, and these were in poor condition. Monk Zheng Longzhuo spent twenty-four years raising contributions and repairing the temple. His disciple Ri En carried on after his death, and attempted to pass control of the temple to his disciple Tun Xun. But another of Zheng Longzhuo's disciples from the expanding Sanxuan Buddhist sect in the home temple, Kaiyuan si, attempted to take over the affairs of the temple and passed control to his disciple, Tun Jun. A split in leadership ensued, and the division was known as the sects of the Eastern and Western towers.

In 1598 the "Six Old Men" (see above) visited the temple and wrote poems praising the scenery. The following year He Qiaoyuan, also a Jinjiang man and a high court official, visited and wrote a record of the reconstruction of the Pavilion of Enlightenment.

In 1622 the Monk Ci Wu led a contribution drive to cast a great bronze drum. The first casting was a failure, and a second successful casting was made in 1630. In 1633 the first gazetteer of the temple was printed with the support of District Magistrate Xu Zibiao and various Anxi gentry (see above). In 1645 Anxi District Magistrate Zhou Dongbi came to the temple to pray for rain and decided to build a gateway to the temple. He placed the four guardian demons in the gateway, whom local legends identify with four of the She minority; demons who escaped Puzu's magical confinement in agreement to serve as guardians of the temple. Meanwhile, the gentry Li Rikun, who had sponsored a printing of the temple gazetteer, directed the repair of the East and West towers.

In 1671, the temple again required repairs and the Directing Monk with the support of the District Magistrate, accomplished the task. Another version of the temple gazetteer was compiled. In 1741 District Magistrate Wang Zhi came to the temple to pray for rain and printed another edition of the gazetteer. In 1761 two monks of the opposing branches, Yi Mao and Ze Feng, joined forces to gather contributions for the repair of the temple and the reedition of the gazetteer. Yi Mao was a gifted poet, and was able to interest literati from Anxi in the republication. Thus he got the District Magistrate and leading gentry to contribute prefaces and poetry. The competition between the two sects continued under the leadership of Monks Mian Qiu and He Dan. They were able to persuade urban gentry like Peng Zhu and Li Qingfu to donate rental lands to the temple.

In 1787–1789 the Taibei Mengjia Zushi Miao was founded. Major reconstruction took place after a fire in 1867. According to Qiu Dezai's 1979 count, there are ninety-eight temples to the god in Taiwan. Another important temple to the god in Taiwan is the famous Zushi Gong temple in Sanxia founded in the Qianlong period (1732–96). A temple in Magong in the Penghu Islands dates from 1729. The earliest dated temple shown on Qiu's list is one in Gaoxiong built in 1689. Gaoxiong in

1979 had sixteen temples; Pingdong, seven; Tainan, thirty-three; Yunlin, three; Zhanghua, seven; Nantou, four; Taoyuan, two; Taibei, twelve; Jilong, four; Yilan, three; and Penghu, two.

In 1812, a massive contribution drive was organized by the purchased licentiate Xu Yucheng, the Linsheng (stipend student) Ling Han, the local military man Lin Dahong, and others, who went to Xiamen and elicited the aid of the Xiamen Naval Governor Wang Delu. The latter, who was involved in similar activities in the Baijiao Baosheng Dadi Temple (see chapter 2), encouraged the Xiamen Prefect Ye Shaopen, the Tongan District Magistrate He Landing, the Anxi District Magistrate Xia Yihuai, and the merchants of Xiamen to donate a total of over three thousand yuan for the repair of the temple. These funds were kept in the Anxi District Warehouse and were later leached away by Magistrate Yang Enjing. Thus the costs of repainting the temple in 1819 had to be raised anew by Lin Dahong, the local military man. Another repair was carried out in 1835, when local gentry, including the juren Chen Xishi, with Ke Daliang and Liu Piaofang, raised twenty-five hundred yuan. In 1850, Chen Xishi reprinted the gazetteer.

In 1871, a monk from Fengshan si in upper Nan'an, ancestral temple of the cult of Guangze Zunwang (on whom see chapter 4 below) named Zhi Hui, was invited to direct the temple, which had fallen into disrepair amid the general corruption of the resident monks. Zhi Hui restored morale and accomplished major repairs in 1899. In 1903 he secured the monetary assistance of an overseas Chinese merchant from Dongxi *xiang* for the purchase of stone dragon pillars, stone lions, and stone pools near the entrance of the temple.

Before his death in 1909, Zhi Hui had taken over seventy disciples, and sent them to take charge of over eleven temples in the area. He was succeeded by Monk Sun Miaoyun. Repairs of the pavilions were conducted in 1926 with funds raised overseas by local men. Just after another reediting of the gazetteer and further repairs in the summer of 1926, directed by a gentry from Zhangping District, war broke out and the temple was neglected. The Director of the Temple Committee, Liu Weili, attempted to open up tea fields on the hillside. He repaired the temple and reprinted the gazetteer.

In 1941, the Monk Li Ben directed the temple. Li Ben had a successful career moving from one temple to another, leading contribution drives and financing repairs. He was invited to the temple and won the aid of the overseas merchant Ke Xianshu and other overseas Chinese. Large-scale repairs were carried out. In 1955, letters were sent out to overseas Chinese from the temple requesting contributions for the repair of the temple roof, and sufficient funds were raised for this purpose.

In 1969 the temple was gutted during the Cultural Revolution. Local

Red Guard bands destroyed the statues and frescoes. One group leader decapitated the ancient statue of the god. He subsequently fell ill and lost the use of one of his legs. In 1987 this same man welcomed the god to his ancestral hall as one of the sponsors of the god's procession described below. It was widely believed that the improvement in his health was attributable to his change of heart.

Recent Restorations

The temple underwent extensive repairs in 1980, mainly funded by overseas Chinese contributions that began pouring in as soon as the Cultural Revolution prohibitions were lifted. The temple is visited by some 600,000 people each year, particularly around the birthday of the god during the Chinese New Year holidays. The local government presently is responsible for the temple. They have a local cadre in charge, and a staff of older caretakers as well as two older monks with eight younger disciples. Until 1985, the proceeds from donations went to the upkeep of the temple and to the local government. But in 1985 the provincial government declared itself interested in making the temple a "provincial tourist site," and clearly they plan to redirect the temple income into provincial coffers. Incense-bearing delegations, *jinxiang tuan*, from offshoot temples of the cult come from all over Fujian, especially from Dehua down to Zhangzhou, and from Guangdong, Zhejiang, and Jiangxi. Many overseas Chinese visit the temple, and there is a reception room where their donations are listed on the walls. The temple is now the object of a power struggle between local and provincial government forces. Moreover, there are more overseas Chinese from Anxi living abroad than there are people in Anxi, so the number of returning family members and tourists is very large.

These overseas Chinese feel a responsibility to their families, and have contributed funds toward the restoration of lineage halls and local temples as a sign of lineage unity. They have elicited the support of trustworthy local people to manage the reconstruction or repair of temples and ancestral halls torn down in the Cultural Revolution. The traditional formal authority structure of extended lineages has been revived, with elders of each generation in hierarchical order. But real decision-making power rests now, as before, in the hands of mature, devoted, and capable men whom the overseas Chinese feel they can trust. Interestingly, the pool from which these people are drawn is often composed of retired accountants. Recall that the accountants were among the only technical people brought into the local governmental apparatus by the Communist party. They were often not party members. Many of them were nevertheless attacked during the Cultural Revolution and driven away from their homes. Many ended up becoming accountants for their new units. These men are now at official retirement age. They are ideally situated, through lifelong training and connections, to profit from the new economic initiatives. This is especially true if they have some young male children to organize into various commercial enterprises. In the poorer areas, including the Penglai valleybed—which was judged to be an impoverished area in 1986 and given special investment aid and a reprieve from taxes for three to five years—the local leaders may not have the resources to capitalize on the new policies. Nonetheless, they gain in community stature through their involvement with these projects. This, in turn, enables them to present an alternative traditional morality to the younger generation. In their view, the gods have brought life back into the valley in a way the collectives and communes never did.

Since the repairs of the main temple were beyond the control of overseas Chinese, they concentrated on smaller, local temples and ancestral halls. However, there was a need to rebuild the Zhongting miao, first built in 1317. The reconstruction required some 50,000 yuan. Every item was meticulously accounted for in lengthy account books, and copies of the books were sent to the principal overseas Chinese sponsors. The temple stands in the center of the valleybed, and has become, along with the pavilion behind it, the center of the local cult of the god. The statue of the god housed there, or in the homes of the following year's headmen (see below), now performs many of the functions denied the god statue in the main temple. But the temple is now also dedicated to the Three Great Ones, the Wangye Zhu, Xing, and Li.

Functions of the God

What does the god do all year when it is not going on inspection of its spiritual territory? In fact the god is seldom still, as it is constantly asked to private homes or into the mountains for a variety of purposes. The god is often invited to the home of a sick person. Then a Taoist invokes the aid of the god in healing the patient and writes a talisman for the patient to consume. Devotees of the Patriarch of the Clear Stream have in fact devoured his buttocks! The statue in the main temple was made of aloewood, which is a valuable ingredient in Chinese medicine. Yang Jun refers to the magnanimity of the god, who willingly allowed devotees to slice pieces off him for medicinal cures. The god is no longer let out of the temple. But doubt remains as to whether the god in the temple is in fact the original god. As I mentioned above, people say that the original god was beheaded during the Cultural Revolution.

Of course there are many statues of the god, some more efficacious than others. Even during the Cultural Revolution, the god occasionally made excursions into the mountains after dark to find herbs. The handlebars of the sedan chair periodically became overwhelmingly heavy and came to rest on some plant on the hillside. The quantities to be administered were determined by divination. The god can also help select the orientation of a home or the placement of a temple by forcing down the handles of the sedan chair.

The Zhongting miao maintains a medium cult that speaks for the god, as well as for the Three Great Ones, the Wangye of the valley. Many village temples also have local mediums who sometimes speak in the voice of the Patriarch. Mediums in the area perform a variety of functions, including healing, exorcising, writing simple protective talismans, answering inquiries, etc. Although they may be present at the same ritual as a Taoist priest, they each perform their discrete roles. Taoists in the area mainly do rituals in honor of the birthday of local gods, perform healings (often alongside a medium), and consecrations of temples and new homes, and write elaborate talismans for a wide variety of day-to-day needs. They do not officiate at funerals, as this portion of the ritual market has been cornered by the Buddhists in the area. In general, the Taoist tradition in this part of Anxi closely resembles the Lushan sect rituals one can see in Northern Taiwan.[11]

Speaking in the voice of the god is the central role of the medium in the cult. The god has spoken through mediums many times through the last nine hundred years. In the thirties the god warned of a flood that devastated half the plain. Those who heeded the words of the god saved their belongings and made offerings to the cult. Those who had not paid heed resolved to mend their ways. Any false message can be due to the mischief of malignant spirits or to the pretention of a false medium. The latest major prophecy of the god states that the god's procession will only be perfect when the hairs on the head of the lion stand straight up. Elders versed in the divinatory arts of geomancy and the interpretation of mediumistic utterances explain that this refers to the hardwood trees planted several years ago on the lion's head–shaped mountain on which the temple stands. The trees will reach maturity in five or six years. Perhaps by that time the procession will proceed undisturbed.

Buddhist Saint or Taoist Deity?

The history of the development of the cult of the Patriarch of the Clear Stream affords an example of the transformation of a Buddhist cult figure into an object of popular worship structured by the Taoist liturgical framework. As described above, the birthday of the god is celebrated inside the temple by practicing Buddhists, either monks or members of scripture recitation societies. But the procession around the valley involving the entire population is initiated, consecrated, and led by Taoist priests.

Further evidence of the Taoist transformation of the Patriarch of the Clear Stream can be found in the incantation included in the appendix to Yang Jun's *Qingshuiyan zhilue*:

> The Perfect One of the Clear Stream
> Is the Transformation Body of the Black Emperor
> Riding upon wind and fire
> He traverses the "World of Sand"
> His Precious Sword of Seven Stars
> Beheads Demons and Sprites
> (He responds to) prayers with rain and shine
> Protects the nation and brings peace to the people
> In the invisible realm his voice is heard
> In the visible realm his fame is great
> Ascending to the Heavens and descending to the Underworld
> He responds to offerings by manifesting his form.

Here one finds the Buddhist Patriarch of the Clear Stream referred to as a Taoist *zhenren* (Perfected Being) and identified as a manifestation of the Dark Warrior of the North, Xuantian Shangdi, an important Taoist deity. The quiet builder of bridges is now a cosmic warrior, wielding a sword of the stars to decimate the demonic ranks.

18. Photo of the Reverent Lord of Broad Compassion distributed
at the Phoenix Mountain Monastery.

FOUR

THE REVERENT LORD OF BROAD COMPASSION:

CONTRADICTORY INTERPRETATIONS OF A GOD

IN RITUAL AND LEGEND

The Prominence of the Cult

DE GROOT (1977, 1:201) remarked that Guo Shengwang (Saintly King Guo, a title commonly used for Guangze Zunwang) could "without hesitation be called the tutelary saint of the province [of Fujian] . . . [T]here he finds his place amongst the domestic gods which are venerated." De Groot also mentioned that the god was the only major local deity among the four gods worshiped on altars in every home in Amoy, the others being Guanyin, the God of Wealth, and the Stove god. He notes that festivals are held for the god on 2/22 and 8/22. After discussing the god's legend in written sources and in popular legend, he goes on to describe the pilgrimages to the god's temple. There are several problems with his descriptions of the cult of the god. First of all, the temple he identifies as the center of the cult, the Weizhen miao in Anxi, is in fact one of thirteen ancillary temples that split off from the main temple in Shishan in Nan'an, the Fengshan si. This temple was the original Weizhen miao, although it was later called the Temple of Guo Mountain, or the Phoenix Mountain (Buddhist) Temple. Even more curious is his failure to mention, except in passing, the sacrifice at the graves of his parents.[1]

As will be seen below, this is one of the central ritual activities of the cult. The procession to the graves and the traditional sacrifice has recently been revived and will be discussed below. Officials of the Fujian Provincial Religious Affairs Office in Fuzhou stated in 1987 that the month-long pilgrimages to the tomb were the largest and most significant expression of popular religious activity in Fujian today.

The tomb was rebuilt in the early 1980s by a group of a dozen young people who had applied unsuccessfully for years to get permission to emigrate to Hong Kong. Since then they have all managed to get there. The ritual sacrifices have been revived as well. They are led, in rotation, by one of the five branches of the Huang lineage that live at the base of Phoenix Mountain in Shishan. In another instance of the interplay between popular cults and ancestral worship in this lineage, each of the five brothers who founded the five branches of the lineage were given as *gan'er* (god-children) to five different deities. Each branch of the lineage not only worships their ancestors on the birth and death dates of their respective branch founders, but also hold ceremonies on the birth and death dates of their respective patron deities. Ancestral halls have been rebuilt for the lineage as a whole and for several of the branches as well. Currently, great efforts are being made to rebuild the tombs of important ancestors. As the involvement of the young people in rebuilding the tomb of the god's parents indicates, leadership in these rituals comes not only from those high in the lineage hierarchy but also from younger activists.

The following announcement was posted on the walls of the Weizhen Temple near the tomb when I visited in spring 1987:

> By Imperial Decree, Loyal and Responsive, Trustworthy and Compassion-ate, Heroic and Martial, Preserver of Peace, King Guo of Broad Mercy.
> In order to sacrifice and sweep; the tombs of the High King and Queen Mother, we have carefully selected the date of 8/26/1985 [and 10/10/85] at the dawn hour to set out from the Longshan Temple and to proceed directly to worship the ancestors at Xingli in Qingxi. The next day, at dawn, we will carry out the sacrifices and sweep the tomb. That same day we will head back with the carriages [in fact the sedan chairs of the gods]. Whosoever amongst the good men and faithful women of the four directions who has a need to express his/her gratitude to the god, you may send funds directly to the Bu-reau of the Master of Sacrifices, which will keep and use it [for the ritual]. (The Bureau of the Master of Sacrifices has been established in the midst of Shishan's main road in Nan'an, Fujian, under the name of XXX.) This is here specially proclaimed. 1985/3/6 and 4/26. Master of Sacrifices: A Compatriot from Taiwan travelling in Macao XXX.

De Groot's remarks on the pilgrimages nevertheless deserve attention because they demonstrate the continuity of the ritual paraphernalia of the cult into the present day:

> Regular pilgrimages are made to his temple every three years, in the eighth month of the civil [lunar] year. This took place in 1883. A traveller passing through the province would have seen on all the roads and footpaths people headed to the temple and the miraculous tomb to which people return. All of them had a small flag attached to their sleeves, a box containing an image of the god on their chests, and a bag of supplies for the trip on their backs. Ordinarily, these pilgrims make arrangements in advance to travel in groups of three or four to keep company. Their little flag is triangular or square and bears the word "command" to indicate that the pilgrim considers it his duty to bring himself before the god. Sometimes there is the inscription "I go to

visit the ancestor." Ordinarily, the statue that they carry with them is the one placed on their domestic altars. However, if they have already made the pilgrimage, they gladly take along a statue belonging to a parent or a friend who could not themselves take part in the pious journey. . . . Certain pilgrims, it seems, think that a lamb is a gift highly agreeable to the god. At least many of them lead one to the temple, having painted the horns and the hooves red, and wearing a small coverlet fitted with small bells. They are consecrated to Guo Shengwang, and are killed later in his home on one of the biannual festivals. However, other people keep these sheep until their natural death. (1977, 2:526–27)

Yang Jun describes the pilgrimages as follows: "There are four paths leading to the god's abode. Each time the year of the visit to the tombs comes round, from spring to autumn all through the day people rub shoulders and march one after the other, while at night they carry torches and continue their visits without rest. Around the mountain one sees four dragons of fire twisting and turning their way to the top. The cult was flourishing" (*Fengshan si zhilue*). Yang Jun provides the following description of the pilgrimage to the tombs:

On the year of the visit to the tombs, whether they be from the nearby provinces of Zhe[jiang] or Yue [Guangdong], or the more distant Si[chuan] or Chu [(Hunan], or even from overseas, white-haired old men and youngsters support one another along the way, undaunted by a journey of a thousand li. Villages within a hundred li of the temple welcome the visiting pilgrims even if they don't know them. They invite them in. They sweep their doorways to welcome them. They dare not think of the expense. If the pilgrims stop to eat or rest somewhere without a place to spend the night, then they leave their belongings in the middle of the road, merely writing the five words *Feng shan si jin xiang* "[On] Pilgrimage to Phoenix Mountain Temple," and there is no need to guard them. The next day each picks up his own belongings, none daring to make mistakes. Should a thief take something [belonging to the pilgrims] he would call out, "I want to return these things to whoever lost them." Only then would he feel calm. Traditionally many people took lambs as offerings. Then they would consult divination blocks. If they should be slaughtered they would kill them. If they should be let free they would be left, at the temple, untied. If the lambs went into someone's house, people would compete to feed them. If someone on the road caught one he would return it to the temple. They were called the lambs of the Venerable Reverent King. (*Fengshan si zhilue*, 1:5b-6a)

Today lambs with dyed-red horns are still brought to the temple by pilgrims bearing sachets of incense and carrying triangular red flags labeled, "Pilgrimage to Phoenix Mountain Temple."

Sources

De Groot went on to translate the legend of the god given in the *Min Shu* and the *Quanzhou fuzhi*. He was unable to consult the *Fengshan si zhilue* of Yang Jun, published in 1888 or the *Guoshan miaozhi*, compiled by the Shishan Hanlin academician, 2d rank Secretary in the Chinese Documents Section of the Inner Secretariat, Dai Fengyi, in 1897. These two gazetteers differ greatly in tone, though for our purposes they compliment one another. Yang Jun includes the *True Scripture of the Stellar Lord Guo* and two mediumistic utterances on filial piety and respect for the written word translated below.[2] Dai provides a more detailed discussion of the rituals performed at the grave of the god's parents. Dai also gives a useful discussion of the various temples and tombs of the cult. His efforts to exhibit a Confucian understanding of the god are both fascinating and problematic. Dai also includes a complete set of reports and memorials surrounding the enhancement of the enfeoffed title of the god in 1883. These materials are translated in the appendix. They reveal the role of the cult in responding to the mid-century secret-society-led rebellions.[3]

Dai Fengyi records a dream in which the god directed him to a copy of the Nan'an District Magistrate's memorial that had led to the addition of the phrase "Protector of Peace" to the god's title in 1871. This memorial reveals the continuities between Song and late Qing canonization methods, as well as the differences (see the materials gathered in appendix II). Clearly, the context and motivation for canonization had changed. The Qing government was attempting to draw upon systems of local power embodied by cults like that of the Reverent Lord of Broad Compassion to reassert social control through a revival of traditional forms of central legitimation of local cults.

These documents reveal certain changes in the canonization process. Reports come up from District Magistrates, with the substance of the report provided by local gentry. The provincial-level administrative system had expanded somewhat since the Song. Fujian was under the direction of the Governor-General of Zhejiang and Fujian as well as the Provincial Governor of Fujian. Each had separate staffs, including Bureaus of Education, all of which had to be consulted in the canonization process. The personal inspection by outside officials of the Song process is lacking, suggesting a routinization of the process. On the other hand, much more weight is put on the testimony of the regional gazetteers, which were far more comprehensive by the Qing. At the court level, the requests appear to have been handled primarily by the Board of Rites.

The Inner Secretariat drafted the *nifeng* (provisional title), which was submitted to the Emperor for his decision. The Jici si (Office of Sacrifices), was also consulted. The title chosen by the Emperor for the Reverent Lord of Broad Compassion was *Bao'an* (Protector of Peace). Altogether, these materials reveal the renewed appeal to sources of ideological support for an Imperial system that was on its last legs.[4]

The Divergent Legends of the God

Both Yang and Dai first provide their own accounts of the god and then quote the versions in the *Min Shu* (ca. 1629) and the *Quanzhou fuzhi* (1776). Based on these sources, the events of Guo Shengwang's short life were as follows:

Guo Zhongfu was born in 963 on the twenty-second day of the second lunar month. Yang and Dai differ as to the location of his birth. Yang says that it was in Qingxi (in Anxi, site of the tomb of the god's parents), while Dai states that it was in Shishan (formerly known as Shantou jie), in a village at the base of Phoenix Mountain in the twelfth division, *du*, of Nan'an district. According to both sources, Guo was a descendant of the Fenyang Wang aristocratic lineage of Guo Ziyi (697–781) of medieval China.[5] Supposedly, a branch of the family led by one Duke Songshan moved first to Fujian, then one Duke Hua moved to the Quanzhou region. The god's mother had a portentous dream announcing his birth. The boy was uncommonly filial and virtuous. He often tended sheep (or, in some versions, cows) in Qingxi for Yang the Elder. His father died and the family was too poor to pay for a tomb.

Here again the accounts in Yang and Dai differ. Yang recounts the popular legend that the god's mother was working as a cook in the Yang household while her son tended the sheep (or the cows).

A geomancer was invited by Elder Yang to select an auspicious spot for his grave. The family mistakenly offered him a meal of a lamb that had fallen into a latrine. The geomancer was angered at its impurity. The god's mother served the geomancer assiduously in washing and combing, and washed his clothes each day. The geomancer asked her, "Have you found a good tomb for your late husband?" She replied,"I barely have time to support my family, how could I hope for such a thing?" She was very upset. The geomancer said, "Would you like to have an audience with the Son of Heaven? Receive blood sacrifices for ten thousand years?" The women urged him to go on. Then he pointed to the sheepfold where her son tended the sheep. "That is a perfect point [*zheng xue*]. Tomorrow morning grind up the bones of your

husband and wash and boil them and bring them here. Then I will pretend
to be angered by their desecrated state and I will slap you on the face. Then
you should burst into tears and spill the bones and ashes onto the ground of
the stockade. Then quickly fetch your son and run off. I too will depart at
that time. You and your son will escape from several battles. When you encounter a great rain shower and see a monk wearing a metal rain-hat, a cow
riding its cowherd, then that will be your former residence, and you may
settle down." They came upon a great downpour and saw a monk with a
copper pot on his head and a cowherd taking shelter from the rain under-
neath a cow. The god's mother said, "This is my old home" [now the site of
the Longshan Temple]. When they went back to the home of Elder Yang,
they learned that the ash and water had all turned into black hornets which
had stung to death everyone in the house. Nowadays, [at the tomb] they first
sacrifice to the Elder, so as not to forget their roots. (*Fengshan si zhilue*,
1:4a-b)

In the version told to De Groot, the father of the god was a slave in the
house of Elder Yang.

A geomancer was invited to the house. The slave served him so well that
upon leaving the geomancer asked him what he desired. The slave said, "Offerings of incense for my descendants for ten thousand years." The geomancer then led him into the mountains and found a spot for a tomb. He
told the slave to bury the bones of his father there. "Wait until you see pass
by someone wearing a metal hat, and an ox riding upon a boy. At that auspicious moment bury the bones of your father, and glory and prosperity will
come to your family." The slave disinterred the bones of his father and
placed them in an urn and went to the assigned spot to wait for [the signs].
At that time it began to rain lightly. A peasant passing by with a metal pot
in his hands happened to use it to block the falling rain, and a boy passing
by with a cow took refuge under the beast. This was obviously the appointed
moment, so the slave began to dig a tomb. As soon as he had placed the urn
in the tomb, it closed up by itself. The slave hurried home to see what would
happen next. Soon thereafter a star shone in his home and a boy was born.
He was destined to become the god of the region. . . . At the age of sixteen
the boy dreamed that he would become a saint. He told this to his mother,
washed and combed himself, and sat down on a chair and died with his legs
crossed. All of a sudden his chair rose up in the air. His mother rushed in at
that instant and prevented his miraculous ascension by pulling on one of his
legs. That is why one always represents this god with one leg folded and the
other hanging down. Other people say however, that he died in the mountains in a tree and that his mother, coming upon him, pulled on his leg to get
him down out of the tree. (De Groot, 1977, 2:521–2)

Dai's version of the life and death of the god is far more restrained.

> As a boy the god was uncommonly virtuous and filial. He tended animals in
> Qingxi for Elder Yang. . . . When his father died it was difficult for them to
> [find the funds to] bury him. The god's heart was grieved. Although he went
> back to tending the animals he wept constantly. A geomancer noticed his
> filial piety and pointed to a mountain belonging to Elder Yang and told him,
> "Bury him there and it will be most auspicious." The god then kowtowed
> before him and thanked him profusely. He asked permission of Elder Yang
> and set up a tomb. Then he returned to the foot of Guo Mountain and
> served his mother until the end of his days. When he was sixteen, he led a
> cow to the top of the mountain. At the setting of the sun he sat upon an old
> wisteria vine and died. When his mother arrived she pulled at his left leg. . . .
> Later when his mother died the people of the Li were so moved by the god's
> perfect filial piety that they decided to worship her at the tomb in Qingxi,
> and buried her together with her husband. They carried out the ritual of
> joint worship of the tomb of the State of Lu. (*Guoshan miaozhi*, 2:2a-b)

The three versions of the origin of the tomb reveal sharply contrasting
representations of the nature of the god. In Yang's account, the ash and
ground bones turn into magical weapons of death and destruction, resulting in the defeat of Elder Yang and the takeover of the geomantic powers
of his land. In De Groot's version, the planting of the god's grandfather's
bones bear fruit in the birth of the god. Here bones reap good fortune.
The class tensions are brought out in the position of the slave and his
enormous wish to transcend his status and achieve a lineage of his own.
In Dai's tamer account, all these conflicts are neutralized by the filial piety
and propriety of the god, who asks and receives permission from Elder
Yang to build a tomb on his land.[6]

As to the manner of the god's death/ascension, early Fujian gazetteers,
such as the *Bamin tongzhi* of 1481 and He Qiaoyuan's *Min Shu* of 1629,
and Qing sources such as the *Quanzhou fuzhi, Nan'an xianzhi, Anxi xianzhi*, and *Fujian tongzhi*, all state that, at the age of ten, or thirteen, or
sixteen, the god climbed Guo Mountain with a jug of wine and a cow. He
sat cross-legged on an old vine. He transformed by sloughing off his body
(a traditional method of leaving the world employed by Taoist adepts;
Robinet, 1979) and was found dead the next day by his mother. The
wine was gone from the jug, and the cow had been devoured, leaving
only the bones. The death/ascension took place during the last years of the
Min dynasty, on the twenty-second day of the eighth lunar month.

Yang Jun comments that the body of the god was first covered with a
layer of gold leaf, and then with a layer of plaster by the local people.
Yang stated that the mummified god was still worshiped in the back hall

bedroom of the Weizhen temple and in Longshan Temple on alternate years. Apparently, when the time came to carry the god-body to visit the tomb of his parents, it was so heavy that it required eight men to lift it. Yang remarks that each time the god-body went to the grave, tears would form in its eyes, due to an overabundance of filial feelings. This miracle is attested to by Dai as well, who saw it himself when he followed the god to the tomb in 1897. When I inquired as to the fate of the mummified god, people were very secretive but indicated that it had been preserved, although the temple was torn down. They said that the time had not yet come for the god to return to the temple.[7] These comments recalled those of a Yongchun man who described how a god statue was protected in his village. The statue was passed from one person to another, with only two people at any one time knowing its whereabouts. This went on for years during the Cultural Revolution. Finally, the god was returned to the restored temple. But in Shishan, the very importance and conspicuousness of the cult center make it difficult to locate the god at this time. Yang Jun adds another interesting anecdote: "When the god was about to transform by sloughing off his body, he asked his mother to bring a gourd [bao, bu in Hokkien, and a book, shu, cu in literary Hokkien]. He sat cross-legged on a vine waiting for her. His mother misunderstood him and brought him a cow [gu in Hokkien] and a pig, [tu in some areas in Hokkien]." She apparently misunderstood gu for bu and tu for cu. I was told the same story to account for the offering of a calf along with a pig and a goat at the birthday of the god in 1986. This combination of offerings is a ritual statement with considerable ramifications, for the sacrifice of an ox is usually reserved for the Great Sacrifices to Heaven and Earth and to Confucius, and is performed by the Emperor or by District Magistrates (Feuchtwang, 1977; Zito, 1984; Da Qing Huidian, 1764, 1888). This problem will be discussed in greater detail below.

The next episode in the god's legend concerns his spirit-marriage to a young woman. De Groot writes that she was identified in the legends he heard as the daughter of a Taoist priest. Yang Jun identifies her as a women of the Huang surname from Youxi. Dai gives her hao as Yide, and remarks that her birthday is celebrated on the twenty-third day of the first lunar month. He also notes that she is believed to have been enfeoffed as the Miaoying Xianfei (Immortal Consort of Miraculous Responses) in the Song Shaoxing period. Dai does not mention the following legend.

Both De Groot and Yang state that the young woman was washing clothes by a stream when she saw a bracelet floating by. (Yang adds that her mother ordered her to retrieve the bracelet.) She picked it up and put it on. Then she found that she could not take it off again. She was betrothed to the god. According to Yang Jun, when her sedan chair passed by the temple, a sudden wind blew her into the temple. She expired inside and thereby became the god's wife. According to the version in De Groot, when she was being carried to the temple to visit her fiancé, the sedan chair suddenly became very light, and then regained its weight. When the bearers arrived at the temple, they discovered that the woman was gone and that a stone had taken her place. (The recently rebuilt temple has preserved the traditional bedroom of the god and goddess behind their altar.) Yang and De Groot remarked that the bed had to be made every morning, and that occasionally one heard the cries of a newborn infant from the bedroom. The next morning a lump of plaster would be found in the temple, and people would quickly form an image of the newborn prince. In this way thirteen princes were formed, and they have been distributed to thirteen auxiliary temples around the Shishan area.

De Groot remarks that the woman's father was a Taoist priest who was very much against the match. In revenge he cast a spell on his wife's spinning wheel, which caused a flood when she spun cloth. The flood threatened the temple and the countryside. But the god emerged from his statue and ordered a traveling peddler staying in the temple to cast his wares one by one into the flood. This forced back the water, and allowed the god to reach his mother-in-law and have her reverse her weaving, which drew the water back to its original borders.

Next, the Taoist waited until the moment of his own death, and had his wife bury smoldering coals at the four corners of his coffin. Just at that moment, the same young man who had emerged from the god's statue reappeared and told his mother-in-law that it would be a desecration of her husband's corpse to allow it to be burned in that way, even if he had asked for it specifically. Unfortunately, she left a tiny morsel of charcoal in one corner by accident, and that is why one corner of the former temple always slowly decays, as though eaten by a slow fire.

Yang Jun feels that these tales are all nonsense, but he adds two interesting details. First, he mentions that some people attribute the decay of the corner of the temple not to the Taoist's magical attack but to the act of a District Magistrate, who, after building a bridge nearby the temple, shot an arrow which struck that corner of the temple. Second, Yang mentions that the Taoist priest used talismans and spells to summon the three gods, Zhu, Xing, and Li, to aid him in his battles against the Reverent Lord of Broad Compassion. His efforts were unsuccessful, as has been seen, and to this day it is considered extremely inauspicious for someone to inadvertently enter the temple while wearing incense from the cult of the Three Gods. These three are in fact the Three Wangye mentioned in chapter 3, who are celebrated by means of jiao community sacrifices in the Penglai valley in Anxi, some forty miles east of Shishan. Fragmentary legends such as these reveal deep-seated tensions among various social groups, temple networks and political groups around the cult, and their religious leaders. The Taoist's opposition to the god in the legend could represent a struggle for resources between two neighboring or overlapping cult networks or their sponsors.[8]

Dai mentions the spirits of two Dukes worshiped alongside the god. The first was the Chongde Zunhou (Reverent Duke of Worshipful Virtue) and the second was the Xianyou Zunhou (Reverent Duke of Manifest Aid). Both were said to have been Song officials who brought the tablets of Imperial investiture with them to the temples. Both are said to have died in the temple so as to serve the god forever. The two other officials represented in some of the Reverent Lord of Broad Compassion temples are Huang Taiwei and General Chen Jiangjun. The former is represented as a civil official, wen, with white hair and beard. He is said to have used a bowl to scoop away ten fathoms of floodwater. He is sometimes called the Duke of the Bowl. General Chen is of course represented as a military official, *wu*.

Dai provides the locations and names of the thirteen principal auxiliary temples housing the Thirteen Princes. All are located within three miles of the cult center. The thirteenth prince stays in the main temple, in the central hall. Interestingly, the cult of Mazu on Meizhou Island is also said to have had a first generation of thirteen statues of the goddess. In the case of the Reverent Lord, there are signs of tensions within the cult visible in the patterns of interaction of these auxiliary gods.

The antagonism between the Prince of the Weizhen temple near the tomb and the parents of the god suggests certain tensions within the cult network. The four principal sites of the cult are: (1) the tomb of the parents of the god in Qingxi some fifteen miles from the main temple; (2) the Weizhen miao (Temple of Awesome Protection) on Guo Mountain, also known as Guoshan miao or Fengshan si (Phoenix Mountain Buddhist Temple); (3) the Longshan gong (Dragon Mountain Temple), about a mile north of the main temple; and (4) another Weizhen miao, about a mile from the tomb of the parents of the god in Qingxi in Anxi. According to Yang Jun, the site of the tomb had the shape of a centipede; the main temple resembled a phoenix with outstretched wings; the Longshan gong looked like a sleeping buffalo; and the Weizhen miao had the image of a water snake. The phoenix of the main temple could visit the centipede of the tomb, but the water snake of the auxiliary temple near the tomb could not visit the centipede-shaped tomb. Thus the prince of the temple near the tomb could not join the sacrifices at the grave. Several other indications in Dai's gazetteer point to conflicts between that temple and the main temple. Dai vigorously denies allegations that the auxiliary temple was in fact the earliest temple to the god. He also denies that the god was born near the temple in Qingxi. Dai explains that the main temple was the original Weizhen miao. Only much later did Buddhists move

19. Blockprint of the temple of the Reverent Lord (from the *Guoshan miaozhi*).

into the temple and set up a statue to Guanyin in the side hall. Later, people began calling the temple "the Phoenix Mountain [Buddhist] Temple." Others called it "the Temple of Guo Mountain." But Dai is adamant about its priority in the cult.

It is understandable how the temple so close to the tomb would seek to expand its own claim on the cult. To this day the god of that temple does not visit the grave, but instead makes a circuit of the villages below it toward Jingu in Anxi on the birthday of the god and at New Year's, when the god of the main temple also parades round Shishan.[9]

A Brief History of the Temple

After his death, the god frequently appeared in dreams to local people, and they soon set up a temple to him, addressing him as "Guo Jiangjun" (General Guo—ca. 939). In 1130 a brigand named Tang led an attack on the area. The god appeared on a white horse and led the brigands into the stream where many drowned, and the region was spared. Sometime in the Shaoxing period (1131–62), a local man was in the capital, carrying the god's incense, when the palace burst into flames. The god appeared on a white horse and put out the fire. Emperor Gaozong (r. 1127–62) enfeoffed the god as "Weizhen Guangze Hou" (Duke of Awesome Protection and Broad Compassion), and bestowed a temple plaque on the thereafter named Weizhen Temple. In the Qiandao period (1165–73), District Magistrate Chen Dafang, and Fugang Chen Yue wrote a stele. In the Shaoxi period (1190–94), the god put out a fire in the Song Palace and Emperor Guangzong (r. 1190–94) enfeoffed the god as "Weizhen zhongying fuhui guangze hou" (Duke of Awesome Protection, Loyal Responses, Trustworthy Kindness, and Broad Compassion), and enlarged the temple. He made the temple's official name Weizhen.

In the Qingyuan period (1195–1200), Emperor Ningzong (r. 1195–1224) enhanced the god's title to Bo (Count) and then to Wang (King, lit. Prince). The full title was "Weizhen zhongying fuhui weiwu yinglie guangze Zunwang" (Reverent King of Awesome Protection, Loyal Responses, Trustworthy Kindness, Awesome Prowess, Martial Energy, and Broad Compassion).

The temple was restored in 1223. At the completion ceremonies in 1226, an official from Jinjiang named Wang Zhou (*jinshi*, 1223, Instructor and later Erudite of the National University, later Controller-general of Huizhou) composed a *Record*, which was written out by Zeng Conglong, who had become Vice Grand Councillor in 1219. (Recall that Zeng also composed a poem at the temple of Qingshui Zushi.)[10] In 1259 the god was enfeoffed by Emperor Lizong (r. 1225–64: this may have been when the title attributed to the Qingyuan period actually was bestowed, as Wang Zhou still refers to the god as a Duke [Wei, 1929]).

In 1561 "Japanese pirates" attacked the area and teamed up with brigands from the Lu surname group (currently living to the north of the temple). The principal lineages of the area built a *bao* (stockade) for protection just north of the temple. The bandits burned the temple, destroying the steles and the three Imperial Enfeoffment Tablets which the Huang lineage had guarded until that time. The bandits had the stockade under siege but tremendous rains attributed to the god drenched their gunpowder and caused them to disperse.

The temple was rebuilt in 1567. Further restoration took place in 1580. In 1588 Chen Xueyi wrote the *Guoshan miaoji* (Record of Guo Mountain). In 1595 a local man named Ye composed a record on the new stairway leading up to the temple.

After a long pause of over 220 years, there is record of a restoration of the temple in 1818, led by the Buddhist monk in charge of the temple, Yu Huan. The consecration of the newly rebuilt temple in 1827 was the occasion of another *Record* by the local man, Lu Tingzong. Then in 1853 the god played a role in the suppression of a number of secret-society-led rebellions, which is detailed in the memorials translated in appendix II. From that point on, the cult seems to have come alive again, with many miracles, scriptures, official documents, religious pamphlets, and temple gazetteers produced up to the turn of the twentieth century. I turn now to a consideration of the two principal gazetteers on the cult.

Taoist versus Confucian Interpretations of the God in Two Temple Gazetteers

Yang Jun states in his 1888 preface to his *Fengshan si zhilue* (Brief Account of the Temple on Phoenix Mountain), that a Jinjiang man named Chen Tiexiang had brought two books on the god to him in Xiamen. The first was the *Puxi jilue* (Brief Record of the Filiations [of the god]) printed by Zeng Shaozhan. The second was a *Fengshan si zhi* (Gazetteer on the Temple of Phoenix Mountain), compiled not long before by one locally recommended juren named Dai (most likely an early version of Dai Fengyi's *Guoshan miaozhi*). Yang copied these books down and personally carried them back to Fuzhou, where he edited and printed his *Brief Account*. He states, "[T]he god is not merely worshiped with offerings in my own family as though he were alive. Every household in Xiamen (Amoy) offers incense to him. In different cities far away he also responds to prayers. People say that this is because he obtained the *zheng xue* [correct geomantic point], in the dragon vein of mountains and rivers. The earth being spiritually charged, the man was extraordinary. Indeed there is truth to this" (*Fengshan si zhilue*, preface). Yang's debt to the god was deep. In his list of the miracles performed by the god in the wake of his role in quelling the mid-nineteenth-century rebellions in Fujian, Yang Jun included the following account: "In 1881, in the 9th month, I, Yang Jun, fell seriously ill. My sons went to [Fengshan si to] worship and prayed for me far away. That very day the crisis passed and I returned to health. I figure that it had been fourteen days since I had passed my bowels. I dreamed that someone was holding a feather-duster which they brushed over my body. When I awoke I felt clear and vigorous" (*Fengshan zhilue*, 4:3b-4a).

As Yang Jun's *Sishen zhilue* begins with the *Fengshan si zhilue*, one would probably be justified in assuming that he published the entire collection as an act of thanksgiving to the god. He included the legends, miracles, scripture, mediumistic utterances, and divinatory poems of the god. He also included the standard sections on the geography, temples, and tombs of the cult, some of the ritual texts for worship at the tomb, as well as an abbreviated ritual protocol for the tomb, the legend of the god and of his attendants, the history of enfeoffments, the excerpts from the Fujian gazetteers, sections on literary writings on the temple and the cult, and miscellaneous remarks.

Dai Fengyi's *Guoshan miaozhi* is a much more elaborate production. Dai was a Hanlin academician from Shishan. Dai had had a direct encounter with the god in the form of a dream, revealing the whereabouts of the god's official dossier (see above). This dream convinced Dai that he must set the record straight. He persuaded the Quanzhou Prefect, Zheng Bingcheng, to write the first preface to his gazetteer on the cult. A second preface was written by Wu Lu (died 1904), a famed calligrapher and the last man from the Quanzhou region to win the *zhuangyuan*, the top score in the Imperial examinations. Dai composed the third preface and had another local official, one Huang Er'ou, a third-rank Brevet Vice Minister and concurrently Secretary of the Zhejiang Bureau of the Ministry of Punishments, write it out for him.

Quanzhou Prefect Zheng's bombastic preface to the *Gazetteer* lashes out at Buddhism (to which he refers in the archaic terminology of the *Shiji* as *shendu zhi jiao* [lit. the Teaching of the Poison of the Body]— *shendu* was an early transcription for "India" found in the *Shi Ji*) and deplores the preposterous carving and worship of icons. Then he attacks the behavior of *Youtai zhi jiao* (lit. Judaic religion), by which he means Christianity; instead of setting up icons, they thoughtlessly discard them and discontinue the ancient domestic rituals. He goes on to state that, upon receiving the Imperial command to proceed to Quanzhou, the first thing he did upon arriving was to worship the officially recognized gods of the prefecture. He points out that Guo Shengwang has long been on the Register of Sacrifices. He praises Dai's work as a historical account which expunges the fantastic and emphasizes the essential. He applauds its Confucian ethical aim of transforming readers by emphasizing the fundamental filial piety of the god. He refers to the great achievements of the god in quelling the Lin Jun and Xie rebellions (see appendix II). He concludes that one should not reject religion, but select what is trustworthy and not comment on the rest. The worship of the god consists basically in the expression of the desire for divine assistance in the maintenance of peace and prosperity.

Dai constantly compares his own work to that of the classic historians. He does this by bringing up wherever possible the locus classicus of the genre or topic about which he was writing at the time. These he refers to as the *shili* (exemplars from the Historians). At one point Dai laments that his talents are shallow, and that he has not been able to "divide incense" from the (Han Shu) *History of the Former Han* of Ban Gu (A.D. 32–92). He beseeches "Master Guo" to come to him in a dream and present him with the "brush of many colors" of Jiang Lang (i.e., Jiang Yan [444–505], a poet of the Six Dynasties period).[11] In compiling a local-level gazetteer, Dai is writing in the tradition of Gu Yanwu (1613–82) and Zhang Xuecheng (1738–1801) (Nivison, 1966).

In his preface, as well as in his "Announcement of the Publication of the Gazetteer," and in his "Preamble to the Publication," Dai reveals his motives in compiling the book. Foremost on his mind is the need to set the record straight on the nature and accomplishments of the god. He includes several harsh criticisms of "certain careless gentlemen," by whom he appears to mean the author of the *Filiations*, Zeng Tianjue, who according to Dai had mixed lowly distortions into their accounts of the god. He also makes several specific attacks on Yang Jun's *Gazetteer*.

His preface presents his Confucian reinterpretation of the god's nature and expands upon his continuing value.

In antiquity the Sages used the *shendao* [Way of the Spirits], to establish their teachings. They regulated it with sacrifices in temples and shrines. Their worship was resplendent in recompense for the bounty of the gods. They depended on the spirits for the well being of the people. However, the spirits had not necessarily accomplished the extraordinary feats of "casting off the bonds of the body" and "ascending to perfection." They need not necessarily have "carried out actions within the pure void of space." Everything depended upon their loyalty, filial piety, humanity, and righteousness. Their morality and good deeds shone throughout the universe. Such traits are adequate to illumine the laying out of sacrifices and the endless offering of incense. Later, offerings of food and drink were made to them in the Register of Sacrifices. People practiced these rituals until they had become standard daily actions. People did not seek for the unusual. Only in later ages did people despise the constant Tao and pretend that "the actions of the lofty, deep, and mysterious" were the work of spirits. Thereupon, those who loved the bizarre and delighted in the absurd, welcomed [the spirits] in from afar and worshipped them. According to my humble opinion, there are but one or two orthodox spirits whose morality and good works are beyond compare. However, wayward people have spoken of them as though they were not thus, and instead claimed that they were to be worshipped as spirits. Alas, how sad. As for the spirit known as Guangze Zunwang of my county, his visits to and sacrifices at the tombs of his parents are the perfection of his filial piety. His saving [the Palace] from fire and his protection of the nation are the perfection of his loyalty. His aiding the people against brigands and pirates was the perfection of his humanity. His not forgetting his former lord's mercy and causing him to be worshipped at the tomb was the perfection of his righteousness. His fame and spiritual power resound, harmonizing the center and the extremities, and gathering them under one roof. This was the comprehensiveness of his morality. His good works were resplendent; they formed into precepts that expanded the labor of the people and fixed the direction of the State. His great nurture swept away all adversity. In all of the Registers of Sacrifice there is not one on which he does not belong. And yet the world does not revere him in this way. Instead they exaggerate and add in all kinds of nonsensical and absurd legends, such as the "sloughing off of the body" and the "self-refining to perfection." Are these not the rumblings of wayward people of decrepit customs who do not realize that in this way they are actually slandering the god? If we do not actively correct this, I fear that people everywhere will grow used to listening to their wayward speech, and will follow after the "lofty, deep and mysterious," neglecting to attend to constant and daily matters. Is not this denial of the Way of the World a burden to one's heart? I have long reserved my doubts before compiling this book. I discovered that the matter of [the boy] "dangling one leg and passing away" was not a matter of "sloughing off the body and transforming into an immortal." Having written an account of his deeds I found that they were all matters of protecting the state and bringing peace to the people. Therefore his life did not involve "abandoning [his duties] and thereby breaking the taboos between master and servant and father and son," in order to "cultivate himself with single-minded attention to attain perfection." Having written down his official titles I know that they do not include such titles as [Master of] "Great Enlightenment," "True Vacuity," "Penetrating Primordiality," and "Coursing through the Void." Moreover, the *Fujian Tongzhi* lists the Guo Temple directly after the City God temple. The *Quanzhou fuzhi* lists the Guo Temple in the section on (Official) Altars and Temples. Thus he is not at all like the Immortal Xu (brothers), . . . Baosheng Dadi or Qingshui Zushi, who all have accounts in the *Fang-wai* section. I saw this with my own eyes and understood it in my heart, so I desired to write it down to inform the world. After I had written the temple gazetteer in eight chapters, I experienced difficulties in printing it. Then the Deputy District Magistrate Hu Chaojin and the Deputy District Magistrate Lei Junsheng each happily offered 100 [yuan] in gold to assist the printing. (*Guoshan miaozhi*, 1:10b-14b)

Watson (1985) has remarked on the political and cultural significance of the recording of a particular temple into the local gazetteer. In Dai's quote one can see how the category and position of the listing within a district gazetteer could assume special significance.

In his "Announcement," Dai first quotes from the *Xiaojing* (the Classic of Filial Piety), and then repeats his condemnation of the interpretation of the Reverent Lord as an "immortal or a Buddha." His work, he claims, will disprove such errors and edit out such distortions. In his "Preamble," he claims that the king is in no way inferior in loyalty and righteousness to Guandi (d.219) (who was officially honored as patron saint of the Qing court) or Yue Fei (1103–41). He again quotes the *Xiaojing*, as well as Confucius, and marvels at the continuity of the cult and the powerful example of filial piety it provides. Assessing the current state of the cult, he remarks:

Now the temple has undergone six restorations, received four Imperial enfeoffments, received visits from people living thousands of miles away, and received offerings of incense from a million households. Records of the temple were written by great statesmen, and the Gazetteers have recorded his deeds. . . . However, recently a *Filiation* of the god was put together which also was fully capable of documenting (the god's) filial piety. However, the selection of materials was not pure, and they constantly added in bizarre and ridiculous phrases. This effort to praise the King actually results in vilifying him. (*Guoshan miaozhi*, 6:18–21)

Dai promises that he will set the record straight and concludes with a plea for contributions toward printing costs. Dai presses his attack against Yang Jun with specific rebuttals of five points raised in Yang's *Fengshan si zhilue*. These were included on two pages interpolated into the text following page two of chapter 7, with the unusual marginal pagination, "a second page two."

First Dai quotes and then ridicules the anecdote on the god's mother's misunderstanding of his requests. Then he quotes and mocks the comments on the "spirit marriage" of the god to Lady Huang. Next, he rejects as preposterous the legend of the weeping of the thirteen princes in the bedchamber of the palace. The thirteen auxiliary temples are merely resting points on the god's processional itinerary, and all this sculpting of prince statues is ridiculous. Finally, he quotes and condemns as unbelievable the anecdotes concerning the vengeful Taoist priest. It seems quite likely that Dai composed his *Gazetteer* specifically to respond to the representation of the god in the *Filiations*, which was quoted in the memorials to the throne of the 1860s, and in Yang's *Brief Account of Phoenix Mountain (Buddhist) Temple*.

The differences between the two gazetteers are borne out in the disparate nature of the sources included in each, after the standard materials had been included. For example, Yang (3:19) quotes a poem by a Jinjiang man named Xu Caohua (1848 *jingyuan*) which identifies the god as a Taoist immortal:

> White rocks, a clear stream, the region is remote.
> The traces of the Immortal linger to this day.
> Long ago he climbed the mountain with wine and a cow,
> Desiring to offer incense to the nine provinces.
> Driving away disaster and overcoming adversity his spiritual power
>   shone forth.
> Brilliant and vast are his fame and power: he is worshiped in the
>   temple.
> Try looking at the cinnabar hill as the outstretched wings of a phoenix
>   in flight.
> The Emperor bestowed it upon him as part of his ritual paraphernalia.
> The Buddha-land of Phoenix Mountain has been there since the
>   opening of heaven.
> The temple has been resplendent since the Northern Song.
> His ancient heroic spirit will never die.
> He broadly disburses virtue and mercy across the earth.
> On the day of his sloughing off the body he left behind a sword and
>   sandals (traditional Taoist emblems).
> The honors accorded him for his good works through the ages are
>   recorded in the histories.
> He causes his powerful *qi* to linger long amongst mankind.
> How could it be limited to the tomb at Xin village?

Dai's *Gazetteer* includes a total of 108 pieces by 100 authors. Dai meticulously identifies the rank and place of origin of the authors, as well as the date of the composition of the poem or essay. These materials provide some insight into the social strata supporting Dai's interpretation of the god.[12]

TABLE 2
Contributors to the Literary Section of the Guoshan Miaozhi
by Rank and Place of Origin

Degree	Place of Origin							
	Shihshan	Nan'an	Jinjiang	Anxi	Hui'an	Fujian	Other	Total
Jinshi	3	2	3			1	2	11
Juren	5	3	7	2		1		18
Total	8	5	10	2		2	2	29
Rank								
Court Official			3	1		2		6
Hanlin or Court Scribe	2	2	4				1	9
Juren without Office	3	3	5					11
District Magistrate	2	1	7				1	11
Education Advisors	3		6	1		4		14
Gongsheng	3	5	7	2	1			18
Shengyuan	1	7	4	1				13
Yamen Official		1					1	2
Monks	2							2
Untitled Commoner	2							2
Total	18	19	36	5	1	6	3	88

Popular Ballads

Dai Fengyi by and large includes poems in his gazetteer that emphasize the god's filial piety, or the sincerity of worship the god arouses. Dai (7:3–4) did however bend his own rules somewhat to include an old-style song on the god, entitled *Guoshan ge* (Song of Guo Mountain), by a relative, Dai Shousong, a Nan'an man who took his material from an old ballad book called *Guoshan yishi*. This song provides an interpretation of the death of the god largely in line with Dai's, but it adds in supernatural elements more attractive to a popular audience. The preface to the song, written by Dai Shousong admits as much when it states that, although Dai Fengyi has produced "an excellent history" of the cult by omitting many of the unsubstantiated legends surrounding it, he has in the process left out many elements of the ancient lore of the temple. So this song was written to aid in the celebration of the expansion of the cult. Each verse is in seven characters, with the exception of exclamations:

Beneath Poetry Mountain in Minnan in the Later Tang
Master Guo had a son but no daughters.
The boy had a lofty nature, quite uncommon.
The family was poor, there was nowhere for him to study.
At the household of Yang the Elder
They received their meals in return for looking after the livestock.
Thinking of his parents, he wept through winter and summer.
August heaven was unkind; he lost his father.
Mother and son stood face to face deep in sadness.
Her dowry could not cover the costs of a grave site.
Leaving a relative unburied, they felt empty and sad.
Who should come along but an old man with white hair.
Stroking his beard by the side of the road he spoke to them.
Their misery and complete filial piety moved him.
He truly showed them a perfect grave site in the shape of a sleeping cow.
The boy went to [Yang] the Elder's home and begged for it.
"No matter how much you beg I won't give it to you."
Then he pitied this young boy of such a perfect nature.
He called him back and listened to him.
"We are in dire straits; wind and rain pierce our secluded hut.
I seek a single grave mound in which to rest the spirit of my ancestor.
When my father was alive, it was hard for me to leave home.
Now that my father is dead, my mother's life is even more difficult.
Depending on others we cannot experience good times.
We eat vegetables and drink water in the side courtyards."
From antiquity perfect sincerity could model Heaven.
The birds planting and the elephants plowing [for the filial paragon Shun]
    were no ordinary events.
How much more so such perfect conduct in one so young.
Mysteriously [his conduct] truly moved Heaven to feel pity.
The Emperor said "Ah, on the earth below there is a filial boy."
He ordered Wu Yang [the legendary physician] to descend and summon
    him, [saying],
"Otherwise I fear he will be consumed by goblins."
In the setting sun he stood in a straw raincoat on the top of the mountain.
"Who is it that comes here?" [It was the] Taishen [Great God—
    Messenger of Heaven],
In embroidered robes riding a horse with feathered cape;
Holding jade court tablets and golden books, he proclaimed the
    Emperor's words.

"I don't want to go to Heaven; I want to stay on earth.
At home I have an old mother who relies on her only son."
But alas, how could the Emperor's order be disregarded?
He sat atop an ancient vine and died with tears streaming down.
The wine was gone from the jar and the cow left only its bones.
The pain of his old mother could not be assuaged.
These strange events indeed coincide with those of antiquity.
By his side were a group of children scared half witless.
The cattle returned and pushed against the thatch fence.
His mother threw down her spinning and rushed to see what had
    happened.
His two eyes shone brilliantly and his left foot hung down.
"My son, after you are gone, how will I live on?"
She wailed and wept in the empty mountains; her tears fell like the rain.
The elders by the roadside knelt down and said,
"Old woman, do not feel so bitter this night.
Your son has transformed this village with his filial piety."
These events were fully recorded.
See how the neighboring women and children brought her food.
Later Heaven sent down a jade casket.
Like the people of Lu, she was jointly buried [with her husband].
From this time on, the power of the King took shape.
Horses of wind and chariots of clouds came down
To express thanks to the people of the village for carrying out his wishes.
In his home region he drives away disaster and sweeps away adversity.
Beginning in the Tang and Sung dynasties and lasting for so many springs
    and autumns,
His magnificent temple stands atop Phoenix Mountain.
He drove away plagues of insects and the demons of drought.
With his deep red banner on his white horse, he routed the rebel leaders.
His heavenly words are resplendent; he is worshiped in the Register of
    Sacrifices.
Living under the care of the True King, people have no worries.
His overflowing virtue and abundant deeds are difficult to recount in full.
Oh sir, look at the edge of the sky where calling birds return.
Crying "Zhou Qiu."

Scriptures and Invocations

The Taoist interpretation of the god finds its fullest expression in *The
True Scripture of the Imperially Enfeoffed Reverent Lord of Broad Compassion*,
translated at the end of this chapter. A copy of this scripture was printed
at the Snowy Seas [Studio] through contributions collected by Yang Jun,

of [Fujian] Commandery and included in Yang Jun's *Gazetteer*. The writing of the scripture may have been part of the rising enthusiasm for the cult that led to the massive pilgrimages described by De Groot. The god is referred to in this scripture with the title bestowed in 1871, Bao'an (Protector of Peace). The scripture may have been composed in 1875 or 1876 following a flood in Fuzhou during which the god is said to have intervened to prevent widespread destruction. I also found a copy of this scripture among a collection of scriptures, liturgical manuscripts, morality books, and collections of spells and talismans gathered during the Cultural Revolution and kept in the Tushanjie Guandi Temple in Quanzhou.

The blend of Three Religions teachings is obvious throughout the scripture, but the identification of the god is unmistakably Taoist. The god is a stellar god positioned in the Palace of Jade Purity, within the Bureau of Responsive Origins, as General of the Bureau of Thunder of the Nine Heavens, in command of the Lightning and Thunder of the Southern Pole. The Thunder Bureau was revealed to be at the center of the magical powers of the Qingwei school of Taoism, founded in the late twelfth century (Boltz, 1987). His Initiatory Master was the Immortal of the Red Cliff from the *Liexian zhuan*. His current Overlord is the Patriarch of Thunder, Leihua Tianzun. He is summoned to his task of salvation by the Yuanyang Wushi Tianzun. His role, affirmed in the major miracles listed in the scripture, is the protection of the community and the court. His primary virtues are loyalty and filial piety.

The Managing Committee of the Xiluo Dian of Tainan published in 1984 a booklet entitled *Nan'an Shishan Fengshan si Nanshi Jie Xiluo Dian Bao'an Guangze Zunwang Zhenjing Yuanchi* (The Origins and True Scripture of Bao'an Guangze Zunwang of Xiluo Dian of Nanshi Road, based on the original scripture and legend of Phoenix Mountain Temple in Shishan in Nan'an). The *True Scripture* included in the booklet is said to have been sent to them from a Buddhist monk in the Phoenix Mountain Temple of Hong Kong, who is said to have obtained it from the original cult center. The scripture was also written after 1871, as it too refers to the god with the title Bao'an, and it seems to be the work of a spirit-medium. However, the new title is mistakenly attributed to the Song dynasty in the scripture. This Taoist scripture identifies the god as a transformation of the Northern Polestar, Master of Fundamental Destiny, which should not surprise the reader by now. The full title of the god is Jiutian Xiaofu Weiling Xianhua Bao'an Guangze Zunwang, Protector of Peace, Reverent Lord of Broad Compassion of the Nine Heavens, [King] of Manifest Transformations, Awesome Spiritual Power, and Fundamental Filial Piety.

The impact of the Imperial Edict of 1871 bestowing the title of Bao'an upon the god was felt throughout the cult network. The new title of the god was soon spread throughout the interconnected pantheon of local deities in the Minnan region served or invoked by a variety of religious specialists. A collection of invocations currently used by a Ritual Master in Tainan contains the following segment:

> I worshipfully invite the Protector of Peace, Saintly King Guo.
> Atop Phoenix Mountain he offered up his body.
> Divinely versed in transformations, he saved the myriad beings.
> Imperially enfeoffed in respect for his ability to settle the State.
> "I am from the Phoenix Mountain Temple of Quanzhou.
> The good work of bringing salvation is what I do.
> The Sacred Ruler bestowed his personal enfeoffment on me.
> The Rescript announced that the words
> "King of the Protection of Peace" be added to my title.
> On Phoenix Mountain I drive away the perverse and filthy.
> My True Form manifests to save the people.
> From antiquity until today my fame has not diminished.
> My illustrious name is known all over the Four Seas.
> People in danger or hardship
> may invite me with spells and talismans.
> Immediately I will manifest myself before them.
> We disciples of the Ritual Teachings especially invite
> The Saintly King, Protector of Peace, to descend
> and draw near. [Ofuchi, 1983, p. 1030]

The God's Self-Criticism (1877)

Immediately following the Taoist scripture in Yang Jun's *Gazetteer* there are two mediumistic utterances recorded in 1877 and 1879 (also translated below). In the first, the conflicting versions of the god's identity are expressed in the god's own words. "Now I hadn't thought that after becoming a Buddha, my *hun* and *po* souls would still stay before my father and mother—that I would become an Immortal, and yet be bowing and kneeling in rites [to my parents] who have had honors repeatedly bestowed upon them. Alas, who is not someones' child?" The god goes on to suggest that he transforms others through the moral example offered by his eternal observances at the grave of his parents. In the second utterance, the god bemoans the lack of regard for the written word evident in the popular worship around his cult. Here he could be any good Confucian speaking. Both of these utterances indicate the degree of interpenetration of Confucian values and divine "Taoist" powers associated with the god.

Confucian Rituals at the Grave of the God's Parents: The Rites

The Confucian interpretation of the god was given ritual form by the sacrifices at the tomb of the god's parent. Dai Fengyi's emphasis on the Confucian rituals that developed around the cult has resulted in the preservation of detailed charts and instructions for the sacrifices, together with documentary forms for the worship of the god's parents, the god's sponsor, the god himself, and the Earth God, Houtu, ruler of the tomb. The descriptions are consciously modeled on the *Wangji*, the *Princely Sacrifices* of the *Liji* (Book of Rites), and the *Da Qing Huidian*. Other notes in the annotations and commentaries refer to Zhu Xi's writings on ritual.

Dai Fengyi attended the sacrifice at the tombs just before the turn of the century and wrote an account of the scene (*Guoshan miaozhi*, 6:15–16):

> Qingxi is one of the outstanding locales in Min. [From here] the spiritual power of the Reverent Lord reverberates afar. People from Min [Fujian], Zhe-[jiang], Wu[Jiangsu], and Yue [Guangdong] compete to visit the tomb. This offering up of incense by all under heaven is no doubt due to their being deeply moved by his filial piety. At the time [of the visit to the tomb] clouds of jade made tinkling sounds and cassia flowers spread their fragrance. Pilgrims coming to present incense covered up the sun with their embroidered banners. They laid out their offerings and withdrew. Their coming and going resembled linked clouds. Some came riding sedan chairs while others came on foot, without ceasing day or night. Before the tombs gentlemen and ladies expressed their sincerity. Suddenly, the moment of the sacrifice arrived. The palanquin of the god appeared with pendants and banners leading the way and carriages and horses crowding behind. The gentlemen and ladies gazed upon the dust and bowed with their incense. The Invoker said, "The Reverent Lord has arrived at the tomb." Cassia wine and peppered soup were first offered at the tomb of Yang the Elder so as not to forget the mercy of the [god's] former lord. They killed the victims by the shrine and when the time of the sacrifice drew near, they laid them out before the tomb to display their purity. [Officiants] in long blue robes with purple sashes poured three libations of wine onto the rushes. The Chief Sacrificer pronounced his sincerity. Those holding sacrificial vessels rushed left and right, assisting in the solemn execution of the sacrifice. When the sacrifice was over and the repast complete, they all turned back the palanquin of the god. Gentlemen and ladies continued their visits without stop. They knew that they were taking part in the sacrifices to the tomb, but they did not necessarily realize the great significance and illustrious teaching of this

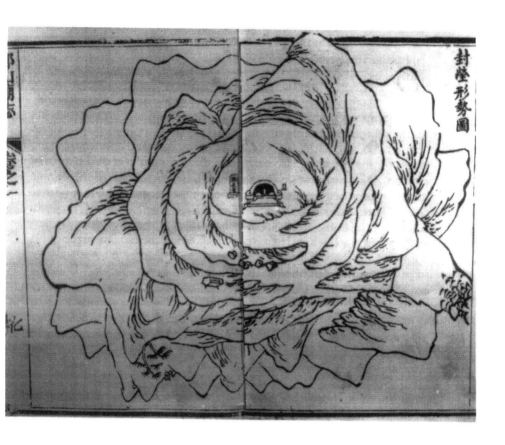

20. Blockprint of the tomb of the parents of the Reverent Lord
(from the *Guoshan miaozhi*).

act. Knowing how to sincerely invoke the Reverent Lord does not necessarily mean realizing that the King has brought filial piety to complete perfection. I went along on a visit to the tomb for the ritual sacrifice. The filial piety of a normal person takes place within a single generation. The filial piety of the Reverent Lord lasts for 10,000 generations. Normal people extend their strength to the utmost to feed their ancestors; their filial piety is still small. The Reverent Lord leads all under heaven to feed his ancestors; his filial piety is much greater. I take up my brush to record this so that later visitors to the tomb may consider my remarks.

Dai begins his discussion of the tombs by noting that very few among the myriad tombs of antiquity have survived into modern times. Moreover, never before has there been a case of the spirits in a tomb receiving incense for hundreds of years because of the staying power of the spirit of their son. "Nowadays when the Reverent Lord pays a visit to the tomb a great mass of people go along. Even though they be from the three [lands of] Wu [Jiangnan] or the hundred [regions of] Yue [Lingnan], they still come, leading lambs, and pour out libations of wine. Thus does the perfect filial piety of the King move people and exalt the hidden virtue of his ancestors."

Dai goes on to describe the tomb, located fifty li (15 miles) from the Anxi district capital in Chongshan li, near the Nan'an border. The mountain path from Shishan takes several hours to walk. Both parents are buried together, as seen above. The tomb is in the shape of a circle, with a Taiji configuration. At the back are two mounds marking the graves. In the center is a stele engraved with the two words "Sacred Edict." The grave faces south. There is a stone marker to the left of the tomb for the Earth god, Houtu, and a grave for Yang the Elder, the patron of Guo's family, to the right. A hundred paces from the tomb is the Tomb Shrine [no longer standing], which was built for the carrying out of the sacrifices. About a mile down the road in the opposite direction from Shishan is the Weizhen miao. A stele on that road states that the path is a "Sacred Way," *shendao*.

The ritual was conducted every three years around the Mid-Autumn Festival, usually in the eighth lunar month. About a year prior to the event, the sacrificial officiants would repair to the Guoshan Temple and determine the exact date of the sacrifice with divination moon-blocks. Then the date would be posted near and far so that people all around would know when to bring their offerings (see charts 1 and 2).

Dai provides detailed instructions for every aspect of the ritual at the tomb.[13] He also provides instructions on the process of the division of the sacrificial meat offered at the tomb. In a gazetteer Dai wrote on

CHART 1
Officiants at the Sacrifice at the Tomb of the Parents of Guangze Zunwang
(Guoshan Miaozhi 5:2a)

Reverent King Guo
Taifei (Mother) Taiwang (Father)
[Spirit Tablets]

	Altar for Offerings	
Libationer	Altar for Incense	Libationer
Silk Official		Silk Official
Prayer Reader		Prayer Reader
	Chief Sacrificial Officiant	
Cantor		Cantor
Attendant Official		Attendant Official

CHART 2
Sacrificial Vessels and Offerings

(a)	(a)	(b)	(b)	(b)	(b)	(b)	(b)
		(c)			(c)		
		(2)			(2)		
	(g)		(e)	(d)		(f)	
13	17	3	1		5	9	
14	18		(h)		6	10	
		two bolts of silk					
15	19				7	11	
			(1)				
16	20	(1) pig	goat		8	12	
	candle	incense	candle	(a)			

Notes to Chart 2 (Sacrificial Vessels and Offerings)
Ritual Recipes

a. *jue*: Metal and porcelain wine decanter. b. *zun*: Metal wine goblet. c. *xing*: Metal broth container. d. *fu*: Square metal container with circular center for panicled millet. e. *ken*: Circular metal container with square center for wheat. f. *bian*: Bamboo baskets for raw fruits of the land and the water such as dates and water chestnuts. g. *dou*: Wooden containers for cooked offerings such as pickled vegetables and minced meat sauces. h. *fei*: Woven bamboo container for silk offerings. i. *zu*: Container 3′3″ long by 2′2″ wide, with red painted sides the Shishan Academy in 1899, he includes an even more detailed list of who should receive just how much of a pig or goat, sacrificed to the spirit of Zhu Xi (1130–1200) and Ouyang Xun (557–641), an early resident of Shishan.[14] Rubie Watson (1985) has shown the uses of the division of sacrificial meat in the marking of relations of class and power within a lineage. Also noteworthy in Dai's ritual instructions is the mention of court robes for participants in the ritual, or fine robes for those "awaiting official appointment." This remark demonstrates the direct involvement of the scholar-gentry official elite in popular worship.

I obtained a set of the ritual instructions for the current sacrifice at the tombs. These are a considerably simplified version of the rites set out in the *Guoshan miaozhi* (5:1–8). According to local informants, the Confucian rites described by Dai were and continue to be performed by leaders of the five branches of the Huang lineage. Although they lead a great procession to the grave of the god's parents, their ritual is exclusive and

---

and black painted wooden planks for setting out offerings. On the incense altar is set the incense burner and lamps. According to the *Huidian* there should also be a Prayer Altar with places for the wine decanters and goblets, and a Silk Altar for the offering of silk. The sacrifice at the grave should consult and employ this arrangement of altars. k. *zhu pan*: Prayerboard: use catalpa or pine wood, 8″ wide by 1′2″ long. Make a separate stand to set it on. Use red paper to write out the prayer, then paste it to the board. At the conclusion of the ritual, tear off the paper and burn it, saving the board and the stand for future use. l. *pan*: Use one wooden plate to hold the hair and blood of the victim. Use a copper plate to hold the reeds and sand. Use a salt platter to hold the purificatory salt. m. *tan*: A prayer carpet, or a red carpet. (1) Goat and Piglet: the sacrificial victims. Prior to the ritual the Chief Sacrificial Officer must inspect the victims to see if they are properly paired and fat, and whether their color is of adequate purity and beauty. When the victims are slaughtered at the shrine by the tomb one must take the blood to announce their death and take their hair to announce their purity. Use a basin and fill it with some blood. In the course of the ritual bury this. (2) *he geng*: The *Zhou Li* states that this is a broth of meat juices with the five flavors added in. It is acceptable to use chicken broth. 1. *shu*: Glutinous millet. 2. *ji*: Panicled millet. 3. *dao*: Rice. 4. *liang*: Sorghum. 5. *xing yan*: Salt shaped in the form of a tiger. 6. *hao yu*: Dried fish. Before using it wash it with warm water and briefly steep it in wine. 7. *zi*: (Red) dates. 8. *su*: Unhusked rice. 9. *shen*: Hazelnut (flat beans [*Dolichos lablab*] may be substituted). 10. *ling*: Caltrop (water chestnut). 11. *qian*: Foxnut (edible seeds of the *Euryale ferox*). 12. *lu fu*: Preserved deer meat. Dice the deer meat, marinate it in wine, then dry it. 13. *jiuju*: Pickled leeks. Remove the top and bottom, keep three inches from the middle. Tie in bunches of four. 14. *qinju*: Pickled celery (prepare as #13 above). 15. *jingju*: Pickled leek-flower (cut into three-inch slices, boil and then pickle). 16. *sunju*: Pickled bamboo shoots. 17. *xihai*: Minced meat sauce (nowadays people dice pork rib-meat, stir in oil, and cook it with salt, scallions, pepper, ginger, soy sauce, dill, star-aniseed, and sesame-oil). 18. *luhai*: Minced deer meat sauce (dice the deer meat or substitute mutton, prepare as in #17). 19. *tuhai*: Minced rabbit meat sauce (prepare as in #17 above. A good substitute is meat from chicken drumsticks). 20. *yuhai*: Minced fish sauce (prepare as in #17). Silk: White silk of official standards, one *zhang* eight feet long, with the words, "Silk made for the God's Rites," embroidered along the edge.

serves to mark their elite status. Other worshipers come and go throughout the eighth lunar month, presenting their own offerings to the grave.
Thus the Confucian rituals of the Huang lineage leaders do not provide
a liturgical framework that brings in all the different social groups in the
community. For such a framework, it is necessary to turn to the Taoist
liturgies celebrated by all the communities of Shishan on the birthday of
the god on the twenty-second day of the second lunar month.

Another example may clarify this issue. In the great Mazu celebrations
at Beigang in Taiwan, an elite group celebrates a traditional Confucian
ritual inside the temple while Taoist ceremonies go on elsewhere inside
the temple and all kinds of popular worship go on outside in the streets.[15]
A similar situation holds true in many major cult temples such as the Xi
Gang triennial *Wangye Jiao* (Liu Chih-wan, 1983; Schipper, 1985c).[16]
Yet the Taoist ceremonies continue to provide the basic framework into
which the Confucian rites are inserted. Moreover, the Taoists move in
and out of the temple, blessing the offerings outside, moving onto the
stage where the theatrical troupe has just displayed the entire popular
pantheon (*banxian*), to announce to the gods and to the people the merit
accrued during the rituals. The Confucian rites may mark the exclusive-
ness of the participants, but they are incapable of generating an inclusive
framework, transcending lineages, for the community.

Nonetheless, elements of the Confucian interpretation of the cult did
manage to influence the legend, ritual and ideology of the cult of the
Reverent Lord of Broad Compassion. In times of severe social turmoil,
the cult could provide a rallying point for local leaders. In the ability of
the cult to demonstrate the loyalty of the locale and in the elaborate attention paid to the cult by highly educated and well-positioned Confucian
scholar-gentry, one sees a collapse of the elite-popular distinction that has
plagued studies of Chinese religion and Chinese culture. This holds true
not only in the field of ritual, "popular worship," and community solidarity, but also in the ideological sphere as well.

Several instances of the merger of the Three Teachings in cult writings
and activities have already been noted above. I have also provided examples of particular ideological investments of certain representations of the
gods by particular groups in a community or subculture. In the Taoist
Memorial translated below even the neo-Confucian sage Zhu Xi (1120–
1200) is invited to the altar, along with other local deities. Recall that
Zhu Xi was also offered a cult in the Shishan Shuyuan. Gernet has recently remarked on the cultlike activities of the Confucian academies
(Gernet, 1985) and Hymes (1986) suggests that a cult to Zhu Xi was
established in the Southern Song to link together Confucian scholars
around the empire.

Taoist Rituals on the Birthday of the God

On the twenty-second day of the second lunar month, communities throughout Shishan, and throughout the Quanzhou region, celebrate the birthday of the Reverent Lord of Broad Compassion. Ironically, the very cult centers that have been the focus for the reestablishment of traditional religious observances are often too conspicuous to openly hold large, public, communal Taoist *jiao* at this time. Thus I have had to gather material on Taoist rituals in smaller temples that have branched off from the major cult centers, or in temples devoted to even more localized cults. I was able to attend one celebration on the Reverent Lord's birthday in 1986 and two more in 1987. I recorded the Taoist *Memorial* recited during one of the 1987 rituals. The following is a translation of that Memorial.

> Eternally receiving great good fortune,
> In supplication we behold,
> The divine radiance shining everywhere.
> Blessing our village and homes with peace.
> The august spirits are moved,
> And raise high the luster of our households.

This year in the Brigade Headquarters of the Seventh [Production] Brigade of Guzhai *bao* of Shishan *chu*, of Qingfeng li of Rongde county of Nan'an district of Quanzhou prefecture of Fujian Province, the resident [surnamed] Li [followed by seventy given names] elders, etc., and their descendants, Sincerely bow one hundred times, And undertake the great task of preparing [a celebration] for the gods. Desiring that the following be cordially invited: The Three Pure Ones of the Great Tao, Master of the Six Chariots, the Ten Thousand Perfected Beings of the Three Realms, the High Saints of the Ten Directions, the spirits of Heaven and Earth, The Nine August Stellar Lords of the Northern Dipper, and of the Sun, the Moon, the Stars and the Dipper. The Three Precious Heavenly Venerables of the Great Net Heaven. The Revered Saintly Ancestral Master of the Marvelous Tao. The Merciful Host, Baosheng Dadi of Haolin Temple, the subsidiary statue of Baosheng Dadi, the Chengwei Baosheng Dadi, the Guangze Zunwang of the Righthand Hall [of Fengshansi], the Guangze Zunwang of the Auxiliary Temple of Yongan *she*, The Miaoying Zhide Immortal Consort, the Primordial Lord Saintly Father, and the Great Immortal Saintly Ancestor [Mother?]. The Golden Immortal of the Fragrant Spirit Tablet, the Two Revered Kings of Illustrious Aid and Worshipful Virtue, General Chen and Commandant Huang, the Two Lads before the Hall who hold the Seal and Sword of the

God, The Merciful Lord Guangze Zunwang of Weixi, Marshall Zhang of Xie'an Tang, the Three Generations of Ancestral Masters of the Yanggan Line, the Revered Lord of Martial Pacification. The Kuixing God of Literature, Wenchang, and Master Zhu Xi of the Hecheng she. Marshal Lu of Houyao. All the Kings and Dukes and Lords of the Realms of the counties near and far. The Guanyin and Earth gods of every residence, and the gods of each well, hearth and doorway, and the Attendant Officers to the left and right, and their underlings. The various gods of the Lamps and the Altar. All lend your aid, let shine your compassionate light. Illumine our vows. Now the headsmen, by order of age, reverently worship the Merciful Lord Baosheng Dadi and Guangze Zunwang, whose golden statues and precious icons have protected this region and preserved it in peace. For the above mentioned god we joyfully recite: A Lingbao Taoist Ritual for the Prolongation of Life. We purify the altar and sweep away all filth. Then we commence the Announcement of the Messages. We burn incense to honor: The arrival here of the Merciful Lord, Guangze Zunwang. We offer incense to him on the first day of every month. Today we honor the Sacred Birthdate with congratulatory celebrations, and so choose this auspicious 23rd day of this month to establish a Sacred [Taoist Altar]. It is fitting that we recite the various True Scriptures, perform the Announcement of the Ten Thousand Spiritual Lamps of the Three Realms ritual, and the laudatory Hundred Lamps and Fundamental Destiny Ritual Texts. Then we shall reverently present the Threefold Offering of the Lamps. After that we will burn and transform Underworld Currency to repay his Divine Radiance. We beseech a harmonious region and peace. We humbly pray that The Brilliance of the Worthy King will shine as long as Heaven and Earth ... that the god's Buddha Power will be efficacious and Shine together with the sun and the moon. Moreover, we beseech protection and tranquility for our village and homes, and peace and quiet for our *li* and *she*. So that people and their animals shall all be healthy. That rain and wind will be seasonal. That Overseas Chinese and Hong Kong and Macao Compatriots will prosper in their business activities. That scholars, farmers, workers, and merchants will all thrive together. That all things will be auspicious and lucky. That the five grains will rise up, the six domesticated animals all flourish, disasters be averted, disease-carrying miasmas not intrude, and all things be fortunate and fine. In all this we forever depend upon Your Divine Radiance and Protection. We reverently memorialize thus for your information. On the date dingmao [1987], in the second month, XX day, we burn incense, kowtow, and memorialize.

The large number of deities, and multiple versions of the Reverent Lord of Broad Compassion invited to what was originally a Baosheng Dadi temple suggests the intricacy of the multiple representations of the god

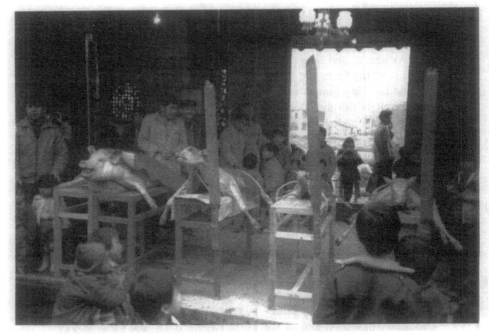

21. Sacrifices for the birthday of the Reverent Lord of Broad Compassion.

marked for different communities and different groups within the same communities. The first group of gods are the abstract Taoist divinities. Then the local gods are invited. Note the traditional address of the location in terms of li and bao with the modern work brigade headquarters added at the end.[17]

As I mentioned above, the offerings on the birthday of the god included a calf, a goat, and a pig. Local people happily recounted the story of the god's mother's misunderstanding of his requests that has resulted in this abrogation of the official ritual code. This is an example of the co-optation of the highest form of official ritual by a local cult.

The cult soon discovered a mechanism to break free of domination by the Huangs. On the god's birthday virtually every village, and certainly major representatives from every one of the six principal lineages, can participate directly in a Taoist Communication of the Lamps ritual for the god.

The True Scripture of the Reverent Lord

(Printed at the Snowy Seas [Studio] through Contributions collected by Yang Jun, of [Fujian] Commandery.)

1. *Sacred Spell to Purify the Heart.*
2. *Sacred Spell to Purify the Mouth Spirit.*
3. *Sacred Spell to Purify the Spirits of the Body.*
4. *Spell to Pacify the Tutelary Divinity.*
5. *Spell to Purify Heaven and Earth.*
6. *Spell to Express Hope via the Spirit of Incense.*
7. *Spell to Control Demons.*
8. *Sacred Spell of Golden Light.*
9. *Invocation*

> *Bowing before the Saint of Phoenix Mountain*
> *Venerable abode of the King of Broad Compassion*
> *His loyal heart pierces the sun and moon*
> *His vermillion liver illumines the qian and kun hexagrams*
> *His filial piety moves the heavenly vault above*
> *His virtue transforms the center of the nation*
> *His mercy extends beyond the Three Realms*
> *He powerfully vouchsafes the courts of the Nine Heavens*
> *He was given by decree the Seal of Thunder and Lightning*
> *Which he uses especially to exterminate the five rebellious emotions*
> *Excising all deviant evil beings*
> *Exorcising pestilence he subdues ghosts and goblins*
> *He captures the masses of demons and sprites*
> *He protects the Emperor and makes peaceful the altars of grain and harvest*
> *He mercifully saves the myriad people.*

10. *Sacred Spell to Open the Scripture.*

> *Silent, empty, quite without ancestors*
> *Empty peaks stretching for a myriad fathoms*
> *Expansively there descended the Writings of the Cavernous Mystery.*
> *Who can fathom their hidden reaches?*
> *Once you have entered the Path of the Great Wheel [Mahayana]*
> *Who can calculate the number of years and kalpas?*
> *Unborn and yet not extinguished*
> *Wishing to be born he followed the lotus blossom*
> *And surpassed the pathways of the Three Realms*
> *His merciful heart liberated from the entanglements of the world.*
> *The Perfected Being's most high merit*
> *[Enables him to be] an immortal for age after age.*

The Marvellous Scripture on the Awakening of the World and the Subduing of Demons by Stellar God Guo, King of Broad Mercy, Numinous Salvation and Universal Virtue, Who Preserves Peace, as proclaimed by the Heavenly Venerable of No Beginnings, the Most High Emperor of Primal Yang.

Formerly, the Heavenly Venerable of No Beginnings, in the Great Luo Heaven, together with all the Imperial Lords of Heaven and the Immortal Sages of the 10 directions, assembled in the Hall of the Ninefold Radiance of the Jade Void, on the Jade Brahma Seven Treasure Stage, and chanted the Cavernous Stanzas and sang Immortal songs, gathering together the Unobstructed Marvellous Tao. They expounded the most precious mystic Writings.

Just at that moment there appeared a spirit in charge of inspecting transgressions. He offered up a document, memorializing:

At this time people below are all being victimized by hordes of demons, all manner of monsters are doing evil and deluding [the people's] hearts. They do not know to turn towards the good, but falsely do wrong. The variety of their crimes would be difficult to describe.

When the immortals had heard the memorial, they broke rank and [rushed] forward, memorializing:

Great is the Mercy of the Heavenly Venerable. Great is the Sageliness of the Heavenly Venerable. You are the Father of all things and the Master of the myriad spirits. Broadly dispense compassion and save the lower realm.

The Heavenly Venerable spoke:

Excellent. Excellent. This class of beings [i.e., humankind] has encountered tribulations. If one wished to subdue the demons and enlighten the masses, then the only one who could accomplish this task is the Stellar Lord Guo of Numinous Salvation and Universal Virtue. He is perfectly loyal and filial, correct, upright and unselfish. As for the Stellar Lord, he is related to the Perfected Immortal Nan Ling. He descended and was born in the Qingxi area of Quanzhou Commandery. He served his mother with perfect filial piety. When he was thirteen years old, he sloughed off his body in the first year of the Tianfu [reign-period] of the Latter Jin Dynasty. He revealed his saintliness atop an ancient vine in Nan'an. By Jade Imperial Decree, [he was enfeoffed as] Stellar Lord Guo of Numinous Salvation and Universal Virtue, Heavenly Venerable Who Protects and Urges Good Conduct Everywhere. [His] Divine Residence is in the Palace of Jade Purity, and he has a position within the Bureau of Responsive Origins. He worships as his Master the High Emperor Red Hill. He has control over the dispensation of the Lightning and Thunder of the Southern Pole and has administrative power over the heavenly responses. In the past he has punished the deviant and the evil. Now he judges the good and the bad. He cuts up demons and sprites beneath the Dipper stars and the Mainstays of Heaven and exorcises pestilence from the center of the nation. From the Song dynasty onwards, he has killed robbers and saved the August Palace from fire. At first he was enfeoffed as "Great General." [His titles] were successively improved to those of Duke and

King. An Edict was issued commanding the construction of a tall and imposing temple with ritual sacrifice to be held in spring and autumn. The fire of incense lasted long. In the Great Ming [Dynasty] the Islander Dwarfs [Japanese pirates] were vicious and wild, and the Lu brigands ran amok. [Then the god] greatly opened forth his divine powers and swept away the masses of ghouls and annihilated all the fiends. He was enfeoffed as Reverent Lord of Broad Compassion, Awesome Martial Heroic Prowess, Loyal Response, and Dependable Benevolence. His cinnabar heart and vermillion liver protect the nation and preserve the people. His loyalty and sincerity transfix the sun. His meritorious acts merge with heaven. Then the Sacred [Qing] Dynasty piled up enfeoffments of kingly honors, decreeing the addition of the words "Protector of Peace." His merit supports the altars of grain and the harvest. His powers are stationed on Phoenix Mountain. He has refined himself to perfection for 1,000 years. No one surpasses his virtue.

When the Immortals heard this, they were all overjoyed. Then the Heavenly Venerable ordered a golden lad to carry a talisman to Phoenix Mountain to summon him. When the Stellar Lord received the summons, he immediately returned and was granted an audience with the Heavenly Venerable. Kowtowing, he memorialized:

Your Servant resides in the Bureau of Thunder. He had been granted [the task] of garrisoning Phoenix Mountain. May I ask for what reason I have had the honor of a summons?

The Heavenly Venerable said:

I today command you to [go to] the lower realm to sweep away demons and ghosts, to save and raise up the masses of living beings, enlighten the world and save the people, protect the Nation so that it will be forever pure.

The Stellar Lord repeatedly bowed, accepted his mission, and descended, transmitting the [following] Order everywhere.

Now, this Sacred Dynasty has a timely Ruler. He is a ruler of intelligence. How could he countenance the likes of ghouls and goblins acting viciously under the light of bright Heaven's transforming sun? I originally punished crimes on behalf of Heaven, cutting down all demons. Now my compassionate heart has been awakened and I open up the road to life. Now all you demons, wash your hearts and cleanse your thoughts. All listen to my words. Return to the correct, cast off evil. Quickly return to the Cavern Headquarters. Face the stone wall and refine yourselves to perfection. Turn your heads back to famous mountains and there sit on your [meditation] mats and become enlightened. Await perfect merit and worshipfully do your work. Then your nature will be calmed and your spirit coalesce. You will be able to prove your worth as a High Perfected and reach the stairway of the Marvellous Tao. Wherever this Order reaches, the King of Demons will be tied at the neck; he will leap to take refuge in the Way. People and Heaven will all be benefited. The nation will know rising peace.

At this time the Stellar Lord again pronounced the precious stanzas and awoke the World, saying: Now, the Great Sages of the Empire established Rites and Music, wrote the [Book of] Songs and the [Book of] History. All of these alter habits and change customs. At this time the people below have lost their original perfection. They are blind to their heavenly nature to the point that neither the ancient stanzas of former Saints nor the Codes and Regulations of former Kings can be recited or held in the heart. On the contrary, they maintain their stubborn, vulgar feelings. They consider the Tao and righteousness to be mere formalities. They take ghosts and spirits to be nonexistent and consider rewards and responses [from the gods] to be empty lies. They do not know that the rewards of good and evil are like a shadow following a shape. If you are good, then heaven rewards you with good fortune. If bad, then heaven besets you with misfortune. Therefore I pronounce the precious stanzas, universally transforming people of the world. I judge good and evil in the minutest measure. Revere ghosts and spirits even in the darkest corners of the room. Never desist from doing something if it is only a little good. Nor do something because it is only a little bad. The standard of good and evil is not set by you, and there is no definite good or evil. Yet still if you can give birth to a heart that follows the good and expels evil, then that is the Way of turning misfortune into good fortune. All you multitudes, listen to my words and refine yourselves. At best, you can prove to be a Saint and complete your perfection. At least, by keeping this command, you will not forsake being a good person and a gentleman. Strive with sincere hearts. The Perfect Tao is before you. The precious stanzas universally transform. The myriad families are raised up and enlightened.

Thereupon he returned to the Gates of Heaven, obtained an audience and beheld the Venerable countenance, and reported back concerning the Imperial command. He bowed in thanks to all the Immortals who sang out in praise and commendation, enabling him to obtain the Most High Wheel of the Law. Thereupon the Heavenly Venerable sang in praise of the Stellar Lord and pronounced this **gatha**:

> The Perfect Saint, King of the Preservation of Peace
> Most High Stellar Lord Guo
> General of the Bureau of Thunder of the Nine Heavens
> Venerable Who Universally Transforms the Ten Directions
> Recounting a Scripture while astride a brocade phoenix
> Upholding the Law grasping a golden whip
> Within his belly the Primal Mechanism is marvelous
> Within the crucible cinnabar and lead are made

Capable of using the power of his wisdom
To subdue all the demons and sprites
Travelling on a tour of inspection beyond the Three Realms
He examines good and evil feelings
Without prejudice or party
His responses are extremely discerning
He propagates the teachings of the Heavenly Venerable.
Awakening and enlightening living beings
If people of the world know to carefully revere him
They will obtain blessing and increase their lifespans
With complete sincerity bow and recite [this scripture]
The myriad nations will all be tranquil.

At this time, the Heavenly Venerable's **gatha** was concluded. He spread it about the Jade Capital. All the Heavenly Emperors and Lords, and the Immortals and Saints from the Ten Directions, were greatly delighted. They made bows and withdrew.

Faithfully keep and worship: The Marvellous Scripture on the Awakening of the World and the subduing of Demons by Stellar God Guo, King of Broad Mercy, Numinous Salvation and Universal Virtue, Who Preserves Peace, as proclaimed by the Heavenly Venerable of No Beginnings, the Most High Emperor of Primal Yang. The end.

Precious Appellation:
  Great Saint of Phoenix Mountain, Orthodox Spirit of the Bureau of Thunder, Ruler of the Nine Lands and Ten Directions of the Three Realms, Controller of the Five Sacred Mountains, the Eight Poles and the Four Mainstays, Ritual Ruler of the Orthodox One, Examiner and Inspector of the Records of Good and Evil, Ruler of the Teaching of Actionless Action, Source of Responses of Good or Bad Fortune, Subduer of Demons and Sprites, Exorciser of Pestilence. All Beings Rely upon Him. Foolish Deeds are put Right by Him. Great is His Loyalty, Great is His Filial Piety, Great is His Saintliness, Great is His Mercy: Heavenly Venerable of the Protection of Peace, Great Stellar Lord Guo, of Numinous Salvation and Universal Virtue, Subduer of the Demons of the Three Realms, Southern Pole Commander of Heaven, King of Broad Compassion, Awesome Martial Heroic Prowess, Dependable Benevolence, and Loyal Response.

Precious Appellation of the Patriarch of Thunder:
  [Within] the Bureau of Response to the Origin of the Nine Heavens, [the] Most High King of Jade Purity. Transforming his Shape he fills the Ten Directions. Discussing the Tao he sits crosslegged on a nine-phoenix car-

riage. Above the Thirty-six Heavens, he reads the Precious satchel, [and] examines the Rosegem Books. Prior to 1500 Kalpas, he established the ortho- dox and the true [and] empowered the great transformations. In his hands he holds a Scepter of Golden Light. He proclaims the Precious Scripture of the Jade Pivot. Those who are disobedient he turns to dust. The announcing of his name [brings results] as swiftly as wind and fire. Using his pure heart he expands his vast vow. Using the power of wisdom he subdues all demons. He is commander in chief of the Five Thunders. Moving his heart through the Three Realms, [he is] Father to the masses of living beings and Master of the myriad immortals. Great is his Mercy, Great is his Compassion, Great is his Vow, [the] Heavenly Venerable of Universal Transformation through the Sound of Thunder of the Response to the Origin of the Nine Heavens, Jade Sovereign of Perfected Tao.

Precious Appellation of the Jade Sovereign [omitted]
Hymn to Conclude the Scripture:

> *Reverent Lord of Broad Compassion*
> *Mystic Door to the Salvation from Distress*
> *From the Peak of Phoenix Mountain you let shine your radiance*
> *All under Heaven have heard of your*
> *Awesome Responses*
> *Delivering from Evil and Prolonging Life*
> *Uphold and recite [this Scripture to ensure] the*
> *Preservation of Peace*

*On the 7th evening of Guangxu **wuyin** [1878] in Fuzhou, Qian Taibao, who exalts and worships Phoenix Mountain Temple in his heart, reverently wrote this. He ordered that it be printed and distributed. Anyone who recites the scripture must first fast and observe prohibitions, lustrate himself, and with a sincere heart fix their breath. After this grind your teeth and pro- nounce the sounds and harmoniously recite it. Communicate to the spiritual powers whatever you feel, and all that you pray for will be responded to.*

Appended Mediumistic Utterances from 1877 and 1879: The Reverent Lord of Broad Compassion's Writing Encouraging Filial Piety, Carved as an Appendix

That which the world does not lack is the Five Relationships. That which a person needs in life is loyalty and filial piety. If you possess loyalty, then you put your heart into serving the nation and the people, revering the court and bring- ing peace to the common people. Such a man has power and rank. As for the word "filial piety," this is the road that every ignorant man or woman must follow. I was born in the Tongguang reign period of the Latter Tang Dynasty

[923–25]. Although young, I indeed displayed exceptional qualities. However, at the time both my parents were impoverished. The Way of our family was meager and simple. When I was little, my heavenly nature was wholehearted. I took filial piety towards my parents as the basis [of my conduct]. I shepherded sheep for people and fed cattle. I used my earnings to provide the amount needed to feed my parents breakfast and dinner. When my father had died but my old mother was still alive, I followed her and moved to Shishan so she would be happy with me sitting at her side, always staying close by. When the cultivation of filial piety was complete, my heavenly nature manifested. The High Emperor was pleased by my loyal, sincere, filial heart. He first ordered immortal lads and friends in the Tao to assist me to accomplish the aim of transcending and slough-ing off [the body]. When it came to the Tianfu reign period of the Latter Tang Dynasty, I sat on an ancient vine and transformed by sloughing [off my body]. Although my Buddha bones had always been intact, still it was my Way of Filial piety that moved the heart of Heaven. Later I protected the nation and the people, frequently manifesting mystic experiences, so the people of the village set up a temple and worshiped in it. The court recorded my merit and enfeoffed me, and [my cult] could be said to have flourished. Now, since I was an accom-plished Immortal Buddha, so my Saintly Father and Saintly Mother too were enfeoffed with honors. They were buried together in the old neighborhood of Qingxi. Now why is it that, year after year, people go up to their graves? This has to do with my father and mother being completely close to me, [yet] I could not live to see many days. When I was just over 10 years old, I transformed by sloughing off my body, so I could not long provide the joy of staying by my par-ents' knees. To this day my heart is still sorrowful. Therefore I composed the Rites for Ascending to the Graves, in order to record [their] mercy which never ceases in a thousand autumns. And everyone comprehends my feelings, so people of the world follow me up to the grave. And they could be said to be very numer-ous. Now I hadn't thought that after becoming a Buddha, my **hun** *and* **po** *souls would still stay before my father and mother. That I would become an Im-mortal, and yet be bowing and kneeling in rites [to my parents] that have had honors repeatedly bestowed upon them. Alas, who is not someone's child? And who has no father or mother, yet can avoid strong selfishness? My protection goes only to good people. If people of the world know how to serve parents well and regularly go up to the graves [of my parents], then I will comfort them and bestow good fortune on them. Yet if there are those who do not know how to serve parents well, and do it all for fame or advantage, yet follow me up to the graves, how could they actually come with me up to the graves and not reflect on my deep feelings? If they can painfully right their former wrongs, and filially revere their parents at home, loving their brothers as friends, single-heartedly with all their might follow the Five Relationships truly, sincerely without dissatisfaction, then they will become complete men between heaven and earth. Yesterday I received the High Emperor's command, ordering me to transmit this message to*

*the people of the world. Now the quality of feeling in one heart can bring all forms of good fortune. That is what I look forward to with this minor expression of my intent. Thus he descended into a medium in the Zhenfu Academy on Guangxu **dingqiu** [1877].*

The Precious Instructions of the Reverent Lord of Broad Compassion

I am the Blue Lotus Lad Spirit. Yesterday, together with some friends in the Tao, we roamed the dusty world. At times the wind made a soughing sound, deep was the color of the moon, and my heart was greatly pleased by this. Suddenly the conversation turned to the sunken ways of the world, and the fallen weakness of human hearts. So I could not stop sighing alas and was endlessly sad. Thereupon I paid a respectful visit to the King of Broad Compassion on Phoenix Mountain. I begged him to send down Precious Instructions to guide the ignorant and the confused. The Reverent Lord said: Excellent! Excellent! I have observed the people of the world. Generally speaking they are disloyal as ministers, unfilial as children, unfriendly as older brothers, disrespectful as younger brothers, unharmonious when married, and unreliable as friends. Either they lie and act false, or they are deviant and hateful. They either cheat orphans and widows, or they deceive good people. Or they act licentiously with unrestrained desires, happily behaving like dogs. Or they abort foetuses and drown daughters, thoughtlessly giving in to their fierce hearts. Or with sharp tongues say what they like, and their phrases harm the harmony of heaven and earth. Or they use knives and brushes at this work, and create sprouts of hills and mountains. Or in the name of sacrificing to spirits they carelessly slaughter livestock. Or with an eye to immediate profits, they slaughter cattle and lambs. The many kinds of their crimes I cannot bear are too numerous to describe in full. Even more despicable, a precious character of but a single brushstroke is a source of great concern to Confucian scholars, but merchants completely disregard [precious words]. Either they display brocade characters on the sides of firecrackers, which when exploded send the ashes flying into the dust and dirt. Or they print "Originary Treasure" on top of gold paper, and after they burn it they cast the ashes into the mud. It has got to the point that men and women coming into the temple to offer incense, also take incense and paper [spirit-money], printed with words, and casually toss them away, treading on them as they come and go. Generally no one can even point out their confused behavior. Ah! At first I would not have thought that under the sun by the rivers and streams things could come to this. Blue Lotus, since you have asked, from now on let there not be such cause for grief. From now on, proclaim this for me to the people of the world. To those who are able to reverently follow my Instructions, I will bring protection, silently in the dark. [I will] change misfortune to good fortune, bestow good luck and remove ill omens. If there still be those who dare ridicule my words, and do not obey my Instructions and teachings, I will come to them silently in the dark and increase my examination [of their conduct], measure the lightness or severity of their crimes, and let fall their punishments. There will not be even a moment of laxity. I have stated this so.

Thereupon [the Blue Lotus Lad] kowtowed, together with his friends in the Tao, to the Reverent Lord. Receiving his command they withdrew, and just now I met up with this noble group of mediums, so I made a special visit to completely recount [this]. You all can sincerely and solemnly follow these Saintly Instructions, and also everywhere exhort the [people of the] realm, causing everyone to rise out of their ignorant straits and obtain immeasurable good fortune. On the date of the full moon of the 7th lunar month, in the jimao year of the Guangxu period, the Blue Lotus Lad Spirit followed orders and descended into a medium in the Kuiyin Academy (August 25, 1879).

22. Local god as Taoist astral deity: from the *True Scripture of the Imperially Enfeoffed Reverent Lord of Broad Compassion*.

CONCLUSION

T HIS STUDY has attempted to document the role of Taoism in the history and revival of local cults in Southeastern China. The tremendous activity within these cults in China today could be termed a revival, although in fact they were never totally suppressed, and the current developments reflect new responses to surrounding social transformations. The struggle for survival of local traditions could be cast in a confrontational fashion, as the emergence of traditional structures of local power that set themselves in opposition to the command structure of the state Communist party. This would ignore the fact of the continuity of these traditions and the complex working arrangements that have been achieved among the Party, local government, and traditional structures in enormously varied communities throughout China. Fieldwork in China is only beginning, while, in the decades in which China was closed off, much energy and perhaps not a little frustration was expended on identifying theoretical points of contradiction within a supposedly inflexible political system.

It is clear, however, that the Communist party has inherited some distinctly Western notions of the nature of religion and its functions in society. These are of course the legacy of Marx, Engels, Lenin and Morgan. The Marxist model of religion and its ideological role in mystifying the people is ultimately based on a late nineteenth-century understanding of the Christian Church in Europe. The impact of Marxist conceptions of religion in China can be seen in the repeated and ultimately misguided demands from the Party that Taoism define itself as a Church and explain its doctrine. These preconceptions often lead to the elaboration of regulations concerning what is "normal religious activity" and what is "feudal superstition" that show little regard for the diffused, but pervasive, highly integrated role of religion in Chinese society (Yang, 1961). One set of definitions was recently detailed in a nationally circulated note from the Zhejiang Provincial CCP Committee's Party Rectification Office:

> In his speech at the National Conference of Party Delegates, Comrade Deng Xiaoping seriously pointed out: "In recent years production has gone up, but the pernicious influence of capitalism and feudalism has not been reduced to a minimum. Instead, some evil things that had long been extinct after liberation have come to life again." This issue warrants our close attention. Some time ago, due to laxities in ideological and political work, feudal superstitions and patriarchal activities gained ground in some localities in our province, particularly in some rural areas, seriously poisoning the minds

of the masses, particularly the younger generation, and affecting the building of socialist spiritual civilization. Some Party members and cadres also joined in the activities. Effective measures should be taken in line with Party rectification in order to resolutely curb and rectify this unhealthy trend. It should be made clear that the "normal religious activities" protected under the Chinese Constitution refer to religious ceremonies of Buddhism, Taoism, Islam, Catholicism, and Christianity performed in religious places in accordance with their respective traditions and customs of religious activities conducted by religious followers in their own homes. These include prostrating oneself before the image of the Buddha, reciting scriptures, burning joss sticks, going to church, saying prayers, expounding Buddhist suttras, giving sermons, hearing Mass, receiving baptism, being initiated into monkhood or nunhood, fasting, celebrating religious festivals, performing last rites, and conducting funeral services. Indiscriminate construction of temples without the approval of the Department concerned and feudal superstitious activities exceeding the limits prescribed by the religious policy must be stopped. Building clan temples, drawing genealogical charts, joining persons of different ancestors to make them bear the same family names, and performing rites in honor of ancestors are feudal, patriarchal activities, impermissible under our Socialist System. Invoking immortals to exorcise evil spirits, praying for rain, divining by the eight trigrams, telling fortunes by analyzing the component parts of chinese characters, and practicing physiognomy and geomancy are feudal superstitious activities which should be resolutely banned. All activities which seriously infringe on the interests of the State and jeopardize the lives and property of the people must be resolutely suppressed. (March 1, 1986, *Guangming ribao*)

From the preceding chapters it will be clear that religion in China is embedded in community and that it contains many features considered unacceptable by the Party. One way to approach this impasse in understanding is to apply comparative perspectives on religion in Asian cultures. Frits Staal (1983) has applied what he calls "the scientific study of Ritual Syntax" to Vedic ritual. He argues elsewhere (Staal, 1991) that Durkheim's division of religion into Belief, Faith, and Ritual reflects Western, post-Reformation developments and is misleading when applied to Asian religion and probably to religion anywhere outside of the Western world. Durkheim stresses that differences in doctrinal beliefs become items of faith to followers of new religious denominations. Rituals are constructed to reflect these new tenets. Marxist views stress the ideological ramifications of Church dogma and organization.

In Asian religion the situation with regard to dogma is often the reverse of that found in the West. A foundation of a wide range of ritual complexes are imbedded in everyday social life. Faith grows out of the constant repetition of ritual. Only with the aid of religious specialists can the ever-elaborating rituals be performed. These same specialists have faith in their ritual traditions, but are seldom concerned with doctrinal implications. The central beliefs of Taoism are again a set of "secret" methods to assure the efficacy of the ritual. Where doctrine is made public, it is generally to emphasize morality, not to differentiate teachings.

This does not deny the elaborate theological efforts of Taoists over the centuries to contend with political threats and encroachments on ritual business by Buddhists. But such debates were often held at the command of the court, and work with rhetorical strategies informed by court discourse. Moreover, internal attacks and reinterpretations within Taoism demonstrate the ability of a tradition to invent new and sometimes contradictory interpretations for ritual actions whose "original meanings," if they ever existed, have been lost. Rather than seeing religion as an ideologically motivated organizational rubric with a feudalist agenda, the Chinese leadership may have to approach it as an underlying, structuring framework for communal organization. This could be done within the context of a more sophisticated Marxian methodology, but so far official discourse on religion talks past the issues.

What is needed, then, is an approach to Asian religion that explores the fundamental role of ritual and liturgy within family, lineage, and communal groups. The principal ritual paradigms of Chinese culture should be identified and their variations throughout the different regions, classes, and social groups of Chinese society explored. Such research should proceed on the basis of careful fieldwork. These studies will eventually open the way for a differential analysis of the impact of Taoism and local traditions on contemporary China. They may one day provide the conceptual vocabulary through which the Party and the people can begin to talk to one another about their cultural heritage.

On the basis of the few examples discussed here it is impossible to do more than suggest the importance of cults at all levels of society in Southeastern China. Temples to local gods provided a mechanism to overcome the conflicts between competing factions or lineages within a single village. Large-scale cult networks, processions, and rituals provided the basis for alliances between villages and lineages in a locale. These alliances could function as peaceful and profitable communications networks. They could also function as military reinforcements in times of need. Perhaps the most significant evidence of the importance of the cults is their survival in the face of the largest expansion of the state apparatus in the history of China. The effort to extend state control to the village level in China has not eliminated the need for unofficial systems of communication within traditionally marked subcultures. On the contrary, the paradoxical strengthening of the natural village which has proceeded simultaneously with the strengthening of the central government under Maoist policies has presented traditional organizational networks with new opportunities and new roles to play.

A consideration of the role of Taoist liturgy in popular cults and local communities raises several important questions. What can be said about the unity of Taoist ritual not only in Fujian and Taiwan, but throughout China? Can this unity be shown to have a historical dimension? How does Taoist ritual mark social hierarchy and reproduce local power? How do the different ritual traditions of China interact? Finally, how do the social units (cults and communities) brought together by Taoist liturgy fit into contemporary Chinese society?

Ritual Unity

While it may not be surprising that certain Taoist ritual traditions and manuscript lineages so closely link groups of Taoists in Fujian and Taiwan, the question remains as to how much unity exists between the actual performance of ritual in Taiwan, Fujian, and the rest of China. To answer this question one would need first of all to access Taoism's role in wider ritual complexes. For example, no treatment of Taoist requiem services would be complete without a consideration of the fundamentally Confucian family liturgical framework into which it is inserted. One would have to describe the kinship system, the five grades of mourning, and the role of affines and agnates in sponsoring different aspects of the funeral rites as well as the prestations and prohibitions linking marriage and funeral rites (De Groot, 1892–1910; Wolf, 1970; Ahern, 1979, 1981; Watson, J., 1982a, 1988; Watson, R., 1985; Ebrey, 1986). The fact is that funeral rites can be performed in the absence of Buddhist or Taoist ritual specialists (Yu, 1981); even though distinctly Buddhist or Taoist elements may still be used, their "original meanings" have long been forgotten. Many life-crisis rituals which usually include Taoist elements are fundamentally shaped by an underlying Confucian framework. Once the different elements are distinguished, this underlying framework can be compared around China (Watson, 1988). With an awareness of their specific role in funeral ritual, Taoist and Buddhist requiem services can also be compared across China.

The Zhengyi Lingbao tradition has maintained a high degree of unity across Southern China. I attended funeral rituals performed by Zhengyi Lingbao Taoists in the Baiyun Guan in Shanghai. Despite differences in dialect, music, and iconography, the fundamental ritual structure and the manuscript tradition were remarkably similar to that of Fujian and Taiwan.

As for the communal jiao sacrifice, the Shanghai and Suzhou Taoists have collaborated in the production of a videotape of their rituals. On the basis of these materials, and discussions with specialists in the Shanghai Academy of Social Sciences, it is possible to assert a high degree of unity between their tradition and certain major traditions of Fujian and Taiwan (Chen Yaoting, 1989).

Much more work needs to be done in other areas of China, not to mention Hong Kong, Singapore, and elsewhere in Southeast Asia (Ofuchi, 1983; Tanaka, 1981, 1983; Kamata, 1986). On the basis of material compiled so far it is possible to identify many structural similarities between these areas and the Fujian/Taiwan traditions. This holds true for communal jiao sacrifices, Buddhist and Taoist funerals, and individual rites. Many overseas Chinese communities such as the Putian *tongxiang hui* (fellow-regional association) described by Tanaka Issei (1983) and the Sanyuan Taoists of Singapore who immigrated from Nan'an, preserve intact the respective traditions of their points of origin in Fujian.

There is growing evidence of the widespread practice of Taoist ritual traditions among the minorities of Yunnan, especially the Bai, the Yao, the Dai, the Yi, and the Naxi (Shiratori, 1975; Strickmann, 1982; Lemoine, 1982). Near Dali I met a Han Chinese Taoist priest who worked with many of the basic liturgical texts used by other Zhengyi Taoists in Fujian. At the communal level, scripture recitation societies of Bai elders sing the Taoist scripture *Wenchang datong tanjing* (KDMSS, 198; Kleeman, 1988). Female groups recite scriptures dedicated to Guanyin. At the temple fairs, Taoists sell traditional box-shaped envelopes with printed prayers to Taoist deities.

The large collection of Taoist documents collected from the Yao peoples of northern Thailand by Shiratori (1975) present positive proof of the unity of the Taoist manuscript tradition across China to the very borders of the Empire (Strickmann, 1982). In 1988 I discovered that Yao Taoist rituals were being performed in Richmond and Oakland, California, by recent immigrants from Thai refugee camps. These rituals include group initiations complete with the investiture of sets of gods and spirit soldiers, all highly reminiscent of medieval Taoist rites documented by Zhang Wanfu (Benn, 1991).

The unity of Taoist ritual traditions over time is an equally important and difficult question (Bell, 1988). Song dynasty ritual texts can be compared element-for-element and in some cases, word-for-word, with related liturgical manuscripts in use today (Schipper, 1975). How can one account for this underlying unity in light of the breakdown of the medieval ecclesia and the unified ordination system of Zhang Wanfu and other Tang Taoists? With the development of local movements in Taoism, beginning (in the available sources) as early as the ninth century, new, local ritual traditions flourished. But each new revelation and consequent ritual elaboration always added its innovations onto the established ritual structure without fundamentally transforming it. The outraged accusations of some Song Lingbao fundamentalists should be seen in this light (Boltz, 1987). This process leaves its traces in modern texts, in which layer after layer of ritual offshoots of new revelations can be peeled away, revealing an unchanged structure. Perhaps the most significant result of the continuity of the structural unity of the Taoist liturgical framework was the degree of unity it imparted to Chinese popular religion.

Social Hierarchy

Readers of the earlier chapters may have been impatient for an assessment of the impact of the "Taoist liturgical framework" on the social hierarchy of particular communities. Are certain groups, such as the traditional *xia jiu liu* (lower nine ways of life), excluded, or relegated to certain onerous tasks? Similarly, were the gentry or scholar-officials afforded special status by their mode of involvement? In the introduction I discussed the ability of the Taoist liturgical framework to accept multiple representations of the local god, each marking a particular social group's involvement in the ritual. This results in a complex whole which dissolves or deliberately ignores the day-to-day distinctions between social groups. A similar melting away of social hierarchy is evident in the selection by divination of representatives from all the households of the community.

There is, however, always structure emerging out of formlessness, as the Taoists know so well. The community representatives have certain ranks and grades. The *Zongli*, or General Manager, is almost invariably a man of great wealth and high social standing. This is because his position makes him liable for tremendous feasting expenses, as well as responsible for any shortage in funds raised toward the cost of the ritual. He also must have the social clout to force compromises on countless details of organization of the ritual. In addition, he must have some pull with the local Party official, who must be persuaded to look the other way and, somehow, at the same time avoid criticism from the local Party Headquarters. The same problems that afflict the General Manager hold true to a lesser extent for the huishou. In the Zhangzhou jiao I observed in 1985, one could sell one's position for six hundred yuan. However, doing so made a person the laughingstock of the community, revealing his social limitations all too clearly before the entire community.

Being a community representative brings many concrete social benefits. They get to have their Lamps of Fundamental Destiny burn before the gods in the temple throughout the ritual. They get to parade about in Qing dynasty long blue robes and, thereby, assert their pride in local tradition and indifference to government antagonism. They get to throw feasts with blessed foodstuffs that heighten their *guanxi* (connections) with many different sectors of local society.

Furthermore, there are many other aspects of the celebration that can be used to demonstrate wealth and status. Theatrical performances can be sponsored by wealthy individuals, while at the same time function as a gift to the gods and to the community. Processional troupes can vie for beauty and extravagance. Offerings at family tables can be particularly sumptuous. Feasts can involve dozens of tables of guests. Even strict Confucian scholars could find a way to participate in a local cult such as Guangze Zunwang's. Although when writing about popular religion and local drama, such scholars invariably write in an extremely condescending tone that suggests that they and their readers are, it goes without saying, above it all, nonetheless a closer examination of their role in sponsoring temples, and actually participating in community rituals, reveals that they had a tremendous stake in local "popular" traditions. Once again, the elite/popular divide seems inapplicable. If one agrees that Taoist liturgy is structuring the entire cult worship, than it is ridiculous to maintain that this should be called "popular" religion as opposed to pure philosophic Taoism or even some nonexistent institutionalized Taoist Church. Taoism should be recognized as the indigenous higher religion of China.

The Taoist liturgical manuscripts are written in elegant Classical Chinese, with whole sections going back to the sixth century and others dating to the Song. Where vernacular elements enter in, as for example in certain plays added as illustrative material to the requiem services in the late Ming, one can look for signs of regional variation. But these elements also have their place determined by the overall liturgical framework.

In the chapters above I have shown how Taoism came to cooperate with local elites organized around local cults by casting local gods as Taoist divinities. At the same time I have shown where Taoist ritual specialists fit into the functionings of cults. They provide the liturgical framework that allows different social groups to find a place in the community rituals. On the one hand their communal jiao sacrifices provide a reinvestiture of the local leadership in the eyes of the highest universal deities of the Taoist pantheon, and before the less privileged members of the community (Schipper, 1982). Taken to an extreme, the desire to mark social standing in the ritual context could lead to the elaboration of exclusive rites for elite groups. The case of the Reverent Lord of Broad Compassion provides an example of the insertion of additional Confucian sacrificial rites and ideology into a popular cult.

The description in chapter 4 of the rituals led by the heads of the Huang lineage branches and offered to Guangze Zunwang at his tomb reveals that Confucian ritual, although an important element particularly for the participation of local elites, does not serve as the unifying liturgical framework for popular religion. Certainly the sacrifice at the tomb is the highpoint of a month of observances there. But the outsiders who visit the tomb in such great numbers are not included in the proceedings. They may send contributions to the Master of Sacrifices, or they may wait their turn, watch the spectacle, and present their own offerings in their own way. The Confucian sacrifice demonstrates the power and importance of the elite of the locality. As such it differs immensely from Taoist liturgy, which finds a place for all the other ritual forms inside its own universal structure.

Many aspects of the proceedings emphasize more democratic, equalizing processes. The god may select at random from among the villagers by divination for the community representatives of his choice. Social groups of low status according to the dictates of traditional Confucian ideology—such as actors, militia bands, mediums, butchers, etc.—all play key roles in the integrated liturgical ensemble. For example, the performance of ritual theater throws a new light on the underlying centrality of the ritual origins of Chinese theater (van der Loon, 1977). Such performances must have deeply affected local attitudes toward actors.

Perhaps the most striking figure of the inversion of social roles in the context of Chinese festival is that of the spirit medium. Such individuals may be ignored during normal times, but they command the complete attention of the entire community when they speak in the voice of the god during the god's festival.

In Late Imperial China merchants could work hand in hand with scholar-gentry in the sponsoring and performance of rituals and the renovations of temples. Class-based conflicts or intralineage oppression within a community could be transformed to a level of solidarity vis-à-vis aggressive outside lineages, rebel groups, or rapacious government officials or government troops. Such solidarity was celebrated in the processions of the gods, in which all the various groups participated, including Taoist and often Buddhist priests, the local elite and selected community representatives, the performing arts troupes, the local militia, and the mass of the faithful villagers following with incense in their hands.

Even larger networks of communication and solidarity developed around the regional cults studied in the preceding chapters. Villages could belong to several such networks. Pilgrimages to the founding temple of major regional cults could bring together an entire community. The relative freedom from harassment for pilgrims en route to these temples (see chapter 4) suggests widespread acceptance of these avenues of communication.

The Bureaucratic Metaphor and the
Taoist Floating Signifier

As suggested in the preceding section, other reasons underlie the unity of Taoist ritual. Taoism has consistently distinguished itself from popular cults by the refusal of blood sacrifice. Instead, Taoism has developed a unique role for the sacrifice of texts, including messages, orders, contracts, scriptures, and symbols of the universe. In fact, however, over the past thousand years, Taoism has developed mechanisms that have allowed it to integrate with popular cult worship despite its rejection, within its own rituals, of bloody sacrifice. In this process, popular cult worship would seem to have undergone a fundamental restructuring by the Taoist liturgical framework. Wilkerson (1990) makes the interesting argument that rituals involving blood sacrifice maintain a separate cosmology proper to shamanism which contradicts certain assumptions of Taoist and lineage ritual and cosmology. He suggests that these contradictory cosmologies are nonetheless integrated within annual liturgical cycles. The point I would like to emphasize is that rather than simply mimicking the imperial order through communications addressed to a celestial bureaucracy, Taoism was attempting to perform contradictory tasks at different levels of society. At the local level, Taoist ritual could serve as a reinvestiture of the local leadership. By this I do not mean to imply that Taoism accomplished legitimation of local elites on behalf of the government. On the contrary, the very ambivalence between central power and local leadership resulted in the emergence of alternative modes of legitimation at the local level.[1]

But Taoism could also serve to integrate a community, and provide transversal flows within and between regions, on the basis of nonhierarchical principles.

The unity and power of the locality (or of specific groups within the community) is often expressed through spirit-possession by mediums working with local gods and local temple organizations (Seaman, 1978). In spirit-possession one can find traces of a primitive code that combines sound (rather than written words), bloody marks on the body of the medium, and the collective eye of the community recording pain (Deleuze and Guattari, 1983). The medium is in fact a sacrifice, and his flowing blood displays the power of the god. Mediums do not kill themselves, however, nor do they sacrifice animals. Recall that in many communities mediums are directed by Ritual Masters who are also connected with the temple. These Ritual Masters instruct mediums in trance techniques and also lead chants describing the legend of the gods, or the passage to the underworld, etc. Thus, under the guidance of the Ritual Master, the mediums are primarily involved in the promotion of the local cults. As the underlying complementarity of their ritual structures with those of classical Taoism reveal, the Ritual Masters have already joined forces with Taoism (Schipper, 1985a).

Although the Ritual Master and the Taoist Master are separated by a set of complementary oppositions, there is considerable interaction between them. Both are often involved in the same communal ritual, although they proceed independently with their own ritual sequences. They tend to borrow rituals from one another, incorporating them into evolving ritual complexes. This is clear in Taoist jiao where one of the officiants will change costume to perform an exorcistic Fashi rite.

Heusch (1985) singles out sacrifice and possession as the principle means of communication between human and nonhuman spirit realms. If the burning of texts in Taoist ritual is a form of sacrifice, then it would appear that the Taoist ritual tradition was profoundly conscious of issues of communication between these realms. Contemporary Taoist ritual texts call for the self-transformation of the chief priest into a god in the Taoist pantheon. Self-transformation implies control over techniques and spells. This is quite the opposite of a medium, who is often forced into trance by the god's insistence, struggling and vomiting. The degree of power attained is also very different. As a Taoist divinity, such as Taishang Laojun or Taiyi Jiuku Tianzun, the priest is in a position to command the legions of heaven and the powers of earth to carry out his ritual goal. In addition, a priest has a list of gods and generals attached to his lu (register), which he receives at his ordination, along with ritual texts and robes. He can summon these gods to assist in the delivery of messages. The priest is also able to summon the gods of his body out of the microcosm to merge with their counterparts in the macrocosm. In short, he knows how to become a god and use divine power.

The medium, on the other hand, is in fact called the "child of the god," and Schipper (1966a) has noted the resemblance of a medium to a puppet in the hands of the Ritual Master. The Ritual Master is always standing by the spirit medium, guiding his journey through the underworld, interpreting his séance. Taoism has always sought to channel the energy of China's shamanic substratum (van der Loon, 1977), its "ecstatic religion" (Strickmann, 1980), into Taoist revelation and Taoist ritual uses. This channeling of popular religion can be seen as a form of overcoding, as evidenced in the writing of scriptures for local gods, their absorption into the Taoist pantheon, and their worship within the Taoist liturgical framework.

Two problems arise here. One concerns the bureaucratic metaphor and Chinese religious ideas about the spiritual realm. The other concerns the modes of communication between these realms. Wolf (1974) has argued on the one hand that there exist profound structural correspondences between gods, ghosts, and ancestors on the one hand, and officials, strangers, and allies on the other. He implies that these categories apply throughout Chinese religious experience. On the other hand, he denies the unity of Chinese religion, positing local difference and atomization by declaring that the religious landscape of the Chinese peasant changes according to where he is situated in it. Ahern (1981a) accepts the importance of the correspondences and discovers political training within ritual process. Sangren (1987) changes the correspondences into structural analogies and extends the hierarchical analogy to the realm of value and spiritual power, discovering an urge for order overcoming the destructive, anarchic potential of spiritual power. Lagerwey (1987a) goes even further and states that there is a hierarchy of mystical attainment differentiating mediums, ritual masters, and Taoist priests. Rather than attempting to determine the values of the elements of the metaphor or analogy, we need to see what it does not say.

The bureaucratic metaphor analyzes the spiritual realm in terms of the human realm. As such it represents an ancient Chinese sociological insight. As Arthur Waley (1943) put it, "The Chinese let the cat out of the bag." But the metaphor is not a complete model of all the modes of communication between the human and the spiritual in Chinese religion. Heusch (1985) notes sacrifice and possession. The Taoist's ritual works around external sacrifice of texts and an internal merging of microcosm and macrocosm. This latter method is another essential mode of communication with the spiritual realm. The ability of Taoist priests to transform themselves into gods through knowledge of the god's secret names, correct visualization, etc., suggests a third mode of interaction with the nonhuman realm overlooked by Heusch. These techniques bear a close resemblance to Tantric meditational and ritual method. The evocation of a god through visualization, recitation of secret names, pacings and mudras, and the subsequent total identification with the god, provides the ritual specialist with tremendous power over the spiritual pantheon, into which he has entered.

Beyond the realm of religious specialists and the insane, the everyday interaction of common people with the gods can have an intensity and immediacy that stretches the bureaucratic metaphor to the breaking point. The devoutness with which a local god is believed to be there for someone in need would be difficult to imagine in dealings with a district magistrate. A man or woman praying in a temple may have a shattering sensation of the god's protection which they would never dream of in connection with government officials.

The continual interaction and communication between the spiritual and the human realm in Chinese religion belies the rigidity of the bureaucratic metaphor, as do the many cases of shifting categories. For example, at one jiao I attended near Zhangzhou, the founding lineage ancestor had become a god (in fact a *Wangye*, considered by Taoists to be demons inspired by calendrical complications, who are exorcised by being pushed out of the cracks in time [Schipper, 1985c]). While Yu Kuang-hung (1987) suggests that all these categories are on a circular continuum, I suspect that the potential for interaction with the spiritual realm can lead to new dimensions and unexpected connections for individuals and groups in China. That Taoist ritual specialists have a stake in harnessing these flows explains their presence in millenarian movements as well as in "standard" village religion.

This can best be explained by looking at the other codes holding Chinese society together in traditional times. The Imperial system gathered up particularistic communities by organizing them along standardized patterns, as bricks in the edifice of empire. The Imperial system entered into every aspect of life and diverted it toward itself. The power of the Imperial system is all in the hands of the despotic signifier—the Emperor's word is Law. Imperial power comes to inform every aspect of society. This is most evident in the bureaucratic metaphor, with its Heavenly palaces and hierarchies, its ranks of immortals, its dangerous ghosts and demons, and its tribunals in the Underworld. As a model for conceiving the world, teaching political truths, or inculcating obedience, the bureaucratic metaphor is omnipotent. And at a more concrete level, the system of ancestral worship worked to infuse family relations with political principles, as Granet (1929) observed. Since nothing can be more powerful than the despotic signifier, then the father of the Emperor must be Heaven itself.

Taoism reacted to this architectonic of the state by scrambling the codes. A fundamental commitment to Nature rather than Culture, to natural process, to chaos and change, allows for a profound ability to absorb contradiction and ambivalence in representations of spiritual power. Taoism took up and built upon widely shared Chinese cosmological beliefs such as the five elements: Yin and Yang, the power of the stars, magical numbers and magical squares, and the existence of a microcosm. Working with these principles, Taoists were working within a Chinese cosmological process-model of spiritual power in which transformations within the microcosm affect the outside world (Granet, 1934; Giradot, 1983; Schipper, 1982).

Taoist liturgy transformed primitive codes by gradually restructuring popular religion into a ritual process complementary to itself, so that the moment of possession could fit in with the timing of the ritual, and the cosmography experienced by the medium would reflect the latest Taoist and Buddhist revelations. In similar ways, Taoist ritual absorbed elements of the imperial metaphor, but put them to very different ends. Instead of reaffirming any structural homology between locale and the state, or family and the state, as in ancestral worship, Taoist ritual generates merit for a specific community, and empowers representatives of the locale, rather than the state. These representatives are not only the wealthy and powerful lineage leaders but also the mediums of the gods, the performers of ritual theater, the members of the martial arts militia, the musicians, and the Taoists themselves.

By providing a ground for the proliferation of different and often contradictory representations of spiritual power within the community, Taoist liturgy releases a floating signifier into the sociocultural system. I have spoken above about the cyclic revelation of Taoist scriptures and the Taoist fascination with the sacrifice of signs. This too grows out of an anarchic rejection of culture and language, leading to an awareness of the multiple dimensions of language. The floating signifier of Taoist ritual is the *fu*, the indecipherable talismanic graph, the origin of language, and the source of scripture. The revelation of the indecipherable, the instruction without words, the return to the undifferentiated.

These fundamental Taoist insights provide lines of flight in Chinese culture from the rigidity of the despotic signifier and the self-absorption of the primitive codes. Such lines of flight could coalesce into revolutionary outbursts. But they could also transform into a destructive plunge into a hopeless rebellion.

Within certain settings, particularly under the tight control of exploitative lineages already acting as agents of the state at the local level, this creative potential in Taoist liturgy could be stifled, the imperial metaphor would win out, and a rerigidification of social relations would be the end result of Taoist ritual. In other circumstances, such as one finds today in contemporary China, Taoist liturgy can provide a rallying ground for cultural forces that may serve to revitalize China.

All the cults described above illustrate the creative use and popular manipulation of cultural symbols. The local Taoists and Baijiao temple elders worked up an awe-inspiring title for the Great Emperor Who Protects Life, in imitation of the imperial favors shown to the Immortal Xu brothers in northern Fujian. The Reverent Lord of Broad Compassion is worshiped by some as a paragon of filial piety, by others as a Taoist god, but all who participate in the cult join in co-opting imperial sacrificial codes to honor their god with a Great Sacrifice. A Buddhist monk, the Patriarch of the Clear Stream, became transformed into a popular cult deity, worshiped through rituals structured by the Taoist liturgical framework. These are all examples of the ability of local-level forces to appropriate official cultural symbols, generating in the process their own complex cultural forms and meanings through ritual. Rather than being passive in the face of elite cultural hegemony, these examples reveal the ability of local communities to define themselves in terms torn from imperial codes. The temple elders in Baijiao were able to exploit the title of Great Emperor, with all its implied imperial favor, honors and prerogatives, despite never having received official canonization. The Great Sacrifice for the Reverent Lord of Broad Compassion represents a similar usurpation of the ritual code. All three cults, including that of the Patriarch of the Clear Stream, were only able to achieve the freedom to define themselves in these ways by first entering into, and becoming empowered by, the Taoist liturgical framework.

As we have seen, ritual remains a powerful engine of cultural reproduction in contemporary China. The cults described above have shown a remarkable ability to regroup social forces, channeling them by means of ancient ritual frameworks into new social meanings. In an intriguing recent instance of popular co-optation of official codes, images of Chairman Mao have been pasted to buses and trucks from Guangdong to Fuzhou. These images are believed to be efficacious in preventing accidents, functioning just like similar images of the gods described above. Like the rituals and processions mentioned in this study, these talismanic images play a paradoxical role in an ongoing, ceaseless cultural revolution.

23. Medium writing talismans that are stamped with the seal of the temple and distributed to every household in the community.

APPENDIX I

FOUR SONG TITLES OF INVESTITURE FOR
THE PATRIARCH OF THE CLEAR STREAM

I. Edict Bestowing [the title of] Great Master of Brilliant Responses (1164) (Yang:2:1a-2b.)

The Department of State Affairs mandates that the Board of Rites' report has been approved and the Department has noted the appended matter of the elder Yao Tian and others of the Clear Water Temple of Anxi District of Quanzhou Prefecture sending up a report begging that an Edict be issued bestowing the title of "Brilliant Responsive Great Master" on Chen Puzu, whose true body transformed in meditation at the Clear Water Temple of this Prefecture. We later approved and sent it to the Bureau for verification, requesting that the Bureau investigate the acceptability [of the request]. On Shaoxing 26:3/23 (4/20/1153), it was decreed that the Secretariat-Chancellery and the Department of State Affairs send it to the Board of Rites. The report has been accepted by the Department. We attach the memorial of the Fiscal Commission of Fujian Circuit, which is based on a report from Anxi district in Quanzhou prefecture, and the report from the elder, Yao Tian and others in Anxi district. [They state that]: [T]he true boddhisatva of the Clear Water Cliff, was originally a Yongchun man [named] Chen Puzu. When young he left home to join the Great Cloud Monastery. He swore his vows, shaved his head, and prepared for a life of hardship. He built a shrine on Gaotai Mountain, where he practiced self-cultivation and meditation. Whenever the district experienced a drought, he prayed for rain and got results. We beg to vouchsafe this memorial to the throne, asking [the court] to specially extend superior rewards.

The office [of the Fiscal Commissioner of Fujian] appointed Fang Pin, an Assistant Magistrate of Longxi District in Zhangzhou Prefecture, to personally go there and investigate. Indeed, there had been spiritual deeds, whose merit reached to the people. [Fang] guarantees the truthfulness [of these facts]. Then we appointed an official in charge of revenue accounting in this Circuit office, Caijiguan Zhao Buwen, to also go there and investigate the facts of the matter. He was able to see that there had really been spiritual deeds and manifestations, and guaranteed that this was the truth. That office having thus guaranteed the truth of the matter, then this Bureau sought out the Court of Imperial Sacrifices to officially inspect the issue. After hearing that, according to the judgment of the Court of

Imperial Sacrifices, ceremonial forms in such a case of a Taoist's or Buddhist's displaying spiritual responses make appropriate the elevation of enfeoffed titles, we have additionally added the two words "Great Master" [to the god's title]. When adding these two words, we examined the guaranteed memorial of the Office of the Fiscal Commissioner of Fujian Circuit [which states that they] "had gone to Clear Water Cliff in Anxi district of Quanzhou prefecture. The man of the Tao, Chen Puzu, prayed [for rain] and received responses. We beg that his title be raised." In the above case it is appropriate to enfeoff him with the two words Great Master. As for the proposal of [bestowing the title of] "Great Master of Brilliant Responses," the Board of Rites wishes to proceed in accordance with the principles of the issue laid out by the Court of Imperial Sacrifices, so this action is even more appropriate. The court so commands, humbly obey this command. On 3/23 (4/20/1153) we received the Imperial [Sacred] Edict in accord with the memorial of the Board of Rites. This Bureau has stamped with approval the request that came from the Elder Yao Tian and others of Quanzhou Commandery, begging that the true transformed body of the Chen Puzu of Clear Water Cliff of that department be presented with a mandate of enfeoffment as the "Great Master of Brilliant Responses." On Shaoxing 26/3/23 (4/20/1153), we commanded that he receive a Taoist and Buddhist enfeoffment as "Great Master." This is appropriate for the Council to bestow. [Furthermore] after our official examination we have issued a mandate and bestowed [the title], as Yao Tian and others begged us to do. Humbly uphold this mandate and order. It has been decreed that the title of "Great Master of Brilliant Responses" be bestowed.

Southern Song Longxing 2/10 (1164).
Can zhizhengshi, Participant in Determining Government Matters
   (Vice Grand Councillor)
Wang [Zhiwang][1] (1103–70)
signature
Can zhizhengshi, Participant in Determining Government Matters
   (Vice Grand Councillor)
Zhou [Kui][2] (1098–1174)
signature

II. Edict Bestowing the Title of Great Master of Merciful Salvation and Brilliant Responses (1184) (Yang:2:2b-7b)

The Vice-Director of the Department of State Affairs, Joint Manager of Affairs with the Secretariat-Chancellery and the Department of State Affairs mandates that the Board of Rites's report has been approved and the

Department has noted the appended memorial from the Fiscal Commission of the Fujian Circuit. That memorial was based primarily on a report from Anxi District in Quanzhou Prefecture, composed by Digonglang zhengshishi, [Gentleman for Meritorious Advancement, rank 9b] Lin Eryan, and others, who together reported that they had humbly observed the imperially enfeoffed Great Master of Brilliant Responses of Clear Water Cliff of Chongshan li of their own District obtain responses to his prayers for rain, and that he had thus accumulated merit among the people. They pleaded that, as in the cases of Tiantong Zhengjue Dashi (Great Master of True Awareness of the Heavenly Child), of Mingzhou District, and the Miaokan Dashi (Great Master of Miraculous Profundity) of Fuzhou's Xuefeng [temple], and the Ciji Dashi (Great Master of Merciful Salvation) of Jiufengshan, etc., that he have a beautiful title added to his original enfeoffment. [They also] asked for a plaque for a stupa, a standard with which to display the manifest powers of the god. The District Office guaranteed their report to the prefectural authorities. [The latter] accordingly authorized Assistant Magistrate and Digonglang, [Gentleman for Meritorious Advancement, rank 9b] of Yongchun District, Huang Guan, to go there and uncover the facts. Now I quote from Huang Guan's report: "I personally went to the grounds of the temple and called together the *xiangsu* (Village Elder) Liu Pixu and others, and investigated the truth of the matter. According to what they said, whenever one worships the Great Master of Brilliant Responses, and begs for rain, then he never fails to respond. Indeed he has spiritual powers, and has accumulated merit amongst the people. I guarantee that this is the truth." Thus he reported to the prefectural authorities. He also submitted a guaranteed report to the Fiscal Commissioner. Accordingly, a mandate was issued appointing an official on duty assignment in the neighboring Xinghua Commandery to go to the region and inspect it. His results confirmed that there had truly been all along such spiritual responses, meritorious deeds, and manifestations. [He claimed that the god's] compassion reached to the people, [his worship] was included in the rituals. This was no licentious cult. "What I have today set forth is the truth. These are no ordinary spiritual encounters. As for the request to enhance the enfeoffed honors, there are no obstacles in this case." Next, he deliberated with the Commandery and guaranteed the truth of his comments in a report. Next, according to the report sent from the Xinghua Commandery, they ordered [an official from] Putian District to also go there and investigate. Now I cite the report of Putian Vice-Magistrate, Gentleman for Meritorious Advancement, Yao Jin:

I personally went to the Clear Water Cliff of Anxi District of Quanzhou Prefecture and called together the village neighbours of the area including Liu Pisu, etc. I discovered that the Great Master of Responsive Manifestations was originally a man of Yongchun District in Quanzhou prefecture. His ancestral surname was Chen, his name was Puzu. During his life building bridges and repairing roads was his work. He built several tens of great stone bridges. He never sought honors. In 1101, after he had transformed into an immortal, his brave spirit still seemed to be present. Whenever anyone had an illness, or if there was a drought from lack of rain, or disorders caused by bandits, as soon as one prayed he was responded to. In Shaoxing 26 (1156), on the basis of his former spiritual accomplishments, the former Elder Yao Tian and others presented a request in a guaranteed memorial that moved the mercy [of the Court to] enfeoff [the god]. . . . In Long(xing) 2/10 (1164) it was decreed that he be enfeoffed as the "Great Master of Responsive Manifestations." The manifestations and accomplishments of the god over the ages have been innumerable. I can not record them all. Today I briefly record the spiritual deeds and manifestations of the last few years:

1. On Long(xing) 2/2/4 (2/28/1164), Zhang Ting of Nan'an District, Chong ren *li*, Jiaokang bao, was blind in both eyes. His father visited the temple and asked for water to wash his eyes with. Within a month's time, he could see as well as ever.

2. Qiandao 2/2/11 (3/15/1166): the Quanshou Lin Zeng and over one hundred people from Nan'an District, Youfengli, Xuangkang, and several other *bao*, visited the temple and burned incense, made prayers and delivered memorials, stating: "Amongst the villagers of our humble *li* plague is spreading, people are afflicted with adversity. We beseech the Great Master's incense fire to come with us to fix and calm the villages of our *li*." Then they asked for ritual water with which to effect a cure. On 3/23 (5/7/1166) Lin Zeng and some two hundred people escorted the Great Master back to the temple, he had invisibly aided them and they expressed thanks for his blessings.

3. Qiandao 2/5/4 (6/24/1166): The Quanshou He Fo'er and some fifty people from Hui'an District's Renli, Jinjie and Yuanqian *bao*, came to the temple and delivered memorials and made prayers, saying that the old and the young of their area were afflicted by the diseases of the moment. They asked for ritual water and incense fire to take back and worship. They begged for peace and tranquility. On 6/13 (7/11/1166), Fo'er and the others came to the temple to hold an offering to express thanks for the mercy of the god.

4. Qiandao 9/5/12 (6/24/1173): Quanshou Ye Wei and over one hundred others from Yongchun District, Shi'an *li*, Xiaobian *bao* came to the temple and delivered a memorial stating that the rice seedlings of their villages were being destroyed by insects, and were inadequate, so that they feared there would be nothing to harvest. The people were hopeless. They worshipfully implored the Great Master's incense fire. They took it with them and so preserved internal order and peacefully raised their crop, kept calm, and maintained tranquility. [The god] particularly guarded over the village well water, and the people accordingly expressed thanks at this [divine] response.

5. Chunxi 1/2/18 (3/23/1174): Weng Dali and others from Youxi District, Datian *bao*, came to the temple and delivered a petition stating that their bao was short of rain, so it was impossible to plant seeds, and cows were dying at a disastrous rate. The people had lost hope. They begged and pleaded for the statue of the god, which they took with them to the country-side and worshiped with burning incense. The god protected their village wells, and when they prayed for rain enough fell to soak [the ground]. Also, Liu Dechong and others from Dehuaxian, Guanhu *li*, came to the temple to ask for the god's statue. They took it with them and worshiped it.

6. Chunxi 2/1 (1175) *Quanshou* from every area, including Weng Dali, held an offering to express thanks for the protection and security offered by the god to every area, and for the peace among the people and the soaking rain which allowed for a harvest every year.

7. Chunxi 6/9 (October 1179): Anxi District experienced a drought. Although the wheat had been planted, the shoots were dried and withered, so the District Magistrate, Gentleman for Managing Affairs, [rank 8a2] Chengshilang, Zhao Xun, on 12/18 (1/17/1180) appointed Assistant Magistrate, Digonglang Cao Wei, to invite the Great Master of Brilliant Responses to the District capital where an altar was built for him. The Magistrate prayed for rain on behalf of the people. On the 20th (1/19/1180) they were blessed with [divine] response. Only after two days [of rain] did the sky clear. The second wheat crop grew and people were able to harvest it.

8. Chunxi 7 (1180): There was a great drought. Wheat and rice seedlings withered and died. The Anxi District Magistrate Zhao Xun again appointed Assistant Magistrate Cao Wei, who climbed the cliff on 6/2 (6/26/1180) to invite the Great Master to pray for rain on behalf of the people. When they were five or six *li* from the District capital, near the Jueyuansi, there was a shower that followed after the cart. So they invited the god into the Jueyuan Temple for a rest, and after a while the skies cleared a bit, and the District officials and elders came out to the suburbs to burn incense, and then escorted the god into the city and prayed to him. On the 4th, they were blessed with his divine response. The people were overjoyed. The elders and others erected a stele to commemorate the occasion, and recorded the spiritual deeds.

Thus we say that there have definitely been these events in which the benevolence and benefits of the god have reached the people. These are no ordinary coincidences. They deserve to be recorded in rituals. Thus this is no licentious cult. This we uphold and guarantee. We recommend to the Commandery that they adopt these suggestions.

The Commandery reported to the Fiscal Commissioner's Circuit Office. They then again ordered an official on duty in Zhangzhou to go and uncover the truth and to make a guaranteed report. Now we quote the report of Zhou Ding, Zhangpu Assistant Magistrate: "I personally visited the Clear Water Cliff in Anxi District, and called together the various local *baojia* [leaders] including Chen Yan. I uncovered evidence that the Great Master of Brilliant Responses when prayed to in the past and nowadays, has indeed performed spiritual deeds whose benevolence and merit extend to the people. These are no ordinary coincidences." He guaranteed the truth of his report to the prefecture.

His guarantee and his report on the truth of the matter have been reported to the Circuit Fiscal Commission Office. [As for] the plea that we act in accordance with his request, we have given our permission. On Chunxi 3/3/25 (5/6/1176) it was decreed that there should be deliberations as to the appropriate elevation of the god's reward, and regulations were compared with the following one, stating that for any Taoist or Buddhist shrine in which there are spiritual responses to prayers, and merit and manifestations that extend benevolence and benefits to the people, and in which these are no ordinary coincidences, then it is appropriate to enhance the enfeoffed rank and title, and to bestow temple plaques. The prefectures should all honor this announcement, and their guaranteed reports should reach the Fiscal Commissioner's Office. These Offices should then appoint an official of the neighboring prefecture to personally conduct an investigation. Then another uninvolved official should be sent to examine the facts and make a guaranteed memorial.

According to the Quanzhou report, it was upheld that the Great Master of Brilliant Responses of Clear Water Cliff of Anxi district had responded to prayers for rain. Therefore they requested an enhancement of the Master's titles, as well as a plaque for a stupa. In accordance with the regulations, a neighboring official from Xinghua Commandery, Putian District Vice-Magistrate Yao Jin, was appointed to investigate, and then Zhangpu Assistant Magistrate Zhou Ding was also appointed to go and re-examine the case. They visited the Great Master of Brilliant Responses and ascertained that there had, in fact, been the above-mentioned spiritual response to prayers for rain, with benevolence and benefit reaching to the people. The officials of [the Fujian Fiscal Commissioner's Office] again officially deliberated over the case, and vouchsafed that it was true. We desire that the Saintly Mercy will kindly make a special grant. After humbly awaiting the edict, the case was approved and sent back to us for deliberation. We reported it to the Department of State Affairs, who passed it down to the Court of Imperial Sacrifices. After they had finished their deliberations, we now, in accordance with the recommendations of the Court of Imperial Sacrifices, on Jianyan 3/1/6 (1/28/1129) send down a proclamation to the temples of the gods, [stating that] wheresoever there be spiritual responses, then one should first send a plaque and next enfeoff [the god] with a title. Each time add two words until you reach an eight-word title. Also in accordance with the statues of the Court of Imperial Sacrifices, whenever a Taoist or a Buddhist has spiritual responses, it is appropriate to enhance his title. One generally adds "Great Master" as the first two words.

Now upon deliberating over the guaranteed memorial of the Fiscal Commission of Fujian Dao, concerning the Great Master of Brilliant Responses of Anxi District in Quanzhou, and requesting the enhancement of his title and the bestowal of a plaque for a stupa, we have deliberated that with the exception of the difficulty that the laws and regulations have nothing in them about plaques for stupas, in accordance with the above-mentioned laws and regulations, it is appropriate to enhance the title by two words. Accordingly, we make him a four-word [title], "Great Master." It is appropriate to issue an edict to this effect. The Bureau has deliberated as well and agreed to act in accordance with the recommendations of the Court of Imperial Sacrifices. They reported upon the matter and received an Imperial Edict bestowing the title of "Great Master of Merciful Benevolence and Brilliant Responses." The mandate has been issued as an edict. Nan Song Chunxi 11/3 (1184).

> Participant in Determining Government Matters (Vice Grand Councillor) Huang Qia[3] (1122–1200), signature.
> Participant in Determining Government Matters (Vice Grand Councillor) Shi Shidian[4] (1124–92), signature.
> Assistant Director of the Right (Grand Councillor) Wang [Huai][5] (1126–89), signature.
> Assistant Director of the Left (Grand Councillor) Zeng,[6] signature.

III. Decree Bestowing the Title of "Great Master of Merciful Salvation, Broad Benevolence, and Brilliant Responses" (1201) (Yang:2:7b-9a.)

The Department of State Affairs mandates that the Board of Rites' report, based on the report of the Court of Imperial Sacrifices, has been examined. The Board of Rites approved on Qingyuan 6:2/27 (3/15/1200), the proclamation of a decree, with an approved report of the Board of Rites and the Court of Imperial Sacrifices, checked by the Department, stating that recently the rains had been somewhat delayed, and memorializing all the Fiscal Commissions of the various circuits and commanderies that wherever there had been acts of merit by spiritual response and subsequently petitions for enhancement of enfeoffments, and which had temporarily been overlooked as insignificant and so not forwarded, and thereby forsook the bestowal of honors and praises, they (i.e., the Fiscal

Commissioners) should within five or six days immediately draft a report and submit it. We now relate the following cases:

1. The Fiscal Commission of Fujian Circuit memorialized that there was a request for the enhancement of the titles of the Yinghu Wulie Zhen Minwang [Heroic Protector, Martial Commander of Min; i.e., Wang Shengzhi, first Emperor of Min], [and his assistants . . .] in Fuzhou's Nantai Wuji Temple.

2. The Fiscal Commission of the Chengdu Prefecture memorialized that there was a request for the enhancement of the titles of the Puji Xianling Zhenjun, [True Lord of Manifest Spiritual Power and Universal Salvation] of Luojiang District in Jinzhou.

3. The Fiscal Commission of Fujian Circuit memorialized that there was a request for the enhancement of the enfeoffment of the Great Master of Merciful Salvation and Brilliant Responses of Anxi District in Quanzhou Prefecture. As for the above god shrines, according to the records of the Bureau of Rites and the Court of Imperial Sacrifices, they have no record of these requests. Although these are not inconsequential matters or insignificant beings, it is appropriate that the respective Fiscal Commissions be contacted and that they record immediately the mandates of enfeoffment already issued, and guarantee their reports. Then again, fearing delays in upholding the commandments of the Court, we shall first bestow the titles and send the [decrees] down together with the orders. Each area made their guarantees, and these arrived. They had carried out their instructions. On 6/29 we received an Imperial Edict, in accord with the report of the Board of Rites and the Court of Imperial Sacrifices, that the officials of the Court of Imperial Sacrifices have examined and approved each case. On Jianyan 3/1/6 (1/28/1129), a decree was issued stating that whenever god temples experience divine deeds and request the bestowal of plaques, and then [ask] for enfeoffment as a Duke, each time bestow two words until you reach a total of eight. For enfeoffments as Kings, each time add two words until you reach eight. As for gods and immortals who have not yet been enfeoffed, if they have accomplished divine deeds, then they should first be enfeoffed as *zhenren* [Perfect Being], and afterward as *zhenjun* [True Lord]. Each time they should have two words added to their titles up to a total of eight words. According to the regulations of the Court of Imperial Sacrifices regarding Taoists and Buddhists, those who have made divine responses and received enhanced enfeoffments, should also have the words "Great Master" added on. Each time add two words to their titles until you reach eight words. Now upon examining the following god temples, on former occasions they have already been granted enfeoffments. Now as for Yinghu Wulie Zhenxianwang of Fuzhou's Nantai Wuji Temple, we now wish to compose his title as "Yinghu Wulie Zhonghui Zhenmin Wang." . . . More-

over, we also command and instruct that the Master of Merciful Salvation and Brilliant Responses of Anxi District in Quanzhou Prefecture of Fujian shall now be known as "Master of Merciful Salvation, Broad Benevolence and Brilliant Responses." It is appropriate to issue this decree, and we expect the Department of State Affairs and the Bureau of Rites to report on the implementation of the Court's decree. The report went to the Bureau, and the Bureau acted in accordance with the recommendation of the Court of Imperial Sacrifices concerning the principles of the case, and humbly upheld the commandments, and so on 3/5 received an Imperial Edict in accordance with the mandate forwarded by the Board of Rites, decreeing that it was appropriate to bestow the title of Master of Merciful Salvation, Broad Benevolence and Brilliant Responses. The mandate has been issued as a decree.

> Nan Song Jiatai 1/3 (1201)
> Administrator of the Bureau of Military Affairs,
> Participant in Determining Government Matters
> (Vice Grand Councillor) He [Dan],[7] signature.
> Grand Councillor, Assistant Director of the Right,
> signature.

IV. Decree Bestowing the Title of "Great Master of Superior Benefits, Merciful Salvation, Broad Benevolence and Brilliant Responses" (1210) (Yang:2:9a-13a.)

The Department of State Affairs mandates that the Board of Rites' report has been approved and the Department has noted the appended memorial of the Fujian Fiscal Commissioner which stated that the Quanzhou Commandery had reported that in Kaixi 3/9 (Oct. 1207), the rains had been somewhat delayed, and so they had gone to the Buddhist temples and Taoist belvederes and the various god temples to pray for rain, but had not obtained any response. Then, in the first month of the [following year] Jiading 1/1 (Jan. 1208), they invited all the Buddhas and all the Gods [lit. god-kings] of all the temples and set up an altar for them and prayed to them, but there was no response. Then a report arrived from Anxi District, stating that the Great Master of Merciful Salvation, Broad Benevolence and Brilliant Responses of the Clear Water Buddhist Temple of their district had brought rain when prayed to and responded to the needs of the prefectural capital. The god was invited on 4/22 (5/9/1208). When he had just reached the city gate, dark clouds gathered on all sides. That night it rained and the next day the peasants planted the crop. Truly this response showed benevolence to the people. The report urged the submission of a guaranteed memorial requesting the enhancement of the enfeoffments of the god. The Circuit Fiscal Commission Office examined the matter and discovered that the Great Master of Brilliant Responses of Clear Water Cliff originally was a man of Mazhang in Yongchun District. His surname was Chen, his name was Puzu. He concentrated on building bridges and repairing roads. He built several tens of great stone bridges. He never sought for honors. He transformed into an immortal in 1101. His responses are like an echo. In the Shaoxing period (1131–62) the district was suffering a long and terrible drought. People prayed for rain, and their prayers were instantaneously answered. The officials of the district erected a stele. The elder Yao Tian and others, on the basis of the stele inscription, made their request for the enfeoffment of the god. In Shaoxing 26 (1156) a decree enfeoffed him as the "Great Master of Brilliant Responses of Clear Water Cliff." Successive prayers produced reactions and extraordinary deeds. So the two words "Merciful Salvation" were added to his title. Afterward he continued to manifest and transform as before, so he was again enfeoffed with the two words "Broad Benevolence." As for the decrees making him the "Master of Merciful Salvation, Broad Benevolence and Brilliant Responses," and the accounts of his benevolence reaching to the people, these documents and protocols are all recorded in the Register of Sacrifices. Thus his is not a licentious cult. After receiving three enhanced enfeoffments, his incense fire became spiritually charged, and its influence grew larger by the day. Benevolence and benefits extended to the people.

Now the district capital had had no rain since the winter of Kaixi 3 (1207). By the spring of Jiading 1 (1208), seeds would not go into the ground. Anxi District officials invited the god to the District Hall where they set up an altar and prayed for rain on behalf of the people. Accordingly, rain fell in sufficiency. Peasants set to work planting. Then these divine deeds were reported to the prefectural capital. They, relying on this report, invited the statue of the Buddha to go with them. They prayed for rain on behalf of the people. When they had barely arrived at the gates of the city, dark clouds rose upon all sides. That night rain fell, and by the next day enough had fallen that the people of seven district cities could plant their crops.

Later, in the same year (1208), in the 6th month, locusts caused a disaster. When they flew up they covered up the sun. When they descended they destroyed the sprouts. The Fulao, Elder Liu Fu and others led a mass of people to invite the god's statue to carry out exorcistic rites and drive away the evils. Within three days the locusts were annihilated. The autumn harvest still had hopes. Truly these are meritorious deeds, which extend benevolence to the people. The prefectural government investigated and upheld the truth of these events in a report to the Circuit Fiscal

Commission. They, in accordance with the regulations, appointed Han Yu, Assistant Magistrate of Xianyou, an official of the neighboring Xinghua Commandery, to go and investigate. Then they also ordered He Bao, the acting District Defender of Changtai, a Zhangzhou official, to uncover the truth. They concluded that there had in fact been the above-mentioned praying for rain and divine response, extending benevolence to the people. The Circuit Office again deliberated, and then upheld the truth of the matter, desiring the [Emperor] in his saintly mercy, specially to bestow [honors]. They humbly awaited the Saintly Edict. Then their request was approved for transmission to the Bureau of Rites for deliberation. They [in turn] reported the matter to the Department of State Affairs. The Bureau then sent the matter to the Court of Imperial Sacrifices for deliberation. Now we quote the recommendation of the Court of Imperial Sacrifices: "Having examined the Essential Rules of the Dynasty, and because the Records do not list this incident, etc. . . . [There follows a great deal of bureaucratic transferring and recopying of files on the god from the Fujian Fiscal Commission Circuit Offices to the offices of the Court of Imperial Sacrifices. The regulations on promotions of deities, including Taoist and Buddhist gods, are quoted at length again. Reference is made to the regulations of Chunxi 14/6/19 (7/27/1187) insisting that Fiscal Commissioners abide by the regulations in their requests for the promotion of local gods. Finally, the edict is prepared and issued, confirming the new title.]

The edict was issued and signed as shown below:
Nan Song Jiading 3/5 (1210)
Canzhengshi, Participant in Determining Government
Matters (Vice Grand Councillor) Lou [Ji][8]
(1133–1211) (signature).
Canzhengshi, Participant in Determining Government Matters
(Vice Grand Councillor) Huang (signature).
Administrator of the Bureau of Military Affairs,
[rank 2a], Participant in Determining Government Matters
(Vice Grand Councillor) Lei [Xiaoyou][9] (signature)

APPENDIX II

THE DOSSIER OF THE REVERENT LORD
OF BROAD COMPASSION

I. Documents Requesting an Enhancement of Enfeoffment

The Department of Yongchun and the District of Nan'an of Quanzhou Prefecture have met together to report on events. We have cautiously sent up the report asking that Guangze Zunwang and the City God of Yongchun be enhanced in rank and that plaques be bestowed. The reasons for this request have been completely recorded below. We have not tolerated any unnecessary remarks in this correct report. We have gathered together all the documents of the request. We ask the Provincial Governor to examine this report. We memorialize requesting an Imperial edict enhancing the titles and an Imperially bestowed plaque in order to respond to the god's protection and the harmony of the realm. This would truly be to the general good. In addition to [sending this report to] the Governor, we humbly request that this report also be sent to the relevant officials. The former report was submitted in the first month of 1869. Approved by Lieutenant Governor of Fujian and other parts, Deng.

II. Investigation of All Gods Who Drive Away Disasters and Overcome Adversities

When mention is made of enfeoffments and the Register of Sacrifices, then one must investigate clearly the facts of the matter and see whether or not the gazetteers have detailed discussions [of the god]. Then one should compile a dossier compiling documents in accordance with the regulations. This [case] has not gone through the proper process of compiling a dossier and including the relevant documents, therefore there are difficulties in determining the proper response. Therefore reassemble and clearly investigate the matter, gathering together the relevant documents into a proper dossier. Send this together with the relevant gazetteers and books to this office for our deliberation. Do not delay in responding to this command. 1/24/1869. To Department Magistrate Weng Xueben and District Magistrate Wu Guanghan.

III. [The former report circulates through the Provincial Administration]

The Deputy Lieutenant Governor, Xia, in accordance with his orders, offers up the former documents to the Governor-General Ying's office. The latter approves the deliberations of the Lieutenant Governor of Fujian regarding the request on the part of Yongchun Department in association with Nan'an district for the enhancement of the title of Guangze Zunwang and the City God of Yongchun. The Governor's Education Bureau approves the handling of the case by the Lieutenant Governor. The Education Bureau of the Governor-General approves the handling of the case by the Lieutenant Governor. Thus in accordance with the joint permission of the Offices of the Governor-General and the Governor, and the deliberations of our Office, we order the compilation of a dossier and the sending up of relevant gazetteers and books to this Office for further deliberation. We call upon the [Yongchun department] officials and yamen runners to immediately obey this command and to meet with the officials of Nan'an to investigate the events and to see whether or not the gazetteers carry detailed discussions. Then compile a dossier with all the relevant documents and report it to this Office without delay. 1869, third month.

IV. The Magistrate's Report

The Department of Yongchun and the District of Nan'an of Quanzhou Prefecture have held a meeting to report on events. According to a report from the *shenshi* (gentry) of Yongchun and Nan'an, entitled "Report on the Divine Spirit's Manifest Responses," we humbly make the following report:
We memorialize requesting an enhancement of the enfeoffment of the gods as well as the bestowal of Imperial plaques, in order to repay the protection of the god. We humbly point out that these included . . . . [there follows a list of the god's early miracles with citations from the various gazetteers, and from the *Filiations of Guangze Zunwang*, by the Nan'an man, Zeng Tianjue]. In 1853 the Small Knives Association rose up in Xiamen, Tongan, and other locations. This was a grave matter, the disturbances were spreading everywhere. In all four corners of Nan'an there was looting and robbing. The government troops encircled the bandits for several months but still the flames of rebellion spread further, wreaking tremendous havoc. The officials and the gentry went to Guo Mountain and prayed to the god. That night in a dream, the god pointed out that the time was right for the gathering together of village militias who should join forces with the government troops

in attacking the bandits. Accordingly, the bandits were pacified. Every time the god was prayed to for rain, he responded. In the fourth month of 1853, the local bandit leader Lin Jun rounded up a band of four or five thousand men, and crept into Yongchun City from Dehua. From dawn until noon the government troops battled the bandits. After they had fought for over four hours, things were at a crisis. Suddenly we saw atop Dapeng Mountain to the north of the city masses of soldiers dressed in armor. There among them were flags and banners with the name "Guo" upon them. When the gentlemen and soldiers saw this, their courage increased one hundred-fold. They attacked with furious strength. The band of thieves was forced together and decimated. Countless heads were chopped off. The bandit leader Lin Jun was forced to run far away. The town and its moat were thus recovered at the hour of noon. The entire region depended on the god for bringing peace. Then in 1864, the bandit leaders Liu Guangju, Xie Xian, and Xie Jin formed a *dang* [secret-society] and called together [a rebel band] in the He Mountain stockade of Yongchun. They disturbed and harmed the people. At that very time, the hairy bandits [of the Taiping Tianguo] had sneakily taken Zhangzhou city and the surroundng countryside. The aforementioned bandits plotted to coordinate with them. After several sieges by government troops on the stockade, they finally broke off their water supply. The bandits broke out of their nest like frightened rats. The leaders Liu and Xie Jin were captured alive and punished according to law [executed on the spot]. Only Xie Xian escaped. In 1867 Xie Xian slunk to the border of Yongchun and Dehua and made alliances with bandit groups, plotting to again raise trouble. Then local civil and military officials, together with local gentry, joined forces to capture and annihilate them. They destroyed the bandit lair. Xie Xian scurried in all directions, running in flight. He would suddenly appear and then disappear; it was impossible to determine his whereabouts in order to capture him. The officials and gentry again made a visit to the Guo Mountain Temple. Within a month Xie Xian was captured and immediately received his heavy punishment. Were it not for the resplendent power of the god how could we have annihilated these demons? Now in the entire Datian, Dehua, Yongchun, Nan'an region, all is calm; the villages and households are at peace. We felt deep thanksgiving and so composed this report. The report has been reworked into a memorial requesting the enhancement of the enfeoffment and the bestowal of Imperial plaques. As for these former matters, the humble [Department and District Magistrates] [Weng] Xueben and [Wu] Weishu, met together and examined the record of Temple sacrifices. We found that this orthodox spirit was in fact able to drive away disaster and overcome adversity. He has merit with the people, and so his case merits a request in the form of a memorial for the enhancement of his title. Now Guangze Zunwang has been repeatedly enfeoffed in the Song dynasty. His deeds are detailed in the gazetteers. In 1853 when the local bandit Lin

Jun was disturbing the region the awesome power of the god shone forth and protected the people. These acts accord in nature and in principle with those listed above under the driving away of disaster and the overcoming of adversity. We have met and gathered together all the documents and now send them to the Provincial Government for inspection.

The Department Magistrate of Yongchun and the District Magistrate of Nan'an submitted a memorial in the first lunar month of 1869 to the Lieutenant Governor of Fujian, detailing the assistance of the god in the quelling of a local rebellion led by Lin Jun in 1853. The god again helped capture rebels in 1864. The memorial requested the enhancement of the titles of the gods. On 1/24 (March 6, 1869) the Lieutenant Governor acknowledged receipt of the memorial but requested further information. In the third lunar month, the Lieutenant Governor's office further quoted the approval of the Governor General, and the Governor, and the favorable responses of their respective Bureaus of Education. The Magistrates of Yongchun and Nan'an were ordered to verify the facts of the matter. Later in the same month, the Magistrates responded with a detailed memorial quoting a report prepared by the local gentry which itself was based on the *Filiations of the God*, by Zeng Tianjue. The Magistrates urged that the enfeoffment request be forwarded to the court. Next, one finds a document dated April 11, 1870, written by the Board of Rites, acknowledging receipt of a memorial from the Governor of Fujian on the matter. An Imperial Rescript authorizing the enhancement of the titles was issued on May 14. The edict arrived in Fujian on December 28. It was announced by the Governor to the Lieutenant Governor and then to the Magistrates on February 25, 1871. The edict was proclaimed by the Magistrate in the temple on March 20, 1872. A stone inscription was carved detailing the events. Plaques were presented by the respective District Magistrates on behalf of the Emperor. The plaque at Fengshan si read "Bao'an" (Preserver of Peace).

保生大帝真經

THE TRUE SCRIPTURE OF THE GREAT EMPEROR

啓請

　　仰啓昊天吳大帝，世居泉郡誕臨漳，威靈勇猛起慈心，以法力故作醫王，於諸衆生多饒益。功成行滿感玉皇，詔問修何因緣行。得正知見道彌彰，敕補醫靈大徽號。仍差仙醫官姓黃，威武舍人江四使，青巾眞人並二童，驅邪力士六丁將，女醫太乙勤小娘，更與飛天大使者，協力扶衰驅病殃。我今至心皈命請，願歆一念降恩光。

開經偈

　　大聖醫靈吳眞君，書符降篆演經文，誓願神咒大威力，興祥集福免災迍。爾時慈濟眞君，朝於太清宮中，三元殿上。衆星諸神，咸皆會集。
　　天尊曰：「吾今下觀三千大千世界，南閻浮提衆生，十惡五逆，不忠不孝，無禮無義，不敬三寶，不知布施，不行方便，多作惡業，殺害衆生，姪盜貪瞋，結諸罪網，撓亂國土。人王匪正，上無道揆，下無法守。是致擾攘，無辜橫死，英爽不散，爲作蜚尸魔鬼。故邊夷人民，刀兵橫起。南夏人民，歲時寒暑，瘴癘瘟黃，瘄瘟暴死。復行蚊疖瘡子，赤眼瀉痢，豬羊牛馬，冒氣而死。山魔蚖蛇，蝮蠍虎象，禽獸海魔，疾風漂船，龍魚鬼浪，城津破壞。多水火災。復遭王法，年逢饑饉，五穀不登。凡爾施爲，事不如意，當知魔種。皆是武夫健卒，勇猛神氣，亦助天神，行雲布氣，風雨及時，禾米大熟，天下太平。今各增長，八萬四千眷屬，忽起風災，水災，火災，四百四病，時氣流行，世間薄福。惡逆衆生，遇災當死。」
　　天尊憫此十善修福之人，乃推窮厤數，考究讖言：
　　青犬吠，
　　木豬鳴，
　　雞兔月，
　　員無晶，
　　三災至，
　　九橫生，
　　甲乙多兵患，丙丁懼火災，戊己蝗瘴疾，庚壬風水災，自甲週癸，上五荒，下五豐，嗟值末世，昙運將終，諸佛涅槃，賢聖隱伏。凡夫愚婦，不覺不知，故傳經法，普救世間，而說偈言：
　　犬吠豬鳴，惡化善生，皈依三寶，持誦此經，
　　隨處供養，永鎮魔兵，天神守護，家國安寧，
　　廣傳經法，散施流行。
　　太上老君曰：「若有善男信女，敬重三寶，歡喜布施，每遇庚申甲子，三元七星主命臘日，齋戒淸心，持誦此經，供養眞文，自有天神擁護

。不遭彼難，欽承功德，獲福延生」。復敕祕訣靈符，一百二十道。告慈濟眞君曰：「汝道全德備，善行淸隆，在天有戒定慧妙力，在地有慈悲濟載大功，在人有孚惠眞君寵號，能通三界，可伏斯魔，傳布經法，救度群生，同歸大道。」太上說已，天尊回馭。衆星諸神，奉辭而退。於是慈濟眞君，承上告言，遄勅妙所。於癸酉四月七日，步罡吀氣，地震三聲，扶降眞童，宣說此經。而作咒曰：

觀音化身，渤海儲精。心潛六合，氣運五行。
慈悲濟世，救疾醫靈。七鹽盂水，寶劍前橫。
步罡呼吸，衆魔皆傾。千災永殄，萬福咸臻。
香煙啓處，聖格騰升。誦吾神咒，即降眞形。
唵；急急如律令。

眞童曰：「吾世居泉郡，顯蹟臨漳。迨今三百餘年，積功累行，嘉寵薦臻。向挽米舟，以濟水旱。復擁神兵，以禦寇盜。近湧甘泉，以祛疾苦。今傳靈寶經法，以救世人。若有男女得吾眞經妙印，信受供養，或請僧道轉誦，或結會讀誦，廣令傳說，求心所願，無不遂意。若人開築井竈，架造宅墓，豬羊牛馬，雞鴨栖欄，或有時氣疾病，可以香花燈茶，異果供養，持通此經。連念吾咒七遍，以朱砂書吾傳示。符訣如法，敕向門上。災鬼自消，人員自泰。所求稱心，咸登道岸。」眞童說已。吀魂而悟。

眞君眞君，治邪斬瘟。行符咒水，普救萬民。
罡步正炁，永斷禍根。威光烜赫，顯號增封。
香火廟食，夙夜虔恭。萬靈有禱，咸沐神功。
誦吾神咒，萬滌群凶。急急如律令。

敕水咒

孚惠眞君，觀音化身。慈悲普濟，隨念降靈。
行雲布炁，治病除迍。火車去毒，水車咸臻。
風車炁車，洞達玄冥。靑龍守木，白虎衛金。
朱雀守火，玄武水神。吾爲土主，道宗混元。
罡步正炁，保衞萬生。功成行滿，與吾同升。
急急如律令。

醫靈寵號廣稱揚，顯赫神機誕臨漳。昔日觀音應化身，世人焚香虔轉誦，千災永弭福壽臻。

相傳此經專治時疫，誦之可爲衆生解厄。□本末附太上說慈濟仙姑救產妙經，俟續刻梭注。

敕封保安廣澤尊王眞經

THE TRUE SCRIPTURE OF THE REVERENT LORD

淨心神咒

太上台星，應變無停，驅邪縛魅，保命護身。智慧明淨，心神安寧。三魂永久，魄無喪傾。急急如律令。

淨口神咒

丹朱口神，吐穢除氛。舌神正倫，通命養神。羅千齒神，卻邪衛眞。喉神虎賁，氣神引津。心神丹元，令我通眞。思神鍊液，道炁長存。急急如律令。

淨身神咒

靈寶天尊，安慰身形。弟子魂魄，五臟玄冥。青龍白虎，隊仗紛紜。朱雀玄武，侍衛我眞。急急如律令。

安土地咒

元始安鎭，普告萬靈。嶽瀆眞官，土地祇靈。左社右稷，不得妄驚。回向正道，內外肅淸。各安方位，備守家庭。太上有命，搜捕邪精。護法神王，保衛誦經。皈依大道，元亨利貞。急急如律令。

淨天地咒

洞中玄虛，晃朗太元。八方威神，使我自然。靈寶符命，普告九天。乾羅答那，洞罡太玄。斬妖縛邪，殺鬼萬千。中山神咒，元始玉文。持誦一遍，卻病延年。按行五嶽，八海知聞。魔王束首，侍衛我軒。凶穢消散，道氣常存。急急如律令。

祝香神咒

道由心學，心假香傳。香爇玉鑪，心存帝前。眞靈下盼，仙佩臨軒。弟子關告，逕達九天。

攝魔神咒

乾坤一氣，育我者七。丹元寂養，妙在勤息。善觀太和，洞監出入。化賊爲良，刺邪如戟。鑒耀金庭，常度五逆。運閉傍觀，洒埽淨室。塵起於土，土安神逸。煙生於火，火降氛滅。金空有聲，聲不亂擊。木堅則榮，守榮則實。水澄則淸，貴淸不溢。五政旣持，利往終吉。二儀在傍，循環赫奕。處暗愈光，交曲始直。綱紀吾身，晨昏怛惕。迴度靈田，精華羅畢。頃刻敷威，群魔自失。皎皎無窮，用之不竭。無強無昧，無妄無弱。以大光明，圓通莫測。能斬非神，能絕六逸。以玉爲章，玉無瑕迹。以金爲章，金焚不洩。傳誦吾章，逍遙太極。

金光神咒

天地玄宗，萬氣本根。廣修億刼，證吾神通。三界內外，惟道獨尊。體有金光，覆映吾身。視之不見，聽之不聞。包羅天地，養育群生。受持萬遍，身有光明。三界侍衛，五帝伺迎。萬神朝禮，役使雷霆。鬼妖喪膽，精怪亡形。內有霹靂，雷神隱名。洞慧交徹，五氣騰騰。金光速現，覆護眞人。急急如律令。

啓請

仰稽鳳山聖，尊居廣澤王。
忠心貫日月，赤膽照乾坤。
孝感蒼穹上，德化國土中。

恩覃三界外，威鎮九天庭。
敕授雷霆印，專滅五逆情。
翦除諸奸惡，報應直分明。
驅瘟降鬼祟，收伏群魔精。
保主安社稷，慈悲救萬民。

開經神咒

寂寂至無宗，虛峙萬仞阿。豁落洞玄文，誰測此幽遐？一入大乘路，孰計年劫多？不生亦不滅，欲生因蓮花。超凌三界途，慈心解世羅。眞人無上德，世世爲仙家。

太上元陽上帝無始天尊說保安廣澤王靈濟普德郭星君攝魔醒世妙經。

爾時無始天尊在大羅天上與諸天帝君、十方仙聖、會於五虛九光之殿、玉梵七寶之臺、朗誦洞章，長吟仙曲。會參無軼之妙道，展聞至寶之玄文。適有司過之神上章啓奏「今時下民俱被群魔作擾，諸怪爲祟，蠱惑其心，不知向善，妄自爲非；種種罪端，實難闡述。」衆仙聞奏，越班而出奏曰：「天尊大慈，天尊大聖，爲群生之父，爲萬神之師。廣發慈悲，以拯下界。」天尊曰：「善哉善哉。此等衆生，遭此苦難，要伏群魔，提醒黎庶，非靈濟普德郭星君，至忠至孝，正直無私，莫勝其任。夫星君係南陵眞仙，降生於泉郡清溪之地，事母至孝。年一十三歲，蛻迹於後晉天福初年。顯聖於南安古藤之上。玉封靈濟普德星君，萬方勸善護佑天尊。神居玉清宮，位列應元府，奉師於朱陵上帝，掌南極雷霆之任，司都天報應之權，誅奸邪於已往，判善惡於當時，翦魔精於斗罡之下，驅瘟疫於國土之中。自宋代淂殺湯賊，救火皇宮，初封大將軍。繼贈提伯王，詔命敕建廟宇軒昂，春秋祀典，香火長存。至大明島倭猖獗，呂寇縱橫，大展神通，埽除群醜，剿滅諸冤，敕封忠應孚惠威武英烈廣澤尊王。丹心赤膽，護國佑民，忠誠貫日，功業參天，及聖朝疊封王爵，敕贈保安。功扶社稷，威鎮鳳山，修眞千載，功莫大焉。衆仙聞說，皆大歡喜。天尊即命金童持符，逕往鳳山召之。星君聞召，隨即朝見天尊。稽首奏曰：「臣居雷部，賜鎮鳳山，蒙召何緣？」天尊言：「吾今敕汝下方埽除魔鬼，救拔衆生，醒世濟民，保國永清。」星君再拜，奉敕而下，傳檄十方。「夫聖朝乃應運之君，聰明之主，豈容此魑魅魍魎之流，猖獗於光天化日之下？吾本代天糾罰，翦滅諸魔，發惻隱之心，放開生路。爾等群魔，洗心滌慮，咸聽吾言，歸正棄邪，速歸洞府，面石壁而修眞。回首名山，坐蒲團而悟道。待至勳崇行著，性靈神融，自可克證高眞，即階妙道。是檄到處，魔王束首，踴躍皈依。人天利益，國土昇平。是時星君復說寶章而醒世，曰：「惟天下之大聖，制禮樂，著詩書，皆可移風而易俗。今時下民失其本眞，昧其天性，以及先聖舊章，前王典制，皆不能口誦心維。反守其固陋之心情，以道義爲具文，以鬼神爲無有，以報應爲虛誣。不知善惡之報，如影隨形。善者天則賜汝以福。惡者天必禍汝以殃。吾故演說妙章，普化世人，判善惡於亳釐，欽鬼神於屋漏。勿以善小而不作，勿以惡小而爲之，蓋天下無爾立之善惡，亦無一定之善惡。能生從善除惡之心，即轉禍爲福之道。爾諸大衆，聽吾言，修己身，上而推之，則可以證聖成眞。下以守之，亦不失善人君子。誠心嚮往，至道在前。寶章普化，萬姓提醒。即赴天闕，朝覲尊顏復旨，禮謝諸仙，讚歎推可，得遇無上法輪。於是天尊讚詠星君而說偈曰：

　　　至聖保安王，無上郭星君。
　　　九天雷府將，十方普化尊。
　　　談經跨錦鳳，持法執金鞭。
　　　腹內元機妙，鑪中丹汞成。
　　　能以智慧力，攝伏諸魔精。
　　　巡遊三界外，糾察善惡情。
　　　無偏亦無黨，感應極分明。
　　　宜揚天尊教，提醒於眾生。
　　　世人知謹奉，獲福且延齡。
　　　虔誠而禮誦，萬國俱咸寧。
是時天尊說偈已畢。旋於玉京。諸天帝君、十方仙聖、皆大歡喜、作禮而退。信受奉行。
太上元陽上帝無始天尊說保安廣澤王靈濟普德郭星君攝魔醒世妙經終

　　寶誥　　志心皈命禮

　　鳳山大聖，雷部正神。主管三界十方九地。掌握五嶽八極四維。正一法王，考較善惡之籍。無為教主，報應禍福之由。攝伏魔精，驅除瘟疫。群生是賴，蠢動咸康。大忠大孝，大聖大慈，忠應孚惠威武英烈，保安廣澤尊王，南極都天，三界降魔，靈濟普德郭大星君，護佑天尊。

　　雷祖寶誥　　志心皈命禮

　　九天應元府，無上玉清王。化形而滿十方，談道而跨九鳳。三十六天之上，閱寶笈，考瓊書。千五百劫之先，位正真，權大化。手舉金光如意，宣說玉樞寶經。不順化作微塵，發號疾如風火，以清淨心而宏大願，以智慧力而伏諸魔。總司五雷，運心三界。群生父，萬靈師。大聖大慈大悲大願，玉皇至道，九天應元，雷聲普化天尊。

　　玉皇寶誥　　志心皈命禮

　　太上彌羅無上天妙有玄真境，渺渺紫金闕，太微玉清宮。無極無上聖，廓落發光明。寂寂浩無宗，玄範總十方。湛寂真常道，恢漠大神通。蒼穹真老，妙圓清靜。智慧辨才，至道至尊，三界師，混元祖，無為勝主，四生慈父，高天上聖，大慈仁者，十號圓滿，萬德周身，無量度人。拔生死昔，諸佛之師，眾聖之王，清淨自然。覺王如來，太上開天，執符御歷，含真體道，金闕雲宮，九穹御歷，萬道無為，通明大殿，昊天金闕，玉皇大天尊，玄穹高上帝。

　　完經讚

　　廣澤尊王，救苦玄門。鳳山頂上放光明。感應普天聞，度厄延生，持誦保安寧。

　　　光緒戊寅七夕榕城問心軒奉鳳山寺錢太保降筆敬書飭頒刊送凡誦經者必先齋
　　　戒盥沐誠心定氣然後叩齒演音和聲朗誦隨感通靈祈無不應。

NOTES

INTRODUCTION

1. "Fujian Sites Restored to Buddhists," *China Daily*, March 25, 1986. Tremendous amounts of money have been donated by Buddhist organizations in Japan, Hong Kong, and Southeast Asia to the reconstruction of temples and the restoration of Buddhist libraries. One example is the Chengtian si, founded in Quanzhou in the Tang dynasty, torn down and replaced with stone factory buildings during the Cultural Revolution. In the last few years the stone factories have been dismantled and relocated, all at the expense of the Singapore Buddhist organization sponsoring the reconstruction. Traditional building techniques and materials were used to rebuild the temple halls at a huge cost. The government has itself spent a great deal on the restoration of major Buddhist sites in Fujian: Fuzhou's Gushan, Putian's Guanghua si, Xiamen's Nan Putuo, and Zhangzhou's Nanshan si, to name a few. Government interest in tourist income seems at least to equal any interest in reviving Buddhist culture, although both Guanghua si and Nan Putuo house major Buddhist academies with three-year study programs. Along with interesting new dimensions to tourism, especially from overseas Chinese groups who sometimes do a complete circuit of the major Buddhist temples of Fujian, there has been a revival of jinxiang pilgrimages to the ancestral temples of god cults by affiliated temples within Fujian. Further evidence from the Chinese press on the resurgence of religious observances can be found in "The Practice of Excessive Restorations of Shrines and Temples in Shehong County (southern Zhejiang)," where we read that in 1986 there were over one hundred newly restored temples in the seventy-five townships of the county. See also Jan (1984). Further evidence comes from periodic articles in local Fujian and Guangdong papers criticizing the large numbers of people burning incense in temples, or announcing the arrest of so-called "god (temple) committees," accused of extorting money from the community, or providing cautionary accounts of women committing suicide rather than go through with a marriage by purchase. (On the state's construction of the negative category of feudal superstition evident in newspaper reports from all over China in the early 1980s, see Agnacost [1987].) These estimates and figures reveal the inadequacy of counts based on listings in regional gazetteers. Eberhard's (1964) study of temple building resulted in a total for Fujian of only 3,113 over a 1300-year period. Eberhard notes the limitations of his data base but still manages to produce interesting comparative results. On the Three-In-One Religion see J. Berling (1980) and Dean (1989b). Hahn (1989) discusses the available figures on Taoists in China and provides a commentary on reports published internally by the Taoist Association of China, entitled "Visiting Taoist Temples in the Wenzhou and Taizhou Areas," which listed 314 Quanzhen Taoists but did not even attempt to estimate the numbers of *huoju daoshi* (hearth-dwelling Taoists) of the southern, Zhengyi tradition in the area. The latter are the predominant group in Southern China. John Lagerwey reports having overheard Religious Affairs officials in Fuzhou quote a figure of four thou-

sand Taoists for Fujian, but he believes this figure is too low (personal communication, Dec. 1989).

2. The principal god-cults that originated in Fujian and northern Guangdong include those to Tianfei or Mazu (960–987), based on Meizhou Island in Putian (temple destroyed in the Cultural Revolution, reconstructed in 1987); Chen Jinggu or Linshui Furen (766–790?, or 904–?), mother temple in Gutian, restored 1981, 1984); Guo Zhongfu, or Guangze Zunwang (926?–939?) based in Nan'-an, Shishan (reconstruction nearing completion, 1987); Wu Tao (979–1035) or Baosheng Dadi (Longhai, Baijiao; repairs on the western temple were completed in 1984; the eastern temple in Qingjiao was repaired in 1989); Chen Puzu or Qingshui Zushi (1045–1101), based in Penglai, Anxi (extensive repairs completed in 1981); Wang Shengzhi or Kaimin Shengwang (Fuzhou), and Chen Yuanguang or Kaizhang Shengwang (Zhangpu); and the Sanshan Guowang (Jiexi, Guangdong, still in ruins in 1986 with reconstruction just beginning). A complete list of the subsidiary temples within Fujian that have branched off from these founding temples has not yet been compiled. The total would very likely run into the thousands (see chap. 2). These temples have well over eight hundred subsidiary temples (fenxiang) in Taiwan, according to a count by Qiu Dezai, *Taiwan Miaoshen zhuan* (1981).

3. I have published a list of the titles of the manuscripts collected up to 1987 (Dean, 1988b). The Taoist liturgical manuscripts that I collected fall into four main groups, with varying coverage for different regions: (1) liturgical manuscripts for communal jiao (sacrifice) services, family gongde (acquisition of merit) requiem services, and individual prophylactic or healing rites; (2) holy scriptures for recitation dedicated to local deities and Taoist gods; (3) a few collections of *wenjian* (documentary forms), and *mijue* (secret instructions); and (4) collections of talismans, mudras, and spells. All these manuscripts have to be considered in terms of the following issues: (a) The date of the composition of the text: The text of many liturgical manuscripts can be traced to similar texts in the Taoist Canon. These canonical texts sometimes provide elements for dating the text. As will be shown below, these manuscripts reveal the continuity of Taoist ritual traditions in Fujian from the Song dynasty to the present day. The origins of many of the rituals in these traditions can be traced much further back into the earlier layers of Taoist ritual included in the Taoist Canon. This work must be done for each important ritual in the tradition; clearly it is beyond the scope of this study. (b) The date of the manuscript copies: A few of these copies date to the early Qing. Another group dates to the mid nineteenth century. The great majority of manuscript copies have been recopied in recent years, in an effort to reassemble manuscript lineages and ritual traditions shattered during the Cultural Revolution. (c) The condition of the manuscript copies: Almost all the manuscripts are in book form, tied at the left with string. A few recent, carefully recopied manuscripts are in accordion-folded-page style. The older manuscripts are beautifully written in the traditional style. All the manuscripts written in the early 1980s, just after the end of the Cultural Revolution, were also written with a brush, but very hastily and with little regard for traditional format. The quality of the paper is generally very coarse. As the cults grew in strength and Taoism began to come back into its own, one can note vast improvements in the manuscripts copied after 1985.

These are more carefully written in the traditional style on better quality paper, and are often in accordion-folded-page form. (d) The attitude of the Taoists toward their manuscripts: Taoists regard ritual texts as the basis of their legitimacy. Texts are traditionally recopied as part of the preparation of a Taoist for his ordination as a high priest, again traditionally an honor accorded only one son in a generation. The scramble to regroup the Taoist tradition in Fujian has led many Taoists to pool manuscripts and copy back and forth, or at least share the use of a manuscript during a ritual they jointly perform. The old jokes are already resurfacing, however, like the Zhangzhou Taoist who said, "Lend a manuscript, and I guarantee you'll get it back in three years." Taoists throughout Fujian showed me great kindness and courtesy in allowing me to photograph their ritual texts. Their attitude seemed to be that, as long as I was doing this out of an interest in researching the Taoist tradition, that was fine. But to give the texts to any local person who showed interest would break a religious prohibition. A less important consideration was that others would try to set themselves up as Taoists. But such illegitimate activity has little chance of enduring success, even under the troubled conditions of the post–Cultural Revolution era. Local elders know what kind of questions to ask about a person's training and qualifications. These manuscripts can be compared to similar collections and published manuscripts from Taiwan and Southeast Asia as well as to sources in the Ming Taoist Canon (Schipper, 1966b; Saso, 1975; Ofuchi, 1983; Kamata, 1986). The manuscripts gathered in Fujian cover the same variety of rituals as are performed on Taiwan. In several cases, I have found evidence of ritual traditions unknown or lost on Taiwan. Nevertheless, there are many continuities between Fujian and Taiwanese Taoist ritual traditions and manuscript lineages. The parallel but independent development of Taoist ritual traditions in Southeast China and Southeast Asia can begin to be documented and studied with the aid of this material. Included among the manuscripts from Fujian are well-known Taoist scriptures such as the (CT1) *Lingbao wuliang durenjing* (The Precious Treasure Invaluable Scripture of the Salvation of Mankind); (CT 1442) *Taishang sanyuan sifu shezui jiefan xiaozai yansheng baoming miaojing* (The Marvelous Scripture on the Preservation of Life, the Prolongation of Years, the Elimination of Disaster, the Eradication of Difficulties, and the Pardoning of Wrongdoing of the Most High Three Primordials and the Four Headquarters); (CT 10, 13) *Gaoshang yuhuang benxing jijing* (Collected Scriptures of the Basic Actions of the Jade Emperor on High); and the (CT 16) *Jiutian yingyuan leisheng puhua tianzun yushu baojing* (The Precious Scripture of the Jade Pivot of the Heavenly Worthy of Universal Transformation by the Sound of Thunder of the Hall of Responses of the Nine Heavens). Here the primary issues are those of the integrity of textual transmission and the function of the scriptures in the different ritual traditions. Although the scriptures devoted to various gods that I collected were not signed, it is obvious that they were the work of either Taoist or Buddhist priests, and most often the former. Some were written by planchette. They were normally printed as an act of devotion by a group of contributors, whose names and titles, if any, would be listed at the end of their editions. These scriptures would be recited during rituals in honor of the gods. Some of the scriptures explicitly call for the formation of lay scripture recitation groups. In times of need, the scriptures call for the employment of Buddhists or Taoists to recite them in the homes of individual devotees. Aside from scriptures re-printed in gazetteers or among Taoist and sectarian manuscript collections, I also found independently printed and distributed scriptures dedicated to local gods. These manuscripts should be compared with the great ritual compendia of the Song included in the Taoist Canon (Boltz, 1987, chap. 1), as well as to earlier collections of the liturgical materials from the Zhengyi and Lingbao traditions. Clearly, the study of Taoist ritual has a great deal of material to draw upon; how-ever, far more work remains to be done in this field.

4. I traveled a great deal around Fujian, partly in order to document the resur-gence of religion around the principal cults, and partly because this seemed to me to be the best way to conduct my research under the circumstances. During 1985–1987, I spent altogether over three months living in villages and temples during religious festivals. Six or seven months were spent traveling on research trips around Fujian. I also frequently went on day trips from Xiamen to conduct fieldwork. The remainder of my time was spent in libraries throughout Fujian and with my family who lived in a residential community with a Chinese family on Gulangyu Island. Unfortunately, until research conditions in China change fun-damentally, it will continue to be difficult to conduct in-depth studies of the tradi-tional religious activities of particular communities.

5. There is a growing body of studies dealing with the history of specific cults in China. The Chinese folklorist Wei Yingqi took up the study of Linshui Furen, Guangze Zunwang, and Tianfei in his *Fujian Sanshenzhi* (1928). The Mazu cult has been examined by Li Xianzhang (1979), Watson (1985), Boltz (1986), and Jiang (1990). Brigitte Berthier (1988) has written a fascinating study of the Lin-shui Furen cult. E. L. Davis (1985) and Lagerwey (1987a) have investigated the cult of the Immortal Xu brothers (fl. 937–946). Schipper (1990) illustrates the development of fenxiang networks with the cult of Baosheng Dadi. Valerie Han-sen (1990) has examined the growth of several regional cults in Huzhou pre-fecture in the Song dynasty. Terry Kleeman (1988) has studied the evolution of the Wenchang cult from its beginnings in Sichuan in the Song dynasty. David Johnson (1985) has focused on the rise of city gods in the Tang and Song dynas-ties. Mano Senryū (1979) traced the evolution of Wudang shan and the cult of Zhenwu; see also Grootaers (1952) and Seaman (1987). The cult of Guandi has been studied by Duara (1988b), while that of Guanyin has been analyzed by Dudbridge (1978) and Yu Chün-fang (1992). Richard van Glahn (1991) and Ursula Cedzich (1985) discussed the Wuxian cult. Zurndorfer (1989) mentions local cults in Huizhou. Other studies are listed in L. Thompson's (1980) bibliog-raphy of Western studies of Chinese religion. Ter Haar (1990) has commented on the origins and developmental patterns of several cults in Fujian, including those of Baosheng Dadi, Qingshui Zushi, and Guangze Zunwang. He suggests that cults often originate around "hungry ghosts," dangerously marginal figures without social moorings who almost accidentally demonstrate supernatural power and develop a following. In this case, the evidence appears to best fit the case of Guangze Zunwang (chap. 4), who, paradoxically but predictably, is the cult most heavily superscribed with Confucian interpretations (see Duara, 1988b). Ter Haar's second point, that the development of the cult follows

the expansion of trade-networks within economic macroregions, is well taken. Ter Haar has unfortunately mistaken the personal name of Wu Zhenren: it should be Wu Tao, not Wu Ben: the character *tao* is written with a *da* (large) on top with a *shi* (ten) below. Moreover, the character is incorrectly printed as *tao* (set) in K. Schipper's article in the same collection (Schipper, 1990: 401).

6. Sivin (1966) comments that alchemical experimentation also should be seen as a scientific process, an effort to manipulate space and time that is an end unto itself, rather than a goal-oriented magical effort. Of course, Chinese religion was multifaceted, and Strickmann has shown how alchemy during the Six Dynasties period became linked with messianic movements into the elaboration of ritual suicide designed to translate the adept instantaneously into the ranks of the immortals (Strickmann, 1979a, 1981). Religion contains contradictory tendencies toward transcendence and the preservation of social order.

7. Susan Mann (1987) has recently applied Weber's concept in her study of merchant and state relations in late Imperial China. Mann (ibid.) raises the important point that boundaries between wealthy merchants and gentry were increasingly meaningless in late Imperial China. I suggest that as leaders of local society, they joined in cult worship. Mann is primarily concerned with an account of the changing relationships between merchant associations practicing "liturgical governance" and state efforts to develop tax farming strategies in the context of modern state building. Mann finds that merchant associations and guilds were traditionally called upon by the state to collect commercial taxes and remit them to the state. Their liturgical functions included the regulation of markets and prices. After 1850 the establishment of the likin tax on the movement of goods represented a deep state intrusion into an area formerly under the control of local merchant associations, which provoked a spirited response. Thus her use of the term "liturgy" is primarily restricted to a discussion of merchant associations, markets, and tax policy. Mann does however remark that although "gentry" were excluded from liturgical tax management in the Qing they continued to perform a wide variety of liturgical services at the local level. Her case study of the Li lineage in Shandong in fact suggests that a gentry-merchant lineage could control a wide range of "liturgical" functions in certain townships. Interestingly, the town maintained a temple to a deified ancestor of the Li lineage. I would suggest that at this level the liturgical activities of local elites can be shown to function within the framework of ritual paradigms.

8. By way of illustration, I list below (table 3) the gods worshiped at the various Fujian district-based merchant associations in Beijing in the 1930s drawn from the *Minzhong huiguan zhi* (Gazetteer of the Landsmannschaften of Fujian [in Beijing]), a source neglected in Niida (1950) and Negeshi (1953). Most *huiguan* also worshiped the spirit-tablets of their founders, along with assorted local sages. The entries on Shaowu are the most complete. These list Guandi, Xuantan Zhao Yuanshuai Laoye, Caishen, District City God, Shaowu City God, Xunxu Houwang, Jianning District City God, Guangze District City God, and the Tudi Gong. Also worshiped were spirit-tablets for three Song sages, three founders of the huiguan, one tablet for "all unworshiped spirits," and one tablet for "all [visitors from Shaowu] who have died in Beijing." The rules of each huiguan are

TABLE 3
Local Gods Worshiped by Fujian Merchant Associations in Beijing

Huiguan	Mazu	Wenchang	Citygod	Caishen	Tudigong	Guandi	Other
Fujian	X						
Zhangzhou	X						
Zhangzhou	X						
Tingzhou	X			X			
Yanshao	X						
Jianning	X						
Tongan		X	X	X			X
Jinjiang		X	X	X	X		X
Longyan		X	X			X	X
Shaowu			X(2)		X	X	X
Quanzhou		X	X		X		X

given, and again the Shaowu rules provide the most detail on the annual rituals, daily worship, fees collected for ritual purposes, and liturgical functions (weddings, funerals, business contacts, etc.) performed by the association.

9. Vandermeersch (1980) has criticized the notion of "magic" as applied to Chinese religion. He suggests instead the importance of an appreciation of the liturgical basis of Chinese "morphological thought" which attempts to comprehend the universe in terms of correspondences. These criticisms apply to Weber's assessment of Taoism as well.

10. Helen Siu has recently (1990) argued that the traditional social networks underlying traditional rituals have been eliminated by state intervention in the Pearl River area of Guangdong, resulting in the fragmentation of the ritual tradition. The fragments have been reassembled into new configurations by people reconstructing contemporary culture and have thereby taken on new meanings. She contrasts these developments with those in Hong Kong and Taiwan, where she points to market forces as responsible for the fragmentation of traditional culture. On the basis of my fieldwork in Fujian and Northeast Guangdong (Chaozhou and Hakka areas), I can state that I have found clear evidence of wide-scale community involvement in festivals for the gods, funerals, marriages, ancestral worship, etc. My impression was that the pace of "restoration" of "traditional" networks and ritual observances in Guangdong was several years behind that of Fujian. Each region of China has its unique social history, and reveals unique social formations. In the case of the Pearl River delta, one might point to the development of high-level religious (and lineage) centers that transcend local ties, paralleled by the proliferation of autonomous households. Intermediate religious and social organizations tied to localities appear to be less significant than is the case for Fujian or Taiwan where one can find clear examples of nested hierarchies of multi-leveled local religious systems. Furthermore, this area has a long history of commercialization, and was the focus of an intense post-1978 planned economic reform. Only a full-scale comparative inquiry into the historical, eco-

nomic, political, and especially the religious forces that have effected developments in various parts of China could provide data for an exploration of the new role of ritual in contemporary China. Certainly the experience of Taiwan in the past few decades suggests that for Minnan culture as a whole, the expansion of market forces need not necessarily slow the scope or power of popular religion.

CHAPTER ONE
TAOISM IN FUJIAN

1. The current population of this area is about ten million. The local dialect is Hokkien, or Southern Min. Regional theater and music, sung in local dialect, and performed during the festivals of the gods, plays a key role in defining the local subculture (Ward, 1979, 1985). The principal theatrical forms sung in this region are Gezai xi, Gaojia xi, Liyuan xi, and marionette Kuilei xi. The first two are relatively recent forms, while the last two retain a portion of the Nanxi Southern Theater repertoire of the Southern Song. The earliest extant scripts date from the early Ming. The local ballad tradition, Nanguan, or Southern Pipes, is related to Liyuan theater, and of similar antiquity. This musical form includes instrumental suites performed by a quartet of vertical bamboo flute, southern *pipa* (lute; horizontally held), plucked two-string banjo, and three-stringed viol played with a bow. A singer joins the ensemble to sing arias reminiscent of troubadour ballads, beating the time with a wooden clacker. The following population distribution and average income statistics for the Zhangzhou-Quanzhou region in 1984 are drawn from *Fujian Diqu jingji* (Fujian Regional Economy, Fuzhou, 1986). The greater Quanzhou region is made up of the city and surroundings of Quanzhou plus 7 districts, divided into 102 counties and 28 towns, with 2,245 villages. Quanzhou region's total population: 5,053,000. Overseas Chinese population: 3,260,000. Average yearly income: workers, 950 yuan; farmers, 320 yuan. The greater Zhangzhou region is made up of the city and 9 districts, 23 towns, 85 counties, and 1,690 villages. Population: 3,760,000. Overseas population: 700,000. Average income: workers, 828 yuan; farmers, 315 yuan. The greater Xiamen region now includes 3 city quarters, a suburban quarter, an outlying quarter, and a Tongan district. The latter district includes the district seat, 2 towns, 11 counties, and 220 villages. Xiamen area total population: 1,005,600. Average income: workers, 1,023 yuan; farmers, 396 yuan. I also mention the Xinghua region, especially in chapter 3. This region is made up of Putian and Xianyou and is now known as the Putian city administrative unit. It contains 2 cities, 37 counties, 8 towns, and 908 villages. Population: 2,351,000. Overseas population: 305,000. Average income: workers, 817 yuan; farmers, 264 yuan. (Official exchange rates in 1987 made the U.S. dollar equal 3.6 yuan but unofficial rates of exchange were closer to 1:6.)

2. The god of Wuyi Mountains is mentioned in *diquan* used in funerals in Nan'an (Dean, 1988a) as well as in *wufang zhenwen* of wood and brick employed in an *Ancu* Consecration of an ancestral temple in Tongan in 1985 (Dean, 1989a). See also Ofuchi, 1983. The early awareness of the mountain and its god may be related to a Han city located in nearby Chongan xian currently under

excavation by an archaeological team from the Fujian Provincial Museum. Several gazetteers have been written on this mountain. Brook (1988:216–18, nos. 17–23) lists seven, dating from 1558, 1576, 1582, 1643, 1710, 1718, and 1753.

3. *Juan* 100, of the *Fujian Tongzhi* of 1868–1871 provides brief biographical notes on some ninety-nine Taoists and seventy-six "immortals" from Fujian. Immortals, as distinguished from Taoists, are those who disappeared by *shijie* (deliverance of the corpse) or by flying off in broad daylight. Taoists, on the other hand, are those who instead merely hid themselves away and transformed while seated (died in meditation), or who acted as specialists in exorcisms, or those who returned to life despite having been properly buried. The biographies are arranged chronologically as follows: Taoists—Tang, 2; Five Dynasties, 3; Song, 44; Yuan, 10; Ming, 38; Qing, 2—Total: 99. Immortals—Antiquity, 1; Shang, 1; Zhou, 1; Qin, 7; Han, 6; Wu, 2; Jin, 2; Liang, 1; Sui, 3; Tang, 20; Five Dynasties, 2; Song, 27; Yuan, 2; Ming, 1—Total: 76. Combined total of Taoists and Immortals: 175.

4. Chen Shouyuan, a Taoist from Minxian, was given the Baohuang gong by the Min Ruler, Wang Yanchun, who made him a Tianshi (Celestial Master). Chen built a Sanqing dian (Hall of the Three Pure Ones) within the palace. He was notably extravagant, using gold to gild the Baohuang Gong. He had statues made of the deified form of Laozi (Wushi Tianzun Lao Jun), and held Taoist rituals day and night (Schafer, 1954: 96–100, quotes the *Wudai Shi* [History of the Five Dynasties], and *Zizhi tongjian*: *juan* 277: 283–84).

5. Berthier (1988) and Wei (1929) quote a Song inscription and some Ming inscriptions on the cult. Little can be found in the Taoist Canon (on which, see further, chap. 1). The *Fujian tongzhi j.* 100 adds little, merely mentioning Lushan in the biography of three Taoists from the Song dynasty named Cheng, Yao, and Yin. The first two were from Ningde, and had refined themselves through inner alchemical meditation on Huodong Mountain, where they had finally attained the elixir and sprouted feathers, and departed this dusty realm. Yin, together with one Yang, were from the Miaoxi region outside Ningde. Both had studied Taoist ritual methods at Lushan. Yin's arts were more refined than Yang's, who felt jealous and went after him. Yin split open a rock and entered Hetong Mountain. There he met an unusual being who transmitted a miraculous method which allowed him to turn into an immortal (100.1.11a). A second mention comes under the Ming, when one Song Jiugong from Fuzhou is said to have studied the ritual methods of Lu shan in a cave in the Guixi cliff before ascending to heaven in broad daylight. Fieldwork reveals a confusing picture of a vibrant ritual tradition originating in northern Fujian that has worked its way into the ritual practice of Taoist priests and Ritual Masters from across Fujian to Taiwan, and across South China to Guangxi and perhaps beyond. The rites of this tradition focus on childbirth, childhood-related dangers, and many individual rites for the correction of ill fortune.

6. Boltz (1987) has briefly outlined the main Taoist movements of the Song dynasty and listed their principal surviving scriptures and liturgies in the Taoist Canon. The Tianxin zhengfa tradition is mentioned in the *Fujian Tongzhi* (1926:100.1.3a) with reference to Tan Zixiao of Quanzhou, a favorite of Chen

Shouyuan, the court Taoist of Wang Yanchun (R. 926–30). Tan claimed to have dug up texts transmitted by Zhang Daoling which he deciphered as the Tianxin zhengfa ritual methods of exorcistic healing. He is said to have employed these methods often on the Min Ruler, who gave him the title of Feathered Guest of the Golden Gate, Master of Orthodox Unity. After the collapse of the Min kingdom, he fled to Lu shan in Jiangxi, where he is said to have conducted a successful interrogation (*kaozhi*) of a specter in a well and to have thereby succeeded in exorcising it. According to Lu You's *Nan Tang shu*, he became a patriarch of the Tianxin school (100.1.3a). The Qingwei (Pure Tenebrity) tradition is represented in the *Fujian tongzhi* by Liu Mengding, a native of Chunnan, in the Song dynasty, who is said to have received the Huang Lei Tu (Yellow Thunder Chart) and the ritual methods of the Qingwei school. He is said to have specialized in the performance of Lingbao Jiao and funerals, and to have presided over a great Yellow Register Zhai Requiem service in the Jiulong Belvedere of Shaowu. Also, one Huang Xianzhong from Dongyang is said to have received a scroll of the secret methods of the Qingwei school from a lunar being, a man of the Tao, while meditating in the Wuyi Mountains. Finally, one Zhang Kezhen, hao, Pingxin, from Fuzhou, received the Yellow Thunder Chart and the ritual methods of the Qingwei school at the Guanghua si in Chongan. He used these to great avail to quell demons, induce rain, and survive dangers (quoting the *Min Shu* of He Qiaoyuan), 100.1.9b. The related Five Thunder Rites (Wu Lei fa), are mentioned in relation to Zhang Zhizong, a Taoist in the Wenchang Belvedere of Songxi district, who lived into his eighties in the Hongzhi period. The Longhu Mountains are mentioned in two Song biographies. Qiu Yundi of Zhangzhou became a Taoist in the year 1000. He resided in the Zhangzhou Taiqing Belvedere. Sometime between 1008 and 1016, he received a Taoist register at Longhushan and was thereafter able to cause demons and spirits to work for him. He received honors and titles in 1046 and in 1054. In the Ming, two Taoists from Min xian are mentioned as having stayed at Longhu shan. These are Lin Jinle and Huang Jietong. The latter was a Taoist in the Chongxi Belvedere there. The biographical notes on Lin Jingle, *zi* Zisu, from Minxian, suggest that at least at the level of officially sanctioned Taoism, there was considerable coordination at a national level. Lin served as an official at Longhu shan. In the Yongle period, he was appointed Taolusi Youyanfa. He held positions successively at Wudang Mountain, Mount Tai, Taihe Mountain, and the Dasheng Nanyangong. He eventually was promoted to the rank of Military Commissioner.

    7. The Taoist Canon has been edited seven or eight times, with one exception always at Imperial command. The earliest catalog of Taoist sources was ordered by Song Mingdi (r. 465–72) and compiled by Lu Xiujing (406–77) in 471. Entitled *Sandong jingshu mulu* (An Index of the Scriptural Writings of the Three Caverns), the work totaled 1,200 *juan* (scrolls *or* chapters). In 748, Emperor Tang Xuanzong (r. 713–56) ordered the compilation and copying of the *Sandong qionggang* (Exquisite Compendium of the Three Caverns), totaling between 3,700 to 7,300 juan. In 990, Emperor Song Zhenzong (r. 998–1022) ordered Wang Qinruo (962–1025) and others, including Zhang Zhunfang (fl. 1008–29), to prepare the *Da Song tiangong baozang* (Precious Canon of the Celestial Palace

of the Great Song) in 4,564 juan (see van der Loon, 1984). In 1114, Emperor Song Huizong (r. 1101–25) ordered the compilation of the *Zhenghe wanshou daozang* (Taoist Canon of Everlasting Life of the Zhenghe period) in 5400 juan. This was the first printed Taoist Canon. The blocks were carved in Fuzhou between 1118–1120, and later transfered to Kaifeng, where they formed the basis for the *Da Jin xuandu baozang* (Precious Canon of the Mystic Capital of the Great Jin), totaling 6,455, completed in 1192. The next Taoist Canon, the *Xuandu Baozang* (Precious Canon of the Mystic Capital), totaling 7,000 juan, was published in 1244 by the Quanzhen Taoist Masters Song Defang (1183–1247) and his disciple Qin Zhian (1188–1244) in Pingyang (Shanxi). Unfortunately, in 1281, Khublai Khan decreed that all Taoist books and printing blocks be burned, with the exception of the *Daodejing*. In 1406 Ming Chengzu (r. 1403–24) ordered the forty-third generation Celestial Master Zhang Yuchu (1361–1410) and Shao Yizheng to compile the *Da Ming Daozang Jing* (Scriptures of the Taoist Canon of the Great Ming) in 5,318 juan. This edition of the Canon is often called the *Zhengtong Taozang* because it was completed in 1444, during the Zhengtong reign period (1436–49). Emperor Ming Shenzong approved the reprinting of this edition in 1598 on behalf of his mother, and soon after ordered the fiftieth generation Celestial Master Zhang Guoxiang (d. 1611) to compile the 240 *juan Xu Daozangjing* (Scriptures in Supplement to the Taoist Canon). This collection was affixed to the Canon in 1607. Only three sets of this Canon appear to have survived into the twentieth century. Two sets were in the *Baiyun guan* in Beijing and Shanghai. Several missing texts in these editions were replaced in 1845 and 1866, respectively (van der Loon, 1984; Boltz, 1987). A complete set is said to be kept in the Chungshansi of Taiyuan.

    8. These inscriptions are among some five hundred unpublished inscriptions that I have gathered in the Minnan region of Fujian in collaboration with Professor Zheng Zhenman of the Institute of Historical Research of Xiamen University. These materials will be combined with extant literary sources and published in separate volumes under the title *Fujian zongjiaoshi beiming huibian* (Epigraphical Materials on the History of Religion in Fujian) by the Fujian Renmin chubanshe in 1993. By way of example, the *Chongxiu gongde beiji* (Stele Inscription on the Merit Won by Restoration [of the Temple]), written in 1793, describes the founding of a Zhenwu temple dedicated to Xuantian Shangdi in Zhangpu district by Taoist Master Li in 976. The temple fell under the protection of the Zhao lineage and had been restored in the Yongzheng period (1723–35) by a lineage leader in consort with a local official. The restoration commemorated in this inscription had taken place sixty years later, with support from many lineage members, but also from various ship's captains, indicating a wider base of support.

    9. A stele from Putian entitled *Chongjian Chenghuangmiao fuji* (Supplementary Record of the Reconstruction of the City God Temple) from 1630 shows the leading role of Taoist priests in the restoration of the City God temple of Xinghua fu, where buildings were set aside for resident Taoists. A stele erected in 1730 in Putian entitled *Chongxiu yuanmiao guan* (Commemorative stele on the Restoration of the Belvedere of Primal Mystery), describes the role of a Taoist priest named [Zhuo] Maoqiao in the construction of a temple to Wenchang, god of

literature and literati, and the Wuxian, gods of the five manifestations, in the grounds of the Belvedere of Primal Mystery. The stele goes on to note that the temple grounds also contained a Temple to the Eastern Peak. The Sanqing dian, Hall of the Three Pure Ones, still stands in Putian, and is one of the few surviving Song dynasty buildings in Fujian. The entry in the *Putian xianzhi* (1926:4:46) on the Belvedere records restorations by the Taoist Fang Rudiao and Li Zhisheng in 1556. A District Magistrate built an entranceway in 1564. In 1581 a number of Taoists including Zhuo Maoqiao and Chen Junyan restored and expanded the belvedere.

The *Chengnan dingjian Xingshengmiao chongji Wuhuang dadi beiji* (Stele Inscription on the Construction of the Temple of Uplifted Sanctity South of the City [of Xianyou] to Worship the Five Great Emperors) erected in 1650 by the resident Taoist priest Xu Lifu, describes a dream-vision that led to the invitation of the cult of the Five Emperor gods from Fuzhou to the temple. This is an example of Taoist priests intervening to help a local cult expand. The *Guchenggong xiangdeng chantianji* (Record of the property and lands for provision of incense and lamp[oil] to the Gucheng Temple) of 1680 indicates a preference for Buddhists over Taoists because the latter keep wives and thus are impure. Several other steles indicate that Buddhist monks have taken charge of a temple with clear Taoist affiliations. A set of steles in the Lingyundian of Putian, dedicated to the cult of *Haotian jinque Yuhuangshangdi* (The High Jade Emperor of the Golden Gate of August Heaven) indicate that a group of thirty-three villages rotated the organization of the costs of the temple, including the upkeep of resident Buddhist monks. The *Shengquangong jinyuebei* (Stele Recording a Prohibition at the Temple of the Saintly Spring) of 1720 records the banning of a resident Taoist because of his illicit sale of temple lands for burial plots.

10. The 1798 edition of the *Tongan xianzhi* (j.10, 14a,b.), remarked that the temple was in poor repair at the time the gazetteer was compiled, and that neighbors were moving into the side halls of the temple. Further major repairs were carried out in 1540 and again in 1747, the latter under the auspices of District Magistrate Zhang Quan. Currently the temple is in very poor condition. The back halls have collapsed or been taken over by neighbors and the original god statues have been destroyed and replaced with names written on red paper.

11. Ōfuchi Ninji, in his *Chūgokujin no shūkyō girei* (1983), provides a description of the Tainan ritual tradition. He also reproduces the texts transformed by burning in the course of Taoist jiao and Taoist funeral services. The latter rituals require some 66 documents: 11 are *die* (Passes); 5 are *shuwen* (various kinds of Memorials); 26 are *guan* (Announcements or Passports); 17 are *fuming* (Talismanic orders); 2 are *sheshu* (Documents of Pardon); 2 are *biao* (Messages); 1 is a *shen* (Recommendation); 2 are *quan* (Contracts); and 2 are *zhuang* (Reports). This is quite a modest number of documents. Some medieval liturgical compilations call for the burning of hundreds of Messages alone. Some of these documents, such as the Memorial, or its posted counterpart, the Proclamation, *bang*, are addressed to the highest gods. They detail the title of the Taoist priest, the name and dates of the deceased, and those of their descendants sponsoring the funeral. The Memorial also lists the rituals that will be performed in the course of

the funeral, and expresses the wishes of the descendants that the soul of the ancestor will ascend to paradise and shower them with good fortune. Other documents command lesser gods under the control of the Taoist priest (and listed on his register [lu]) to transmit messages or to guide the soul to the altar from the dark underworld or, subsequently, along the treacherous path to paradise. Some are addressed to the soul of the dead, referred to over the course of the ritual first as *wanghun* (lost soul), and then, as more and more steps are taken to ensure the purification, consecration, and repayment of the debt of the soul, as *zhenghun* (correct soul).

12. Ch'u Kun-liang [Qiu Kunliang] (1986) has studied the ritual repertoire of Chinese theater. He has discussed the varying repertoire of different local theatrical traditions on Taiwan. These are, for Beiguan theater in Taiwan: (1) (a) *Tianguan cifu* (the Heavenly Officer bestows good fortune); (b) *Zui baxian* (the Eight Drunken Immortals); (c) *Pantao hui* (the Banquet of Peaches); and (d) *Fengxiang* (the Enfeoffment of the Minister); (2) *Tiao jiaguan* (masked mime of "the Promotion of the Official"); (3) *Jinbang* (The Pantheon Honors the Stage); and (4) the dance of Chong Kui (Chu, 1986). In the Zhangzhou region of Fujian, *Xiangju*, or *Gezaixi*, has preserved a richer ritual repertoire than the similar groups in Taiwan. They usually perform the following three short acts: (1) *Tianfei songzi* (The Heavenly Maiden Sends a Child); (2) *Tiao Jiaguan* (see above); and (3) *Baxian* (Dean, 1986). I have already mentioned the dance of Xiang Gong in the Quanzhou Marionette theater above. The "Heavenly Maiden Sends a Child" involves the Queen Mother of the West, *Xi Wangmu*, sending a *xiucai*, a young scholar with his wife and her handmaiden from the stage into the temple, where they place a dollbaby on the altar, a godchild for the god. Repeated performances of this ritual were sponsored by individuals, who would thereby accrue merit. Like the *Tiao Jiaguan* this scene emphasizes the close relationship of the traditional scholar-gentry elite with the gods. The theatrical troupe sometimes would join the processions of the gods or take part in certain of the rituals. For example, In Anxi I was told that actors from the *Gaojia xi* troupes at religious occasions would accompany a procession of Taoist priests to a nearby stream to perform the "Invitation of Water" rite. Ward and Tanaka Issei (1985) have examined the values portrayed in opera performances held invariably on stages facing the doors of the temple of the local gods during religious celebrations. Piet van de Loon has underlined the ritual origins and functions of Chinese theater (1977). Schipper (1966a) has commented on parallels between marionettes and mediums, and a second parallel between Taoist priests and the god of marionettes as joking intermediaries between men and the gods. See the description of the simultaneous performance of Mulian plays by Taoists and Buddhist monks engaged in ritual competition during parallel funeral rites in Nan'an (Dean, 1990a). The study of regional opera in its fundamentally liturgical context will provide new understandings of this essential dimension of Chinese popular culture. During three of the jiao rituals I observed near Zhangzhou, the ritual repertoire was performed by the *Gezai xi* troupe just prior to the Presentation of the Memorial. In a five-day jiao near Zhangzhou, conducted in 1985 by a family of Taoists from southern Anxi, these performances coincided on the second and third day with the outdoor Noon Offering performed by the priests (Dean, 1990b).

CHAPTER TWO
THE GREAT EMPEROR WHO PROTECTS LIFE

1. Schafer (1954) describes the career of Wang Shengzhi. Epigraphical material on Wang Shengzhi (r. 909–25) is included in Chen Qiren (1934). This includes:

1. *Wangshengzhi dezheng bei* (Inscription on the Virtuous Governing of Wang Shengzhi). Fuzhou. A.D. 906. 2:12b-18b.
2. *Chongxiu zhongyiwang miaobei* (Inscription on the Restoration of the Temple of the Loyal and Lovely King). Fuzhou. A.D. 976. 3:3b-12b.

The original steles and artifacts from his tomb can be seen at his shrine in Fuzhou and at the Fujian Provincial Museum in Fuzhou. A man from Nan'an told me that in his village there were two principal lineages, the Ye and the Wang. The Ye were far more numerous and powerful and each year at New Year's held a procession of their deified ancestor, Huize Zunwang (see chap. 4). However, the Wang were becoming more powerful and so they planned to carry their statue of Kaimin Shengwang Wang Shengzhi, whom they took to be their clan ancestor, on a procession at New Year's for the first time ever.

2. According to a legend told at both the Baijiao and the Qingjiao temple, the front halls of the Qingjiao temple were torn down by Zheng Chenggong to secure wood for the construction of masts for his fleet. It is difficult to say what lies behind this story. Accounts at Baijiao maintain that the village supported Zheng and sent a large group of villagers with him to Taiwan. They further maintain that Qing forces encircled Baijiao and were preparing to destroy the village when Zheng's forces arrived from Xiamen and drove them back. They do say, however, that the people of Baijiao tore down their houses to provide materials for the defense of Haicheng against Qing forces. Perhaps this latter incident underlies the legend?

3. Yang Jun received his juren degree in 1852. He was a keen observer of the enormous midcentury revolts. He wrote congratulatory letters to Zeng Guofan (1811–72) and Zeng Guoquan (1824–80) after the defeat of the Taiping troops in Nanjing. Then he presented his views on the crisis in Fujian, brought on by invading remnant Taiping armies and large-scale local revolts under secret-society leadership, to Zuo Zongtang (1812–85), who had been assigned the task of defeating the Taipings in Zhejiang and Fujian in 1863–1866. He saw the effects of the warfare on common people and complained about government troop excesses in some of his poems. Zuo appointed him to head the Zhengyi tang shuzhu Publishing House set up in 1864 in Fuzhou. In 1867 Yang accompanied Zeng on his campaign west to Shenxi and Gansu. According to a student's account in the preface to his posthumously collected parallel prose, Yang held a position equivalent to a military advisor. But Yang returned when news of his wife's death reached him. His letter of resignation and thanks was written in 1875. Probably during his travels west and back to Fujian, he visited major Taoist sanctuaries and famous mountains, writing poems to record his impressions. Upon his return he was offered a position by the Xiamen military commander to organize his countrymen in Jinjiang into self-defense units and military camps. Apparently he declined,

preferring to spend a few years teaching in Confucian academies in Zhangzhou, Jinmen, and Xiamen. In 1881 he suffered from illness, and one of his three sons made a special trip to Fengshan si (see chap. 4) to ask for the god's assistance. This was granted, and Yang reports feeling great relief and thanksgiving upon recovering. Yang also sponsored the publication of five Chan Buddhist scriptures. He wrote a manuscript of a collection of notes and poems on Fujian by several authors, including himself. A copy survives in the Beijing University Rare Books collection. He included a divinatory text for the interpretation of astral phenomena. Yang is said to have built up a collection of seventy thousand volumes. He was especially fond of inscriptions and calligraphy. He died in 1890, and his sons organized the publication of his collected works in 1892. These were called the *Guanhuitang wenji* (Literary Collection of the Hall of Regret over the Official Cap). They include his collected poetry, ryhme prose, parallel prose, couplets, and standard prose. The latter category includes a number of *Memorials* written for Buddhist and Taoist rituals, as well as a *Proclamation for a Pudu for the Universal Salvation of All of Fujian*.

4. Sources for the study of the Baosheng Dadi cult:

   (1) *Ciji miaoji* (The Temple of Benevolent Salvation [in Baijiao]), by Zhuang Xia (*jinshi*, 1181, died 1217, ultimately Vice Director of the Ministry of War) is included in the *Haicheng xianzhi* (1762), the *Quanzhou fuzhi* (1763), the *Tong an xianzhi* (1929), and in Yang Jun's *Sishen zhi: Baijiao zhilue* (1872).

   (2) *Cijigong bei* (Palace-Temple of Benevolent Salvation Inscription [in Qingjiao]), written in 1209 by Yang Zhi (*jinshi* 1208), an Instructor in Gaozhou, later District Magistrate of Changxi, and finally Vice Prefect of Guangzhou. Found in the *Haicheng xianzhi* (1762), the *Zhangzhou fuzhi* (1877), and excerpted in Yang Jun (1872).

   (3) *Song huiyao jigao* (Collected Drafts of the Essentials of the Song Dynasty), edited by Xu Song (1781–1848), Taipei, Shijie shuju, 1964, vol. 2, pp. 848, 865. Two entries on enfeoffments of the god and the bestowal of plaques to the temple in 1166 and 1207. 4. The *Bamin tongzhi* (1483 ed. in the Library of Congress) briefly mentions the Cijigong.

   (4) He Qiaoyuan's (1567–89) *Min Shu* (1621–29) provides information on many of the legends that grew around the cult.

   (5) *Haicheng xianzhi* (1762): (a) an account of jinxiang processions from Haicheng to Qingjiao under the Annual Customs Section, 15:14a-b; (b) description of the temple, 17:3a; (c) hagiography of the god in the *Fangwai* section, listed among the "Immortals," and including comments on the nature of the god, 19:7a; (d) *Temple Inscriptions* includes (1) and (2) above in the *Literature Section*, 22:1, 5.

   (6) *Quanzhou fuzhi* (1763): (a) an account of the procession of the god together with Tianfei (Mazu) during the Lantern Festival in the *Annual Customs* section, 20:19a-20b; (b) accounts of the principal temples in Baijiao and Quanzhou, 16:15a, 72a-b; (c) the Zhuang Xia Inscription (1), appended to the account of the temple in 1672; (d) a hagiography of the god, in the *Fangwai* section, 65:38b-39b.

   (7) *Tongan xianzhi* (1798): (a) description of Cijigong in Baijiao and a listing of other temples where the god was worshiped in Tongan, 10:8–11.

(The most important of these was the Zhenjun miao which contained an undated inscription entitled *Wuzhen jun ji* [Record of the True Lord Wu] by one Yan Lan.) (b) hagiography of the god identical to that in (5)d, 26:19.

(8) *Xiamen zhi* (1832): mentions the Cijigong temple and several other offshoot temples in a list of seventy-eight temples in the area, 2:45–50.

(9) *Zhangzhou fuzhi* (1877): (a) mentions Cijigong in Zhao'an, and Haicheng (Qingjiao), 40:30a; (b) Yang Zhi's *Inscription* (2), 43:24.

(10) J.J.M. de Groot's *Les Fetes Annuellement Celebres a Emoui (Amoy)* (1979: [1886]), gives a vivid description of the jinxiang processions on the birthday of the god observed in 1877.

(11) Yang Jun's *Sishen zhilue: Baijiao zhilue* (1887–89): (a) notes on the setting and temples of the cult and the life of the god, followed by material on his followers and honors; (b) review of the gazetteer literature, cites (4), (5), and (7) above; (c) literature section reprints (1) and excerpts (2); (d) continues with a praise-poem by He Shanyan carved in stone by Zeng Guanghou in Quanzhou in 1815; (e) Yang Jun refers in his preface to the *Baijiao zhilue* dated 1888, to a volume entitled *Wu Dadi chuanwen* (A Life of Great Emperor Wu), by Lin Tinggui of Xiamen, which was widely read in Xiamen and the Zhanghou area. This book consisted mainly of quotes from the *Record of the True Lord Wu* by Yan Lan (in [7] and [13]). However, Yang deleted the twenty-eight, seven-character annotated quatrains at the end of Lin's book, which he stated had little to do with the god's cult. Yang included Lin's praise-poem, dated 1821. Yang also included a preface to a later edition of Lin's work on the god by Yan Qingying, entitled *Preface to an Account of Baosheng Dadi*, written in 1848; (f). Yang Jun reprints the *Summary Account of the Filiations of Baosheng Dadi*, written by Huang Huaji preceded by a preface written in 1831 by Xu Bangguang. Yang Jun states that both the preface and the *Filiations* were inscribed on separate steles in the Quanzhou Huaqiao gong, in the hand of one Zheng Yuan a Provincial Surveillance Commissioner from Changle; (g) an appendix gives the *True Scripture of the Great Emperor Who Preserves Life* (see translation above) and the *Divinatory Poems* of the god.

(12) *Maxiang tingzhi* (expanded version of 1893), contains in the appendix, pp. 82–89, the *Investigation of the True Facts concerning the Investitures (with Titles and Honors) of The Perfected One, Wu (Tao)*, by Huang Jiading. This essay cites (1) and (2), as well as inscriptions by Qing scholars Li Guangdi and Yan Lan (see [7] and [13a]). He mentions Huang Huaji's *Summary Account of the Filiations of Baosheng Dadi* (12e) as well as Yang Jun's *Baijiao zhilue* (11). He also alludes to (7), (8), and (9), as well as the *Anxi xianzhi*, and the *Fujian tongzhi*.

(13) *Tongan xianzhi* (1929 version). (a) *Ciji miao ji* (1): descriptions of the main Baosheng Dadi temple in Tongan City, the Zhenjun True Lord Temple, with an appended *Record of the True Lord Wu* by Yan Lan, 24:17–8, locations of the other Baosheng Dadi temples in Tong an, and a brief mention of the Baijiao Cijigong 24:19; (b) Hagiography of the god with a discussion of the enfeoffments of the gods almost entirely drawn, with acknowledgments, from Huang Jiading's essay (12) 40:1–4; (c) Mentions (1)

and gives Zhuang Xia's dates, (d) Ten Superstitions. The first, second, and fifth all relate to the cult of Baosheng Dadi.

(14) *Fujian tongzhi*, 1878 edition; (a) *ce* 15, *Tanmiao zhi* 3:7 mentions the Quanzhou Huaqiao gong, Flower Bridge Temple; (b) 3:9b: mentions a Cijigong in Nan'an xian; (c) 3:13b., 14a: mentions the Zhenjun miao, as well as the Cijigong and quotes (11) on the Baosheng Dadi temples around Maxiang; (d) 4:2b: mentions the Cijigong in Zhangzhou, Longxi, Qingjiao; (e) 4:12b: lists a Cijigong in Changtai.

(15) *Dadao zhenjing jipian fajie*, (Collected edition of the True Scripture of the [Duke] of the Great Dao, with Ritual Score), published by devotees of the Tainan DaGuanyinting xingjigong (the Great Guanyin pavilion of the Temple of Flourishing Salvation) (No date).

(16) *Taibei Bao'an gongzhi* (Gazetteer of the Bao'an Temple in Taibei), collated by Zhang Gaohuai, edited by Zhang Jieren, 1981, published by the Temple Committee of the Bao'an gong in commemoration of the thousandth birthday of the god in 1979, 416 pp.

(17) Other modern sources include *Taiwan shentan* (1965), *Taiwan miaoshen juan* (1979), *Taiwan nanbu beiwen ji* (1966), and Wang Xuesong's pamphlet, *Summary Account of the Temple of Merciful Salvation of Baijiao: A Short Record of the Life of The Divine Doctor Wu Tao* (1981).

In addition to these printed sources there are the following epigraphical sources:

Steles in the Baijiao Cijigong (Western Temple)

a. *Juan ti xingshi beiji* (Record of the Contributions by Family Name) (1799): 4' wide by 8' high, 24 columns of text, dated Jiaqing sinian siyue chongxiu (repaired in the 4th year of the Jiaqing period).

b. See above. (1799): 4' × 8', 22 columns in 7 rows, 154 entries, including over thirty temples; concludes with "Jiaqing sinian wuyue li tibiao juanyin" (Erected in the 5th month of the 4th year of the Jiaqing reign-period, a list of money contributed).

c. *Baijiao zugong chongxiu juanti xingshi luyin beiji* (Record of the Family Names of Contributors and the Amounts [Given toward the] Repair of the Baijiao Ancestral Temple). (1816): 3'3" × 7'3", erected in the 21st year of the Jiaqing period in the summer, stone inscription recording the names of contributors and the amounts donated to the repair of the Baijiao Cijigong temple.

d. See above. (1815): 6' × 10', Erected on an auspicious day in the summer of 1815 (in commemoration of) the repairs conducted by the heads of the clan of the village of Baijiao in 1814.

e. *Zugong chongxiu juanti lu* (Record of contributions to the repair of the Ancestral temple) (1816): 10' × 1'3".

f. (1840) 3' × 6'. (contributors and amounts donated toward repairs).

g. *Chongxiu cijizugong juankuan xingshi beiji* (Record of the Contributions by Family to the Restoration of the Ancestral Temple of Merciful Salvation) (1878): 8' × 8'.

h. *Chongxiu cijizugong beiji* (Record of the Restoration of the Ancestral Temple of Merciful Salvation) (1878): 8' × 8', second half of above inscription.

i. *Chongxiu cijizugong juankuan xingshi beizhi* (Account of the Contributing Patrons [involved in the] Restoration of the Ancestral Temple of Merciful Salvation) (1923): 10′ × 6′, list of contributors.

j. *Chongxiu cijizugong juankuan xingshi beizhi* (Account of the Contributing Patrons [involved in the] Restoration of the Ancestral Temple of Merciful Salvation) (1923): 10′ × 6′ (second part of above inscription).

k. (1981) 2′6″ × 4′: "1981, 2d month, Overseas Compatriot Hong Kong Chinese Lin Rongjui of the Dongshan clan in Jiaomei, ordered the carving of a statue of Baosheng Dadi and a throne. This stele has been erected to record our thanks to him."

l. *Cijigong chongxiu juan ti xingming lu kuan beiji* (Record of the Contributions to the Restoration of the Temple of Merciful Salvation Listing the Full Names [of Patrons] and the Amounts [Offered]) (1984): 8′ × 4′, erected on an auspicious day in winter of 1984 to record the names and contributions for the repair of Cijigong.

Steles in the Qingjiao Ciji Gong (Eastern Temple)

a. *Baguo yuanzhu beiji* (A Record of the Patrons from Batavia) (1697). Schipper (1990) reads the first character of this stele as a variant of *yi*, city, or state, and so translates the inscription as "Record of the Patrons of Our Kingdom," which he interprets as testimony to the independent nature of cult territories. Another reading of the character would be as *ba*, in the term *baguo*, a term that is used for Batavia in several stone inscriptions collected in Claudine Salmon and Denys Lombard, *Les Chinois de Jakarta: Temples et vie collective* (Etudes insulindiennes—Archipel 1, Maison des Sciences de l'Homme), UMI, Ann Arbor, Michigan, 1980: 222, 231. The text of the stele refers to a number of captains who have donated funds to the restoration of the temple, which would seem to suggest an overseas trade connection with Southeast Asia.

b. *Chongxiu cijizugong beiwen* (Stone Inscription recording the Restoration of the Ancestral Temple of Merciful Salvation) (1814): 3′ × 6′, individuals and amounts.

c. *Chongxiu dongong beiji* (Record of the Repairs to the Eastern Temple) (1814): 3′ × 6′, continuation of (b) above; fenxiang temples and their contributions.

d. *Chongxiu cijizugong beiji* (Record of the Restoration of the Ancestral Temple of Merciful Salvation) (1854): 8′ × 5′.

e. *Chongxiu cijizugong beiji* (Record of the Restoration of the Ancestral Temple of Merciful Salvation) (1896): 8′ × 6′.

f. *Chongxiu cijizugong beiji* (Record of the Restoration of the Ancestral Temple of Merciful Salvation) (1896): 8′ × 6′, continuation of (e) above.

g. (1987): lists of jinxiang temples that visited in '87 and amounts donated, posted on three sheets of red paper kept in a display case behind glass.

h. Stele inscriptions reprinted in *Taiwan nanbu beiwen wenji* (1966).

i. *Cijigong yuanye beiji* (Record of the Karmic Work on the Temple of Merciful Salvation) (1744): Tainan xian, Fengjia Xuejia temple: A temple committee made up of twelve villages complain about poaching of temple lands and rents in a fragmentary inscription: 38–39.

j. *Chongxiu xingjigong beiji* (Record of the Restoration of the Tainan Xingji Temple) (1797): contributors and amounts, mention of a Buddhist monk as Director of the Temple: 547–48.

k. *Chongxiu lianghuanggong xu* (Preface on the Restoration of the Lianghuang gong in Tainan) (1810): contributors, costs. The temple is declared the equal in beauty to nearby Buddhist temples: 192–93.

l. *Xingjigong xinmaonian chongxiu beiji* (Repair of the [Tainan] Xingji Temple in the Xinmao Year) (1837): contributors and costs. Note that exactly sixty years had passed since the last repairs were carried out: 625–26.

m. *Baosheng Dadi beiji* (Record of the Baosheng Dadi Temple [in Jiayi (Chia-i)]) (1875): The inscription details the temple fields, rental units, etc., and the amounts they should produce for the maintenance of rituals at the temple: 499–501. Further material is available on the spread of the cult in Taiwan in the Japanese census taken in the 1920s (Schipper, 1990).

5. On Xi Wangmu see Loewe (1979). Schipper (1965) employed the term "hierogamy" in his study of the legend of the encounter between Han Wudi and Xi Wangmu in the *Han Wudi Neizhuan*. Strickmann (1981) emphasized the role of the divine instructress Wei Huacun in the Maoshan revelations. See also Schafer (1977).

6. These officials renouncing their functions and joining the god serve to underscore one of the greatest ironies in the history of the cult—namely, that Zhu Xi was Assistant Magistrate in Tongan at the time the cult was first achieving prominence. Unfortunately, Zhu Xi's disciple Chen Chun (1159–1222) did not write about Baosheng Dadi in his *Beixi ciyi* (trans. by Wing-tsit Chan, 1986). Perhaps Zhu and Zhen would have tolerated the cult in its immediate cultural area. They were strongly opposed, however, to the regionalization of cults. Thus Zhen objected strongly to the worship of Mazu in the Zhangzhou area while he accepted the cult of Kaizhang Shengwang, Chen Yuanguang. It is important to note that although Putian is only 120 miles north of Zhangzhou, the dialect and many of the local customs of the two regions are completely different. It is also ironic that Zhu Xi would himself become the object of a literati cult linking Confucian Academies across wide regions (Hymes, 1986).

7. Yan Shilu, *zi* Jisheng, (1119–93) is mentioned in *Song Shi* 389a. He was from Qingjiao. He earned his jinshi in 1142, and served as Investigating Censor, later as Chancellor of the Directorate of Education, and finally as Minister of the Ministry of Personnel. He was then appointed Auxiliary Academician of the Dragon Diagram Hall, and was made Manager of the Affairs of Quanzhou after 1182.

8. The use of messianic prophecy in Taoist texts is best known from the repeated claims for the imminent arrival of the Lord Li in such texts as the *Dongyuan shenzhoujing* (Mollier, 1991). For further examples connected with major political events see the *Lidai Chongdaoji* of Du Guangting (Verellen, 1989; Benn, 1977; Seidel, 1970; Strickmann, 1981).

9. David Jordan has given the best description of the rituals and functions of the Five Camps of the Spirit Soldiers in Minnan village religion in his *Gods, Ghosts and Ancestors* (1972).

10. This scripture is KD.MSS.176.PT.31: *Chifeng Tianhou Shengmu Zhen-*

jing. This version of the scripture differs somewhat from the version translated by Judith Boltz (one of four extant versions of CT 649: *Taishang laojun shuo Tianfei jiuku lingyan jing,* the earliest dating to around 1414), and from KD.MSS. 177.PT.32. *Tianshang Shengmu Zhenjing,* included in Yang Jun's *Sishen zhilue, Meizhouyu zhilue.* The latter is more closely related to the Daozang version.

11. The other deities in this group are Pu'an Fo, Longshu Wang, Shangdi Ye, Guandi Jun, and Mazu Po.

12. Naquin and Rawski (1987), in their otherwise excellent overview of eighteenth-century Chinese society, make the following remark:

> These highly personal and somewhat ad hoc [temple] organizations functioned best for small communities where decisions could be made by consensus between a few leaders. Most temple communities were relatively small in size and territory. Moreover, each was a separate, independent unit: there was little relationship between temples, even those of the same deity. (It is not clear if the idea that we see in Taiwan of newer temples being the offspring of older temples from which their incense had come was commonplace elsewhere.) Temple organization thus provided no framework for linking large numbers of people and worked poorly when the community was not a homogenous one. (Pp. 42–43)

In light of the material I have presented above, it is clear that cults had established wide networks in Southeast China and that these were linked to Taiwan and Southeast Asia. Whether or not these networks took on all the functions of temple networks in Taiwan such as those described in Chuang Ying-chang (1973), Hsu Chia-min (1973), and especially Ch'en Ch'i-nan (1981) is difficult to determine at this stage of research. It is clear, however, that they mobilized enormous social and cultural resources.

13. Sources on Wang Delu include *Qingshigao* 1.356.3b., *Qingshi liezhuan* 2.39.29b., *Guochao qixian shuzheng* 3.303.4a., *Xubei chuanji* 5.49.17a., and *Fujian tongzhi,* ce. 70, j.6.45a-47b.

14. Lamley (1977a) and Feuchtwang (1974a) discuss the Bao'an gong in Taibei and the subethnic feuding that from time to time enveloped it. The attacks of 1853 were actually launched by segments of the Quanzhou region which had divided into hostile Tongan, three-counties (Jinjiang, Hui'an, and Nan'an), and Anxi groups. The 1858 conflicts pitted Quanzhou groups against Zhangzhou groups.

15. Personal communication from David Jordan, May 1988. On the Mazu pilgrimages within Taiwan see Sangren (1987). For a description with photographs of the traditional Dajia pilgrimage to Beigang see *Minsu Quyi* (1983), vol. 27.

16. As I mentioned in the introduction, tremendous pressure has been brought to bear on the traditional religious practices of the Chinese since 1949 and especially during the Cultural Revolution. The onslaught actually began at the turn of the century, when Western-influenced rationalist administrators of the Republic banned many forms of popular religion and attempted to convert most temples into schools and government office buildings. The struggle for survival of these traditions has had mixed results. Tongan has always had a strong tradition of mediumism, and this appears to have been transmitted intact to the younger

generation. The Putian Xianyou area also has a rich tradition of mediumism, and one town in which I conducted fieldwork in 1987 had just completed training large groups of children, neighborhood by neighborhood, in the seven major temples of the town. The training sessions had lasted for a week, and consisted mainly in the old generation of mediums, now in their sixties, teaching the young boys the chants and dance steps of the gods. Exciting processions between these temples have been going on since 1979 at Chinese New Year celebrations, and several of the children have demonstrated an ability to go into a trance. It should be noted, however, that mediums in this town rarely turn weapons on themselves, although one older medium showed me a collection of skewers he claimed to stick through his skin on such occasions. In addition to the large-scale mediumistic practices I have described above in connection with the Baosheng Dadi cult, I observed mediums in Tongan, Anxi, Xianyou, and Hui'an on several occasions.

17. The Conferences of the Gods include the following: 1st Mazu conference, 1986; 2d Mazu conference, 1988; 1st Wu Tao conference (Zhangzhou), April 1988; 1st Wu Tao conference (Xiamen), April 1988; 1st Lin Longjiang (Three-in-One Religion) conference, April 1989; 3d (International) Mazu conference, April 1990; 2d Wu Tao conference (Xiamen), April 1990); and the 1st Kaizhang Shengwang (Chen Yuanguang) conference, Dec. 1990.

CHAPTER THREE
THE PATRIARCH OF THE CLEAR STREAM

1. On emigration from Fujian see Chen Ch'i-lu (1972).

2. This description of the bustling activity of the procession prior to 1949 is based on oral accounts gathered during fieldwork in Penglai.

3. David Hawkes (1967), basing himself on sources including the *Lisao* and the *Yuanyou* in Qu Yuan's *Chu Ci* (Songs of the South) describes these tours around the spiritual boundaries of the territory of the god, the corners of the empire, and the edges of the cosmos as "divine itineraria."

4. My fieldwork on the Qingshui Zushi procession was conducted in 1986 and 1987, during the Chinese New Year. Both years I accompanied the procession throughout its itinerary. Hsu Chia-ming (1973) discusses the use of multiple statues of the same divinity to mark different social groups during the god's processions in the Zhanghua plains. The best discussion of anthropological terminology of kinship in relation to the Chinese material is in J. Watson (1982b). There he asserts that a true lineage must own common property with the proceeds maintaining rituals or other lineage activities, conduct common rituals, have a sense of group solidarity, and be able to demonstrate (usually through a genealogical record) direct descent along the patrilineal line. In his concluding essay to a study of kinship organization in late Imperial China (Ebrey and Watson, 1986), however, he notes that the Southeastern lineages appear to represent the exception rather than the rule for Chinese kinship organization, and points to the growing appreciation of the paramount role of ritual in forging a sense of kinship. Certainly since the Land Reform Movement and especially during the Cultural Revolution, lineages in Southeast China have not owned common property. Nevertheless, they have preserved rituals and maintained solidarity.

5. Material on feuds is widely scattered through the memorials and collected writings of officials who served in Fujian. Niida (1954) has gathered a group of sources. Freedman (1966) describes the stylized nature of feud combat and the system of substitutes. Sasaki (1963), Lamley (1977b), and Ownby (1988) discuss the evolution of the feuding patterns in Fujian as society began to fall apart in the latter part of the eighteenth century. Increasingly, lineage groups became the victims of mercenaries exploiting social tensions for their own profits. Ownby (1988) has examined the criminal archival evidence for explanations of these transformations.

6. Earlier gazetteers on the temple include one compiled in 1633 by Anxi District Magistrate Xu Zibiao, and several Anxi urban gentry including Li Rikun, Li Guanglong, and Wang Zhengnan. According to Xu's preface, quoted in Yang Jun's *Gazetteer*, he based his edition on a manuscript copy of an earlier temple gazetteer. The monks in charge of the temple had passed down a single manuscript copy, which Xu found to contain many errors and omissions. Other editions or versions of the gazetteer were composed in 1671 by District Magistrate Xie Hongchen and by District Magistrate Wang Zhi in 1741. Li Qingfang, an official in the Board of War, together with Zhao Yuanhui, an Anxi juren and official in Sichuan, and Song Yinglin, District Magistrate of Anxi, printed a version of the gazetteer in 1761. A three-volume edition of the gazetteer was printed in 1812 by Anxi District Magistrate Xia Yihuai. A manuscript copy of that edition is in the Fuzhou Provincial Library. An expanded version of the temple gazetteer was printed in 1850 by Chen Xishi, an Anxi juren. In 1929, after the temple had suffered serious neglect during the confusion of the times, a gazetteer was compiled on the basis of earlier editions by the local gentry, Chen Jiazhen (in charge of collating), Zhang Dianlong, Chen Dingyuan, and Lin Xiangyuan (in charge of illustrations). Yang Jun states that he had been unable to locate the 1633 edition, but he does not say from which edition he made his selections. It must have been the 1850 version as he mentions poems composed in 1832. An edition of the temple gazetteer was smuggled into Anxi by overseas Chinese from various Southeast Asian Anxi native-place associations. First, copies went to local leaders of the revival of local traditions, then a copy was officially presented to the cadres in charge of the temple. From there a copy made its way to Xiamen University's library.

7. The following sources are included in Yang Jun's *Qingshuiyan zhilue*, j.3 and 4:

a. *Postscript to a Prayer to the Ancestral Master for Rain* (1210), by Yu Keji, an Anxi man serving at the time as the District Magistrate of Chang Tai, subsequently worshiped among the Local Sages.

b. *Record of the Precious Stupa on Clear Water (Cliff)* (1211), by Yu Keji (see above), and written on stone in the hand of Chen Mi (1171–1230), according to Yang Jun currently the Anxi District Magistrate, and a disciple of Zhu Xi (1130–1200) from Putian.

c. *Ritual Memorial Praying for Rain* (1216), by Zhen Dexiu (1178–1235, *jinshi*, 1212) Prefect of Quanzhou and later of Fuzhou, subsequently a Hanlin academician and finally Grand Councilor; posthumously named Wenzhong, and worshiped in the Confucian temples.

d. *Record of the Construction of Clear Water Temple* (1263), by Xu Mingshu (*jinshi*, 1232) Officer in Zhangzhou and later Prefect in Chaozhou, finally Vice-Director of the Board of War and Abbot of the Jade Bureau Taoist Temple in Chengdu Prefecture.

e. *Sacrificial Address to the Great Master* (1269), by Lin Yong (*jinshi*, 1253), Anxi District Magistrate.

f. *Record of the Repairs to Clear Water Cliff* (1317), by Monk Fu Yuan.

g. *Brief Account of Prayers for Rain* (1332), by Chang Juren, Anxi District Magistrate.

h. *Record of the Taking up of Residence in the Clear Water Cliff by the Orthodox Branch of the Kaiyuan Temple* (1565), by Chan Yangbi, an Anxi man (*jinshi*, 1565), Chief Minister of the Bureau of Punishments, posthumously worshiped among the Local Sages.

i. *Record of the Pavilion for Studies*, by He Qiaoyuan, a Jinjiang man (1558–1632; *jinshi*, 1586), Official in the Bureau of Population and the Bureau of Works, posthumously worshiped among the Local Sages.

j. *Preface to the Gazetteer of Clear Water Cliff* (1633), by Xu Zibiao, Anxi District Magistrate.

k. *Preface to the Hundred Foot Tower and the Eastern Tower of the Clear Water Temple* (1633), by Li Rikun, Guozijian xuezheng (Instructor Second Class in the Directorate of Education).

l. *Brief Record of the Construction of the Mountain Gateway* (1645), by Zhou Zongbi, Anxi District Magistrate.

m. *Preface to the Gazetteer of Clear Water Cliff* (1671), by Xie Zhenchuan (*jinshi*, 1654), Anxi District Magistrate.

n. *Preface to the Gazetteer of Clear Water Cliff* (1742), by Wang Zhi (1727 Hanlin Academician), Anxi District Magistrate.

o. *Ritual Memorial Praying for Rain*, by Wang Zhi.

p. *Preface to the Gazetteer of Clear Water Cliff* (1761), by Li Qingfang, later Vice-Minister of the Ministry of War.

q. *Preface to the Gazetteer of Clear Water Cliff* (1760), by Zhao Yuanhui, an Anxi man (1724 juren); later District Magistrate in Longchang District, Sichuan.

r. *Preface to the Gazetteer of Clear Water Cliff* (1760), by Song Yinglin.

s. *Preface to the Gazetteer of Clear Water Cliff* (1831), Li Bianding, Anxi District Magistrate (1835 juren).

t. *Record of Repairs to the Clear Water Cliff Temple*, by Zhang Jiqing (1831 jueyuan).

u. *Brief Account of Repairs to the Clear Water Cliff Temple*, by Chen Xishi (1835 yayuan), with a postface by Zhang Weizheng.

v. *Account of Repairs to the Yangzhong Pavilion*, by Liu Xuanqing.

7. For information on the local cultures of Southeast China see Eberhard (1968). On the Han expansion into She territory in Southeast China see Lu Xisheng (1982). Further information on the She is given in the 1927 edition of the *Yongchun xianzhi*. She minority groups can still be found in four locations in central and northern Fujian. The employment of four escaped She "demons" as guardians recalls the tradition of "holy places" discussed in Granet (1926) where a cult is established on the tomb of the vanquished enemy.

8. The Provincial Library of Fujian and the major Buddhist temples of Fujian have preserved a wealth of material for the study of the local history of Buddhism in Fujian, including temple gazetteers on ten major temples and the founding temple of the Obaku Zen cult. There is also the monograph on the Kaiyuan si by Ecke and Demieville (1935). The latter taught Sanskrit at Xiamen University for two years. Chen Qiren's 1934 *Minzhong jinshilu* includes a large number of inscriptions from the Tang onward taken from temples all over Fujian. Japanese scholarship on Fujian Buddhism includes the essays of Chikusa Misaaki (collected in Chikusa, 1982). For other references see Strickmann (1980), pp. 243–44; for modern developments see Welch (1967, 1968, 1972), and Fan (1985).

9. On the development of Fujian bureaucratic lineages see Sadao (1962). For the wider context of social transformations and evolving lineage strategies see Hartwell (1982) and Hymes (1986).

10. Zeng Conglong, *zi* Junxi, and *ming* Yilong, a Jinjiang man. IBMFS 4.2831. (*jinshi*, 1199). Fourth-generation descendant of Zeng Gongliang (999–1078). Successively made Supervisory Secretary and concomitantly Auxiliary Academician. In the Jiading period (1208–27) he was first made Hunan Military Commissioner. Then in 1215 he was promoted to Minister of the Ministry of Rites and in 1219 made Administrator of the Bureau of Military Affairs and Vice Grand Councillor. Zeng also wrote a stele inscription set up in the central temple of the cult of Guangze Zunwang, discussed in chapter 4 below.

11. On the Lushan ritual traditions see Liu Chih-wan (1974); Schipper (1985a); Berthier (1987, 1988); Lagerwey (1987b); and Saso (1975). See also the comments in the introduction above. More research is required before the development and impact of this tradition can be fully assessed.

CHAPTER FOUR
THE REVERENT LORD OF BROAD COMPASSION

1. De Groot published an early version of this account in the *China Review*, vol. 7, July 1878–79, pp. 91–97, under the title, "The Idol Kwoh Shing Wang." In this article he included a few details in his description of the cult that were left out of his account in *Les Fetes Annuellement Celebrees a Emoui (Amoy)*, 1886. He mentions the pilgrimages to the tomb and states that every three years the god statue was carried to the tomb on the twenty-second day of the eighth lunar month, "or on some date not far from that date, the priests of the temple resort to the famous grave carrying along the image, and lay it down there in front on its belly. This is done because they think it necessary to give an opportunity to the idol for making his due prostrations towards his grandfather. This ceremony is performed with much pomp and splendour although, according to Chinese fashion, most of the assistants appear in ragged and dirty garments" [1977:97]. The Fujian historian Wei Yinglin recalls that, as a boy, he was presented with a statue of Guo Shengwang by his maternal uncle. He includes a chapter on the god, drawing extensively on Dai's *Gazetteer*, in his 1929 study, *Fujian Sanshen kao* (A Study of Three Gods of Fujian), pp. 51–66. He quotes the petitions and memorials surrounding the enfeoffment of the god, but does not provide much background to the incident.

2. The literary sections of Yang Jun's *Gazetteer* include seven prose pieces, including the Song *Record* of Wang Zhou, the Ming *Record* of Chen Xueyi, two discussions of excursions to the temple in the Qing by Chen Qianhe, two Qing records of repairs to the temple, the preface to the *Filiations* mentioned above by Huang Zonghan (*jinshi*, 1835, subsequently Governor-General of Sichuan, then of Guangdong and Guangxi, and finally Minster of the Ministry of Finance), and the Yongchun District Magistrate's *Memorial* requesting the enhancement of the god's title following the rebellions of the 1850s and 1860s. Yang includes about twenty poems on the cult, along with some plaque inscriptions and inscriptions on pillars at the temple. The entire gazetteer fills only fifty-nine folded pages, and was bound with string in a slim volume, one of a set of six volumes in the collection covered with wooden end-pieces.

3. Dai's *Gazetteer* included the following sections: Charts and Illustrations; the Basic Legend; Titles of Enfeoffment; the Documents Requesting Enhancement of Enfeoffment; the Temples; the Tomb; Chart of the Sacrificants and the Offerings; Ritual Texts for the Tomb; Houtu; Yang the Elder; Commentaries; Literary Collectanea divided into Stele Inscriptions; Travel Accounts; Prefaces; Announcements; Preambles; and Poetry in ten different genres. Next, he provides a comprehensive section on temple plaques and couplets written on doorways and pillars of the temple. Finally, he gives a Miscellaneous Account, with sections on "The Correction of Errors Regarding the Former Events of the Venerable King's Life," and lists of recent miracles; the affiliated temple network of the cult; notes on the god's attendant divinities; the divinatory poems; and an appendix entitled, "The Life of Huize Zunwang, Venerable King of Merciful Benevolence." The latter was the god of a cult bordering that of Guangze Zunwang. The genres of poetry in the *Gazetteer* begin with ancient-style songs; then four-characters-per-line poems; then five-characters-per-line ancient-style poems; then seven-characters-per-line ancient-style poems; then five-characters-per-line quatrains; then seven-characters-per-line quatrains; then five-characters-per-line regulated verse; then seven-characters-per-line regulated verse; then five-characters-per-line parallel regulated verse; then seven-characters-per-line parallel regulated verse; and finally, verse written to a pre-established rhyme scheme (for a description of these poetic forms see Liu, 1967).

4. Information on Lin Jun's rebellion can be found in Zhu Weigan (1985), Zhuang Weiji (1985), the *Shejibian*, and the *Dashizhi* (Monograph on Major Events) of the 1929 *Yongchun xianzhi*. See also *Qing shilu: Wenzong Shilu: Xianfeng 3*.

5. Johnson (1977) mentions the Fenyang lineage of Guo Ziyi (fl. 755–780: biography in *Jiu Tangshu*, 120; *Xin Tangshu*, 137), and other major lines of the aristocratic medieval period. On the social transformations in kinship structure after the Tang see Hartwell (1982), Ebrey and Watson (1986), and Hymes (1986).

6. Granet (1926) remarked on the establishment of "lieu sacré" (sacred places) on the tombs of vanquished rivals in ancient China. In the first version of the story, the hostility between the Guos and their overlord explodes into violence. In the second version this violence is mitigated by transposing the underlying conflict back one generation—now the god's father seeks a gravesite for his father—but the desire to transcend his class limitations are powerful. The last

version has removed all trace of violence and conflict—the overlord graciously consents to the request for a superior geomantic site and is himself buried alongside his servant! As we know from Chinese sources (collected and analyzed in Niida, 1954; Sasaki, 1963; Lamley, 1977b) and contemporary accounts of ethnographers and missionaries (Hughes, 1872; Scarth, 1860; De Groot, 1982; Pitcher, 1909), as well as the anthropological literature on China (esp. Freedman, 1966), conflict over geomantic sites was a principal source of violence in Southeast China.

7. Needham (1974, pp. 294–304) describes the process of preparing the "terminal incorruptibility" of mummified religious figures.

8. Political tensions between groups in a community are often expressed through spirit-mediums or other religious leaders as Seaman (1978) has demonstrated. The sources do not allow us to differentiate Taoist Masters from Ritual Masters, or the latter from spirit-mediums. In certain areas these distinctions will not be clearly marked (see chap. 1).

9. Geomantic antagonisms are yet another mode of expressing tensions and rivalries within a cult. See note 3 above. A famous example of rivalry within a cult network is the long-standing quarrel between the Mazu gong of Luermen and the Tucheng Shengmu miao outside Tainan as to which temple was the first to be founded by Zheng Chenggong.

10. On Zeng Conglong see chap. 3, note 10 above.

11. Ban Gu (A.D. 32–92) wrote *The History of the Former Han Dynasty*, translated by Homer Dubs (New York: Columbia University Press, 1966). Jiang Yan (444–505), a Six Dynasties poet, wrote with a "brush of many colors" bestowed upon him in a dream by the poet Guo Pu (276–324), here referred to as Master Guo. Note that Dai also played a major role in the establishment of the Shishan Shuyuan in the 1890s, helping to purchase the school's land and build its halls and dormitories. He wrote a *Gazetteer of the Shihshan Academy* in 1905.

12. The categories of "scholar-gentry" rank and their presumed social class ramifications are described in Ho (1962) and Chang (1955).

13. Dai provides the texts of the *Ji fenying wen* (Ritual Text for the Sacrifice at the Tomb), the *Ji Houtushen wen* (Ritual Text for the Sacrifice to the Earth Spirit, Houtu), and the *Ji Yang Zhangzhe wen* (Ritual Text for the Sacrifice to Yang the Elder). The liturgical text for the order of worship at the tomb is also provided, along with a chart of the positions of the officiants and the placement of the offerings and sacrifices. An extensive commentary on the sacrificial items and rites refers to the *Wang Ji* (Princely Sacrifices) section of the *Liji* (Book of Rites) and the *Da Qing Hui Dian* (Statutes of the Great Qing Dynasty), and to Zhu Xi's *Jia Li* (Family Ritual).

14. The sacrifice to Zhu Xi and to Ouyang Xun, as well as those to Guandi and Tudi gong, are detailed in Dai Fengyi's *Shishan shuyuanzhi*. This gazetteer could be characterized as a charter written upon the establishment of the Academy by Dai and others. Dai is eager to make a clear record of all the school lands donated to the upkeep of the Academy. Almost a third of the *Gazetteer* consists of sketches of the numerous scattered plots belonging to the school.

15. Personal communication, K. M. Schipper, 1988.

16. Sources on the Xi Gang *Wangye jiao* include Liu Chih-wan (1974), Schipper (1985c), and Jordan (1976). I attended the jiao in 1985.

17. Brook (1985) makes an argument for the continuity of subadministrative political units in local society. Several of the units are included in this address. Wilkerson (1990) has demonstrated the continuing role of such units in the Penghu Islands.

CONCLUSION

1. Recently, questions have been raised about the centrality of the burning of texts or talismans in early Taoist ritual. Seidel (1988) and Cedzich (1987) note alternative modes of dispersal of texts in early ritual, modeled on imperial bureaucratic procedures. They also remark the marginality of jiao sacrifice in early ritual. To further complicate matters, Schipper (paper presented to the Franco-Japonais colloque, 1988) has noted the sacrifice of a white goose in the early CT 388 *Taishang Lingbao Wufuxu* (Preface to the Five Talismans of Most High Spiritual Treasure). Regardless of the origins or evolution of early Taoist ritual, one can argue that by the Lingbao codification of ritual in the 5th century, the sacrifice of signs, the translation and actualization of texts through burning, and the exclusion or marginalization of bloody sacrifice are dominant features of Taoist ritual.

APPENDIX I

1. Wang Zhiwang (1103–70), *Songren chuanji ziliao soyin* (Index of Biographical Materials on Figures of the Sung), Taibei, 1974; hereafter abbreviated as IBMFS: 1.255. (*jinshi*, 1138). Successively Vice Minister of the Court of the Imperial Treasury, Minister of the Ministry of Population, Pacification Commissioner for Sichuan and Shenxi, and then Vice Grand Councillor briefly in 1164 (*Song Shi*, 212.5570.) The same year that he signed this edict he was appointed Fujian Military Commissioner, and subsequently became Administrator of Wenzhou.

2. Zhou Kui (1098–1174), *zi* Liyi, H. Qingxi. IBMFS, 2.1454. (*jinshi*, 1124). First served as a Judge in Huizhou, later promoted to Censor. Made a Grand Councillor under Gaozong (*Song Shi*, 212.5570) and honored as a Grand Academician in the Hall for Aid in Governance.

3. Huang Qia (1122–1200), *zi* Derun, from Houguan in Fujian. IBMFS, 4.2846. SS, 387.1. Entered the National University in 1163. Subsequently made a Censor, and later a Vice Grand Councillor from 1183–1189 (*Song Shi*, 213. 5586).

4. Shi Shidian (1124–92), *zi* Shengyu. IBMFS, 2.1534. Hanlin Academician promoted to Vice Grand Councillor in 1183 (*Song Shi*, 213.5584).

5. Wang Huai (1126–1189), *zi* Jihai. IBMFS, 1.156. (*jinshi*, 1145). After serving as Taizhou Linhai Wei, he served in various court offices and as a Hanlin academician. He was made a Vice Grand Councillor in 1175 and a Grand Councillor in 1181. He was an opponent of Zhu Xi. (*Song Shi*, 213).

6. It is difficult to determine who this Zeng could have been. Zeng Huai (1106–74), *zi* Qintao, from Jinjiang in Fujian was made a jinshi and appointed Vice Grand Councillor in 1172 and later became Grand Councillor on the Right, but he died in 1174, ten years too early to have signed this edict. Nor could it be Zeng Conglong, another Vice Grand Councillor from Fujian, who attained that position twenty years later in 1219. This may be a scribal error.

7. He Dan, *zi* Ziran (*jinshi*, 1166). Made Vice Grand Councillor in 1200. IBMFS, 2,1265 (*Song Shi*, 213.5592). A victim of court intrigue, he happily spent twenty years out of office. The Right Prime Minister in 1201 was Xie Shenfu (*jinshi*, 1195), a supporter of Zhu Xi.

8. Lou Ji (1133–1211), *zi* Yanfa. IBMFS, 3.2717 (*jinshi*, 1166). Worked his way up from a Salt Commissioner to Vice Minister of Personnel to Minister of Rites, until becoming Vice Grand Councillor in 1208, despite falling into disfavor and being driven out of office by Han Jou. Lou Ji became Administrator of Fuzhou in 1210. It is possible that the signature was not his but that of one Lou Yue, who also became a Vice Grand Councillor in 1208 (*Song Shi*, 213.5598) but about whom there is no information in IBMFS. The identity of Vice Grand Councillor Huang is difficult to determine for this period on the basis of the Charts of Grand Councillors in the *Song Shi*, 210–14.

9. Lei Xiaoyou, *zi* Jizhong. IBMFS, 4.3090 (*jinshi*, 1169). An Erudite in the National University, he later became Provisional Vice Minister of the Board of Personnel. He worked on the *True Edicts* and *Dynastic History* and became Vice Grand Councillor in 1208.

GLOSSARY

Ancuo (Minnan: ancu)　安厝
antang　庵堂
Anrenli　安仁里
Anxi　安溪
Baijiao　白礁
Bai Yuchan　白玉蟾
Baiyunguan　白雲觀
Ban Gu　班固
bang　榜
Banji　版籍
banxian　扮仙
bao　堡
Bao'an gong　堡安宮
Baohuang gong　寶皇宮
baojia　保甲
Beigang　北港
Beiguan　北管
Biancun　便村
biao　表
bing (no.)　丙
bing (soldier)　兵
Bo　伯
Bohai　渤海
buzhengsi jingli　布政司經歷
Cai Qian　蔡牽
Caijiguan Zhao buwen
　財計官趙不紊
Caishen　財神
Cao Wei　曹緯
Chan Yangbi　詹仰庇
Changle　長樂
Chaotian gong　朝天宮
Chaoyuan Guan　朝元觀
Chaozhou　潮州
Chen Chun　陳淳
Chen Dafang　陳大方
Chen Dingyuan　陳定遠
Chen Jiazhen　陳家珍
Chen Jinggu　陳靖姑

Chen Jun　陳均
Chen Mi　陳宓
Chen Puzu　陳普足
Chen Rongsheng　陳榮盛
Chen Shouyuan　陳守元
Chen Tiexiang 陳鐵香
Chen Xishi　陳希實
Chen Xueyi　陳學伊
Chen Yaoting　陳耀庭
Chen Yining　陳一寧
Ch'en Yong-sheng　*See Chen Rongsheng*
Chen Yuanguang　陳元光
chengbao　承包
Chengshilang　承仕郎
Chengtiansi　承天寺
Chengzu　成祖
Chong Yuan　崇遠
Chongan　崇安
Chongshanli　崇善里
Chongshansi　崇善寺
Chongxiguan　崇禧觀
Chu Ci　楚詞
Chuanghong　傳鴻
chuding　出丁
Chunxi　淳熙
Ci Wu　慈悟
Ciji gong　慈濟宮
cu (Minnan: cu)　厝
Da Guanyinting xingjigong
　大觀音亭興吉宮
dadeng　大燈
dagu　大鼓
Daguan miao　大官廟
Dai Fengyi　戴鳳儀
Dajia　大甲
Dajing　大靜
Dalian　大連
dang　黨

daoshi　道士
Datian　大田
daxuesheng　大學生
Dazang lou　大藏樓
Dehua　德化
diquan　地券
die　牒
Digonglang zhengshishi
　迪功郎政事仕
ding　丁
dingmao　丁卯
dingyou　丁酉
Dingzhou　汀洲
Dongou Zhou Zongbi　東甌周宗壁
Dongxi xiang　東西廂
Dongyang　東陽
Dongyue miao　東岳廟
dou　豆
doudeng　斗燈
duhuitong　都會統
Duren jing　度人經
Fang Guangweng　方廣翁
Fang Hui　方會
Fang lue　方略
Fang Qiao　方嶠
Fang Zhaobing　方昭並
Fangwai　方外
Fashi　法師
Faxuan　法玄
Fengjia Cijigong　逢田慈濟宮
fengqi　封旗
Fengshansi　鳳山寺
Fengxiang　封相
fenxiang　分香
Fotoucu　佛頭厝
Fu　符
fu　簠
Fugan Chen Yue　撫幹陳說
Fujian　福建
fuming　符命
Fuqing　福清
Fushi Ouyang Mo　副使歐陽模
Fuzhou　福州
gan'er　干兒

Gaojia xi　高甲戲
Gaotai　高太
Gaoxiong　高雄
Gaozong　高宗
Ge Chaofu　葛巢甫
geng　庚
gengshen　庚申
getihu　個體戶
Gezai xi　歌仔戲
gong　宮
gongde　功德
gongsheng　貢生
gu (Minnan)　牛
Gu Huishi　顧惠實
Gu Yanwu　顧炎武
gua-hiong (Minnan)　割香
guan　關
guanchashi　觀察使
Guandi　關帝
Guanghua si　廣化寺
Guanghua si　光化寺
Guangxu　光緒
guanli tai　觀禮臺
guanxi　關係
Guanyin　觀音
Guanyin can　觀音讚
gui　癸
guihuli　貴湖里
Guixi　貴溪
Guixiyan　龜溪巖
guiyou　癸酉
Gukou　谷口
Gulangyu　鼓浪嶼
Guo Boyin　郭伯蔭
Guo Pu　郭樸
Guo Shengwang　郭聖王
Guo Zhongfu　郭忠福
Guo Ziyi　郭子儀
guohuo　過火
Gushan　鼓山
Gutian　古田
Haicang　海滄
Haicheng　海澄
Haijiao　海醮

Haikou　海口
Han Yu　韓淤
hao　號
He Bao　何保
He Dan　何澹
He Fo'er　何佛兒
He Landing　何蘭汀
He Qiaoyan　何喬遠
He Shanyan　何善言
Helin guan　鶴林觀
Heming shan　鶴鳴山
Hetong　霍童
Hong Mai　洪邁
Hongguang　弘光
Honggun miao　紅滾廟
Honglo　洪羅
Hongwu　洪武
Houguan　候官
Houju　火居
Houtu　后土
Hu Chaojin　胡朝覲
huagu　花鼓
Huaqiao　花橋
Huang Er'ou　董爾漚
Huang Fengxiang　黃鳳翔
Huang Guan　黃慣
Huang Huaji　黃化機
Huang Jiading　黃家鼎
Huang Jietong　黃介通
Huang Qia　黃洽
Huang Taiwei　黃太尉
Huang Xianzhong　黃咸中
Huang Yu　黃馭
Huang Zonghan　黃宗漢
Hui'an　惠安
huibi　迴避
huiguan　會館
huishou　會首
Huitang gong　會堂宮
Huizhou　惠州
hun　魂
ji　祭
jia　甲
jiabidan (Minnan: gabidan)　甲必丹

Jiang Shaofeng　江少峰
Jiang Si shi　江四使
Jiang Xianguan　江仙宮
Jiang Yan　江淹
Jiangkou　江口
Jiangsu　江蘇
Jiangxi　江西
Jianjian　建劍
Jianyan　建炎
Jianyang　建陽
jiao　醮
Jiaokang bao　焦坑保
Jiaqing　嘉慶
Jiatai　嘉泰
Jiaxi　嘉熙
Jiayi (Chia-i)　嘉義
jiazi　甲子
Jici si　祠祭司
jiefotou　接佛頭
Jiexi　揭西
Jilong　基隆
Jin　金
Jinbang　金榜
Jinbiao　進表
Jinbiao tan　進表壇
jinding　進丁
jing　境
jingshi　精室
Jingyu　景裕
Jinjiang　晉江
Jinman
jinshi　進士
jinshi pangyan　進士榜眼
Jinxiang　金相
jinxiang　進香
jinxiang tuan　進香團
Jinzhou　錦州
jinzhi　金紙
jiqi　祭旗
Jiufengshan　九峰山
Jiulong　九龍
Jueyuansi　覺苑寺
juren　舉人
Kaiguang　開光

kaiguang dianyan　開光點眼
kailu　開路
Kaixi　開禧
kaixiang　開香
Kaiyuan si　開元寺
Kangxi　康熙
kaozhi　考治
Ke Daliang　柯大樑
Ke Xianshu　柯賢樹
ken　簋
Kou Laigong　寇萊公
Kuilei xi　傀儡戲
Kunlun　崑崙
Lanxi　蘭溪
li　里
Li Ben　禮本
Li Changgeng　李長庚
Li Kun　李焜
Li Guangdi　李光地
Li Guanglong　李光龍
Li Qingfang　李淸芳
Li Qingfu　李淸馥
Liang Kejia　梁克家
Liang Zheng Gong　梁鄭公
Liangzhe jinshi　兩浙金石志
Liansheng Ling Han　廩生凌翰
Lin Dahong　林大鴻
Lin Jinle　林靖樂　字紕素
Lin Jun　林俊
Lin Lingsu　林靈素
Lin Longjiang　林龍江
Lin Qian　林謙
Lin Qiaoxiang　林喬相
Lin Shiyan　林時彥
Lin Shuangwen　林雙文
Lin Sishui　林泗水
Lin Sizhen　林嗣眞
Lin Tinggui　林廷瑰
Lin Xiangyuan　林向源
Lin Yong　林泳
Lin Yuncheng　林雲程
Lin Zeng　林贈
Lin Zhao'en　林兆恩
ling　靈
Lingbao　靈寶

Lingbaoguan　靈寶觀
Lingpai　靈牌
Lingyi si　靈醫寺
Lisao　離騷
Liu Beixu　劉丕續
Liu Dechong　劉德崇
Liu Fu　劉輔
Liu Gongrui　劉公銳
Liu Guangju　劉光居
Liu Mengding　劉夢鼎
Liu Piaofang　劉飄芳
Liu Xuanqing　劉選靑
Liu Weili　劉維立
Liyuan xi　梨園戲
Lizong　理宗
Longhai　龍海
Longhu shan　龍虎山
Longjin　龍津
Longjinqiao　龍津橋
Longqiu　龍湫
Longshan si　龍山寺
Longxi　龍溪
Lou Ji　婁機
Lou Yue　婁岳
lu　籙
Lu shan　閭山
Lu Tingzong　呂廷宗
Lu Xiujing　陸修靜
Lu You　陸游
Luojiang　羅江
Ma Zhenhua　馬振華
Man Lin　滿林
Mao Ying　矛盈
Maoshan　茅山
Mazhang　麻章
Mazu　媽祖
Mazupo　媽祖婆
Meizhou　湄洲
Mengjia Zushi Miao　艋舺祖師廟
Mian Qiu　勉求
miao　廟
Miaoxi　渺溪
mijue　宓訣
Ming Tang　明堂
minbei mindong　閩北閩東

Mingdao 明道
Minnan 閩南
Minxian 閩縣
mu 畝
Mulian 目蓮
Nan Foguo 南佛國
Nan Putuo 南普陀
Nanan 南安
nanbeiguan 南北管
Nanguan 南管
Nanjing 南靖
Nantou 南投
nifeng 擬封
Ningde 寧德
Ningzhenjing Jingxuantan
　　凝眞境經玄壇
nongshi 弄獅
Ouyang Xun 歐陽詢
Pangu 盤古
Pantao hui 盤桃會
Peng Zu 彭祖
Penghu 蓬壺
Penglai 蓬萊
Pingdong 屏東
Pinghe 平和
Pingyang 平陽
pipa 琵琶
po 陂
Pucheng 浦城
Pudu 普度
Putian 莆田
Puyang 莆陽
qi 氣
Qian Taibao 錢太保
Qiandao 乾道
Qianlong 乾隆
Qin Zhian 秦志安
Qing Shui yan 清水巖
Qingjiao 清醮
Qingwei 清微
Qingxi 清溪
Qingxi gong 清溪宮
Qingxuan 清玄
Qingyuan 清源
Qingyuan 慶元

qitou qishou 旗頭旗手
Qiu Yundi 邱允迪
Qu Yuan 屈原
quan 券
Quan zhen 全眞
Quanshou 勸首
Quanzhou 泉州
ren 壬
Rende 仁德
Renzong 仁宗
Ri En 日恩
ruyi 如意
San Daren 三大人
Sandong jingshu mulu
　　三洞經書目錄
Sandong qionggang 三洞瓊綱
Sanfoqi 三佛齊
Sanping Zushigong 三坪祖師宮
Sanqing 三清
Sanqing dian 三清殿
Santai 三台
Sanyi gong 三義宮
Sanyi jiao 三一教
shang 上
Shangjie 上街
Shantou 山頭
Shantoujie 山頭街
Shao Yizheng 邵以正
Shaowu 邵武
Shaoxi 紹熙
Shaoxing 紹興
she 社
She 舍
Shehong 射茫
shen 申
shendao 神道
shendu zhi jiao 身毒之教
sheng 聖
shengyuan 生員
shenshi 紳士
Shenxiao 神霄
sheshu 赦書
Shi Daoming 施道明
Shi Shidian 施師點
Shida 師大

shiji 史記
shijie 尸解
Shili 史例
Shima 石碼
Shimenguang Wuzhenren si
  石門光吳眞人祠
Shishan 詩山
Shishan Shuyuan 詩山書院
shizhu 施主
shu 書
shuwen 疏文
shuyuan 書院
si 寺
siguan 寺觀
sona 嗩吶
Song Defang 宋德方
Song Huiyao 宋會要
Song Huizong 宋徽宗
Song Jiang 宋江
Song Jiugong 宋九公
Song Mingdi 宋明帝
Song Yinglin 宋應麟
Song Zhenzong 宋眞宗
Songshangong 崧山公
Songxi 松溪
suijinshi 歲進士
Sun Miaoyun 孫妙雲
Sun Simiao 孫思邈
Tai Zu 太祖
Taidong 台東
Taifei 太妃
Taihe shan 太和山
Taiji 太極
Taikou 汰口
Taimu 太姥
Tainan 台南
Taiping Tianguo 太平天國
Taipingxingguo 太平興國
Taiqing 太淸
Taishou 太守
Taiwan Shentan 臺灣神壇
Taiwang 太王
Taixuan 太玄
Taiyi Qin 太乙勤
Taiyuan 太原

Taizhong 台中
Taizu 太祖
Tan 壇
Tan Zixiao 譚紫霄
Tao Hongjing 陶弘景
Taoyuan 桃園
Tianfei songzi 天妃送子
Tianfu 天府
tiangang 天罡
Tianguan cifu 天官賜福
Tianqing guan 天慶觀
Tianshi fu 天師府
Tianxin 天心
Tiao jiaguan 跳加官
Tongan 同安
Tongquan 通泉
Tongshan 桐山
tongxiang hui 同鄉會
Tongzhi 通治
Tudi Gong 土地公
Tun Jun 疊俊
Tun Xun 疊勳
Wang Delu 王德錄
Wang Huai 王淮
Wang Qinruo 王欽若
Wang Ruhua 王汝華
Wang Ruizhang 王瑞章
Wang Shenzhi 王審知
Wang Yanjun 王延鈞
Wang Yeqiao 王爺醮
Wang Zhengnan 王正南
Wang Zhi 王植
Wang Zhiwang 王之忘
Wang Zhou 王胄
wanghun 亡魂
Wangji 王祭
Wangye 王爺
Wanli 萬歷
Wanshou gong 萬壽宮
wei 薇
wei 微
Wei Huacun 魏華存
Wei Yuanjun 魏元君
Weizhen miao 威鎭廟
wen (civil official) 文

Wen Qu　文曲
Wen Yuanshuai　溫元帥
Wenchang　文昌
Weng Dali　翁大立
wenjian　文檢
wenzhou　溫州
wu (military official)　武
wu (no.)　戊
wu dou mi　五斗米
Wu Lu　吳魯
Wu Meng　吳猛
Wu Tao　吳夲
Wu Yang　巫陽
Wu Zexu　伍澤旭
Wu Zhong　吳鍾
Wu'an　武安
Wudang shan　武當山
wufang zhenwen　五方鎮文
wuxing　五性
Wuxing jinshi　吳興金石志
Wuyi shan　武夷山
wuyin　戊寅
Xi Wangmu　西王母
-xian　縣
xia　下
xia jiu liu　下九流
Xia Yihuai　夏以槐
Xiamen　厦門
xiang zhi fulao　卿之父老
xiangjinshi　卿進士
Xiangju　薌劇
Xiangshan Fanmu　香山梵母
Xianyou　仙遊
xiao　小
Xiaobian bao　小邊保
xiaofa　小法
Xie Chenquan　謝宸荃
Xie Jin　謝近
Xie Xian　謝險
Xigang　西港
Xiluo Dian　西羅殿
Xing　邢
Xinghua　興化
Xingji　興濟
Xin zhu　新竹

Xinmao　辛卯
Xinshengjie Zhenjun an
　新盛街眞君庵
xinshi　信士
xinyou　辛酉
xiucai　秀才
Xu Bangguang　許邦光
Xu Caohua　許藻華
Xu Daozang　續道藏
Xu Mingshu　徐明叔
Xu Song　徐松
Xu Xingfu　許星甫
Xu Xun　徐遜
Xu Yucheng　許玉成
Xu Zhi'e　徐知諤
Xu Zhizheng　徐知證
Xu Zibiao　許自表
Xuandu baozang　玄都寶藏
Xuangkeng bao　雙坑保
Xuefeng　雪峰
Xuejia　學甲
Yan Lan　顏蘭
Yan Qingying　顏清瑩
Yan Shilu　顏師魯
Yan Zhongying　顏仲英
Yang Daozhouming　楊道周明
Yang Enjing　楊恩敬
Yang Jin (法師) 楊謹
Yang Jun　楊浚
Yang Xi　楊羲
Yang Zhi　楊志
yanghang　洋行
Yangong　言功
Yangzhongting　洋中亭
Yao Jin　姚僅
Yao Tian　姚添
yaogu　腰鼓
Ye Shaopen　葉紹盆
Ye Wei　葉尾
yi　乙
Yi Mao　奕茂
Yide　懿德
Yiguo Shangren　一果上人
Yilan　宜蘭
Yinghui　英惠

yong 愿
Yongcheng 雍正
Yongchun 永春
Yongjia 永嘉
Yongle 永樂
Youfengli 由風里
Youtai zhi jiao 猶太之敎
Youxi 尤溪
Yu Huan 玉環
Yu Keji 余克濟
Yuanbao gong 元保宮
Yuanmiao gong 元妙宮
Yuanqian bao 院前保
Yuantan Gong 元壇宮
Yuanyou 遠游
Yue Fei 岳飛
Yuhuang 玉皇
Yuli 玉曆
Yunlin 雲林
Yunqiao yuan 雲橋院
Yunxiao 雲霄
yuqian qingchu 御前清曲
Yuqing wanshou gong 玉清萬壽宮
Yushengtang 玉生堂
Yutou miao 漁頭廟
Ze Feng 澤峰
Zeng Conglong 曾從龍
Zeng Gongliang 曾公良
Zeng Guanghou 曾光侯
Zeng guoquan 曾國荃
Zeng Guofan 曾國藩
Zeng Huai 僧懷
Zeng Shaozhan 曾少瞻
Zeng Tianjue 曾天爵
zhai 齋
Zhang Daoyuan 張道陵
Zhang Dianlong 張典龍
Zhang Guoxiang 張國祥
Zhang Kezhen 張克眞・平心
Zhang Quan 漳泉
Zhang Tianshi 張天師
Zhang Tinggan 張廷幹
Zhang Wanfu 張萬福
Zhang Xuecheng 張學誠
Zhang Yuchu 張宇初

Zhang Yuqing 張宇淸
Zhang Zhizong 章志宗
Zhanghua 漳化
Zhangping 漳平
Zhangpu 漳浦
Zhangyan 張嚴
Zhangzhou 漳州
Zhao Buwen 趙不紊
Zhao Gongming 趙公明
Zhao Xun 趙勛
Zhao Ya 趙涯
Zhao Yan
Zhao Yuanhui 趙元慧
Zhao Zunfu 趙鐏夫
Zhao'an 詔安
zhasha 袈裟
Zhejiang 浙江
zheng (calligraphy) 正
zheng xue 正穴
Zheng Bingcheng 鄭秉成
Zheng Chenggong 鄭成功
Zheng Longzhuo 正隆卓
Zheng Yuan 鄭元
Zhenghe Wanshou Daozang 正和萬壽道藏
zhenghun 正魂
Zhengtong 正統
Zhengtong Daozang 正統道藏
Zhengyi 正一
Zhengyitang shuju 正義堂書局
zhenjun 眞君
Zhenmiao 眞妙
zhenren 眞人
Zhenwu 眞武
Zhi Hui 智慧
Zhifu 知府
zhong 中
Zhong Kui 鍾魁
Zhongting 中亭
Zhongting miao 中亭廟
Zhou Ding 周鼎
Zhou Zongbi 周宗壁
Zhou kui 周葵
zhou qiu 喎啾
zhouwen 咒文

Zhu 朱
Zhu (Nanan Minnan: du) 豬
Zhu Fang 朱紡
Zhu Gaoshi 朱高熾
zhuang 狀
zhuang chunguan 裝春官
zhuang gelou 裝歌樓
zhuang zhaojun 裝昭君
Zhuang Guozhen 莊國楨
Zhuang Xia 莊夏
zhuangguan 裝官
zhuangyuan 狀元

Zhuluo 諸羅
Zhuo Maoqiao 桌茂高
zi 字
Ziji gong 紫極宮
Ziwei 紫微
Zongli 總理
Zui baxian 醉八仙
zuo wei 做衛
Zuo Zongtang 左宗棠
zuodawei 做大衛
zupai 祖派
Zushanshe 祖山社

TITLES

Baosheng Dadi 保生大帝
Beidou Xingjun 北斗星居
Chongying zhenren 沖應眞人
Chongde zunhou 崇德尊侯
Ciji dashi 慈濟大師
Ciji lingguan 慈濟靈官
Ciji zhenjun 慈濟眞君
Ciji zhenren 慈濟眞人
Daluhuachi Tuohulu
　達魯花赤禿忽魯
Daode tianzun 道德天尊
Daolusi youyanfa 道錄司右演法
Enzhu haotian yiling miaodao zhenjun
　wanshou wuji baosheng dadi 恩主
　昊天靈醫沙道萬壽無極保生大帝
Faxuan 法玄
Fuhui miaodao zhenjun
　孚惠妙道眞君
Fuhui zhenjun 孚惠眞君
Fuhui zhenren 孚惠眞人
Guanghui zhenren 廣惠眞人
Guangze Zunwang 廣澤尊王
Haotian jinque Yuhuang shangdi
　昊天金闕玉皇上帝
Haotian jinque yushi ciji yiling chong-
　ying huoguo fuhui puyou miaodao
　zhenjun wanshou wuji baosheng
　dadi 吳玉金闕御史慈濟靈醫沖

應穫國孚惠普祐妙道眞君萬壽無
極保生大帝
Haotian yushi yiling zhenjun
　昊天御史醫靈眞君
Huang Lei Tu 黃雷圖
Huiqing Shangren 惠溍上人
Jinque yushi wanshou wuji baosheng
　dadi
　金闕御史萬壽無極保生大帝
Jinque yushi yiling puji miaodao da-
　zhenjun 金闕御史醫靈普濟妙道
　大眞君
Jiutian Siming Baosheng Dadi 九天
　司命保生大帝
Jiutian Siming Cangguang Baosheng
　Dadi 九天司命滄光保生大帝
Jiutian Xiaofu Weiling Xianhua Bao'an
　Guangze Zunwang 九天孝輔威靈
　顯化保安廣澤尊
Kaimin Shengwang 開閩聖王
Kaizhang Shengwang 開漳聖王
Kangyou hou 康祐侯
Kunshen Qingshui Zushi
　鯤鯓清水祖師
Leihua Tianzun 雷化天尊
Leisheng Puhua Tianzun
　雷聲普化天尊
Lingbao Jiao 靈寶醮

Lingbao tianzun　靈寶天尊
Linshui furen　臨水夫人
Linshui zhenren　臨水眞人
Miaodao zhenjun　妙道眞君
Miaokan dashi　妙湛大師
Miaoying xianfei　妙應仙妃
Nanling Shizhe　南陵使者
Ningzhenjing jingxuantan
　凝眞境經玄壇
Puji xianling zhenjun　普濟顯靈眞君
Puyou zhenjun　普祐眞君
Qingshui Zushi　清水祖師
Qingwei　清微
Sanping Zushi　三坪祖師
Sanshan guowang　三山國王
Shangdi ye　上帝爺
Shenxiao yufu zhangjiao xianguan zhi
　beiji fumo fuzhangshi taishang
　zhengyi mengwei jinglu jiutian jin-
　que shiyudaifu yufujiaochashi　神宵
　玉府掌敎仙官知北極伏魔副使事
　太上正一盟威經錄九天金闕使御
　大夫玉府糾察使
Taishang laojun　太上老君
Taiyi jiuku Tianzun　太乙救苦天尊
Tianfei　天妃
Tianhou　天后
Tianshi　天師
Tiantong zhengjue dashi
　天童正覺大師
Tianxin Zhengfa　天心正法
Wanshou wuji baosheng dadi　萬壽
　無極保生大帝
Wanshou wuji dadi　萬壽無極大帝
Weizhen Guangze Hou　威鎮廣澤候
Weizhen zhongying fuhui guangze
　hou　威鎮忠應孚惠廣澤候
Weizhen zhongying fuhui weiwu ying-
　lie guangze zunwang　威鎮忠應孚
　惠威武英烈廣澤尊王
Wenchang　文昌

Wu Zhenren　吳眞人
Wushi tianzun Lao Jun
　無始天尊老君
Wuxian　五顯
Xianyou zunhou　顯佑尊侯
Xuantan Zhao Yuanshuai Laoye
　玄壇趙元帥老爺
Xuantian Shangdi　玄天上帝
Yiling zhenren　醫靈眞人
Yinghu wulie zhenminwang
　英護武烈眞閩王
Yinghu wulie zhenxianwang
　英護武烈眞顯王
Yinghu wulie zhonghui zhenminwang
　英護武烈忠惠鎮閩王
Yinghui hou　英惠侯
Yuanshi tianzun　元始天尊
Taishang Yuanyang shangdi Wushi
　Tianzun　太上元陽上帝無始天尊
Yuhuang shangdi　玉皇上帝
Zhaoying guanghui ciji shanhe dashi
　昭應廣惠慈濟善和大師
Zhengyi Lingbao　正一靈寶
Zhengyi mengwei jinglu xuanhua da
　shi xianguan kaozhao youmin
　xianshi　正一盟威經錄玄化大侍
　仙官考召幽暝仙侍
Zhengyi mengwei jing lu jiutian jinque
　shiyu daifu qingwei hongdaoshi jusi-
　yuanfushi yishizhizhi　正一盟威經
　錄九天金闕使御大夫清微弘道使
　知諸司院府宜事之識
zhenjun　眞君
zhenren　眞人
Zhongxian hou　忠顯侯
Zhongxian yinghui hou　忠顯英惠侯
Zhoutian xingzhu beiji ziwei dadi
　周天星主北極紫微大帝
Ziwei dadi　紫微大帝
Ziwei Shenren　紫微神人

STELES

Baguo yuanzhu bei 吧國綠主碑

Baijiao zugong chongxiu juanti xingshi luyin beiji 白礁祖師宮重修捐題姓氏錄銀碑記

Baosheng Dadi beiji 保生大帝碑記

Chengnan dingjian Xiangxianmiao chongsi Wuhaung dadi beiji 城南鼎建興賢廟崇祀五皇大帝碑記

Chongjian Chenghuangmiao fuji 重建城隍廟附記

Chongxiu chaoyuanguan bei 重修朝元觀碑

Chongxiu Chaoyuan guan ji 重修朝元觀記

Chongxiu cijigong beiji 重修慈濟宮碑記

Chongxiu cijizugong beiwen 重修慈濟祖宮碑文

Chongxiu cijigong juankuan xingshi beiji 重修慈濟宮捐款姓氏碑記

Chongxiu cijigong juankuan xingshi beizhi 重修慈濟宮捐款姓氏碑志

Chongxiu dongong beiji 重修東宮碑記

Chongxiu lianghuanggong xu 重修良皇宮碑記

Chongxiu lingyundian juanzi juantian bei 重修凌雲殿捐資捐田碑

Chongxiu lingyundian zhengdian bing jian canmen tijuan bei 重修凌雲殿正殿幷建參門碑

Chongxiu xingjigong beiji 重修興濟宮碑記

Chongxiu yuanmiao guan 重修元廟觀

Chongxiu yuhuan baoian bei 重修玉環寶殿碑

Chongxiu zhongyiwang miaobei 重修忠義王廟碑

Chuangjian lingyundian fangming bei 創建凌雲殿芳名碑

Ciji miaoji 慈濟廟記

Cijigong bei 慈濟宮碑

Cijigong chongxiu juan ti xingming lu kuan beiji 慈濟宮重修捐題姓名錄款碑記

Cijigong yuanye beiji 慈濟宮緣業碑記

Guchenggong xiangdeng chantianji 谷城宮香燈產田記

Huangdi chiyu Wuyishan Chongyouguan juchi ji Daozhongrendeng 皇帝敕諭武夷山冲佑觀主持及道衆人等

Hui'anxian zhengtang xushijin 惠安縣正堂許示禁

Ji fengying wen 祭墳塋文

Juan ti xingshi beiji 捐題姓氏碑記

Lingyun baodian xiangdeng chantian beiji 靈雲寶殿香燈產田碑記

Lingyun chuanxuandian tijuan ji 靈雲傳宣殿題捐碑

Lingyun dian juanjian shizhu fangmingbei 靈雲殿捐建石柱芳名碑

Lingyun dian qingzhu shendan fangmingbei 靈雲殿慶祝神誕芳名碑

Lingyun dian xiangdeng zu e bei 靈雲殿香燈租額碑

Shengguangong jinyuebei 聖泉宮禁約碑

Quanzhou jinsuguan ji 泉州紫帽山金粟觀記

Xingjigong xinmaonian chongxiu beiji 興濟宮辛卯年重修碑

Wang Shengzhi dezheng bei 王審知德政碑

Zhangpuxian Shengzudian ji 漳浦縣聖祖殿記

Zugong chongxiu juanti lu 祖宮重修捐題錄

BIBLIOGRAPHY

PRIMARY SOURCES: FUJIAN PROVINCIAL, DISTRICT, LOCAL, TEMPLE,
AND ACADEMY GAZETTEERS; OFFICIAL DOCUMENTS, AND REGIONAL
LITERATURE, SOURCES FROM THE TAOIST CANON

Anxi Qingshui yanzhi 安溪清水巖志 (Gazetteer of the Clear Water Cliff of
Anxi). Xia Yihuai 夏以槐, 1812.
Anxi xianzhi 安溪縣志 (District Gazetteer of Anxi), 1673 edition; reprinted and
supplemented in 1969 edition.
Anxi xianzhi 安溪縣志 (District Gazetteer of Anxi), 1757 edition.
Bamin tongzhi 八閩通志 (General Gazetteer of Eight Districts of Min), 1490
edition.
Baijiao zhilue 白礁志略 (Brief Record of Baijiao), 1887. Yang Jun 楊浚.
Beixi ciyi 北溪詞義 [Neo-Confucian Terms Explained]. Chen Chun 陳淳 (1153–
1223).
Buziqianzhai mancun 不自慊漫存 Xu Gengbi 徐賡陛 (1882). In *Jindai
Zhongguo shiliaocongkan* 近代中國史料叢刊, vol. 78, ed. Shen Yunlong,
Taibei: Wenhai, 1972 edition.
Da Qing Huidian 大清會典 (Collected Statutes of the Qing); (1) Kangxi
edition, 1690; (2) Yongzheng edition, 248 j., 1732; (3) Qianlong edition, 120
j., 1764; (4) Guangxu edition, 384 j., 1888.
Da Qing shichao shengxun 大清十朝聖訓 (Sacred Instructions and Edicts of Ten
Qing Emperors), 922 juan, 1880.
Daoshan jilue 道山紀略 (Record of [the Temples and Shrines] of the Taoist
Mountain [of Wushishan]), 1672 edition.
Fengshan si zhilue 鳳山寺志略 (Brief Record of the Phoenix Mountain Temple),
compiled by Yang Jun 楊浚, 1888.
Fujian tongzhi 福建通志 (Fujian Provincial Gazetteer), 1868–1871 edition.
Gantang baozhi 甘棠堡志 (Local Gazetteer of Gantang bao [in Fu'an district])
Chen Yikui 陳一葵, 2 volume manuscript, written in 1927.
Guanyue sidian 關岳祀典 (Rituals for Guan [Yu] and Yue [Fei]). 1941 edition of
a late Qing work in three juan by Lin Gaoxiang 林高翔.
Guanyue sidian fubei kao 關岳祀典附備考 (Appended Notes to the Rituals for
Guan [Yu] and Yue [Fei], by Su Dashan 蘇大山, 1942.
Guoshan miaozhi 郭山廟志 (Gazetteer of the Guo Mountain Temple). Compiled
by Dai Fengyi 戴鳳儀, 1897.
Gutian xianzhi 古田縣志 (District Gazetteer of Gutian).
Haicheng xianzhi 海澄縣志 (District Gazetteer of Haicheng), 1762 edition.
Huangchao jingshi wenbian 皇朝經世文編 Compiled by He Changling 賀長齡.
Taibei: Guofeng. 1963 reprint.

Hui'an xianzhi 惠安縣志 (District Gazetteer of Hui'an), 1803 edition.

Huian zhengshu (fu: Chongwusuochengzhi) 惠安政書附崇武所城志 (Writings on the Governance of Hui'an) by Ye Chunji 葉春及 (1551 *juren*): also the (Chongwu walled city Gazetteer, edited in the Ming Jiaqing, Chengde, and Republican times). 1987 reprint. Fuzhou: Fujian Renmin chubanshe.

Jinjiang xianzhi 晉江縣志 (District Gazetteer of Jinjiang), 1765 edition.

Jinjiang xinzhi 晉江新志 (New Gazetteer of Jinjiang) by Zhuang Weiji 莊爲機.

Jiulihu zhi 九里湖志 ([Temple] Gazetteer of Jiuli Lake), 1929 edition.

Longxi xianzhi 龍溪縣志 (District Gazetteer of Longxi), 1762 edition, 1835 reprint.

Maxiang tingzhi 馬巷廳志 (Subprefectural Gazetteer of Maxiang), 1777 edition, supplemented in 1893 by Huang Jiading 黃家鼎.

Meizhou yu zhilue 湄洲嶼志略 (Brief Record of Meizhou Island [Tianhou Temple]). Yang Jun 楊浚, 1888.

Min Shu 閩書 (The History of Min [Fujian]), 1629 edition, by He Qiaoyuan 何喬遠.

Min Zaji 閩雜記 (Miscellaneous Accounts of Fujian) by Shi Hongbao 施鴻保, 1878.

Muquan Chengtiansi wanyuan pudu 募勸承天寺萬緣普度 (Pamphlet soliciting contributions to the Wanyuan Pudu ritual held in Quanzhou's Chengtiansi in 1986).

Nanan xianzhi 南安縣志 (District Gazetteer of Nanan), 1672 edition, supplemented in 1963.

Puyang shuilizhi 莆陽水利志 (Gazetteer of the Irrigation System of Puyang [Putian]), 1875 edition, by Chen Chiyang 陳池養.

Qingbai leichao 清稗類鈔 Xu Ke 徐珂, 1917; Taipei, 1966.

Qingshigao jiaoju 清史稿校註 (Annotated Draft Standard History of the Qing) Zhao Erxun (1844–1927) et al., Taipei.

Qingshi liezhuan 清史列傳, Shanghai, 1928.

Qingshuiyan zhi 清水岩志, 1989. Quanzhou: Quanzhou wenwu guanli weiyuanhui.

Qingshuiyan zhilue 清水嚴志略 (Brief Record of the Clear Stream Cliff). Yang Jun 楊浚, 1888.

Quanzhou fuzhi 泉州府志 (Prefectural Gazetteer of Quanzhou), 1870 edition.

Quanzhou Tonghuai Guanyuemiao zhi 泉州通准關岳廟志 (Record of the Quanzhou Tonghaui Guanyue Temple), 1986. Compiled by Zeng Huanzhi 曾煥智 and Fu Jinxing 傅金星.

Sanshanzhi 三山志 (Gazetteer of Three Mountains, compiled by Liang Kejia 梁克家 in 1182, printed in 1240).

Sheji bian 舌擊編 (Tonguelashings), by Chen Chu 陳儲.

Shihshan shuyuanzhi 詩山書院志 (Gazetteer of the Shishan Academy) by Dai Fengyi 戴鳳儀. Preface, 1905.

Sishen zhilue 四神志略 (Brief Record of Four Gods). Yang Jun 楊浚, 1887–1889.

Song Huiyao jigao 宋會要輯稿 (Collected Drafts of the Essentials of the Song Dynasty), compiled by Xu Song 徐松. Taipei, 1964 edition. Shijie shuju.

Tianhou zhi 天后志 (Record of the Empress of Heaven), 2 vols., 1843 edition of a book compiled by Lin Qingbiao 林淸標 (1741 *jinshi*).

Tongan xianzhi 同安縣志 (District Gazetteer of Tongan), 1798 edition.

Tongan xianzhi 同安縣志 (District Gazetteer of Tongan), 1929 edition.

Wushi shanzhi 烏石山志 (Gazetteer of the [Temples on] Wushi Mountain), 1842 edition.

Wuyi shan zhi 武夷山志 (Gazetteer of the Wuyi Mountains), 1751 edition, reprinted in 1847/ 1981.

Xiamen zhi 廈門志 (Gazetteer of Xiamen), 1832 edition.

Yijian zhi. 4 vols. Hong Mai (1123–1202). Beijing. Zhonghua.

Yongchun xianzhi 永春縣志 (District Gazetteer of Yongchun), 1927 edition.

Zhangzhou xianzhi 漳州縣志 (District Gazetteer of Zhangzhou), 1877 edition.

Sources from the Taoist Canon
(CT = Concordance du Taotsang, Schipper, 1975)
(HY = Daozang zimu yinde, Weng Dujian, Harvard-Yenching Institute Sinological Index Series, no. 25, Beijing, 1935)

CT 1 = HY 1: *Lingbao wuliang durenjing* 靈寶無量度人經.

CT 10, 13 = HY 10, 13: *Gaoshang yuhuang benxing jijing* 高上玉皇本行集經

CT 16 = HY 16: *Jiutian yingyuan leisheng puhua tianzun yushu baojing* 九天應元雷聲普化天尊玉樞寶經

CT 219 = HY 219: *Lingbao wuliang duren shangjing dafa* 靈寶無量度人上經大法, 72 juan (13th century).

CT 263 = HY 263: *Xiuzhen shishu* 修眞十書.

CT 317 = HY 317: *Lingbao tianzun shuo Hongen lingji zhenjun miaojing* 靈寶天尊說洪恩靈濟眞君妙經 (1420).

CT 374 = HY 374: *Taishang dongxuan lingbao jiuku miaojing* 太上詞玄靈寶天尊說救苦妙經註解 (postface, 1124).

CT 388 = HY 388: *Taishang lingbao wufu xu* 太上靈寶五符序 (4th century).

CT 399 = HY 399: *Taishang dongxuan lingbao tianzun shuo jiuku miaojing zhujie* 太上詞玄靈寶天尊說救苦妙經註解 (Commentary by Lu Dongyang (13th century?).

CT 468 = HY 468: *Hongen lingji zhenjun ziran xingdaoyi* 洪恩靈濟眞君自然行道儀.

CT 469 = HY 469: *Hongen lingji zhenjun jifu suqiyi* 洪恩靈濟眞君集福宿啓儀.

CT 470 = HY 470: *Hongen lingji zhenjun zaochaoyi* 洪恩靈濟眞君早朝儀.

CT 471 = HY 471: *Hongen lingji zhenjun wuchaoyi* 洪恩靈濟眞君午朝儀.

CT 472 = HY 472: *Hongen lingji zhenjun wanchaoyi* 洪恩靈濟眞君晚朝儀.

CT 473 = HY 473: *Hongen lingji zhenjun qixie shejiaoke* 洪恩靈濟眞君祈謝設醮科.

CT 474 = HY 474: *Hongen lingji zhenjun liyuanwen* 洪恩靈濟眞君禮願文.

CT 475 = HY 475: *Hongen lingji zhenjun qizheng xingdengyi* 洪恩靈濟眞君七正星燈儀.

CT 476 = HY 476: *Hongen lingji zhenjun shishi* 洪恩靈濟眞君事實 (1417).

CT 508 = HY 508: *Wushang huanglu dazhai lichengyi* 無上黃籙大齋立成儀 Jiang Shuyu (1162–1223); postface by Jiang Xi and Jiang Yan (1223).

CT 649 = HY 649: *Taishang laojun shuo Tianfei jiuku lingyan jing* 太上老君說 天妃救苦靈驗經 (15th century).

CT 780 = HY 781: *Dichi shangjiang Wen Taibao juan* 地祇上將溫太保傳. Huang Gongjin 黃公瑾 (fl. 1274).

CT 1127 = HY 1119: *Lu Xiansheng Daomen kelue* 陸先生道門科略. Lu Xiujing 陸修靜 (406–77).

CT 1138 = HY 1130: *Wushang biyao* 無上秘要, 100 juan. (ca. 580).

CT 1212 = HY 1202: *Jiao sandong zhenwen wufa zhengyi mengwei lu lichengyi* 醮 三洞眞文五法正一盟威籙立成儀 (Zhang Wanfu 張萬福, f. 712).

CT 1220 = HY 1210: *Taofa huiyuan* 道法會元, 268 juan (mid-14th century).

CT 1221 = HY 1211: *Shangqing lingbao dafa* 上淸靈寶大法, 66 juan, Wang Qizhen 王契眞 (late 13th century).

CT 1223 = HY 1213: *Shangqing lingbao dafa* 上淸靈寶大法, 44 juan. Jin Yunzhong 金允中 (fl. 1225).

CT 1241 = HY 1231: *Chuanshou sandong jingjie falu lueshuo* 傳授三洞經戒法 籙略說. Zhang Wanfu (fl. 712).

CT 1301 = HY 1291: *Lingji zhenjun lingqian* 靈濟眞君靈籤.

CT 1302 = HY 1292: *Lingji zhenjun jushengtang lingqian* 靈濟眞君注生堂靈 籤.

CT 1442 = HY 1430. *Taishang sanyuan sifu shezuijiefan xiaozai yansheng baoming miaojing* 太上三元賜福赦罪解厄謝災延生保命妙經.

CT 1468 = HY 1456: *Xuxian hancuo* 徐仙翰藻.

CT 1469 = HY 1457: *Canling ji* 贊靈集.

CT 1470 = HY 1458: *Xuxian zhenlu* 徐仙眞錄. (ca. 1486).

SECONDARY SOURCES

Agnacost, Ann S. 1987. "Politics and Magic in Contemporary China." *Modern China*: 13.1:40–61.

Ahern, Emily Martin. 1973. *The Cult of the Dead in a Chinese Village*. Stanford: Stanford University Press.

———. 1981a. *Chinese Ritual and Politics*. London: Cambridge University Press.

———.1981b. "The Tai Ti Kong Festival." In *The Anthropology of Taiwanese Society*, edited by E. M. Ahern and Hill Gates. Stanford: Stanford University Press: 397–426.

Ahern, Emily Martin, and Hill Gates, eds. 1981. *The Anthropology of Taiwanese Society*. Stanford: Stanford University Press.

Akizuki Kan'ei 秋月觀映. 1978. *Chūgoku kinsei Dōkyō no keisei: Jōmeidō no kisoteki kenkyū* 中國近世道教の形成: 淨明道の基礎的研究 (The Development of Taoism in Modern China: Studies of the Way of Filial Piety). Tokyo: Sōbun-sha.

Baity, Philip Chesley. 1975. *Religion in a Chinese Town*. Taipei: The Orient Cultural Service.

Bell, Catherine. 1988. "The Ritualization of Texts and the Textualization of Ritual in the Codification of Taoist Liturgy." *History of Religion* 27.4:366–92.

Benn, Charles D. 1977. "Taoism as Ideology in the Reign of Emperor Hsuan-tsung (712–755)." Ph.D. diss., University of Michigan, Ann Arbor.

———. 1991. *The Cavern-Mystery Transmission: A Taoist Ordination Rite of A.D. 711*. Honolulu: University of Hawaii Press.

Berling, Judith. 1980. *The Syncretic Religion of Lin Chao-en*. New York: Columbia University Press.

———. 1985. "Religion and Popular Culture: The Management of Moral Capital in The Romance of the Three Teachings." In *Popular Culture in Late Imperial China*, edited by David Johnson, A. J. Nathan, and E. S. Rawski. Berkeley: University of California Press, 188–219.

Berthier, Brigitte. 1987. "Enfants de divination, voyageur du destin." *L'Homme* XXVII, no. 101 (Janvier–Mars): 86–100.

———. 1988. *La Dame-du-bord-de-l'eau*. Nanterre, Paris: Societé d'Ethnologie.

Bielenstein, Hans. 1959. "The Chinese Colonization of Fujian until the End of T'ang." *Studia-Serica Bernhard Karlgren Dedicata*. Copenhagen: Ejnar Munksgaard.

Biot, Edouard. 1851. *Le Tcheou-Li ou Rites des Tcheou [Zhou]*. 3 vols. Imp. Nat., Paris. (Photolithographically reproduced Wentienko, Peiping, 1930).

Bodde, Derk. 1975. *Festivals in Classical China: New Year and other annual observances during the Han dynasty, 206 B.C.–A.D. 220*. Princeton: Princeton University Press.

Bokenkamp, Stephen R. 1983. "Sources of the Ling-pao Scriptures." In *Tantric and Taoist Studies in Honor of R. A. Stein*, edited by M. Strickmann. Mélanges chinois et bouddhiques, vol. 21:434–86. Brussels.

Boltz, Judith. 1983. "Opening the Gates of Purgatory: A Twelfth-century Taoist Meditation Technique for the Salvation of Lost Souls." In *Tantric and Taoist Studies in Honor of R. A. Stein*, edited by M. Strickmann. Mélanges chinois et bouddhiques, vol. 21:488–510. Brussels.

———. 1985. "Taoist Rites of Exorcism." Ph.D. thesis, University of California, Berkeley.

———. 1986. "In Homage to T'ien-fei." *Journal of the American Oriental Society*, vol. 106, no.1: 211–32.

———. 1987. *A Survey of Taoist Literature: Tenth to Seventeenth Century*. Berkeley: China Research Monographs, Institute of East Asian Studies.

Brim, John A. 1974. "Village Alliance Temples in Hong Kong." In *Religion and Ritual in Chinese Society*, edited by A. Wolf. Stanford: Stanford University Press.

Brook, Timothy. 1985. "The Spatial Structure of Ming Local Administration." *Late Imperial China*, vol. 6., no.1: 1–55.

———. 1988. *Geographical Sources of Ming-Qing History*. Ann Arbor: Center for East Asian Studies: University of Michigan.

Brown, Peter. 1981. *The Cult of the Saints: Its Rise and Function in Latin*

Christianity. Chicago: University of Chicago Press.

Bush, Richard C. 1970. *Religion in Communist China*. Abingdon Press: Nashville and New York.

Cedzich, Ursala-Angelika. 1985. "Wu-t'ung: Zur bewegten Geschichte eines Kultes." In *Religion und Philosophie in Ostasien: Festschrift für Hans Steininger zum 65. Geburtstag*, Würzburg: Königshausen & Neumann.

———. 1987. *Das Ritual der Himmelmeister im Spiegel früher Quellen-übersetzung und Untersuchung des liturgischen Materials im dritten chüan des Teng-chen yin-chüeh*. Ph.D. diss. Julius-Maxmilians-Universität, Würzburg.,

Chan, Anita, Richard Madsen, and Johnathan Unger. 1984. *Chen Village: The Recent History of a Peasant Community in Mao's China*. Berkeley: University of California Press.

Chan, Wing-tsit, trans., ed., and intro. 1986. *Neo-Confucian Terms Explained: (The Pei-hsi tzu-i by Ch'en Ch'un, 1159–1222)*. New York: Columbia University Press.

Chang, Chung-li. 1955. *The Chinese Gentry: Studies of Their Role in Nineteenth-Century Chinese Society*. Seattle: University of Washington Press.

Chavannes, Eduoard. 1910. *Le Tai Chan: Essai de monographie d'un culte chinoise*. Paris: Ernest Leroux. Reprint., Taipei: Ch'engwen, 1970.

———. 1919. "Le jet des dragons." *Mémoires concernant l'Asie orientale* 3:53–220.

Ch'en Ch'i-lu. 1972. "History of Immigration into Taiwan." *Bulletin of the Institute of Ethnology. Academia Sinica* 33:119–54.

Ch'en Ch'i-nan 陳其南. 1/1981. "Qingdai Taiwan shehui de jiegou bianqian" 清代台灣社會的結構變遷 (The Structural Transformation of Chinese Society in Taiwan During the Ch'ing Period). *Bulletin of the Institute of Ethnology. Academia Sinica* 49:115–47.

Chen Guofu 陳國符. 1963. *Daozang yuanliu kao* 道藏源流考 (Investigations of the origins of the Taoist Canon), 2 vols. Beijing: Zhonghua Shuju.

———. 1983. *Daozang yuanliu xukao* 道藏源流續考 (Supplementary Investigations of the origins of the Taoist Canon). Taipei: Mingwen. Introduction by Jao Tsung-i.

Chen Qiren 陳棨仁. 1934. *Minzhong jinshilue* 閩中金石略 (Record of the Epigraphy of the Central Min Region). Zhonghua Shuju.

Chen Yaoting 陳曜廷. 1989. "Shanghai Daojiao Zhaijiao he Jinbiao keyi gaishu" 上海道教齋醮和進表科儀概說述 (Introduction to the Presentation of the Memorial and Shanghai Taoist Ritual). In *Studies of Taoist Ritual and Music of Today*, edited by P. Y. Tsao and D. Law. Hong Kong: Society for Ethnomusicological Research in Hong Kong.

Chen Yuan 陳垣, Chen Zhichao 陳智超, and Zeng Qingying 曾慶瑛. 1988. *Daojia jishilue* 道家金石略 (Record of Taoist Epigraphy). Beijing: Wenwu.

Chen Zhiping 陳支平 1989. *Qingdai fuyi zhidu yanbian xintan* 清代賦役制度演變新探 (A New Study of the Transformations in the Qing Taxation System). Xiamen: Xiamen University Press.

Chikusa, Masaaki 竺沙雅章. 1982. *Chūgoku bukkyō shakaishi kenkyū* 中國佛敎社

會史研究 (Studies in the social history of Chinese Buddhism). Kyoto: Doho-sha.

Chin Chung-shu (Jin Zhongshu) 金中樞. 1966–67. "Lun Beisong monian zhi chongshang Daojiao" 論北宋末年之崇向道教 (The rise of Taoist worship in the last years of the Northern Song dynasty), pts. 1, 2 *Hsin-ya hsueh-pao* 新亞學報 7.2:324–414; 8.1:187–257.

Ch'iu Te-ts'ai (Qiu Dezai) 仇德哉. 1981. *Taiwan miaoshen zhuan* 臺灣廟神傳 (Legends of Taiwan Temples), Chia-i: Fu-lo. 3d printing.

Ch'u Kun-liang (Qiu Kunliang) 邱坤良, 1986. "Le Repetoire Rituel du Théâtre Chinois." Thèse de doctorat. Paris: École Pratique des Hautes Etudes.

Ch'u T'ung-tsu. 1961. *Local Government Under the Ch'ing*. Cambridge, Mass.: Harvard University Press.

Chuang Ying-chang 莊英章.1973. "Temples, Ancestral Halls and Patterns of Settlement in Chusan" 臺灣漢人宗族發展的若干問題 (in Chinese). *Bulletin of the Institute of Ethnology, Academia Sinica*. No. 36 (Ethnological Studies of the Choshui-tatu Valleys Project): 113–40.

Cohen, Myron. 1968. "The Hakka or "Guest People": Dialect as a Sociocultural Variable in Southeastern China." *Ethnohistory* 8, no. 2: 167–82.

Couvreur, F. S. 1928. *I Li: Ceremonial; Texte Chinois et Traduction*. Sienhsien [Xianxian]: Impremerie de la Mission Catholique.

Davis, Edward L. 1985. Arms and the Tao: Hero Cult and Empire in Traditional China." In *Sōdai no shakai to shūkyō* 宋代の社会と宗教 (Society and Religion in the Song). Sōdaishi kenkyūkai kenkyū hōkoku 宋代研究会研究報告. 2:1–56.

Dean, Kenneth. 1986. "Field Notes on Two Taoist *jiao* Observed in Zhangzhou in December, 1985," *Cahiers d'Extrême-Asie*, 2:191–209.

———. 1988a. "Funerals in Fujian," *Cahiers d'Extrême-Asie*, 4:19–78.

———. 1988b. "Manuscripts from Fujian," *Cahiers d'Extrême-Asie*, 4:217–26.

———. 1988c. "Taoist Ritual and Popular Religion in Southeastern China," Ph.D. thesis. Stanford University.

———. 1989a. "Taoism in Southern Fujian." In *Studies of Taoist Ritual and Music of Today*, edited by P. Y. Tsao and D. Law. Hong Kong, Society for Ethnomusicological Research in Hong Kong: 74–89.

———(Ding Hesheng) 丁荷生 and Lin Guoping 林國平. 1989b. "'Sanyi Jiao' zai Fujian de lishi yizhi chukao" 三一教在福建的歷史遺址初考 (A Preliminary Investigation of the Historical Remains of the Three-in-One Religion in Fujian). *Fujian luntan* 福建論壇 *(Fujian Forum)*, (13, 14), 1989: 114–19.

———. 1990a. "Mu-lien and Lei Yu-sheng ("Thunder is Noisy") in the Theatrical and Funerary Traditions of Fukien." In *Ritual Opera Operatic Ritual: "Mu-lien Rescues His Mother" in Chinese Popular Culture*, edited by D. Johnson. U. C. Berkeley: Institute of East Asian Studies, 1990:46–104.

———. 1990b. "The revival of religious practices in Fujian: A case study." In *The Turning of the Tide: The Religious Situation in Contemporary China*, edited by J. Pas. Hong Kong Royal Asiatic Society, Oxford University Press, 1990: 51–78.

Dean, Kenneth, and Brian Massumi. 1992. *First and Last Emperors: The Absolute State and the Body of the Despot*. New York: Semiotext(e) Autonomedia.

Dean, Kenneth, and Zheng Zhenman 鄭振滿. "Min Tai Daojiao yu minjian zhu-shen chungbai chukao" 閩台道教與民間諸神崇拜初考 (A Preliminary Study of Fujianese and Taiwanese Taoism in relation to popular religious worship), *Bulletin of the Institute of Ethnology, Academia Sinica*, forthcoming.

———. 1993–. *Fujian zongjiaoshi beiming huibian: Putian, Quanzhou, Xiamen, Zhangzhou fence* 福建宗教史碑銘彙編: 莆田, 泉州, 厦門, 漳州分冊 (Selected Inscriptions on the Religious History of Fujian: Putian, Quanzhou, Xiamen, Zhangzhou Regions), Fuzhou: Fujian Peoples Press.

DeGlopper, David. 1974. "Religion and Ritual in Lukang." In *Religion and Ritual in Chinese Society*, edited by A. Wolf. Stanford: Stanford University Press.

Deleuze, Giles and Felix Guattari. 1983. *Anti-Oedipus: Capitalism and Schizophrenia*. Preface by Michel Foucault, trans. by R. Hurley, M. Seem, and H. R. Lane. Minneapolis: University of Minnesota Press.

———. 1987. *A Thousand Plateaus: Capitalism and Schizophrenia*. Preface and trans. by Brian Massumi. Minneapolis: University of Minnesota Press.

Doolittle, Rev. Justus. 1865. *Social Life of the Chinese; With Some Account of Their Religious, Governmental, Educational and Business Customs and Opinions, with special but not exclusive reference to Fuhchau*, 2 vols. New York: Harper and Brothers.

Doré, Henri, S.J. 1911–29. *Recherches sur les superstitions en Chine*. Shanghai: Variétés Sinologiques, nos. 32, 34, 36, 39, 41, 42, 44–46, 48, 49, 51, and 57. [Translated into English by M. Kennelly, *Researches into Chinese Superstitions*. 13 vols. Shanghai: Tusewei Press.

Dou Jiliang. 1943. *Tongxiangzuzhi zhi yanjiu* 同鄉會組織之研究 (Studies on Native Place Associations). Chongking.

Duara, Prasenjit. 1988. *Culture, Power, and the State: Rural North China, 1900–1942*. Stanford: Stanford University Press.

———. 1988b. "Superscribing Symbols: The Myth of Guandi, the Chinese God of War." *Journal of Asian Studies* 47.4:778–95.

———. 1991. "Knowledge and Power in the Discourse of Modernity: The campaigns against Popular Religion in Early Twentieth-Century China." *Journal of Asian Studies* 50.1:67–83.

Dudbridge, Glen. 1978. *The Legend of Miao-shan*. Oxford Oriental Monographs, no. 1. London: Ithica Press.

———. 1982. "Miao-shan on Stone: Two Early Inscriptions." *Harvard Journal of Asiatic Studies*, 42.2:589–614.

Dumont, Louis. 1970. *Religion, politics, and history in India*. Paris: Mounton.

Eberhard, Wolfram, 1964. "Temple-building activities in Medieval and Modern China." *Monumentica Serica* 23:264–318.

———. 1968. *The Local Cultures of South and East China*. Trans. Alide Eberhard. Leiden: E. J. Brill.

Ebrey, Patricia and J. Watson, eds. 1986. *Kinship Organization in Late Imperial China*. Berkeley: University of California Press.

Ecke, Gustav and Paul Demieville. 1935. *The Twin Pagodas of Zayton*. Harvard-

Yenching Monograph Series No. 11. Cambridge, Mass.: Harvard University Press.

Elliot, Alan. 1955. *Chinese Spirit-Medium Cults in Singapore*. London: University of London Press.

Elvin, Mark. 1973. *The Pattern of the Chinese Past*. Stanford: Stanford University Press.

Elvin, Mark, and G. W. Skinner, eds. 1974. *The Chinese City between Two Worlds*. Stanford: Stanford University Press.

Embree, Bernhard L. M. ed., 1973, rpt. 1984. *A Dictionary of Southern Min (Taiwanese-English Dictionary)*. Taibei: Taipei Language Institute.

Fairbanks, John K. 1969 [1953]. *Trade and Diplomacy on the China Coast: The Opening of the Treaty Ports, 1842-1854*. Stanford: Stanford University Press.

Fan Hui 梵輝. 1985. *Fujianmingshan dasi congtan* 福建名山大寺叢談 (Remarks on the Great Buddhist Temples of the Famous Mountains of Fujian). Fuzhou: Fujian Yixian yiyuan.

Feuchtwang, Stephen. 1974a. "City Temples in Taipei under Three Regimes." In *The Chinese City between Two Worlds*, edited by M. Elvin and G. W. Skinner. Stanford: Stanford University Press: 263–302.

————. 1974b. "Domestic and Communal Worship in Taiwan." In *Religion and Ritual in Chinese Society*, edited by A. P. Wolf. Stanford: Stanford University Press: 105–30.

————. 1977. "School-Temple and City God." In *The City in Late Imperial China*, edited by G. W. Skinner. Stanford: Stanford University Press.

Freedman, Maurice. 1958. *Lineage Organization in Southeast China*. London School of Economics Monographs on Social Anthropology 18, London: The Athlone Press, University of London.

————. 1966. *Chinese Lineage and Society: Fukien and Kwangtung*. London School of Economics Monographs on Social Anthropology 33, London: The Athlone Press, University of London.

————. 1974. "On the Sociological Study of Chinese Religion." In *Religion and Ritual in Chinese Society*, edited by A. P. Wolf. Stanford: Stanford University Press: 19–42.

Fukui Kōjun 福井康須. 1958. *Dōkyō no kisoteki kenkyū* 道教基礎的研究 (Fundamental Research on Taoism). Tokyo: Shoseki Bumbutsu Ryutsūkai.

———— et al., eds. 1983. *Dōkyō* 道教 (Taoism). 3 vols. Tokyo: Hirakawa Shuppansha.

Fu Yiling 傅衣凌. 1948. "Qingdai qianqi Xiamen yanghang kao." 清代前期廈門洋行考 (An Investigation of the Foreign Trade Guilds of Amoy during the Ch'ing). In *Fujian duiwai maoyishi yanjiu* 福建對外貿易史研究, edited by Sa Shiwu et al. Fujian.

————. 1961. *Ming Qing ningcun shehui jingji* 明清農村社會經濟 (Rural Society and Economy in the Ming-Qing Period). Beijing: Sanlian.

————. 1956. *Ming Qing shidai shangren ji shangye ziben* 明清時代商人及商業資本 (Merchants and Mercantile Capital in Ming and Qing Times). Beijing: Renmin chubanshe.

Fu Yiling, and Yang Guozhen 楊國楨, eds. 1987. *Ming Qing Fujian shehui yu xiang cun jingji* 明清福建社會與鄉村經濟 (Fujian Society and Village Economy in Ming and Qing Times). Xiamen: Xiamen University Press.

Gallin, Bernard, 1966. *Hsin Hsing, Taiwan: A Chinese Village in Change*. Berkeley: University of California Press.

Gates, Hill. 1987. "Money for the Gods: The Commoditization of the Spirit." *Modern China* 13.3: 259–77.

Gernet, Jacques. 1985. [1982] *China and the Christian Impact: a Conflict of Cultures*. Trans. Janet Lloyd. Cambridge: Cambridge University Press.

Giradot, Norman. 1983. *Myth and Meaning in Early Taoism: The Theme of Chaos*. Berkeley: University of California Press.

Golas, Peter J. 1977. "Early Ch'ing Guilds." In *The City in Late Imperial China*, edited by G. W. Skinner. Stanford: Stanford University Press: 555–80.

Goodrich, L. Carrington, and Chaoyang Fang, eds. 1976. *Dictionary of Ming Biography, 1368–1644*. 2 vols. New York: Columbia University Press.

Granet, Marcel. 1926. *Danses et légendes de la Chine ancienne*. 2 vols. Paris: Félix Alcan. Rpt. 1959 P.U.F.

———. 1934. *La pensée Chinoise*. Paris: Albin Michel. Reprint. 1968.

———. 1929. *La civilisation chinois: la vie publique et la vie privé*. Paris: la Renaissance du livre.

Groot, J. J. M. de. 1878. "The Idol Kwoh Shing Wang." *China Review*, vol. 7:91–97 (July 1878–79).

———. 1884. "Buddhist Masses for the Dead at Amoy: An Ethnological Essay," *Travaux de la 6e session du Congrès International des Orientalists à Leyde*, vol. II: 1-120.

———. 1977 [1886]. *Les Fêtes Annuellement Célébrés à Emoui (Amoy)* 2 vols. (early version published in 1883 in Batavia), revised version trans. by C. J. Chavannes. Annales de Musée Guimet, vols. 11–12. Paris: Leroux. reprint.

———. 1982 [1892–1910]. *The Religious System of China, Its Ancient Forms, Evolution, History and Present Aspect, Manners, Customs and Social Institutions Connected Therewith*. 6 vols. Leyden: E. J. Brill. [Rpt. by Southern Materials Center, Inc., Taipei, 1982, 6 vols.]

———. 1903-4. *Sectarianism and Religious Persecution in China*. 2 vols. Amsterdam: Johannes Muller. Rpt. Taipei, Ch'eng-wen, 1971.

Grootaers, William A. 1952. "The Hagiography of the Chinese God Chen-wu." *Folklore Studies* 11.2:139–182.

Guo Tianyuan 國天沅, Rare Books Division of the Fujian Teachers College 福建師范大學圖書館古籍組編. 1986. *Fujian difang wenxian ji minren zhuoshu zonglu* 福建地方文獻及閩人著述綜錄 (A Comprehensive Bibliography of Fujian Regional Literature and the Writings of Fujian Authors), Bamin congshu zhi yi, Fuzhou: Fujian Shifan Daxue Press. Internal Publication.

Hansen, Valerie Lynn. 1990. *Changing Gods in Medieval China, 1127–1276*. Princeton: Princeton University Press.

Hartwell, Robert M. 1982. "Demographic, Political and Social Transformations of China, 750–1150." *Harvard Journal of Asiatic Studies* 42.2:365–442.

Hawkes, David. 1967. "The Quest of the Goddess." *Asia Major* 13.

Heusch, Luc de. 1985. *Sacrifice in Africa*. Bloomington: University of Indiana Press.

Ho, Ping-ti. 1962. *The Ladder of Success in Imperial China: Aspects of Social Mobility, 1368–1911*. New York: Columbia University Press.

Ho Ts'ui-p'ing. 1987. "Prestations in Hokkien Taiwanese Marriage Rituals." Paper presented in the session "Exchange and Sacrifice in Chinese Society" at the Annual Meeting of the American Anthropological Association, Nov. 1987, Chicago.

Hou Ch'ing-lang. 1975. *Monnaies d'offrande et la notion de trésorerie dans la religion chinoise*. Mémoires de l'Institut des Hautes Études Chinoises, vol. 1, Paris.

———. 1979. "The Chinese Belief in Baleful Stars." In *Facets of Taoism*, edited by H. Welch and A. Seidel. New Haven: Yale University Press: 193–228.

Hsiao, Kung-ch'uan. 1960. *Rural China: Imperial Control in the Nineteenth Century*. Seattle: University of Washington Press.

Hsu Chia-ming 許嘉明. 1973. "Territorialized Organization of Hoklorized Hakka in the Changhua Plain" 彰化平原福佬客的地域組織 (in Chinese), *Bulletin of the Institute of Ethnology, Academia Sinica*. No. 36 (Ethnological Studies of the Choshui-tatu Valleys Project):165–90.

Hsu, Francis L. K. 1983. *Exorcising the Trouble Makers: Science and Culture*. Westport, Connecticut: Greenwood Press.

Hubert, Henri, and Marcel Mauss. 1964 [1898]. *Sacrifice: Its Nature and Function*. Trans. by W. D. Halls. Chicago: University of Chicago Press.

Hucker, Charles O. 1985. *A Dictionary of Official Titles in Imperial China*. Stanford: Stanford University Press.

Hughes, George. 1872. *Amoy and the Surrounding Districts*. Hong Kong: De Souza.

———. 1873. "The Small Knife Rebels" [An Unpublished Chapter of Amoy History]. *China Review* 1:244–48.

Hummel, Arthur W., ed. 1943. *Eminent Chinese of the Ch'ing Period (1644–1912)*. Washington, D.C., United States Government Printing Office.

Hymes, Robert P. 1986. *Statesmen and Gentlemen: The Elite of Fu-chou, Chiang-hsi, in Northern and Southern Song*. Cambridge: Cambridge University Press.

Jan Yun-hua. 1984. "The Religious Situation and the Studies of Buddhism and Taoism in China: An Incomplete and Imbalanced Picture." *Journal of Chinese Religions* 12 (Fall): 37–64.

Jiang Weitan 蔣淮鍱. 1990. *Mazu wenxian ziliao* 媽祖文獻資料 (Documentary Materials on Mazu), Fuzhou, Fujian People's Press.

Johnson, David. 1977. *The Medieval Chinese Oligarchy*. Boulder: Westview Press.

———. 1985. "The City Gods of T'ang and Sung China." *Harvard Journal of Asiatic Studies*, 45.2:363–58.

———. 1985. "Communication, Class and Consciousness in Late Imperial China." In *Popular Culture in Late Imperial China*, edited by David Johnson, Andrew J. Nathan, and Evelyn S. Rawski. Berkeley: University of California Press: 34–72.

Jordan, David K. 1972. *Gods, Ghosts, and Ancestors: Folk Religion in a Taiwanese Village*. Berkeley: University of California Press.

———. 1976. "The Jiaw of Shigaang (Taiwan): An Essay in Folk Interpretation." *Asian Folklore Studies* 35: 81–107.

Jordan, David K., and Daniel L. Overmyer, 1986. *The Flying Phoenix: Aspects of Chinese Sectarianism in Taiwan*. Princeton, Princeton University Press.

Kagan, Alan. 1989. "Eight Immortals' Longevity Blessings: symbol and ritual." In *Studies of Taoist Ritual and Music of Today*, edited by P. Y. Tsao and D. Law. Hong Kong: Society for Ethnomusicological Research in Hong Kong.

Kaltenmark, Max, trans. 1953. *Le Lie-sien tchouan*. Beijing. Université de Paris, Publications du Centre d'Études sinologiques de Pékin.

———. 1960. "Ling-pao: Note sur un terme du taoïsme religieux." *Mélanges publiées par l'Institut des Hautes Études Chinoises* 2: 559–88.

———. 1979. "The Ideology of the T'ai-p'ing ching." In *Facets of Taoism*, edited by H. Welch and A. Seidel. New Haven: Yale University Press: 19–52.

Kamata Shigeo 鎌田茂雄. 1986. *China's Buddhist Ceremonies*. Tokyo: Daizō.

Kanai, Noriyuki 金井德幸. 1979. "Sōdai no sonsha to shashin" 宋代の村社と社神 (The village *she* and the god of the *she* in the Song dynasty). *Tōyōshi kenkyū* 東洋史研究 38.2:61–87.

Karlgren, Bernhard. 1946. "Myths and Legends of Ancient China," Stockholm: *Bulletin of the Museum of Far Eastern Antiquities* 18:199–386.

Kleeman, Terry, 1984. "Land Contracts and Related Documents." *Chūgoku no shūkyō-shisō to kagaku* 中國の宗教思想と科學 (Religion, Thought and Science in China, Volume in Honor of Professor Makio Ryokai). Tokyo: 33–48.

———. 1988. "Wenchang and the Viper: The Creation of a Chinese National God." Ph.D. thesis, University of California, Berkeley.

Kubo Noritada 窪德忠. 1977. *Dōkyō-shi* 道教史 (History of Taoism). Tokyo: Yamakawa Shuppansha.

Kuhn, Philip. 1970. *Rebellion and Its Enemies in Late Imperial China: Militarization and Social Structure, 1796–1864*. Cambridge, Mass.: Harvard University Press.

———. 1990. *Soulstealers: the Chinese Sorcery Scare of 1768*. Cambridge, Mass.: Harvard University Press.

Lagerwey, John. 1981. *Wu-shang pi-yao, somme taoïste de VIe siècle*. Paris: Publications de l'École Française d'Extrême-Orient, vol. 124.

———. 1987a. *Taoist Ritual in Chinese Society and History*. New York: Macmillan.

———. 1987b. "Les têtês les démons tombent par les milliers: Le fachang, rituel exorciste du nord de Taiwan." *L'Homme* XXVII, no. 101 (Janvier–Mars): 101–16.

———. 1988. "Les lignes taoïstes du nord de Taiwan." *Cahiers d'Extrême-Asie*, 4: 127–43.

———. 1989–90. "Les lignes taoïstes du nord de Taiwan (suite et fin)." *Cahiers d'Extrême-Asie*, 5:355–68.

Lamley, Harry J. 1977a. "The Formation of Cities: Initiative and Motivation in the Building of Three Walled Cities in Taiwan." In *The City in Late Imperial*

China, edited by G. W. Skinner. Stanford: Stanford University Press: 155–211.

———. 1977b "Hsieh-tou: The Pathology of Violence in Southeastern China." *Ch'ing-shih wen-t'i* 3, no. 7:1–39.

———. 1981. "Subethnic Rivalry in the Ch'ing Period." In *The Anthropology of Taiwanese Society*, edited by E. M. Ahern and Hill Gates. Stanford: Stanford University Press: 282–318.

Legge, James. 1885. *The Texts of Confucianism, Part III. The 'Li Chi'*. 2 vols. Oxford: Reprinted as *Li Chi: Book of Rites; An Encyclopedia of Ancient Ceremonial Usages, Religious Creeds, and Social Institutions*, edited by C. Chai, and W. Chai. New York: University Park. 1967.

Lemoine, Jacques.1982. *Yao Ceremonial Paintings*. Bangkok: White Lotus.

Li Xianzhang 李獻璋. 1968. "The Development of Taoist Jiao Rituals and Present-Day Jiao Rituals" 道教醮儀的開展與現代的醮. *Chūgoku gakushi* 中国学誌 5:201–62.

———. 1979. 媽祖信仰の研究 *Boso shinkō no kenkyū* (Studies in Belief in Mazu), Tōkyō: Taizan Bumbutsusha.

Lin Qing 林清. 1989. "Fujiansheng Daojiao gaikuang" 福建省道教概況 (The condition of Taoism in Fujian Province). *Zhongguo Daojiao* 中國道教 9 (1989.1:10)

Liu Chih-wan 劉志萬. 1967. *Taipei shih Sungshan ch'i-an chien-chiao chi-tien: Taiwan ch'i-an chiao-chi hsi-su yan-chiu chih i* 臺北市松山祈安建醮祭典: 臺灣祈安醮祭習俗研究之一 (A Communal Sacrifice for Peace in Songshan District of Taibei: Research on Taiwan *jiao* rituals). Institute of Ethnology, Academia Sinica, Taiwan.

———. 1974. *Chung-guo min-chien lun-wen chi* 中國民間信仰論文集 (Essays on Chinese Popular Beliefs) Monograph of the Institute of Ethnology, Academia Sinica, no. 22, Taipei, Taiwan.

———. 1983. *Tai-wan min-chien hsin-yang lun-wen-chi*. 臺灣民間信仰論文集 (Essays on Taiwanese Popular Beliefs). Taipei: Lianjing.

———. 1984. *Chūgoku Dōkyō no matsuri to shinkō* 中國道教の祭と信仰 (The Festivals and Beliefs of Chinese Taoism). 2 vols. Tokyo: Eifusha.

Liu Hsing-t'ang 劉興唐. 1936. "Fujian di xuezu zuzhi" 福建的血族組織 (The Organization of Fujian Lineages), *Shih-huo* 食貨 4:8.

Liu, James J. Y. 1962. *The art of Chinese Poetry*. Chicago: University of Chicago Press.

Liu, Kuang-chih, ed. 1990. *Orthodoxy in Late Imperial China*. Berkeley: University of California Press.

Liu Ts'un-yan 柳存仁. 1976. *Selected Papers from the Hall of Harmonious Wind*. Leiden: E. J. Brill.

———. 1984. *New Excursions from the Hall of Harmonious Winds*. Leiden: E. J. Brill.

Loewe, Michael.1979. *Ways to Paradise: The Chinese Quest for Immortality*. London: George Allen & Unwin.

van der Loon, Piet. 1977. "Les origines rituelles du théâtre chinois." *Journal Asiatique* 265:141–68.

van der Loon, Piet. 1984. *Taoist Books in the Libraries of the Sung Period: A Critical Study and Index*. Oxford Oriental Institute Monographs, no. 7. London: Ithica Press.

Lu Xisheng. 1982. "Ming Qing shiqi Shezu dui Zhenan shanqu di kaifa 明清時期舍族對浙南山區的開發 (The She People and the Development of the Mountains of Southern Zhejiang in Ming and Qing). *Zhongyang minzu xueyuan xuebao* 中央民族學院學報 2:90–91.

MacInnis, Donald E. 1972. *Religious Policy and Practise in Communist China: A Documentary History*. New York: Macmillan.

———. 1989. *Religion in China Today: Policy and Practise*. Maryknoll, N.Y.: Orbis Books.

Mann, Susan J. 1987. *Local Merchants and the Chinese Bureaucracy (1750–1950)*. Stanford: Stanford University Press.

Mann Jones, Susan, ed., 1978–79. *Political Leadership and Social Change at the Local Level from 1850 to the Present: Select Papers from the Center for Far Eastern Studies*. Chicago: University of Chicago Press.

Mano Senryū 間野潛龍. 1979. *Mindai bunkashi kenkyū* 明代文化史研究 (Studies in Ming Cultural History), Kyoto: Dōhōsha.

Maspero, Henri. N.d. "The Mythology of Modern China." In *Asiatic Mythology: A Detailed Description of the Mythologies of all the Great Nations of Asia*, edited by J. Hackin et al. New York: Cresent Books.

———. 1981. *Taoism and Chinese Religion*. Trans. by Frank A. Kierman, Jr. Amherst: University of Massachusetts Press.

Mather, Richard. 1979. "K'ou Chien-chih and the Taoist Theocracy at the Northern Wei Court, 425–451." In *Facets of Taoism*, edited by H. Welch and A. Seidel. New Haven: Yale University Press: 103–22.

Meskill, Johanna Menzel. 1979. *A Chinese Pioneer Family: The Lins of Wu-feng, Taiwan 1729–1895*. Princeton: Princeton University Press.

Michaels, Franz, and Chung-li Chang, 1966. *The Taiping Rebellion: History and Documents*. 3 vols. Seattle: University of Washington Press.

Miki Satoshi 三木聰. 1979. "The Baojia system in Fujian in the late Ming" 明末の福建における保甲制, *Tōyō gakuhō* 東洋学報 61.

———. 1982. "Rent Refusal in Qing Fujian" 清代前期福建抗租と國家權力. *Shigaku zasshi* 史学雑誌 91.8.

Miyakawa, Hisayuki 宮川尙志.1964. *Rikuchosei kenkyū: shūkyō hen* 六朝史研究一宗敎編 (Studies in Six Dynasties: Religious History). Kyoto.

———. 1979. "Local Cults around Mount Lu at the Time of Sun En's Rebellion." In *Facets of Taoism*, edited by H. Welch and A. Seidel. New Haven: Yale University Press: 83–101.

———. 1983. *Chūgoku shūkyōshi kenkyū* 中國宗敎史研究 (Studies in Chinese Religious History). Kyoto: Dōhōsha.

Mollier, Christine. 1991. *Une Apocalypse taoiste du Ve siècle: Étude du Dongyuan shenzhou jing*. Mémoires de l'Institut des Hautes Études Chinois, Paris.

Moser, Leo. 1985. *The Chinese Mosaic: The Peoples and Provinces of China*. Boulder and London: Westview Press.

Naquin, Susan. 1976. *Millenarian Rebellion in China: The Eight Trigrams Uprising of 1813*. New Haven: Yale University Press.

———. 1981. *Shantung Rebellion: The Wang Lun Uprising of 1774*. New Haven: Yale University Press.

———. 1985. "The Transmission of White Lotus Sectarianism." In *Popular Culture in Late Imperial China*, edited by David Johnson, Andrew J. Nathan, and Evelyn S. Rawski. Berkeley: University of California Press.

Naquin, Susan, and Evelyn S. Rawski. 1987. *Chinese Society in the Eighteenth Century*. New Haven: Yale University Press.

Naquin, Susan, and Yu Chün-fang, eds. 1992. *Pilgrims and Sacred Sites in China*. Berkeley: University of California Press.

Needham, Joseph, and Lu Gwei-Djen. 1974. *Science and Civilization in China. Vol. 5., Chemistry and Chemical Technology: Spagyrical Discovery and Invention, Part II: Magisteries of Gold and Immortality*. Cambridge: Cambridge University Press.

Negeshi Tadashi 根岸信. 1953. *Chūgoku no girudo* 中国のギリド (The Guilds of China). Tokyo.

Ng, Chin-keong. 1983. *Trade and Society: The Amoy Network on the China Coast 1683–1735*. Singapore: Singapore University Press.

Ngo, Van Xuyet. 1976. *Divination, magie, et politique dans la Chine ancienne*. Paris: PUF.

Niida Noberu 仁井田陞. 1950. "The Industrial and Commercial Guilds of Peking and Religion and Fellow-Countrymanship as Elements of their Coherence." *Folklore Studies* 9:179–206.

———. 1954. *Chūgoku no nōson kazoku* 中國の農村家族 (The Clans of Rural China). Tokyo.

Nivison, David. 1966. *The Life and Thought of Chang Hsueh-ch'eng (1738–1801)*. Stanford: Stanford University Press.

Ōfuchi Ninji 大淵忍爾. 1974. "On Ku Ling-pao ching" *Acta Asiatica* 27:33–56.

———. 1978. *Tonkō Dōkyō: mokuroku-hen* 敦煌道經: 目錄篇 (Dunhuang Taoist Texts: Index) Tokyo: Fukutake Shoten.

———. 1979. *Tonkō Dōkyō: zuroku-hen* 敦煌道經: 圖錄篇 (Dunhuang Taoist Texts) Tokyo: Fukutake Shoten.

———. 1983. *Chūgokujin no shūkyō girei* 中國人の宗教儀禮 (Chinese Religious Ritual) Okayama: Fukutake Shuten.

Overmyer, Daniel. 1976. *Folk Buddhist Religion: Dissenting Sects in Late Traditional China*. Cambridge, Mass.: Harvard University Press: 219–54.

———. 1985. "Values in Chinese Sectarian Literature: Ming and Ch'ing Pao-chuan in Late Imperial China." In *Popular Culture in Late Imperial China*, edited by David Johnson, Andrew J. Nathan, and Evelyn S. Rawski. Berkeley: University of California Press: 219–254.

Ownby, David. 1988. "The Evolution of Lineage Feuds in Fujian." Unpublished manuscript.

Pang, Duane. 1977. "The Pudu Ritual: A Celebration of the Chinese Community of Honolulu." In *Buddhist and Taoist Studies I*, edited by M. Saso and

D. W. Chappell. Honolulu: University of Hawaii Press: 95–112.

Parish, William L., and Martin King Whyte. 1978. *Village and Family in Contemporary China*. Chicago: University of Chicago Press.

———. 1986. *Urban Life in Contemporary China*. Chicago: University of Chicago Press.

Pasternak, Burton. 1972. *Kinship and Community in Two Chinese Villages*. Stanford: Stanford University Press.

Perry, Elizabeth. 1984. "Collective Violence in China." *Theory and Society* 13:427–54.

———. 1985. "Rural Collective Violence: The Fruits of Recent Reforms." In *The Political-Economy of Reform in Post-Mao China*. Harvard Contemporary China Series 2, The Council on East Asian Studies. Cambridge, Mass., and London: Harvard University Press: 175–92, 305–8.

———. 1986. "The Shanghai Small Knives Revolt and Tax Rebellions." *Imperial China*.

Pitcher, Rev. Philip Wilson. 1909. *In and About Amoy: Some Historical and Other Facts Connected with one of the First Open Ports in China*. Shanghai and Foochow: The Methodist Publishing House in China.

Potter, Jack M. 1974. "Cantonese Shamanism." In *Religion and Ritual in Chinese Society*, edited by A. Wolf. Stanford: Stanford University Press: 207–32.

Qin Baoqi 秦寶琦, Renmin daxue Qingshi yanjiusuo, and Zhongguo diyi lishi danganguan, ed., 1980–86. *Tiandihui* 天地會, vols. 1–5. Beijing: Renmin chubanshe.

Quanzhou City Government Editorial Staff of the Quanzhou Gazetteer, ed., 1985. *Quanzhou jiufengsu ziliao huipian* 泉州舊風俗資料匯編. Quanzhou. Internal Publication.

Rawski, Evelyn S. 1972. *Agricultural Change and the Peasant Economy of South China*. Cambridge, Mass.: Harvard University Press.

———. 1979. *Education and Popular Literacy in Ch'ing China*. Ann Arbor: University of Michigan Press.

Robinet, Isabelle. 1979. *Méditation taoïste*. Paris: Dervy-livres.

———. 1984. *La révélation du Shangqing dans l'histoire du taoïsme*. 2 vols. Paris: Publications de l'École Française d'Extrême-Orient, vol. 137.

Rowe, William T. 1985. "Approaches to Modern Chinese History." In *Reliving the Past: The Worlds of Social History*, edited by O. Zinz. Chapel Hill: University of North Carolina Press: 236–96.

Sadao Aoyama. 1962. "The Newly-risen Bureaucrats in Fukien at the Five-Dynasty-Sung Period, with Special Reference to their Genealogies." *Memoirs of the Toyo Bunko (The Oriental Library)*, no. 21:1–49.

Sakai Tadao 酒井忠夫. 1960. *Chūgoku zensho no kenkyū* (Researches on Chinese Morality Books). Tokyo: Kōbundō.

Sangren, P. Steven. 1987. *History and Magical Power in a Chinese Town*. Stanford: Stanford University Press.

Sasaki, Masaya 佐々木正哉. 1963. "Kampo Sannen Amoi Shotokai no Hanran" 咸豐三年廈門小刀會の叛亂 [1853 Small Knife Society Uprising at Amoy], *Tōyō gakuhō* 45.4 (March): 87–112.

Saso, Michael. 1975. *Chuang Lin hsu Tao-tsang* 莊林續道藏 (The Appended Taoist Canon of Chuang-Lin). Taipei: Cheng-wen.

———. 1978a. *The Teachings of Taoist Master Chuang*. New Haven: Yale University Press.

———. 1978b. *Dōkyō hiketsu shūsei* 道教秘訣集成 (Collection of Taoist Secret Instructions). Tokyo: Ryūkei Shosha.

Sawada Mizuho 澤田瑞穗. 1975. *Zōho Hokan no kenkyū* 增補寶卷の研究 (Expanded Researches on Baojuan). Tokyo: Kokusho kankokai, 1975.

Scarth, John. 1860. *Twelve Years in China: The People, the Rebels, and the Mandarins, by a British Resident*. Edinburgh: Thomas Constable and Co., reprint. Wilmington, Delaware: Scholarly Resources, Inc., 1972.

Schafer, Edward. 1954. *The Empire of Min*. Rutland, Vermont: Charles E. Tuttle.

———. 1977. *Pacing the Void: T'ang Approaches to the Stars*. Berkeley: University of California Press.

Schipper, Kristofer M. 1965. *L'Empereur Wou des Han dans la légende taoïste: Han Wou-ti nci-tchouan*. Paris: École Française d'Extrême-Orient, vol. 58.

———. 1966a. "The Divine Jester: Some Remarks on the Gods of the Chinese Marionette Theater." *Bulletin of the Institute of History and Philology, Academia Sinica* 21 (Spring): 81–94.

———. (Shi Bo'er 施博爾) 1966b. "Taiwan zhi Daojiao wenxian" 臺灣道教文獻 (Taoist documents from Taiwan). In *Taiwan wenxian* 臺灣文獻 17.3: 173–92.

———. 1974. "The Written Memorial in Taoist Ceremonies." In *Religion and Ritual in Chinese Society*, edited by A. Wolf. Stanford: Stanford University Press: 309–24.

———. 1975. *Concordance du Tao-tsang, titres des ouvrages*. Publications de l'École Française d'Extrême-Orient, vol. 102, Paris. (abbreviated as CT)

———. 1975. *Le Fen-teng: rituel taoïste*. Publications de l'École Française d'Extrême-Orient, vol. 104, Paris.

———. 1977. "Neighborhood cult associations in traditional Tainan." In *The City in Late Imperial China*, edited by G. W. Skinner. Stanford: Stanford University Press: 651–76.

———. 1982. *Le corps taoïste: corps physique-corps social*. Paris: Fayard.

———. 1984. "An Outline of Taoist Ritual." Forthcoming in *Classical Asian Rituals and the Theory of Ritual*. Religionsgeschichtliche Versuche und Vorarbeiten 39, edited by M. Strickmann. Proceedings of the Conference on Ritual and Theory, Berlin, June 1984.

———. 1985a. "Vernacular and Classical Ritual in Taiwan." In *Journal of Asian Studies* 45:21–57.

———. 1985b. "Taoist Ordination Ranks in the Tunhuang Manuscripts." In *Religion und Philosophie in Ostasien: Festschrift für Hans Steiniger zum 65. Geburtstag*, edited by G. Naundorf, K. Pohl, and H. Schmidt. Würzburg: Könighausen und Neumann: 127–48.

———. 1985c. "Seigneurs Royaux, Dieux des Epidemies." In *Archives de Sciences Sociales des Religions*, no. 59.1:31–40.

———. 1985d. "Taoist Ritual and the Local Cults of the T'ang Dynasty." In

Tantric and Taoist Studies in Honor of R. A. Stein, edited by M. Strickmann. Brussels; Mélanges chinois et bouddhiques, vol. 3: 812–24.

Schipper, Kristofer M. 1990. "The Cult of Pao-sheng Ta-ti and its spreading to Taiwan: A Case Study of *fen-hsiang*." In *Development and Decline of Fukien Province in the 17th and 18th Centuries*, edited by E. B. Vermeer. Leiden: E. J. Brill: 397–416.

Seaman, Gary. 1978. *Temple Organization in a Chinese Town*. Taipei: The Orient Cultural Service.

———. 1981. "The Sexual Politics of Karmic Retribution." In *The Anthropology of Taiwanese Society*, edited by E. M. Ahern and Hill Gates. Stanford: Stanford University Press: 381–96.

———. 1987. *Journey to the North: An Ethnohistorical Analysis and Annotated Translation of the Chinese Folk Novel Pei-yu-chi*. Berkeley: University of California Press.

Seidel, Anna. 1969. *La divinisation de Lao Tseu dans le taoïsme des Han*. Publications de l'École Française d'Extrême-Orient, vol. 71, Paris.

———. 1970. "The Image of the Perfect Ruler in Early Taoist Messianism: Lao-tzu and Li Hung." *History of Religions* 9.2–3 (1970): 216–47.

———. 1975. "Buying One's Way to Heaven: The Celestial Treasury in Chinese Religion." *History of Religion* 17.3 (Feb.–May): 419–31. Review of Hou Ch'ing-lang.

———. 1978. "Das neue Testament des Tao: Lao-tzu und die Entstehung der taoistischen Religion am Ende der Han-Zeit." *Saeculum* 29:147–72.

———. 1983. "Imperial Treasures and Taoist Sacraments: Taoist Roots in the Apocrypha. In *Tantric and Taoist Studies in Honor of R. A. Stein*, edited by M. Strickmann. Brussels. Mélanges chinois et bouddhiques, vol. 21: 291–371.

———. 1984. "La Sūttra merveilleux de Ling-pao Suprême." In *Contributions aux études de Touen-houang*, vol. 3, edited by M. Soymie. Paris: Publications de l'École Française d'Extrême-Orient, vol. 135: 305–52.

———. 1987. "Traces of Han Religion in Funeral Texts Found in Tombs." In Hirosaki Daigaku Tōyōshi Kenkyūshitsu 弘前大學東洋史研究室, *Akizuki Kan'ei hakase taikan kinen ronshu* 秋月觀映博師退宮記念論集 (Taoism and Religious Culture: Festschrift in Honor of Prof. Akizuki Kanei). Dōkyō to shūkyō bunka 道教と宗教文化. Tokyo: Hirakawa Shuppan: 21–57.

———. "Early Taoist Ritual" (Review of Cedzich 1987). *Cahiers d'Extrême-Asie*, 4:199–204.

———. 1990. "Chronicle of Taoist Studies:1950–1990." *Cahiers d'Extrême-Asie*, 5:223–347.

Shih Chen-min 施振民 (See Chinben). 1973. Religious Sphere and Social Organization: An Explanatory Model on the Settlement of the Changhua Plain 祭祀圈與社會組織 (in Chinese). *Bulletin of the Institute of Ethnology, Academia Sinica*. No. 36 (Ethnological Studies of the Choshui-tatu Valleys Project): 191–208.

Shiratori Yoshiro 白鳥芳郎. 1975. *Yōjin bunsho* 傜人文書 (Yao Documents). Tokyo: Kodansho.

Siu, Helen. 1990. "Recycling Rituals: Politics and Popular Culture in Contemporary Rural China." In *Unofficial Culture: Popular Culture and Thought in the People's Republic*, edited by P. Link, R. Madsen, and P. Pickowicz. Boulder: Westview Press: 121–37.

Sivin, Nathan. 1966. "Chinese Concepts of Time." *Earlham Review*, 1966.1.

———. 1968. *Chinese Alchemy: Preliminary Studies*. Cambridge, Mass.: Harvard University Press.

Skinner, G. William. 1964–65. "Marketing and Social Structure in Rural China." 3 parts. *Journal of Asian Studies* 24:3–43, 195–228, 363–99.

———. 1971. "Chinese Peasants and the Closed Community: An Open and Shut Case." *Comparative Studies in History and Society* 13:270–81.

———. 1977. "Introduction: Urban Development in Imperial China," "Introduction: Urban and Rural in Imperial China," "Cities and the Hierarchy of Local Systems," "Introduction: Urban Social Structure in Qing China." In *The City in Late Imperial China*, edited by G. W. Skinner. Stanford: Stanford University Press: 3–31, 253–73, 275–352, 521–53.

———. 1985. "The Structure of Chinese History." *Journal of Asian Studies* 44:271–92.

Skinner, G. William, and Edwin A. Winckler. 1969. "Compliance Succession in Rural Communist China: A Cyclical Theory." In *Complex Organizations: A Sociological Reader*, edited by A. Etzioni. New York: Holt, Rinehart and Winston.

Staal, Frits, ed. 1983. *Agni: The Vedic Ritual of the Fire Altar*. Berkeley: Asian Humanities Press.

———. 1986. "The Sound of Religion." *Numen*, vol. 33, Fasc. 1:33–64 and 2:185–224.

———. 1991. *Jouer avec le feu*. Paris: College de France.

Stein, Rolf. 1963. "Remarques sur les mouvements du taoïsme politico-religieux au IIe siècle apres J.-C.," *T'oung Pao* 50:1–78.

———. 1967–68. "Textes taoïste relatifs a la transmission de livres révélés," *Annuaire du College de France* 68.

———. 1979. "Religious Taoism and Popular Religion from the Second to the Seventh Centuries." In *Facets of Taoism*, edited by H. Welch and A. Seidel. New Haven: Yale University Press: 53–81.

Strickmann, Michel. 1975. "Sōdai no raigi: Shinshō undō to Dōka nanshū ni tsuite no ryakusetsu" 宋代の雷儀: 神宵運動と道家南宋についての略説. *Tōhō shūkyō* 46: 15–28.

———. 1977. "The Mao Shan Revelations: Taoism and the Aristocracy." *T'oung Pao* 63: 1–64.

———. 1978. "The Longest Taoist Scripture." *History of Religions* 17: 331–54.

———. 1979a. "On the Alchemy of T'ao Hung-ching." In *Facets of Taoism*, edited by H. Welch and A. Seidel. New Haven: Yale University Press: 123–92.

———. 1979b. "The Taoist Renaissance of the Twelfth Century." Paper presented at the Third International Conference on Taoist Studies, Unteraegeri, Switzerland.

———. 1980. "History, Anthropology and Chinese Religion." *Harvard Journal of Asiatic Studies* 40: 201–48. Review of Saso, 1978a.

Strickmann, Michel. 1981. *Le taoïsme du Mao Chan, chronique d'une révélation*. Mémoires de l'Institut des Hautes Études Chinoises, vol. 17, Paris.

———. 1982. "The Tao Amongst the Yao: Taoism and the Sinification of South China." *Rekishi ni okeru minshū to bunka* [Sakai Tadao Festscrift]: 22–30.

Sun Ko-kuan 孫克寬 1965. *Song Yuan Daojiao zhi fazhan* 宋元道教之發展 (The Development of Taoism in the Song and Yuan) Taichung: Tunghai University.

———. 1977. *Hanyuan daolun* 寒原道論 (Taoist Essays from the Cold Stream) Taibei. Lianjing.

Tanaka Issei 田仲一成, 1981. *Chūgoku saishi engaki kenkyū* 中國祭祀演戲研究 (Research on Chinese ritual drama). Tokyo: Toyo bunka kenkyujo.

———. 1983. *Chūgoku zonzo to engaki kenkyū* 中國宗族と演戲研究 (Research on Chinese Lineages and Theater). Tokyo: Toyo bunka kenkyūjo.

———. 1985. "The Social and Historical Context of Ming-Ch'ing Local Drama." In *Popular Culture in Late Imperial China*, edited by David Johnson, A. J. Nathan, and E. S. Rawski. Berkeley: University of California Press: 143–60.

Taylor, Rodney. 1990. "Official and Popular Religion and the Political Organization of Chinese Society in the Ming." In *Orthodoxy in Late Imperial China*, edited by K. C. Liu. Berkeley: University of California Press: 126–57.

Teiser, Stephen. 1988. *The Ghost Festival in Medieval China*. Princeton: Princeton University Press.

Ter Haar, Barend J., "The Genesis and Spread of Temple Cults in Fukien." In *Development and Decline of Fukien Province in the 17th and 18th Centuries*, edited by E. B. Vermeer. Leiden: E. J. Brill, 1990: 349–96.

Thompson, Lawrence G. 1980. *Chinese Religion in Western Languages: A Comprehensive Bibliography of Publications in English, French and German through 1980*. AAS Monograph No. XLI. Tuscon: University of Arizona Press.

Tien Ju-k'ang (Tian Rukang). 1990. "The Decadence of Buddhist Temples in Fu-chien in late Ming and early Ch'ing." In *Development and Decline of Fukien Province in the 17th and 18th Centuries*, edited by E. B. Vermeer. Leiden: E. J. Brill: 83–100.

Topley, Marjorie, 1963. "The Great Way of Former Heaven: A Group of Chinese Secret Religious Sects." *Bulletin of the School of Oriental and African Studies* 26:362–92.

Turner, Victor. 1969. *The Ritual Process: Structure and Anti-Structure*. Ithaca: Cornell University Press.

Turner, Victor, and Edith Turner. 1978. *Image and Pilgrimage in Christian Culture: Anthropological Perspectives*. New York.

Vandermeersch, Leon. 1980. *Wangdao ou la voie royale: Recherche sur l'espirit des institutions de la chine archaique. 2 vols. Tome 1. Structures cultuelles et structures familiales. Tome 2. Structures politiques. Les rites*. Paris: École Française d'Extrême-Orient.

Verellen, Franciscus. 1989. *Du Guangting (850–933): taoiste de cour à la fin de la Chine médiévale*. Mémoires de l'Institut des Hautes Études Chinoises, vol. 30, Paris: De Broccard.

Vermeer, Eduard B., ed., *Development and Decline of Fukien Province in the 17th and 18th Centuries*, Leiden: E. J. Brill, 1990.

———. 1991. *Chinese Local History: Stone Inscriptions from Fukien in the Sung to Ch'ing Periods.* Boulder: Westview Press.

Von Glahn, Richard. 1991. "The Enchantment of Wealth: The God Wutong in the Social History of Jiangnan." *Harvard Journal of Asiatic Studies*, vol. 51.2: 651–714.

Wakeman, Frederick. 1975. "Introduction." In *Conflict and Control in Late Imperial China*, edited by F. Wakeman and C. Grant. Berkeley: University of California Press.

Waley, Arthur. 1943. *Monkey: Wu Ch'eng-en.* New York: Grove Press.

Wang Shih-ch'ing. 1974. "Religious Organization in the History of a Taiwanese Town." In *Religion and Ritual in Chinese Society*, edited by A. Wolf. Stanford: Stanford University Press.

Ward, Barbara. 1979. "Not Merely Players: Drama, Act and Ritual in Traditional China." *Man* 14.1:18–39.

———. 1985. "Regional Operas and Their Audiences: Evidence from Hong Kong." In *Popular Culture in Late Imperial China*, edited by David Johnson, A. J. Nathan, and E. S. Rawski. Berkeley: University of California Press: 161–87.

Watson, James. 1976. "Anthropological Analyses of Chinese Religion." *China Quarterly* 66: 355–64.

———. 1982a. "Death pollution in Cantonese society." In *Death and the Regeneration of Life*, edited by M. Bloch and J. Perry. Cambridge: Cambridge University Press: 155–86.

———. 1982b. "Chinese Kinship Reconsidered: Anthropological Perspectives on Historical Research." *China Quarterly* 92: 589–622.

———. 1985. "Standardizing the Gods: The Promotion of T'ien Hou ('Empress of Heaven') Along the South China Coast, 960–1960." In *Popular Culture in Late Imperial China*, edited by David Johnson, Andrew J. Nathan, and Evelyn S. Rawski. Berkeley: University of California Press, 1985.

Watson, James, and Evelyn S. Rawski, eds. 1988. *Death Ritual in Late Imperial China.* Berkeley: University of California Press.

Watson, Rubie. 1985. *Unequal Brothers: Class and Kinship in South China.* Cambridge: Cambridge University Press.

Watt, John R. 1972. *The District Magistrate in Late Imperial China.* New York: Columbia University Press.

Weber, Max. 1951. *The Religion of China.* Trans. H. H. Gerth. New York: The Free Press (Collier-Macmillan ed., 1964).

———. 1979. *Economy and Society: an outline of interpretive sociology.* Ed. by G. Roth and C. Wittich; trans. by E. Fischoff. Berkeley: University of California Press.

Wei Yingqi 魏應麒, ed., 1929. *Fujian sanshen kao* 福建三神考 (A Study of Three Gods of Fujian).

Welch, Holmes. 1967. *The Practise of Chinese Buddhism, 1900–1950.* Cambridge, Mass.: Harvard University Press.

Welch, Holmes. 1968. *The Buddhist Revival in China*. Cambridge, Mass.: Harvard University Press.

———. 1972. *Buddhism under Mao*. Cambridge, Mass.: Harvard University Press.

Weller, Robert. 1987. *Unities and Diversities in Chinese Religion*. Seattle: University of Washington Press.

Weng Dujian 翁獨健. 1935. *Daozang zimu yinde* 道藏子目引得 (Index of Titles in the Taoist Canon). Beijing: Harvard-Yenching Institute Sinological Index Series, no. 25. Rpt. Taibei, 1966.

White, David. 1987. "*Dakkhina* and *agnicayana*: an extended application of Paul Mus's typology." *History of Religion* 26.2: 188–213.

Wilkerson, James. 1990. *Other Islands of Chinese History and Religion*. Ph.D. thesis, University of Virginia.

Wolf, Arthur P. 1970. "Chinese kinship and mourning dress." In *Family and Kinship in Chinese Society*, edited by Maurice Freedman. Stanford: Stanford University Press, 189–207.

———. 1974. "Gods, Ghosts and Ancestors." In *Religion and Ritual in Chinese Society*, edited by A. Wolf. Stanford: Stanford University Press.

Xiamen University Institute of Chinese Linguistics, Small Group on Chinese Dialectology. 1982. *Putonghua Minnan fangyan cidian* 普通話閩南方言辭典 (Dictionary of Standard Mandarin and Minnan Dialect), 1982. Shanghai: Fujian renmin chubanshe.

Xiamen University Institute of Historical Research, Chinese Socio-economic History Research Group, ed., 1989. *Fujian jingji fazhanshi* 福建經濟發展史 (History of the Economic Development of Fujian). Xiamen: Xiamen University Press.

Yang, Ch'ing-k'un. 1961. *Religion in Chinese Society*. Berkeley: University of California Press.

Yang Guozhen 楊國楨 and Chen Zhiping 陳支平, "Ming Qing Fujian tubao bulun" 明清福建土堡補論 (Supplemental Discussion of Local Fortresses in Ming and Qing Fujian), in Fu Yiling and Yang Guozhen, eds., 1987. *Ming Qing Fujian shehui yu xiang cun jingji* (Fujian Society and Village Economy in Ming and Qing Times). Xiamen: Xiamen University Press.

Yoshioka, Yoshitoya 吉岡義豐. 1955. *Dōkyō kyoten shiron* 道教經典史論 (Historical Studies of Taoist Scriptures). Tokyo: Dokyo Kankokai.

———. 1959 and 1970. *Dōkyō to Bukkyō* 道教と佛教 (Taoism and Buddhism). 2 vols. Tokyo: Toshima shobo.

Yu Chün-fang, see Naquin, S. and Yu Chün-fang, 1992.

Yu Kuang-hung 余光弘. 1/1981. "Lu-dao te sang-tsang i-shih" 綠島的喪葬儀式 (Funeral Rites of Lutau Island, Taiwan). *Bulletin of the Institute of Ethnology. Academia Sinica* 49:149–74.

———. 1987. "Making a Malefactor into a Benefactor." *Bulletin of the Institute of Ethnology. Academia Sinica*

Yu Jiaxi 余嘉錫. 1980. *Siku tiyao bianzheng* 四庫提要辨正 (Corrections to the Annotated Bibliography of the Four Repositories). 4 vols. Beijing: Zhonghua Shuju.

Zhang Jiyu 張繼禹. 1989. "Fujian Daojiao jianwen 福建道教見聞 (Observations on Fujian Taoism), *Zhongguo Daojiao* 中国道教 11 (1089.3:6–7, 48).

Zhang Ruiyao 張瑞堯 and Lu Cengrong 盧增榮, eds. 1986. *Fujian diqu jingji* 福建地區經濟 (Fujian Regional Economy) Fuzhou: Fujian Renmin chubanshe.

Zheng Zhenman 鄭振滿. 1992. *Ming Qing Fujian jiazu zuzhi yu shehui bianqian* 明清福建家族組織與社會變遷 (Ming Qing Fujian Lineage Organization and Social Change), Hunan: Hunan Educational Press.

Zhu Weiguan 朱維幹. 1986. *Fujian shigao* 福建史稿 (Draft History of Fujian). 2 vols. Fuzhou: Fujian jiaoyu chubanshe.

Zhuang Hongyi (Chuang Hung-i) 莊宏誼.1986. *Mingdai Daojiao zhengyipai* 明代道教正一派 (The Orthodox Unity Taoist Sect in the Ming Dynasty). Taibei: Xuesheng Shuju.

Zhuang Weiji 莊為璣.1985. *Jinjiang xinzhi* 晉江新志 (New Gazetteer of Jinjiang). 2 vols. Quanzhou: Quanzhou shi Jiaoyu Yinshushe.

Zito, Angela. 1984. "Re-presenting Sacrifice: Cosmology and the Editing of Texts." *Ch'ing-shih wen-t'i*, 5.2:47–78.

———. 1987. "City Gods, Filiality, and Hegemony in Late Imperial China." *Modern China*. Vol. 13, no. 3. July 1987:333–71.

Zurcher, Erik. 1959. *The Buddhist Conquest of China*. Leiden: E. J. Brill.

———. 1980. "Buddhist Influence on Early Taoism." *T'oung Pao* 66:84–147.

———. 1981. "Eschatology and Messianism in Early Chinese Buddhism." In *Leyden Studies in Sinology*, edited by W. L. Idema. Leiden: E. J. Brill: 34–56.

———. 1983. "Prince Moonlight: Messianism and Eschatology in Early Medieval Chinese Buddhism." *T'oung-pao* 68, 1–3: 1–75.

Zurndorfer, Harriet T. 1989. *Change and Continuity in Chinese Local History: The Development of Hui-zhou Prefecture 800–1800*. Leiden: E. J. Brill.

INDEX

Ahern, Emily, 48, 183
Akizuki, Kan'ei, 12–13
alchemy, 14, 215
altars:
  as geographical term, 101, 115, 117;
  home, gods worshipped on, 131;
  at Qingshui Zushi festival, 111;
  in Taoist rites, 46–47, 49, 63
Amoy. *See* Xiamen
ancestor worship, 4–5, 132, 174
Announcement of Merit (Yangong), 46, 52
antang ("altars," regional divisions), 101,
  115, 117
Anxi (Fujian), 8, 79, 83–85, 90, 123, 131,
  212, 222, 230;
  overseas Chinese from, 126;
  population of, 99–100;
  Qingshui Zushi gong in, 100
Anxi Gazetteer (Anxi Xianzhi) (published in
  Taipei 1969), 105, 117, 123
Anxi xianxhi (previous gazetteer), 137
Audience Rituals, 46–47

Bai minority, 177
Bai Yu-chan, 24, 28
Baijiao Cijigong (Western Temple), 60,
  62–69, 185–86;
  construction of, 74;
  contemporary observances at, 64–69;
  medical clinic at, 91;
  restorations of, 84, 86–88, 91;
  steles at, 85–87, 226–27
Baijiao zhilue, 78
Bamin tongzhi, 137
Ban Gu, 145, 235
banxian, 159
Bao'an gong (Bao'an Temple), 86, 89, 229
Baohuang Gong, 218
baojia system, 14, 15
Baosheng Dadi (the Great Emperor Who
  Protects Life), 17–18, 31, 60–97, 160,
  161, 212, 214;
  contemporary observances at temple of,
  64–69;
  description of temple of, 62–64;
  as Divine Doctor, 72, 90–91;
  history of cult of, 74–76, 83–90;
  legend of, 70–83;

  Mazu and, 83, 88–89;
  popular names of, 89;
  scriptures of, 78–83;
  sources on cult of, 69–70, 224–26;
  titles given to, 74–78, 79
Baxian, 222
Beidou Xingjun, 71
Beigang (Taiwan), 67, 92, 159
Beiguan musical theater, 51, 118, 222
Beijing:
  gods worshipped at Fujian merchant associations in, 215–16;
  religious origin of guilds in, 15;
  temple to Xu brothers in, 30–31
Beixi ciyi, 29, 228
Berthier, Brigitte, 28
Bielenstein, Hans, 21
blood sacrifices:
  in Guangze Zunwang cult, 131, 133,
  154–58, 162;
  of oxes, 138;
  at Qingshui Zushi festival, 105, 111;
  at San Daren festival, 101;
  Taoism and, 17, 181
Bohai Island, 79, 95
Boltz, Judith, 31, 79, 218
Buddha houses (Fotoucu), 115, 118
Buddhism:
  academies of, 211;
  accused of profit-seeking, 40;
  arrest of monks of, 110;
  Baosheng Dadi cult and, 79, 81, 83;
  Confucian attack on, 144;
  cult's origin in, 18;
  debates between Taoism and, 175;
  Fujian monasteries of, 32–33;
  gongde funerals performed by, 42;
  Lingbao revelations and, 27;
  overlapping between Taoism and, 100;
  overseas donations for, 211;
  Pudu rites of, 7, 14, 50, 100;
  Shenxiao revelations as attack on, 35;
  temple consecration by, 100.
  See also temples; Three Teachings
buzhengsi jingli, 86

Cai Qian, 88
Cai Weishan, 86

Tao Hongjing, 27
Taoism:
accused of profit-seeking, 40;
bureaucratic metaphor of, 181–86;
culture and language rejected by, 184–85;
definition of, 3;
dogma not imposed in, 13–14, 175;
Taoism, *continued:*
encyclopedia of, 27;
in Fujian (*see* Fujian—Taoism in);
as higher religion of China, 15, 179;
overlapping between Buddhism and, 100;
in revitalization of China, 185;
rituals of:
Communication of the Lamps, 162;
Confucian participation, 88, 159, 179–80;
costumes, 51–52, 65, 66, 69;
floating signifier of, 185;
forms of, 41–42;
funding of, 50;
purification, 13, 46;
Ritual Masters, 3, 32, 66, 69, 181–82;
San Daren festival, 101–2;
structural features, 45–49;
structuring of community involvement, 50–53, 180, 181;
symbolism, 53;
unity throughout world, 176–78, 181;
See also jiao communal sacrifices
special written characters of, 43;
texts of, 7, 212–14;
Classical Chinese and vernacular elements, 179;
Khubilai Khan's destruction of, 220;
messianic prophecy in, 228;
ritual burning of, 46–48, 182;
Song dynasty, 177–78;
usual elements in, 81.
See also divination; immortals; Taoist Canon; Three Teachings
Taoist Association of China, 211
Taoist Canon, 7, 15, 212–14;
editions of, 219–20;
Huizong's, 29, 34, 220;
Ming, 29–31, 220;
first printed, 220;
first scripture in, 48;
supplement to, 220

"Taoist liturgical framework," author's use of term, 14
Taoists (Taoist Masters):
arrests of, 105, 110, 211;
debates between Buddhists and, 175;
in disguise, 110–11;
as divinities, 182, 183;
in fire rites, 67;
functions of, 13;
ordination of
certificate, 45, 53–58;
lists of gods and generals given, 182;
Tang princesses, 12
Ritual Masters and, 182
Taolusi Youyanfa, 219
Taoyuan (Taiwan), 125
taxes on ritual expenditure, 5
Temple of the Eastern Peak (near Tongan), 43
Temple of the Eastern Peak (Putian), 35, 221
Temple of the Eastern Peak (Zhangzhou), 82
temples:
bells in, 63;
Buddhists in, 39, 121, 129, 221;
committees of, 11, 34, 66, 67;
consecration of, 4, 7, 13, 26, 100, 128;
description of, 46;
historical inscriptions at, 7–8;
with multiple deities, 34, 127;
as religious centers, 15;
restoration of, 26, 63, 211;
Baijiao and Qingjiao temples, 80, 84, 86–88, 91;
Fengshan si, 143;
government money for, 69;
number of, 4;
Qingshui Zushi gong, 100;
Qingshuiyan, 123–27
Taoists in, 26, 39, 221;
in Wuyi Mountain, 24
Temples of the Eastern Peak (Dongyue Miao), 6, 38
Ten Superstitions, 61, 90, 226
Ter Haar, Barend J., 214–15
Thailand, Yao Taoists in, 177
theater, ritual, 5, 17, 46, 159, 180, 217;
for Baosheng Dadi, 61, 67, 89;
description of, 50–51;

Wu Zexu, 91
Wu Zhenren (Wu Tao), 62, 74, 89, 215.
 See also Baosheng Dadi
Wu Zhenren si, 83
Wu Zhong, 86
Wudang shan (Wudang Mountain), 214,
 219
Wudi (Han emperor), 228
Wushang biyao, 27
Wushi Tianzun Lao Jun, 218
Wuxian, 214, 221
wuxing, 105
Wuyi ji, 29
Wuyi Mountains, 24, 28–29, 38, 217,
 219

Xang Xi, 27
Xi Gang, 159
Xi Wangmu. *See* Queen Mother of the West
Xia Yihuai, 125, 231
Xiamen (Amoy, Fujian), 6, 21, 23, 61–65,
 84, 85, 125, 202, 211, 224, 230;
 Baosheng Dadi—Mazu temples in, 88–
 89;
 Guangze Zunwang cult in, 143
Xiamen shi, 88, 225
Xiang Gong, 222
xiang zhi fulao, 74
xiangjinshizi, 86
Xiangju, 222
Xiangshan Fanmu, 107
Xiangying miaoji, 35
Xianyou (Fujian), 4, 42, 49, 230
Xianyou Zunhou, 140
xiaofu rites, 41, 42
Xiaojing, 147
Xie Hongchen, 231
Xie rebellion, 145, 203
Xie Shenfu, 236
Xie Zhenchuan, 232
xiedou (feuds), 23, 117, 231
Xiluo Dian, 152
Xingdao (Walking the Way), 46
Xinghua fu, 220
Xingji Temple, 81
Xinsheng jie Zhenjun an, 83
xinshi, 86
Xintai (Fujian), 83
xiucai, 222
Xiuzhen shishu, 29
Xu Bangguang, 225

Xu brothers, 7, 30, 32, 75, 78, 185, 214
Xu Caohua, 148
Xu family, 27
Xu Lifu, 221
Xu Mingshu, 232
Xu Song, 224
Xu Taozang, 29–30
Xu Xun, 12–13, 83
Xu Yucheng, 125
Xu Zhi'e. *See* Xu brothers
Xu Zhizheng. *See* Xu brothers
Xu Zibiao, 124, 231, 232
Xuan Zong (Tang emperor), 219
Xuantan Zhao Yuanshuai Laoye, 215
Xuantian Shangdi, 43, 46, 101, 130, 220
Xuejia gong, 86, 92
Xunxu Houwang, 215

Yan Lan, 71–73, 80, 225
Yan Qingying, 76, 80, 225
Yan Shilu, 74, 76, 80, 86, 87, 228
Yan Zhongying, 86, 87
Yang Daozhouming, 119
Yang Enjing, 125
Yang Jun, 8, 69–71, 74–76, 78, 93, 97,
 118–19, 122, 127, 129, 133–39, 143,
 145, 147–48, 151–53, 162, 223–25,
 231, 234
Yang the Elder, 135–37, 154, 156
Yang Xi, 27
Yang Zhi, 70, 72–74, 76, 224
Yang Zhongyi, 123
yanghang, 88
Yangong (Announcement of Merit), 46,
 52
Yanshao (Fujian), 216
Yao (Song Taoist), 218
Yao Jin, 191, 194
Yao minority, 177
Yao Tian, 189, 192
Ye Keji, 231
Ye Shaopen, 125
Ye Wei, 192
Yellow Register Zhai Requiem service,
 219
Yellow Thunder Chart (Huang Lei Tu),
 219
Yi Mao, 124
Yi minority, 177
Yiguo Shangren, 123
Yijianzhi, 29

Made in the USA